Education and
the Making of
Modern Iran

DAVID MENASHRI

Education and the Making of Modern Iran

PUBLISHED IN COOPERATION WITH THE
MOSHE DAYAN CENTER FOR MIDDLE EASTERN
AND AFRICAN STUDIES AT TEL AVIV UNIVERSITY

CORNELL UNIVERSITY PRESS

ITHACA AND LONDON

Copyright © 1992 by Cornell University

All rights reserved. Except for brief quotations in a review, this book, or parts thereof, must not be reproduced in any form without permission in writing from the publisher. For information, address Cornell University Press, 124 Roberts Place, Ithaca, New York 14850.

First published 1992 by Cornell University Press.

International Standard Book Number 0-8014-2612-X
Library of Congress Catalog Card Number 91-55567

Printed in the United States of America

Librarians: Library of Congress cataloging information appears on the last page of the book.

⊗The paper in this book meets the minimum requirements of the American National Standard for Information Sciences—Permanence of Paper for Printed Library Materials, ANSI Z39.48–1984.

TO MY WIFE, GILA

Contents

List of Tables   ix
Preface   xi
Abbreviations   xv
A Note on Transliteration and Dates   xvii

Introduction   1

Part One   The Qajar Period

1. The New Education   27
2. Early Experiments   46
3. The Educated Class as a Motor for Change   66
4. The Constitutional Regime   76

Part Two   Education under Reza Shah

5. Aims and Dilemmas   91
6. Iranian Students Abroad   125
7. The Founding of Tehran University   143

Part Three   Education under Mohammad Reza Shah

8. The "Blessings" of Education   163
9. Pre-University Education   172
10. Higher Education   210
11. Social Origins of the Student Population   241
12. Education—The Badge of the New Elites   269
13. The Struggle for Academic Freedom   282

    Conclusion   300

Epilogue   307
Sources   329
Index   343

Tables

1. Students in *maktabs* and *madreses* as compared with public schools, in selected years between 1924/5 and 1946/7   102

2. Expansion of elementary and secondary education according to sex, in selected years between 1922/3 and 1941/2   110

3. Growth of elementary and secondary schools as compared with that of the population, in selected years between 1922/3 and 1940/1   121

4. Number of students attending Tehran University between 1934/5 and 1940/1   151

5. Students at elementary schools, in selected years between 1941/2 and 1977/8   186

6. Growth of elementary and secondary education in comparison with population growth, in selected years between 1941/2 and 1977/8   191

7. Percentage of children of elementary- and secondary-school age in schools in Iran, Egypt, and Turkey in 1960 and 1975   192

8. Growth of secondary education in selected years between 1941/2 and 1978/9   192

9. Comparative index of growth of elementary, secondary, and higher education between 1941/2 and 1970/1   193

10. Breakdown by province of students at elementary and
    secondary schools in 1973/4 as compared with the
    provincial population (1976 survey)   194

11. Number of vocational school students compared with total
    high school students, in selected years between 1941/2
    and 1976/7   199

12. Number of high school graduates compared with
    university admissions between 1961/2 and 1978/9   207

13. Iranian universities in 1976/7   213

14. Number of university and college students in selected
    years between 1941/2 and 1976/7   216

15. Tuition payment or exemption in 1974/5 according to types
    of institutions   255

16. Tuition payment or exemption of students of medicine, the
    humanities, and social science in 1974/5   256

17. Students in 1971/2 according to province of birth and of
    matriculation   259

18. Place of birth and matriculation of students in 1971/2 by
    types of settlements   260

19. Education of parents of 1971/2 students and 1972/3
    candidates   263

20. Education of fathers of students at Tehran University by
    faculties in 1973/4   264

21. Education of people listed in the 1976 *Who's Who in Iran*   271

22. Education of Majlis members   274

23. Education of ministers (1906–1971)   277

24. Percentage of university graduates among different elite
    groups at the end of Mohammad Reza Shah's reign   280

Preface

The progressive deterioration of Iran's internal situation and its vastly expanding contacts with the West since the early nineteenth century promoted in Iran—much as in the Ottoman Empire and Egypt—the twin process of imitation and change. The West provided both the model for imitation and the impetus for change. A central role in this process was assumed by the educational system, which was both a catalyst of and litmus test for change, as well as an element itself subject to change.

To analyze the role of education in the making of modern Iran, this book examines the contribution of education to the overall process of social, economic, and political change in the two centuries since the country was first exposed to western schooling. The volume looks at the various meanings and goals assigned to education by the shahs of Iran and the top Iranian politicians, educators, and intellectuals, the socioeconomic elites (including the heads of the clerical institution), and the wide strata of the society. It studies the objectives of the "new education," the details and implementation of the policy designed both to advance education (qualitatively and quantitatively) and to use it as a lever for the progress of the country; and it assesses the contribution (as well as the limits) of the educational reform to the making of modern Iran. Although the primary focus of this book is higher education, it also examines concepts in the educational system at large, and discusses developments in pre-university schooling that influenced the quantitative and qualitative development at the higher level.

The volume begins with the initial Iranian efforts to adapt the achievements of western schooling, early in the nineteenth century, and concludes with the collapse of the monarchy in 1979. The Epilogue, however, does discuss the changes in educational philosophy and policy since the Islamic Revolution and up to recent days.

The period studied is divided into three historical subperiods: the Qajar period (1779–1925); the rule of Reza Shah (1925–1941); and the era of Mohammad Reza Shah (1941–1979). The Epilogue discusses the Islamic Republic. Since most of the expansion of the educational system occurred under Mohammad Reza Shah, a great part of the book is devoted to the third subperiod.

This book has been prepared within the discipline of history. The book follows in the tradition of those works that attempt to study the history of a region while examining the interrelationship between the development of the country and the development of the educational system. Some examples are the studies by J. Heyworth-Dunne, Joseph Szyliowicz, Reza Arasteh, and Haggai Erlich.[1] My main approach can be summed up in the words of Edward Carr, who stressed that the more the study of history is sociological, and the more sociology is historical—the better for both.[2]

In this regard, the present book may, I hope, fill some vacuum in the study of Iranian history. Previous studies of the educational system have concentrated mostly on the examination of the system per se. Szyliowicz and Arasteh did examine the interrelationship between education and the process of modernization of Iran, but their studies were too general and did not make extensive use of the primary sources available to me.

Four main types of sources have been used in this book: The first type is primary archival sources, including official studies and surveys, most of which have not been previously examined (and following the revolution are not available to foreign analysts). Second, I personally observed the functioning of the institutions of higher learning during two years of field study in Iran (in fall 1974 and from July 1975 to October 1977). During this period I conducted hundreds of interviews with professors, students, chancellors, and members of the administrative staff of the different universities, as well as with officials at the ministries of education, labor, economic affairs, the Plan and Budget

1. J. Heyworth-Dunne, *An Introduction to the History of Education in Modern Egypt* (London: Frank Cass, 1968); Joseph Szyliowicz, *Education and Modernization in the Middle East* (Ithaca: Cornell University Press, 1973); Reza Arasteh, *Education and Social Awakening in Iran: 1850–1968* (Leiden: Brill, 1968); Haggai Erlich, *Students and University in 20th Century Egyptian Politics* (London: Frank Cass, 1989).

2. Edward H. Carr, *What Is History?* (Harmondsworth: Penguin Books, 1964), 66.

Organization, and research institutions. Third, the journals, periodicals, and newspapers appearing since the late nineteenth century were carefully studied. Finally, most of the secondary sources on the topic, published in Iran and elsewhere, were used as well.

This book will, I hope, be of interest to readers from the field of educational studies (with no special interest in Iranian affairs), from the field of development research in general (but not Iranian studies in particular), and from the field of Iranian history and politics (with no specialized knowledge of educational affairs). Some things will inevitably strike certain readers as overexplained, and others as underexplained. I can only point to the difficulty of the materials' availability and appeal for patience.

It would be impossible to thank personally all those who in one way or another helped me in this long journey into the study of Iranian education. I should begin by expressing gratitude to the many Iranian experts who offered important insights into the subject matters discussed in this book. This was done in Iran in the years 1975–1977. I was given institutional help by the Ministries of Science and Higher Education, the Ministry of Education, the Plan and Budget Organization, the Royal Institute for Research on Education, the universities of Tehran and Pahlavi (at Shiraz) and some other research or governmental institutions, whose heads at the time provided additional help by instructing several of their employees and ministry officials to share their expertise with me.

I am grateful to two professors at Tel Aviv University, Michael Khen and Shimon Shamir, for their encouragement, academic advice, and generous friendship, and for their guidance and support throughout the stages of the preparation of this book. Ervand Abrahamian (Baruch College, New York), Fouad Ajami (Johns Hopkins University), Roy Mottehadeh (Harvard University), Arye Shmuelevits (Tel Aviv University), Hava Lazarus Yafe (Hebrew University, Jerusalem), Michael Winter (Tel Aviv University), and David Yerushalmi (Tel Aviv University) read the earlier versions of the manuscript; for their useful criticism and suggestions, received in the course of revision, I am indebted to them all.

I also thank three men associated with the Moshe Dayan Center for Middle Eastern and African Studies: Itamar Rabinovich (rector of Tel Aviv University and former head of the Center), Haim Shaked (former head of the Center), and Asher Suser (current head of the Center). I wish to express my deepest appreciation also to Daniel Dishon for his valuable editing of the manuscript. He has been a sophisticated and keen reader. His comments and questions, in addition to his superb editing skills, made their mark throughout this book. I likewise take pleasure in thanking Lydia Gareh, who painstakingly prepared the manuscript, and Edna Liftman, Amira Margalit, and Ilana Greenberg for their help. Thanks also go to my research assistants, Avia Oleivski, Miriam Nisimove, Sigal Dagan, and Rinat Meiraz, and to my colleagues at the Moshe Dayan Center's documentation system, who provided all possible assistance. Holly Bailey, Kay Scheuer, and Joanne Hindman at Cornell University Press and copyeditor Victoria Haire should be singled out for their help in the publication of this book.

I owe a special debt to the following institutions and individuals for supporting my research. The Israeli Foundation Trustees (Ford Foundation) gave me a generous grant to conduct field study in Iran (1975–1977). The U.S.-Israel Educational Foundation (Fulbright Foundation) provided a grant that enabled me to carry out research at Princeton and Cornell universities (1984–1986), during which time, inter alia, this book was prepared and written. I am also grateful for the generous support of Oscar Van Leer, and the Alice and Benno Gitter Fund for Research, as well as for the help and encouragement of my dear friend Uri Lubrani during my field study in Iran.

Finally I would like to express my deepest appreciation and gratitude to my wife, Gila, for her patience and encouragement throughout my endless quest for better understanding of the land and people of Iran.

DAVID MENASHRI

Tel Aviv

Abbreviations

AP	*Amuzesh va Parvaresh*
DR	*Daily Report, The Middle East and North Africa*
DT	Daneshgah-e Tabriz
IJMES	*International Journal of Middle Eastern Studies*
ILO	International Labor Organization
IRNA	Islamic Revolution News Agency
JI	*Jomhuriye Islami*
KAEA	*Konferans-e Arzyabi-ye Enqelab-e Amuzeshi*
KH	*Kayhan Hava'i*
KI	*Kayhan International*
MA	Markaz-e Amar, Sazeman-e Barname va Budje
MAM	Markaz-e Asnad va Madarek, Darbar-e Shahanshahi
MEJ	*Middle East Journal*
MES	*Middle Eastern Studies*
MM	*Modhakerat-e Majlis-e Shura-ye Melli*
MQ	*Majmu'e-ye Qavanin, Majlis-e Shura-ye Melli*
MTBRA	Mo'assese-ye Tahqiqat va Barname Rizi 'Ilmi va Amuzeshi, Vezarat-e 'Ulum
MTE	Mo'assese-ye Motale'at va Tahqiqat-e Ejtema'i, Daneshgah-e Tehran
NIOC	National Iranian Oil Company
NYT	*New York Times*
OECD	Organization for Economic Co-operation and Development
PO	Plan and Budget Organization

SBB   Sazeman-e Barname va Budje
SSHBA   Sazeman-e Shahanshahi Bazresi Amuzesh-e ʿAli va
         Pezhuhesh-e ʿIlmi, Darbar-e Shahanshahi
SWB   *Summary of World Broadcast*/BBC
TT   *Taʿlim va Tarbiyyat*
TU   Tehran University (Daneshgah-e Tehran)
VAP   Vezarat-e Amuzesh va Parvaresh
VD   Vezarat-e Darbar
VʿU   Vezarat-e ʿUlum

A Note on Transliteration and Dates

I have used a simplified system of Persian transliteration, making allowances for pronunciation. Some Persian and Arabic consonants and vowels have been transliterated differently, when pronunciation so demanded (e.g., *va*, Reza, and Mohammad in Persian but *wa*, Rida, and Muhammad in Arabic). I have omitted diacritical marks, but have retained the *ayn* and *hamza*. Names of individuals are rendered in the way they are most commonly known. Thus appellations and titles often serve as family names (e.g., Sepahsalar, Malek al-Motakallemin, and Rafsanjani).

The citation of dates has proved a thorny problem in a work that includes dates from different calendars (solar and lunar *hejri*, imperial Iranian calendar, etc.). As a rule, I provide the equivalent Christian years. In the Sources section I give both the original dates and the Christian years.

Unless otherwise indicated, all translations are my own.

Education and the Making of Modern Iran

Introduction

The Islamic Revolution in Iran has undoubtedly been one of the most momentous developments in the Middle East—and in human history at large—in recent decades. Some of its unique features, such as its revolutionary ideology, massive popular participation, the leadership of the ulama, the nature of clerical rule, the policies of the new regime, and its modus operandi, have made Iran (and Shiʿi Islam) into a focus of public attention since the late 1970s.

Indeed, in many ways, the Islamic revolution presented a new prototype of power seizure, significantly different from the many coups the Middle East has known. It had mass support, it was led by clerics (rather than army officers), and its "new" ideology was actually the return to a glorious old one: Islam in its pristine form. A revolution by the masses in which the people take the destiny of their country in hand is not a common event in human history. The total disintegration of the shah's regime, the loyalty of the armed forces and the support of the United States notwithstanding, added to the astonishment of the outside world. So did the fact that the revolution was led by an aged cleric who had been in exile some fourteen years and that such an outburst of hatred toward the West occurred after so many years of westernization. The unique nature of the Islamic state and the attempt to base the "new Iran" on the old philosophies of Islam gave the revolution further original features.

Students of the Middle East are now accustomed to being asked (and probably ask themselves): "Was this revolution religious, political, social, economic—or what?" A leading expert in Iranian studies replied

1

to this question: "The only good answer is that it was all of these . . . economic, social and political discontent have developed over the decades and coalesced in the past few years, while added to the central Islamic identity felt by the majority of the popular classes were new interpretations of religion that justified revolutionary ideas and became widespread in society."[1]

Such a perception raises the question of the ways in which the revolution was in fact "Islamic." No doubt, the ulama were the main force behind it and supplied the coherent ideology around which all the different—often divergent—elements in the coalition that brought Ayatollah Ruhollah Khomeyni to power could unite. But in calling the revolution "Islamic," one must bear in mind that it was not narrowly so in the western sense of the word. Much like other popular uprisings over the last hundred years (such as the Tobacco Rebellion of 1891–92, the Constitutional Revolution of 1905–1911, and the opposition movement led by Mohammad Mosaddeq in 1951–1953), the 1978–79 movement was a coalition of groupings that had come together in a common struggle from varying, often contradictory, motives and goals. As in the previous instances, many pressing social, economic, cultural, and political problems combined to make the situation explosive. Education had its share in the ferment—partly through its achievements, partly through its failures.

Resentment deriving from educational problems centered on two major areas: (a) shortcomings of the educational system itself both qualitative and quantitative (the low level of teaching, insufficient vacancies in institutions of higher learning, lack of coordination between overall manpower needs and educational programs, the concomitant dependence on foreign experts, and the persistence of social gaps); and (b) more basically, the philosophies underlying the educational system and the ideologies it strove to impart (mainly the atmosphere of *gharbzadegi*, "West-strickenness"), which had "contaminated" Iranian thinking, educating Iranians—so it was now claimed—to view themselves as inferior to westerners, turning the young generation away from traditional religious convictions and instilling alien philosophies in them. The clerics, the intellectuals, and some of their partners in the revolutionary movement thought the second set of problems the more harmful and dangerous, but the first category was no less significant in fomenting popular discontent. Each had its share in fos-

---

1. Nikki R. Keddie, *Roots of Revolution: An Interpretive History of Modern Iran* (New Haven: Yale University Press, 1981), 1.

tering resentment and was instrumental in preparing the ground for the revolution.

For all their radical differences, the philosophies of Khomeyni and Shah Mohammad Reza Pahlavi (1941–1979) had one thing in common: their appreciation for education. Both leaders viewed it as a major vehicle for implementing their ideology, advancing their people, and perpetuating their rule. Both made extensive use of education to cast "modern Iran" in the mold of their vision. Yet each led it along an entirely different path: one toward rapid westernization, the other toward radical Islamization.

This book does not specifically deal with whether, or how much, modern education added to public discontent or prepared the ground for the revolution. Rather, it aims to examine the contributions education has made to the overall process of social, economic, and political change in the two centuries since Iran was exposed to the impact of western schooling. Education's particular role in augmenting ferment will, I hope, become evident as the story evolves.

Indeed, the passing of traditional society in the nineteenth- and twentieth-century Middle East generated profound changes in the realm of education. These, in turn, promoted modernization and generated further change. Nonetheless, historians of the modern Middle East have given comparatively little attention to the fate and functions of the "new" education. The study of that complex process known variously as "modernization," "westernization," or simply "development" has focused largely on political change and its impact on social, economic, administrative, and intellectual affairs. The contribution of education has yet to be fully appreciated, primarily because education has been cast in a supporting role. Here the gradual transformation of education in Iran and its role in society are primary. On a more general level, I seek to examine education in Iran as a catalyst and litmus test for change, as well as an element itself subject to change.

Two of the terms in the title of this book— "education" and "modern Iran"—are not fully self-explanatory. Neither is the term "development," used often in the study. To set the limits of our theme these terms all need to be more closely defined.

In definitions of "education," prescriptive and descriptive notions have often been at odds. Some definitions of the former type reflect subjective preferences for what is held to be desirable or "appropriate"; in short they are "saturated with value."[2] Descriptive ones, on the

2. Cole S. Brembeck and Marvin Grandstaff, "What Shall We Mean by 'Education'?,"

other hand, have at times been as general as "[Education is] whatever helps to shape the human being."[3] This book is deliberately limited to that narrow segment of the educational process often called schooling; that is (to quote one current descriptive definition), to "the work of certain special agencies, such as the tutor and the school, which presumably are devoted exclusively to the twofold task of teaching and learning."[4]

But governments and intellectuals, and often enough large segments of the population, think of education not solely in terms of descriptive definitions but also in terms of value judgments and of educational policies, that is, norms and prescriptions they wish to lay down or want to see applied. I will therefore try to make visible the aims officials and educationalists set themselves in formulating policy, to examine the considerations that motivate them, and to evaluate their success in terms of their chosen objectives. The accent will be on higher education, but much space will also be given to primary and secondary education and their influence (both quantitative and qualitative) on higher education.

"Development" has similarly been defined along descriptive and subjective lines. One definition of the former type asserts that "development" subsumes any "consecutive" and "continuous" change over time. Definitions of the latter type, by contrast, tend to assume that each subsequent stage in a chain of development is "better" than the preceding ones. Their adherents end up equating development first with progress and advancement,[5] and next with "modernization" in the current sense of emulating the model of the West.

In fact, some sociologists have often used the terms "development," "change," and "modernization" interchangeably.[6] Their studies have

---

and Jerome Bruner, "Education as Knowledge Transmission," in C. Brembeck and M. Grandstaff, eds., *Social Foundation of Education* (New York: Wiley, 1969), 9–10 and 11–17.

3. From J. S. Mill's Inaugural Address at St. Andrews, 1867, cited in Frank Smith and A. S. Harrison, *Principles of Class Teaching* (London: Macmillan, 1954), 3.

4. *Encyclopaedia of the Social Sciences* (New York: Macmillan), 5:403. See also Christophere J. Hurn, *The Limits and Possibilities of Schooling: An Introduction to the Sociology of Education* (Boston: Allyn and Bacon, 1978), 38–57.

5. Yeshayahu Leibowitz, entry "Development," *The Hebrew Encyclopaedia* (Jerusalem: Encyclopaedia Publishing Company), 15:703–5.

6. S. N. Eisenstadt, "Social Change and Development," E. Shils, "Political Development in the New States: The Will to Be Modern," and G. Balandier, "Socio-cultural Unbalance and Modernization in the Underdeveloped Countries," in S. N. Eisenstadt, ed., *Readings in Social Evolution and Development* (London: Pergamon, 1966), 3–33, 379–419, and 361–78; K. Deutsch, "Social Mobilization and Political Development," *American Political Science Review*, 55 (September 1961), 463–515.

shown that change in developing states went together with higher indexes of modernization.[7] Although this is not sufficient reason to equate change and modernization with westernization (implying that development per se means bringing nonwestern countries in line with western society), the fact remains that change in the Middle East was often motivated by a desire to emulate the West and its successes. The term "development" as used here therefore relates to that process of change in social, political, and economic life that was promoted predominantly by increasing ties with the West and that had the West as its model.

"Modern" Iran is not a clear-cut notion either. Authors who used the term in the title of their books—or studied the process of modernization[8]—have tended to point to the first half of the nineteenth century as the time of the initial western impact.[9] Some disagreement exists as to the beginnings of the specific impact on education. 'Isa Sadiq, Amin Banani, and Mohammad Reza Shah viewed the inauguration of Dar al-Fonun in 1851 as the start of the "new education."[10] Some official publications of the Iranian Ministry of Education as well as some scholars (such as Reza Arasteh) pointed to the inauguration of the new elementary schools toward the end of the century as marking the first stage.[11] Each version has much to be said for it. But, having

---

7. S. N. Eisenstadt, *An Analysis of Modernization Processes* (in Hebrew; Jerusalem: Akademon, 1967/8), 22; Deutsch.

8. Issa Khan Sadiq, *Modern Persia and Her Educational System* (New York: Columbia University Press, 1931); C. J. Wills, *In the Land of the Lion and Sun, or Modern Persia* (London: Ward and Lock, 1891); Peter Avery, *Modern Iran* (London: Ernest Benn, 1967); Hafez Farman Farmayan, "The Forces of Modernization in Nineteenth Century Iran: A Historical Survey," in William Polk and Richard Chambers, eds., *Beginning of Modernization in the Middle East: The Nineteenth Century* (Chicago: University of Chicago Press, 1968), 115–51; John H. Lorentz, "Modernization and Political Change in Nineteenth Century Iran: The Role of Amir Kabir" (Ph.D. diss., Princeton University, 1974); Hamid Algar, *Mirza Malkum Khan: A Study in the History of Iranian Modernization* (Berkeley: University of California Press, 1973).

9. Despite Iran's long history of ties with Europe, there is almost no meaningful sign of earlier cultural influences from the West. See Ali Akbar Siassi, *La Perse au contact de l'Occident: Etude historique et sociale* (Paris: Ernest Leroux, 1931); Ann K. Lambton, "The Impact of the West on Persia," *International Affairs*, 33 (1957), 12–25.

10. 'Isa Sadiq, *Tarikh-e Farhang-e Iran*, 7th ed. (Tehran: Daneshgah-e Tehran, 1976); Amin Banani, *The Modernization of Iran: 1921–1941* (Stanford: Stanford University Press, 1961); Mohammad Reza Pahlavi, *Mission for My Country* (London: Hutchinson, 1961). An Iranian educationalist typically describes "modern higher education" as "teaching sciences in line with the style of the Europeans": Dhabihollah Safa, "Madrese," in *Iranshahr* (Tehran: Daneshgah-e Tehran, 1963/4), 1:714–44.

11. Dowlat-e Shahanshahi-ye Iran, Vezarat-e Ma'aref va Awqaf, *Salname-ye 1311/12*

made the study of higher education the particular focus of this book, I begin my review with the dispatch of the first Iranian students to Europe, early in the nineteenth century. Limited though their numbers were, their journey west represents the first important step in acquiring a knowledge of western science and bringing it to Iran.

The final point of this study is the fall of the monarchy and the establishment of the Islamic Republic in 1979. The Islamic Revolution was carried forward on a wave of resentment against and rejection of the West. Reacting against the rapid and all-embracing change of the preceding decades, it upheld a "pure" Islam unadulterated by the West. This, rather than imitation of the West, would restore Islam to its natural place of leadership in human history. The educational system, as hitherto a major, if not the major, instrument for advancing westernization, now came to be regarded as a tool for advancing "Islamization." Educational concepts and educational policy had come full circle.

To place this account in the context of present educational theories, we must briefly examine some current interpretations of what scholars have called "the educational revolution."[12] Until the 1960s at least, versions of a traditional functional theory as to the nature of education were dominant. Then, a new radical theory—the "conflict theory"— emerged, challenging some basic assumptions of the functional theory.[13] Neither is, of course, of a piece, and there are many variations of the main themes, some of which occupy intermediate ground. But some general characteristics stand out.

The functional theory was formulated in the early 1950s.[14] It posits

---

(Tehran, n.d.); "Farhang-e Now Chegune Aghaz Shod," *AP*, 1951/2, 460–62; Reza Arasteh, *Education and Social Awakening in Iran, 1850–1968*, 2d ed. (Leiden: Brill, 1968).

12. See Talcott Parsons, "Some Considerations on the Comparative Sociology," in Joseph Fischer, ed., *The Social Sciences and the Comparative Study of Educational Systems* (Scranton: International Textbook, 1970), 201–20. Similarly: D. F. Drucker, "The Educational Revolution," in A. Etzioni and E. Etzioni, eds., *Social Changes: Sources Patterns and Consequences* (New York: Basic Books, 1964), 236–42; Hurn, 58–60. For an attempt to explain the growth of mass education, see: Francisco Ramirez and John Boli, "The Political Construction of Mass Schooling: European Origins and Worldwide Institutionalization," *Sociology of Education*, 60 (January 1987), 2–17; John Meyer and Francisco Ramirez, "The World's Educational Revolution: 1950–70," in J. Meyer and Michael Hannan, eds., *National Development and the World System: Educational, Economic and Political Change: 1950–1979* (Chicago: The University of Chicago Press, 1979), 37–55.

13. For a survey of the two theories, see: Hurn, 1–84; Jerome Karabel and A. Halsey, "Educational Research: A Review and an Interpretation," in J. Karabel and A. Halsey, eds., *Power and Ideology in Education* (New York: Oxford University Press, 1977), 1–85.

14. Some of the main proponents and their principal works were: Talcott Parsons, "The School Class as a Social System: Some of Its Functions in American Society," *Harvard*

that the "function" of education in society is to provide a rational way for sorting out and selecting the most talented individuals, regardless of their social origins and inherited privileges, and awarding them the status commensurate with their merits. Education equips students with the cognitive skills needed in a society increasingly based on expertism and transmits the values and ideals of the older generation. It is therefore a vital factor in the functioning of a modern democratic and meritocratic society,[15] and the schools are its crucial agencies.[16]

In ascribing to education the triple task of selecting talents, providing expert knowledge, and transmitting values, the functionalists take their stand in a chain of tradition reaching back to ancient Greece. Their tenets, as Christopher Hurn puts it, have long been "part of the working assumptions of the great majority of all who have thought and written about schooling in western societies until quite recently."[17] They all shared an appreciation for the contribution of education to the political and social advancement of man and society.[18] In the eighteenth and nineteenth centuries, economists from Adam Smith to Alfred Marshall added their voices in praise of education as instrumental for economic growth.

Social, political, and economic considerations of this kind furnished the justification for greater investments in education. Sociologists pointed mainly to education's role in furthering equal opportunities and in opening the way toward a meritocratic society where descent and privilege would count for little, talent and effort for a great deal.[19] Political scientists emphasized its importance for political socialization, recruitment, and integration as well as for nation building.[20] The econ-

Educational Review, 29 (Fall 1959), 297–318; Edward Shils, "Plentitude and Scarcity: The Anatomy of an International Culture Crisis," *Encounter*, 32 (May 1969), 37–57; Robert K. Merton, *Social Theory and Social Structure* (Glencoe: Free Press, 1968).

15. Hurn, 21–22, 33. For the growing need for education in an era of expanding expertism, see Burton Clark, *Educating the Expert Society* (San Francisco: Chandler, 1962).

16. Emile Durkheim, *Moral Education* (Glencoe: Free Press, 1956); Robert Dreeben, "The Contribution of Schooling to the Learning of Norms," in Karabel and Halsey, 544–49.

17. Hurn, 32.

18. For a historical survey of such educational thought, see John S. Brubacher, *A History of the Problems of Education* (New York: McGraw-Hill, 1947), 1–74.

19. E.g., K. Davis and W. Moore, "Some Principles of Stratification," *American Sociological Review*, 10, no. 2 (1945), 242–49, as quoted by Hurn, 3.

20. E.g., Gabriel Almond and Sidney Verba, *The Civic Culture* (Princeton: Princeton University Press, 1963); D. Easton, "Function of Formal Education in Political System," *School Review*, 65 (1957), 304–16; V. O. Key, Jr., *Public Opinion and American Democracy* (New York: Knopf, 1961); Herbert H. Hyman, *Political Socialization* (Glencoe: Free Press, 1959); James S. Coleman, *Education and Political Development* (Princeton: Princeton Uni-

omists stressed the economic gain likely to be created by educated "human resources." The "human capital theory" provided the economic justification for the vast expenditure required to finance a rapidly expanding educational system.[21] So did studies of the correlation between the development of education and economic growth. The conclusions of the economists were supported by studies commissioned by UNESCO and the OECD.[22]

Typical of this trend are formulations such as the remark included in the OECD study of 1961 to the effect that "investment in education is an indispensable prerequisite of future economic growth,"[23] or Dean Rusk's dictum that "democratic institutions cannot exist without education.... Education makes possible the economic democracy that raises social mobility."[24] They reflected and added to the optimistic mood widely current in the early 1960s. For many, the acceptance of education as the master determinant for development had become "almost an article of faith."[25]

Soon enough, however, a series of empirical studies of the actual contribution of education to greater equality (whether between social strata or between races or the sexes) challenged one of the basic principles of the functional theories. Their inspiration came from egalitarian philosophies and from the conflict theories of education.[26] Among

versity Press, 1965), mainly 3–32. See also Gunner Myrdal, *Asian Drama: A Study into the Poverty of Nations* (Clinton: Penguin, 1968), 3:1621–24.

21. Theodore Schultz, "Investment in Human Capital," *American Economic Review*, 51 (March 1961), 1–16; Thomas Joster, ed., *Education, Income and Human Behavior* (New York: McGraw-Hill, 1975); Gary Becker, *Human Capital* (New York: National Bureau of Economic Research, 1964).

22. Don Adams and Robert M. Bjork, *Education in Developing Areas* (New York: McKay, 1969); Frederick Harbison and Charles S. Myeres, *Education, Manpower and Economic Growth* (New York: McGraw-Hill, 1964); UNESCO, *Economic and Social Aspects of Educational Planning* (Paris, 1964); OECD, *Policy Conference on Economic Co-operation and Development: Summary Report* (Washington, D.C., 1961); Dies Hocheitner, "Educational Planning," in the UNESCO volume, 85–97.

23. OECD, 5; see also Hocheitner, 85.

24. Michel Debeauvais, "Problems of Costs and Opportunities," *Prospects*, 3, no. 3 (1973), 307–17, as quoted in Martin Carnoy, "International Educational Reform: The Ideology of Efficiency," in Carnoy and Henry Levin, *The Limits of Educational Reform* (New York: Longman, 1976), 245.

25. James S. Coleman, "Introduction to Part One," in Coleman, *Education and Political Development*, 5; Hurn, 3.

26. Some of the more important examples were: Peter M. Blau and Otis D. Duncan, *The American Occupational Structure* (New York: Wiley, 1967); James S. Coleman et al., *Equality of Educational Opportunity* (Washington D.C.: Government Printing Office, 1966); Christopher Jenckes et al., *Inequality: A Reassessment of the Effect of Family and Schooling in America* (New York: Basic Books, 1972); A. H. Halsey, "Sociology and the Equality

their main findings were that the past expansion of education had failed to create equal educational opportunities, let alone actual equality; that the social background of children still significantly influenced the length of their schooling and their eventual occupational status; and that cognitive skill per se did not decisively promote occupational mobility. While they tended to confirm that superior status was no longer directly inherited, but must be legitimated by actual achievements that are socially acknowledged,[27] they also concluded that achievement in itself still depended on the student's family background. In other words, status was no longer transferred through the inheritance of material assets, but rather (to quote Pierre Bourdieu) by the transmission of "cultural capital" from parents to children.[28]

Writers of this school came to distinguish between passive equality (of opportunities) and actual equality (of results); the former did not necessarily lead to the latter. They did not deny the power of education to determine status. But they argued that what mattered most for occupational mobility was not cognitive *skill* but the educational *credentials* that schools provided. They found that no clear correlation existed between educational achievement and occupational status or the income of graduates, and that parental income was still significant for the educational opportunities of young people; in short, fathers still pass on much of their occupational advantage (or disadvantage) to their children.[29] Even those among them who conceded that motivation

---

Debate," *Oxford Review of Education*, 1, no. 1 (1975), 9–23; J. W. B. Douglas, *The Home and the School* (London: MacGibbon and Kee, 1964); Raymond Boudon, *Education, Opportunity and Social Inequality* (New York: Wiley, 1974), Pierre Bourdieu, "Cultural Reproduction and Social Reproduction," in Karable and Halsey, 487–511; Torsten Husen, *Talent, Equality and Meritocracy* (The Hague: Martinus Nijhoff, 1974).

27. Blau and Duncan, 429–30.

28. Bourdieu, 488.

29. Coleman, *Equality*, 66–98. (In 1975, however, Coleman argued against the utility of the distinction between passive and actual equality for policy purposes: Karable and Halsey, 21.) See also: Jean Floud, A. H. Halsey and F. M. Merton, *Social Class and Educational Opportunity* (London: Heinemann, 1956); Douglas, *The Home and the School*; C. A. Moser, *Inequality in Educational Opportunities* (London, 1965); David Byrne, Bill Williamson, and Barbara Fletcher, *The Poverty of Education: A Study in the Politics of Opportunity* (London: Robertson, 1975); Janckes, see mainly 19–33, 109–10, 179–92, 253–56; James Guthrie et al., *Schools and Inequality* (Cambridge: MIT Press, 1971); L. C. Comber and John Keeves, *Science Education in Nineteen Countries* (New York: Wiley, 1973), and Alan Purves, *Literature Education in Ten Countries* (New York: Wiley, 1973) (both are quoted in Hurn, 42–43); William H. Sewell and Vimal P. Shah, "Socioeconomic Status, Inequality and the Attainment of Higher Education," *Sociology of Education*, 40 (Winter 1969), 1–23; Lester C. Thurow, "Education and Economic Equality," *The Public Interest*, 28 (Summer

is a significant factor in success held that stronger motivation for success and mobility were imparted in schools frequented by the children of middle- and upper-class parents.[30]

More radical writers[31] took the argument a step farther: modern education had not only failed to promote equality but operated to perpetuate existing gaps. In contrast to the functional theorists, these proponents of the conflict paradigm viewed education as being controlled by existing elites and designed primarily to serve their interests. Rather than fostering cognitive skills and serving as a lever for mobility, education confers credentials on elite children and thus helps perpetuate existing social barriers (as its controllers intend it to do). Lower-class children who managed to get a good schooling are "educated" to acknowledge their "inferiority."

Similarly, the conflict theory has a totally different explanation for the rapid growth of the school system. Elementary education expanded because of the elites' desire to train more efficient but obedient workers, not from a liberal-reformist impulse to promote mobility. The growth of higher education stemmed from similar utilitarian considerations, leaving the elites free to assure their own children a place in the most prestigious institutions, to secure higher degrees for them, and to direct them to the more distinguished fields so as to preserve their superior status. A fundamental restructuring of society and of the economy was a prerequisite of educational reform, not its outcome. The message was often encapsulated in the titles proponents of this school chose for their books, for instance: Ivan Illich's *Deschooling Society*, Colin Greer's *Great School Legend*, Samuel Bowles and Herbert Gintis's *Schooling in Capitalist America*, Martin Carnoy and Henry Levin's *Limits of Educational Reform*,

1972), 66–81; Richard B. Dobson, "Social Status and Inequality of Access to Higher Education in the USSR," in Karable and Halsey, 254–75.

30. Talcott Parsons, "General Theory in Sociology," in R. K. Merton et al., eds., *Sociology Today* (New York: Basic Books, 1958), 3–38; Joseph A. Kahl, "Educational and Occupational Aspirations of 'Common Man' Boys," *Harvard Educational Review*, 23 (Summer 1953), 156–203.

31. For example, Samuel Bowles and Herbert Gintis, *Schooling in Capitalist America* (New York: Basic Books, 1976); Rendall Collins, "Functional and Conflict Theories of Educational Statification," *American Sociological Review*, 36 (December 1971), 1002–19, and "Where the Functional Requirement of Employment Is Highest?" *Sociology of Education*, 47 (Fall 1974), 419–42; Martin Carnoy, *Education as Cultural Imperialism* (New York: McKay, 1974); Carnoy and Levin, *Educational Reforms*; Maurice Levitas, *Marxist Perspective in Sociology of Education* (London: Routledge and Kegan, 1974); Michael Katz, *Class Bureaucracy and Schools* (New York: Praeger, 1975) and *The Irony of Early School Reform* (Cambridge: Harvard University Press, 1968); Colin Greer, *The Great School Legend* (New York: Basic Books, 1972).

Carnoy's *Education and Cultural Capitalism*, David Byrne's *Poverty of Education*, and James Guthrie's *Schools and Inequality*. They questioned, as Carnoy and Levin put it, the assumption that "educational reform can resolve social dilemmas that arise out of the basic nature of the economic, political, and social system itself." As long as education was based on capitalist ideology, it would fail to operate against social barriers: "To the contrary, the schools will tend to reproduce the inequalities in order to contribute to the legitimation of adult society."[32] In the face of these challenges, the functional theories "lost some of the taken-for-granted character" they had previously possessed.[33]

The two schools of thought (and their many subdivisions), sketched all too briefly above here, sprang up in the West and dealt initially with education in the West. Inevitably, however, they were applied to developing countries as well. There, the versions of functional theory viewed the weakness of the local school system as the prime cause of backwardness and consequently considered educational expansion the key to advancement. The underlying assumption was that once education was expanding, most other problems would be resolved. Functionalists asserted that education is the key that unlocks the door to modernization.[34] Backwardness of education was the principal reason for countries "developing" rather than being developed.[35] UNESCO and OECD studies generally took the same line.[36] Western consultants urged the governments of nonwestern countries to consider the advancement of education as the single most important motor of development. The United States Act of International Development (1961) stated that "until the requisite knowledge and skills have been developed" in countries aided by the United States, "capital facilities for purposes other than the development of educational and human resources shall be given a lower priority."[37] In 1965 the secretary-general of UNESCO summed up his organization's philosophy by saying that "a country will never be developed unless education is developed. It is through education that the maximum use can be made of human

32. Carnoy and Levin, "Introduction," in Carnoy and Levin, 4.
33. Hurn, 31.
34. Harbison and Myeres, 181.
35. Adams and Bjork, 45. Similarly: Don Adams, ed., *Education and National Development* (London: Routledge and Kegan, 1971), 1–10; John Hanson and Cole Brembeck, *Education and Development of Nations* (New York, 1966), 1–14; Barton Perry, *Realms of Value* (Cambridge: Harvard University Press, 1954), 411–12.
36. See, for example, UNESCO, *Educational Planning*, 84; OECD, 1.
37. U.S. government, Department of Health, Education, and Welfare, *Education and Development of Human Technology* (Washington, D.C.: Government Printing Office, 1962), 1.

resources, in which the developing countries are so rich."[38] Rusk put it as follows: "In underdeveloped economies education itself stimulates development . . . by demonstrating that tomorrow need not be the same as yesterday, that change can take place, that the outlook is hopeful" (cf. above). In short, education, development, and change were presented as interrelated, if not synonymous.

By contrast, at least some of the conflict theorists believed that the backwardness of Third World states stemmed not from the weakness of their school system but rather from international capitalism, which had made them dependent on the developed countries and wished to keep them so. Just as education cannot in itself better the condition of the lower classes in any given individual state, so it cannot change the status of developing countries as long as the fundamental structure of the international economy remains what it is. To quote Martin Carnoy, capitalism "has created structures that prevent the mass of people in the world from achieving the fulfillment of their needs and goals."[39] It follows, according to Theodor Hanf and Karl Amman, that "formal education in Africa and Asia in its present form tends to impede economic growth and promote political instability; in short, education in Africa and Asia today is an obstacle to development."[40]

By and large, it was the optimism of the West, rather than the pessimistic outlook inherent in the conflict theories, that registered with politicians, educationalists, and much of the general public in the developing states themselves. If they came to believe in the omnipotence of education, it was, one may assume, through the combined impact of the following:

First, the more optimistic view had been dominant in the West for decades and was more readily accessible to, and absorbed by, foreign students coming to western universities. They, in turn, then influenced public opinion in their own countries.

Second, observers in the developing countries generally accepted the high standard of education of developed countries as the "secret" of their progress. Studies of the correlation of education and development in Japan, Russia, Britain, the United States, and elsewhere

38. UNESCO Chronicle, 9 (May 1965), 171, as quoted in Howard Hayden, Higher Education and Development in South-East Asia, vol. 1, Director's Report (Paris: UNESCO, 1967), 94.

39. Carnoy, "International Educational Reform," in Carnoy and Levin, 245–258.

40. Theodor Hanf, Karl A. Amman, et al., "Education—an Obstacle to Development? Reflections on the Political Function of Education in Asia and Africa," Comparative Education Review, 19 (February 1975), 68–87.

supported this conviction. Other preconditions of development tended to be ignored.

Third, the combination of the first and second points gave developing countries much comfort: it held out hope of rapid and, as it were, easy progress. As against the view of many western educationalists that society and education were mirror images of each other, Third World thinkers clung to the belief that educational methods and institutions were easily transferable from one culture to another.

Fourth, to quote F. Ramirez, "the European model of a national society" had become "deeply institutionalized as a world order." State—and nation—building in themselves had become "a sufficient condition to induce the newly independent state to devote a large proportion of its effort to constructing a secular, compulsory mass education system." A national commitment to mass schooling was thus "imposed" by the world order and supported by such transnational organizations as the United Nations and the World Bank. "No matter how impoverished or fragmented, every candidate national society must present itself to the world as one committed to establishing a system of mass schooling."[41]

Finally, in Muslim countries, the value thus placed on education and the belief in its power were all the more readily received as they struck a chord of recognition. Similar concepts were deeply imbedded in their native philosophy and had been a formative experience in their own long history. This was one of few areas where western models and indigenous tradition could reinforce rather than battle each other.

Both the pre-Islamic and the Islamic tradition of Iran commended education. Both understood it as a twofold process: the acquisition of knowledge (*danesh*, according to a Persian word root; or *'ilm*, according to a loan word from Arabic), as well as character formation and training in good manners. This is well reflected in two expressions used to connote the educational process as a whole: *ta'lim va tarbiyyat* (loan words from Arabic; *ta'lim* derives from *'ilm*) and *amuzesh va parvaresh* (a neologism derived from old Persian roots). The first terms in both expressions relate to the acquisition of knowledge; the second terms originally had to do with the nursing and training of animals or infants, then acquired the meaning of moral and religious teaching, and, in more modern times, came to denote character formation and the training of the mind.

The Avesta, the Zoroastrian holy book, contains many appreciative references to education and educated people. Greek historians who

41. Ramirez and Boli, 14–15; Meyer and Ramirez, 53.

wrote about Iran, among them Herodotus and Xenophon, stressed the value placed on knowledge under Achaemenid rule (550–330 B.C.). Contemporary Iranian scholars of both the Achaemenian and Sassanian periods (224–651), who were already influenced by modern thinking on education, came to similar conclusions.[42]

In their prayers, Zoroastrians used to ask Ahura-Mazda to grant them "educated children" possessing "culture (ba-tarbiyyat) and knowledge (dana)." The Avesta made teaching the illiterate a religious duty. In an appeal to his son, often quoted in modern Iranian writings, Zoroaster's father said: "The most esteemed divine gift is knowledge; wealth and status are transitional . . . but danesh and tarbiyyat persist."[43] The Avesta's ideal was: "Correct thought (pondar-e nik), correct talk (goftar-e nik) and correct behavior (raftar-e nik)." Acquiring these would make the believer a "useful member" ('ozv-e mofid) of society as well as ensure individual happiness. But, in a society as strictly structured as ancient Iran is, this must not be taken to mean that education was regarded as a conduit for social mobility.[44]

The stress on religion and ethics as educational ideals did not preclude the development of the sciences, particularly under the Sassanians. Both Greek and Indian influence contributed to its development. And, as far as medicine was concerned, so did the great importance Zoroastrianism attached to physical health. The Gondi Shapur academic center, established at the time of Shapur II and flourishing particularly under Anushirvan, was the main scientific institution existing on the eve of the Arab conquest.

In a major study of education in ancient Iran (published in 1972) the author, 'Ali Reza Hekmat, concludes that "many of the traditions and practices" in today's Iran have their origins in the pre-Islamic era.[45] Under the last two shahs, when the regime endeavored to make pre-Islamic Iran an element of cohesion in Iranian modern nationalism, it

<hr>

42. 'Ali Reza Hekmat, *Amuzesh va Parvaresh dar Iran Bastan* (Tehran: MTBRA, 1972); Sadiq, *Farhang*, 31–91; Safa, "'Ilm," *Iranshahr*, 1:695–713; A. Dinshah, *Akhlaq-e Iran Bastan* (Tehran: Rasti, 1955); A. Bizhan, *Cheshmandaz Tarbiyyat dar Iran qabl az Islam* (Tehran, 1963); Hamid Nir-Nuri, *Sahm-e Iran dar Tamaddon-e Jehan* (Tehran: Sherekat-e Naft, 1966); 'A. Ghaffari, *Tamaddon-e Shesh-Hezar Sal-e Iran Bastan* (Tehran: Ibn Sina, 1938); Mohammad Mashkur, *Tarikh-e Ejtema'i-ye Iran dar 'Ahd-e Bastan* (Tehran: Daneshsara-ye 'Ali, 1968); Arasteh, 1–23. So also such foreign scholars as Christane Sun, *Iran dar Zaman-e Sassaniyan* (Tehran, 1938); William Jackson, *Zoroastrian Studies* (New York: Columbia University Press, 1928).

43. 'Ali Reza Hekmat, 77–95; Dinshah, 46–47.

44. Sadiq, *Farhang*, 55–66.

45. 'Ali Reza Hekmat, 80.

was more convenient for the regime to relate its educational policy to pre-Islamic traditions than to the Islamic era. Hekmat's book, following shortly on celebrations of the 2500th anniversary of the Iranian monarchy, is in itself one link in the attempt to establish such a chain.

Even more important, and certainly of greater relevance for the realities of modern Iran, was the place of knowledge in Islamic tradition. Franz Rosenthal writes in his definitive study on 'ilm (knowledge) that in Islam, "the concept of knowledge enjoyed an importance unparalleled in other civilizations."[46] Islamic tradition makes the search for knowledge (talab al-'ilm) a duty of all Muslim men and women (farida 'ala kul Muslim wa Muslima) throughout their life (min al-mahd 'ala al-lahd; "from the cradle to the grave"), and in any place (falau fi al-Sin; "even in China"). The Qur'an speaks repeatedly of its importance: 'ilm and its derivations "make up around one percent of its vocabulary."[47]

Even greater importance is attached to 'ilm in the tradition of the Shi'a—the official religion of Iran since 1501. "Knowledge" was one of the qualifications required in a caliph in the Sunni tradition but was not nearly as central and all-important as it was with respect to Shi'i imams. Even now, one of the main qualifications required for the marja'-e taqlid ("source of [religious] imitation") is to be the "most learned" (a'lam) cleric. An apocryphal hadith (presumably of Shi'a inspiration) makes the Prophet say: "I am the city of knowledge, and 'Ali is its gate." According to Shi'i lore, 'Ali was the "most knowledgeable" Muslim of all times, anywhere. His knowledge bestowed upon him by the grace of God, was passed on to the imams, whose ultimate raison d'être was to spread it. Rosenthal concludes: "This surely constitutes an apotheosis of the concept of knowledge hardly matched elsewhere in the Muslim environment."[48]

Moreover, Islamic tradition linked knowledge and status. According to Shi'i tradition: "knowledge lifts the lowly person to the heights. Ignorance keeps the youth of noble birth immobile."[49] Islam did not encourage the search for knowledge merely for the sake of status. But prestige and status were expected to come to those who engaged in

---

46. Franz Rosenthal, Knowledge Triumphant: The Concept of Knowledge in Medieval Islam (Leiden: Brill, 1970), 334.

47. In all its derivations, there are 750 occurrences of the root 'ilm (out of a total of roughly 78,000 words): Rosenthal, 20. But then, 'ilm had a religious rather than scientific connotation.

48. Rosenthal, 142–50, 251–55.

49. Al-Raghib al-Isfahani, Muhadarat, 1:17; Ibn 'Abd al-Barr, Jami, 1:18—both sources quoted in Rosenthal, 322–24.

it. Acquiring *'ilm* continued to be the main avenue for mobility within the religious establishment until recent years.[50] The ultimate aim of *'ilm*, in Islam as well as in pre-Islamic Iran, was the knowledge of God. In fact in the Qur'an *'ilm* and *iman* (faith) often served as synonyms.[51] In traditional schools, then—whether elementary (*maktab*) or higher (*madrese*)—the focus was on religious subjects. Teaching science in the schools was looked at with a measure of mistrust by the ulama. Gustav von Grunebaum argues that their objections to science became stronger in the late Middle Ages, not only because of its subject matter but also because it derived from non-Islamic sources.[52] But after the Muslim conquest, too, hospitals remained centers of scientific inquiry. Some scientists and philosophers from Iran became famous throughout the Muslim world. The names of Ibn Sina (Avicenna, 980–1037), Khaje Naser al-Din Tusi (1200–1273), and 'Abd al-Rahman Jami (1414–1492) come to mind. They, and many others, upheld the ideal of *talab al-'ilm*, and some developed educational theories that gained wide currency. Teaching religion (*din*) remained central to them, but instruction for the life of this world (*donya*) had its place, too.[53]

The loving admiration Iranians have for classical Persian literature was a further element in shaping the educational ideal. In a society where few were literate, poetry was an important channel for transmitting symbols and ideals. Even those who did not master Persian were able to memorize and quote verses from Ferdowsi, Hafez, Sa'di, or 'Omar Khayyam. The poets themselves stressed the importance of knowledge and its acquisition. Sa'di, for example, devoted an entire chapter in his famous *Golestan* to *tarbiyyat*. Man's ability (*tavangari*), he says, is based on knowledge, not on wealth. Although taking the traditional view that education is primarily an instrument for accomplishing religious perfection, not for gaining temporal profits (*az bahre-ye donya khordan*), he does not neglect its day-to-day function for practical life: "Knowledge divorced of action" (*'ilm bi-'amal*) is like a "tree without fruit" (*derakht bi-bar*) or a "bee without honey" (*zanbur bi-'asal*). And again: "Knowledge, no matter how much you study, if there is no action accompanying it, illiterate you remain." The following phrase

50. Michael M. J. Fischer, *Iran: From Religious Dispute to Revolution* (Cambridge: Harvard University Press, 1980), 88–89.

51. For a discussion of the interrelations between the two terms, see Rosenthal, 97–108.

52. Gustav von Grunebaum, "Islam in Humanistic Education," *The Journal of General Education*, 4 (October 1949), 22.

53. Sadiq, *Farhang*, 136–230.

from Ferdowsi's *Shahname* became the motto of the Ministry of Education in the 1930s: "Capable is the one who possesses knowledge (*tavana bavad an ke dana bavad*); knowledge makes old men's hearts young."

All these proud traditions notwithstanding, the school system such as it existed at the starting point of this study had deteriorated badly.[54] Certainly it was incapable of helping the nation respond to the new challenges posed by the technological-military superiority of the West. Thus, despite the Islamic ideal of *talab al-'ilm* and the deep roots of similar concepts in pre-Islamic Iranian history, the motivation for educational reform and expansion—in Iran as elsewhere in the Middle East—came from contact with the West and from a desire to discover the "secret" of its strength (most particularly of its military strength). As in other segments of life, the West not only encouraged such change but also proffered its own model for imitation. But imitating the western school system could not be divorced from the overall tension between the powers of tradition and change, a tension which characterized the entire period discussed in this book. As in other fields, westernization reached its peak under Mohammad Reza Shah, to be utterly and totally reversed under the Islamic Republic. And yet Iran again tried to separate western culture, which it totally rejects, from western science and technology, which it is willing to absorb. The thought that one may not be had without the other is not allowed to penetrate public consciousness.

54. For a description of traditional schooling in modern Iran, see Fischer, 59–61.

PART ONE

The Qajar Period

Two strands of development stand out in the Qajar period (1779–1925), to whose early decades we can trace back the first beginnings of modern education: a progressive deterioration of Iran's internal situation, and vastly expanding contacts with the West. Both alike sustained the growing awareness among Iranians of their country's weakness as compared with the West, particularly in military and technological terms. This in turn promoted—much as it did at the same time in the Ottoman Empire and in semi-independent Egypt—the twin process of imitation and change. The West provided both the impetus toward change and the model for imitation, generating the conspicuous and characteristic tension between the urge to reject and the desire to emulate.[1] While conservative forces preached clinging to the old system (whether for the sake of the traditional values or from sheer pragmatism), support for change gradually won out.

Leading ulama, as well as other social and economic elites and, more often than not, the political establishment, vigorously opposed any change likely to prejudice their values, let alone their status. The most adamant, most genuine challenge to westernization came from the ulama. Several factors had strengthened the relationship between the faithful and the clerics in Iranian Shi'i society and had added to the power of the latter: the strong religious sentiment of most of the pop-

1. Gustav von Grunebaum, "Acculturation and Self-Realization," in B. Rivlin and J. S. Szyliowicz, eds., *The Contemporary Middle East* (New York: Random House, 1965), 141–42.

ulation; the right of *ejtehad* given to Shiʿi ulama (unlike their Sunni counterparts) whereby they alone decided matters relating to religious law; the *usuli* doctrine, increasingly prevalent since the eighteenth century, that each believer (*moqalled*) must follow a living *mojtahed* (*moqallad*) and accept his rulings as binding; the fact that the *mojtaheds'* livelihood came from the contribution of the faithful rather than from the coffers of the state; the political responsibilities the ulama had assumed during the prolonged period of political vacuum in the mideighteenth century; and finally, the residence, since the nineteenth century, of the most prominent ulama in Iraq (under a government hostile to Iran), which could also add to their willingness to involve themselves in oppositionary activities.[2] The following assessment by a British observer, who traveled extensively in Iran early in the nineteenth century, illustrates the power they already had at that time: "It is not easy to describe persons who fill no office, receive no appointment, who have no specific duties, but who are called, from their superior learning, piety and virtue, by the silent but unanimous suffrage of the inhabitants . . . to be their guides in religion, and their protectors against the violence and oppression of their rulers, and who receive from those by whose feelings they are elevated a respect and duty which lead the proudest king to join the popular voice."[3]

Referring to the same period, the annalist Reza Qoli Hedayat wrote: "The decrees of the Ulama had preference over those of the shah. . . . Had the shah felt compelled to oppose their policies, the people would have toppled the monarchy."[4] Contemporary travelers[5] as well as later scholars[6] have made similar observations.

2. For discussions of the influence of these developments on the growing power of the ulama, see: Nikki R. Keddie, "The Roots of the Ulama's Power in Modern Iran," Nikki R. Keddie, ed., *Scholars, Saints and Sufis: Muslim Religious Institutions in the Middle East since 1500* (Berkeley: University of California Press, 1972), 211–27; Ann K. Lambton, "A Reconsideration of the Position of the Marjaʿ al-Taqlid and the Religious Institutions," *Studia Islamica*, 20 (1965), 115–35, and *Qajar Persia* (Austin: University of Texas Press, 1987), 277–300; Vanessa Martin, *Islam and Modernism: The Iranian Revolution of 1906* (Syracuse: Syracuse University Press, 1989), 11–64.

3. John Malcolm, *History of Persia* (London: Murray, 1815), 2:432.

4. Reza Qoli Hedayat, *Rowzat al-Safaʾ-ye Naseri* (Tehran, 1960/61), 9:647.

5. For example, Jacob E. Polak, *Persian: Das Land und seine Bewohner* (Leipzig, 1865), 1:128 and 2:55, 271; E. G. Browne, *A Year amongst the Persians* (London: Adam and Black, 1893), 370–71; George N. Curzon, *Persia and the Persian Question* (London: Longman, 1892); Wills, *In the Land of the Lion and Sun*. More in the nature of a caricature is the description given by J. J. Morier, *Haji Baba of Isfahan* (New York: Heritage, 1947), 7, 42–48, 278–82, 303–14.

6. Hamid Algar, *Religion and State in Iran, 1785–1906* (Berkeley: University of California Press, 1969); Shahrough Akhavi, *Religion and Politics in Contemporary Iran: Clergy-State*

The clerics could not deny the gap between the idealized view of Islam's superiority in history and the present reality of backwardness if measured against the material strength of the West. But in their view it was through the return to true Islam, rather than through westernization, that the glorious past could be recovered.[7] Innovation they rejected as un-Islamic. In traditional Muslim usage, bid'a (innovation) was the converse of sunna (connoting the accepted practice of the orthodox) and eventually became a synonym for heresy. A saying attributed to the Prophet ran: "The worst things are those that are novelties, every novelty is an innovation, every innovation is an error and every error leads to hell-fire."[8] Resistance to change was explained by a leading Iranian intellectual late in the nineteenth century who said his countrymen regarded it as their "religious obligation to oppose any idea imported from the West."[9]

Not only did mass sentiment reflect and support clerical attitudes, but political leaders, too, resorted to arguments from the arsenal of the ulama. 'Abbas Mirza, for example, complained in 1812 that his brother and political rival, Mohammad 'Ali, had rendered him and his nezam-e jadid (new order) odious by arguing that "in adopting the customs of the infidels he was subverting... Islam."[10]

Other power groups also rejected change, each for its own reasons. These included the Qajar shah and the royal princes (shahzadegan), influential courtiers (darbaris), leading notables (a'yan), and aristocrats (ashraf) from whose midst came army commanders, governors and "titled officials," major landowners (malekin), and the tribal chiefs (khans). The wealthy Bazar merchants (tojjar) and heads of the guilds (asnaf) held similar views. The most prominent among the elites were the so called thousand families who wielded great power.[11] Like similar

Relations in the Pahlavi Period (New York: SUNY Press, 1980); Nikki R. Keddie, Religion and Rebellion in Iran: The Tobacco Protest of 1891–1892 (London: Frank Cass, 1966).

7. Von Grunebaum, "Education," 12–31.

8. Bernard Lewis, "Some Observations on the Significance of Heresy in the History of Islam," Studia Islamica, 1 (1953), 52 ff.

9. A lecture by Malkom Khan in London, cited in Fereshte Nura'i, Tahqiq dar Bare-ye Afkar-e Mirza Malkom Khan, Nazem al-Dowla (Tehran: Ketabha-ye Jibi, 1973/4), 48–52.

10. James Morier, A Second Journey through Persia, Armenia and Asia Minor (London: Longman, 1818), 213.

11. For an analysis of Iran's social structure in the early nineteenth century, see: Ervand Abrahamian, Iran: Between Two Revolutions (Princeton: Princeton University Press, 1982), 9–36; James A. Bill, The Politics of Iran: Groups, Classes, and Modernization (Columbus: Merrill, 1972), 1–51. Referring to the landlords and the tribal Khans, Lambton wrote that they were "the most powerful element in the kingdom." Malcolm said the same about the leading Bazar merchants, and Morier about the courtiers: Ann K. S. Lambton, Land-

elites in other traditional imperial societies,[12] they supported only such orientations as were in keeping with their corporate identity. They conceived of change—of any kind—as a threat to their interests and status. The reformist trend, James Morier wrote early in the nineteenth century, "had not indeed the Janisaries to oppose it, as in Turkey, but it was cried down by some of the princes, and derided by many of the Nobles."[13] The shah, still enjoying significant power,[14] refused in most cases to make reform legitimate by giving it his consent. Even if he wished to support certain reforms, the elite groups often denied him the freedom to do so.[15]

Moreover, social mobility scarcely existed. Most individuals lived out their lives in the class into which they were born. "No person," Morier wrote, "is ignorant of his proper situation and to the several etiquette attached to it."[16] A royal decree by Mohammad Shah, in 1836/7, stated that social differences (*marateb* and *maqamat*, *tafavoq* and *tafavot*) were "necessary" for "orderly government."[17] Court ideologues went so far as to argue that classes were created by God, who had given to the shah the duty of preserving the barriers between them.[18] Throughout the century the social elites and the political leadership opposed any reforms likely to change the social order, detract from their status, or call their values into question.

Yet some channels for infiltration of new ideas gradually opened

---

lords and Peasants in Persia (London: Oxford University Press, 1953), 140; Malcolm, 2:430; Morier, *Second Journey*, 211.

12. Eisenstadt, *Social Evolution*, 74–75.

13. Morier, *Second Journey*, 211.

14. Although the power of the monarchy declined somewhat at the turn of the century (mainly during the struggle against the Tobacco concession, 1891–1892, and later during the Constitutional Revolution, 1905–1911), it was still powerful in the early nineteenth century. Morier (*Second Journey*, 173) noted then that Persians "allow to their monarch a great character of sanctity, calling him the *Zel Allah*, the shadow of the Almighty, they pay him almost divine honours." Several decades later, Lord Curzon summed up the shah's power by saying, with some exaggeration: "The king may do what he pleases" (Curzon, 2:433).

15. Thus, referring to Mozaffar al-Din Shah, Hedayat wrote: "The shah wants to carry out reforms, but reforms are conceived by those who surround him as contradicting their interests; they will not let him" (Mehdi Qoli Hedayat, *Khaterat va Khatarat* [Tehran: Rangin, 1950/1], 183).

16. James Morier, *A Journey through Persia, Armenia and Asia Minor* (London: 1812), 285.

17. A. Piemontese, "The Status of the Qajar Orders of Knighthood," *East and West*, 19 (September–December 1968), 439–40.

18. Abrahamian, 34.

during the century.[19] As in the Ottoman Empire and Egypt, such trends did not result from conscious preference but were the outgrowth of political and international—mostly military—realities. The policy of inward-looking isolation from the rest of the world (western and Muslim alike), a legacy of the Safavi dynasty, gradually came to an end. The growing importance of Iran's strategic location and the growing involvement and presence of European powers in Iran entailed broader and more frequent contacts; and Iran's manifest weakness quickened the will to imitate the West.

Although Britain had long had an interest in Iran, it was only late in the eighteenth century that the country became important in London's calculations. The establishment in Afghanistan of Zaman Shah (1793–1800) and the threat he posed to India, Napoleon's occupation of Egypt (1798–1801) and the fear that he, too, might turn toward India, made Iran an important link in guarding British interests. The same reasons rendered Iran more important to Russia—Britain's rival in the region. France, too, stepped up its contacts with Iran, particularly during its occupation of Egypt. However, while French interests receded after the Treaty of Tilsit (1807), the interests (and consequently the involvement and presence) of both Britain and Russia became increasingly important during the nineteenth century.[20]

The earliest steps in following western models were entirely in the military field. Defeat in the wars against Russia and the humiliating treaties of Golestan (1813) and Turkmanchay (1828) stimulated in Iran—as the treaties of Karlowitz (1699) and Passarowitz (1718) had done in the Ottoman Empire—the awareness of western superiority and spurred (although to a lesser degree than in the Ottoman Empire) the desire to adopt western methods.[21] Consequently, Iran turned to Europe for military training. A French training mission operated in Tehran

19. Although the main influence came from western Europe, some ideas also came in via the Ottoman Empire and Egypt. Some others, particularly in Azerbayjan, where Turkish was the native tongue, came from Russian Transcaucasia. See Nikki R. Keddie, "Religion and Irreligion in Early Iranian Nationalism," *Comparative Studies in Society and History*, 4 (1962), 265–95.

20. The superpowers' attempts to increase their influence in Iran is discussed by 'Ali Akbar-Niya, *Tarikh-e Siyasi va Diplomasi-ye Iran* (Tehran: Daneshgah-e Tehran, 1969/70); and Avery, *Modern Iran*, 23–45.

21. For the awareness of military weakness as an incentive for adoption of western technology, see: Sadiq, *Farhang*, 303; idem, *Modern Persia*, 17; Hoseyn Makki, *Zendegani-ye Mirza Taqi Khan, Amir Kabir* (Tehran: 'Ilmi, 1958), 183; Fereydun Adamiyyat, *Fekr-e Azadi va Moqaddame-ye Nehzat-e Mashrutiyyat* (Tehran: Sokhan, 1961/2), 20; Mojtabi Minovi, "Avvalin Karavan-e Ma'refat," *Yaghma*, 1953/4, 4:182–83.

from 1807 to 1809,[22] to be followed by a British one. Inescapably, however, the task of running the new armies led to demands for educational, administrative, and economic reform.[23]

Diplomacy was next. In 1809, the first Iranian diplomatic mission was set up in London, to be followed by resident embassies in other European capitals. Living in Europe for long periods, the diplomats, their secretaries, and companions not only became acquainted with western culture and politics and reported back about them to Iran, but also—and most important in the long run—learned foreign languages. They were followed by students, the first of whom came to Europe in 1811. In their years at western universities, during the often stormy period of the early nineteenth century, they learned much about the West. Following the military, the diplomats, and the students, the shahs began visiting the newly discovered West. Naser al-Din was the first shah to visit Europe as a tourist, making three tours (in 1873, 1878, and 1889), followed by the trip of his son, Mozaffar al-Din (in 1902). Their impressions,[24] the European attempts to take advantage of these visits to strengthen western ties with Iran, and the endeavors of Iranian reformists to use them to promote westernization[25] added new elements to Iran's links with Europe. Individual Iranian travelers now also began to pay visits to western states.

Economic ties were also beginning to expand. Growing military expenditure, administrative inefficiency, and the extravagance of the shah's court had greatly damaged the economy. To balance the budget, Iran granted, mainly in the second half of the century, generous concessions to foreign firms and governments. In 1872, for example, Julius de Reuter was granted the first major concession (on a scale never to be surpassed) including the right to construct railways throughout the country, work mines, and set up a national bank. In 1889, G. F. Talbot was given a monopoly for the curing and sale of Iran's entire tobacco crop.[26] Economic ties in turn led to visits by foreign experts and the

22. Sadiq, *Farhang*, 305; "Tarikhche-ye Ma'aref-e Iran," *TT*, 1934/5, 4:360–62. This was a monthly publication of the Ministry of Education. Beginning with the seventh volume (1937/8) its name was changed to *Amuzesh va Parvaresh*.

23. For the interrelationship between these processes, see Bernard Lewis, *The Middle East and the West* (New York: Harper and Row, 1964), 37.

24. See diaries of the trips: manuscripts 19/510–13 in the Majlis Library.

25. Thus, for example, Mirza Hoseyn Khan Sepahsalar encouraged Naser al-Din to visit Europe and made sure that Iranian intellectuals accompanied him: Sadiq, *Farhang*, 303, 360–61.

26. For the concessions and their impact on the economy, see Curzon, 1:480–84; and Henry Rawlinson, *England and Russia in the East* (London: 1875), 371–94.

introduction of new means of communication (such as the telegraph), thereby opening yet other channels for westernization.

In the course of the century, and largely as a result of the growing contact with the West, a number of reformist politicians emerged. As was the case throughout Iran's modern history, reform often depended on individual modernizing leaders. Most prominent among them were the crown prince ʿAbbas Mirza, and his chief minister, Mirza Abu-Qasem Qaʾem-maqam, early in the century, Mirza Taqi Khan Amir Kabir in midcentury, and Hajj Mirza Hoseyn Khan Sepahsalar in the 1870s.[27] A growing number of intellectuals, most of them graduates of foreign universities, joined their entourage and guided and encouraged them.

In short, in Iran as in other Muslim countries of the Middle East, the attitude of "ignorant complacency," which had characterized the attitude toward the West for many centuries, came to an end early in the nineteenth century. But it was not yet being replaced by the "anxious emulation" so prominent later on. For the time being, the ambivalent approach of simultaneously wishing to adopt and reject the ways of the strong—but infidel—West still characterized their attitude. Obviously, the East could no longer ignore the threatening strength of the West; rather it sought, as Bernard Lewis put it, to "discover and apply the illusive secret of its greatness and strength."[28] In the view of a growing number of Iranian thinkers, education was one of the main secret sources of western progress. For them, its imitation was no longer an innovation tantamount to an error but rather the high road to salvation.

27. Morier (*Second Journey*, 211) was undoubtedly right when he said of the early nineteenth-century reform movement that "if it had not been for the personal exertions of ʿAbbas Mirza, it must have fallen." The influence of the others was similar.
28. Lewis, *The Middle East and the West*, 45.

1

The New Education

Gradually, a few intellectuals,[1] in Iran as well as in other Muslim countries, came to realize that modern military techniques and technologies could not be implanted into an otherwise unchanged society; it was the whole fabric of the social, economic, and political order (*nazm*) that needed to be reshaped. Above all, some of them concluded that Muslims needed to make the western concept of freedom (*azadi*) their own. As Bernard Lewis has noted, it was a view common at the end of the ninetieth century among Middle Eastern explorers of Europe "that political freedom was the secret source of Western power and success, the Aladdin's lamp with which the East might conjure up the genie of progress and win the fabulous treasures of the gorgeous and mysterious Occident."[2] Some Muslim intellectuals regarded the expansion of education as the prerequisite of freedom, others as its inevitable result. For both alike, progress, freedom, and education were intertwined and inseparable.

The acknowledgment that western education was vital for the

1. "Intellectuals" is a term not easily defined. Broad definitions are those of W. C. Smith ("one who uses his mind to see the world as it is") and of Raymond Aron ("all nonmanual workers"). In this book the term is used to denote what Aron termed "experts and men of letters" and mainly those of the "inner circle" who "live by and for the exercise of the intellect": Raymond Aron, *The Opium of the Intellectuals* (New York: Doubleday, 1957), 203–5; W. C. Smith, "The Intellectuals in the Modern Development of the Islamic World," in Sidney N. Fischer, ed., *Social Forces in the Middle East* (New York: Cornell University Press, 1955), 203–4.
2. Lewis, *The Middle East and the West*, 47.

achievement of progress and freedom became current among Muslim intellectuals around the middle of the nineteenth century. Sadeq Rif'at Pasha and Seyyed Mostafa Sami (in the 1840s) and the Young Ottomans (in the 1860s and 1870s) in the Ottoman Empire;[3] Rifa'a Rafi' al-Tahtawi (1840s), Muhammad 'Abduh and Lutfi al-Sayyid (toward the end of the century)[4] in Egypt; and Khayr al-Din Pasha (in midcentury) in Tunisia[5] gave profound expression to such views. Similar ideas were expressed by Iranians: Mirza Saleh Shirazi (in the 1810s), Mostafa Khan Afshar (in the late 1820s), and Amir Kabir (in the 1840s). But in Iran, as in other parts of the Muslim Middle East, they became widespread only in the second half of the century with the emergence of a new group of thinkers educated in Europe. To achieve political freedom and socioeconomic progress, they argued, the country must adopt the methods of western education.

Though not entirely divorced from their Iranian-Muslim heritage, these thinkers found inspiration for their views on education primarily in the West. Their writings show traces of French eighteenth-century thought on education (Rousseau, Condorcet) and of Pestalozzi's theories. Some also betray the influence of the founding fathers of the United States (Thomas Jefferson, James Madison, John Hancock, John Adams), who held that freedom and illiteracy were irreconcilable. Others reflect the views of Adam Smith on the economic importance of education. However, given the prevalent religious ambience and their own traditional upbringing, they sought—often enough unconvincingly or awkwardly—to accommodate western ideas with Islam. (Some exceptions were Mirza Fath 'Ali Akhundzade, who suffered *takfir* [i.e., was declared a heretic] for his secularist views; 'Abd al-Rahim Talebov [Talebzade]; and Mirza Aqa Khan Kermani.) Early in the century, 'Abbas Mirza admitted that to allay opposition to his proposed reforms, he used quotations from Islamic religious literature and had them "approved by the chiefs of the [religious] law . . . and disseminated throughout the country."[6] In 1876, Nazem al-Dowla Malkom Khan proposed that reformists should present all the innovations they wished to introduce in Islamic terms, and so make them more easily

3. Bernard Lewis, *The Emergence of Modern Turkey*, 2d ed. (London: Oxford University Press, 1965), 111–16, 130–32.

4. Albert Hourani, *Arabic Thought in the Liberal Age: 1798–1939* (London: Oxford University Press, 1962), 155–59, 173–75.

5. According to him, the roots of Europe's strength and prosperity were "political institutions based on justice and freedom," but he knew that these in turn depended on education (Hourani, 90–93).

6. Morier, *Second Journey*, 213.

acceptable to the people.[7] He labeled his approach "reformation of Islam,"[8]—which is reminiscent of Muhammad ʿAbduh's "Islamic modernism." Many of his colleagues held this to be the most appropriate way to gain support for their novel ideas. But though they often couched their advocacy for educational reform in traditional Islamic vocabulary, it was undoubtedly the European model that influenced and inspired them most.

Intellectuals on the New Education

Among the Iranian intellectuals who came to think of education as the principal pre-condition for freedom and progress, Malkom Khan (1833–1908),[9] stands out as the most original, profound, and influential. Malkom studied in Paris and lived abroad (mainly in Paris, Istanbul, and London) for many years. He was well acquainted with the thought and life-style of the West, which he aspired to imitate in Iran. He was, in fact, the first advocate of comprehensive educational change, as one can learn from his first treatise (published in the late 1850s), *Ketabche-ye Gheybi* (Booklet Inspired from the Unseen World), better known as *Daftar-e Tanzimat* (The Book of Reforms).

Apparently under the influence of Darwin and of eighteenth-century humanism, Malkom spoke in his treatise *Osul-e Adamiyyat* (Principles of Humanism) of three stages in the development in nature: inanimate, animal, and human. Man's ability to rise from the animal stage to that

7. A letter to Sepahsalar, P.R.O., F.O. (Public Record Office, Foreign Office of the British Foreign Ministry), 65.

8. Wilfrid S. Blunt, *Secret History of the English Occupation of Egypt* (London, 1907), 83–84.

9. Malkom was born to an Armenian family from Julfa. His father had converted to Islam, presumably because of practical considerations. At the age of ten, Malkon left for Paris and later, with recommendations from Amir Kabir, studied political science there. Upon his return to Iran (1851), he entered government service and worked as a teacher and translator at the newly established Dar al-Fonun (1852) and as personal interpreter to the shah (from 1856). He was accused of being "irreligious" and forced into exile. He spent a short period in Baghdad (1863) and then in Istanbul from where, owing to Sepahsalar's patronage, he was later able to submit his reform projects to the government. He then returned to be appointed adviser to Sepahsalar (then the prime minister) and was elevated to the nobility with the rank of *Nazem al-Dowla*. In 1873, when the shah was about to leave for his first European tour, Malkom was nominated consul, and later ambassador, to London, where he stayed for sixteen years. His involvement in financial scandals led to his dismissal. He remained in Europe until appointed ambassador to Rome (1902). On Malkom and his thought, see: Algar, *Malkom*; Nuraʾi; Adamiyyat, *Azadi*, 94–108; Malek Khan Sasani, *Siyasatgaran-e Dowre-ye Qajar* (Tehran, 1959/60), 127–47.

of humanism (adamiyyat) depended on acquiring knowledge ('ilm): as long as people did not "enjoy the lightness of knowledge," they could not "elevate themselves to the stage of humanism."[10] Elsewhere, presumably under the influence of Kant, he discerned three other stages in the development of human civilization—religious, philosophical, and scientific—parallel to childhood, adolescence, and maturity. To achieve the highest level, societies, just like individuals, must acquire knowledge.[11] The celebrated preacher Mirza Nasrollah Esfahani Malek al-Motakallemin followed suit, pointing to education as making the difference between the human and the animal state. Whereas ancient thinkers had believed that what distinguished man from animal was his ability "to express his thoughts," today's scholars thought that "the difference between them is in their knowledge," he wrote in 1901. Only by knowledge could man "subordinate the powers of nature to his command."[12]

Sepahsalar (1826–1881)[13] is known for his political rather than his intellectual career. Nevertheless, he played an influential role in the country's intellectual development, mainly by supporting intellectuals, newspapers, and cultural activities. He was motivated by a profound admiration for the West and a strong desire to imitate its civilization. To him, European civilization was civilization par excellence and "anyone who wished to become civilized had to emulate [it]."[14] But the Iranians, he complained, believed that they had already "reached the highest degree of progress" and that their affairs needed no improvement.[15] The treatises 'Ilm va Jahl (Knowledge and Ignorance) and Tar-

10. Nazem al-Dowla Malkom Khan, Kolliyyat-e Malkom (Tehran, 1907), 232–34, 238–44.

11. Nura'i, 200.

12. Mehdi Malekzade, Tarikh-e Enqelab-e Mashrutiyyat-e Iran (Tehran, 1948/9), 1: 152–54.

13. Sepahsalar spent many years abroad (by the age of forty-three he had spent a total of twenty-two years out of the country). He studied in Paris and at Dar al-Fonun and served as consul in Bombay and as ambassador in Istanbul during the hectic years 1858–1870. He was appointed minister of justice, and of war, and commander-in-chief of the army before becoming prime minister in 1871. He later held important positions as minister of war and foreign affairs. On the man and his thought, see: Fereydun Adamiyyat, Andishe-ye Taraqqi va Hokumat-e Qanun 'Asr-e Sepahsalar (Tehran: Kharazmi, 1972/3), 144–53; idem, Ideolozhi-ye Nehzat-e Mashrutiyyat-e Iran (Tehran: Payam, 1976/7), 25, 104–9; Guity Nashat, The Origins of Modern Reform in Iran, 1870–1880 (Urbana: University of Illinois Press, 1982); Shaul Bakhash, Iran: Monarchy, Bureaucracy and Reform under the Qajars: 1858–1896 (London: Ithaca Press, 1978).

14. Nashat, 137.

15. Letter of 16 July 1869, archives, Ministry of Foreign Affairs, Tehran, as quoted by Nashat, 35–36.

biyyat (Culture) reflect his views best.[16] In the first, inspired by the Muslim historian Ibn Khaldun, he contrasts nomadic with settled living as indicating the level of development. At first, in the state of "wildness and lack of education," man is engaged only in securing his basic livelihood; with the beginning of education the second phase sets in, but people are not yet able "to utilize science and technology"; then follows the "phase of civilization (*tamaddon*)" in which education develops sufficiently for man to subordinate nature.[17]

Already in 1825/6, a writer by the name of Ja'far Ibn Ishaq argued that "learned people" (*ahl-e danesh*) were "God's superior creatures." "Knowledge," he stressed, "is more vital than worship." But he distinguished between religious and scientific knowledge. Those possessing only the former, he denounced as "bad people" and "creatures of the devil . . . knowledgeable in their speech but ignorant in their hearts"—people who declare "truth to be falsehood and vice versa."[18]

Such perceptions underlay the calls for compulsory education, made as early as the 1870s. Against the background of almost total illiteracy and an inflexible class structure, some intellectuals advocated mass education for the advancement of society as a whole, as well as of the individual—in line with the principles of liberal education. The author of *Tarbiyyat* argued that it was "the duty" of every government to oblige parents to send their children to school for the benefit "of the state and the people." He concluded that this was "the principal cause" of progress.[19] Similar views were set forth by Mirza Yusef Khan Mostashar al-Dowla.[20] In his treatise *Yek Kalame* (A Single Word), he urged the adoption of the "essential principles" of French law, including compulsory, state-run education, free for those unable to pay for it.[21] A

16. Apparently he did not write these pieces himself, but they are believed to have been inspired by him and to reflect his ideas (Adamiyyat, *Taraqqi*, 145–53).

17. Ibid., 148–49.

18. Ja'far Ibn Ishaq, "Tahaffot al-Moluk," manuscript, 1825/6, cited in a collection of unpublished sources from the Qajar period: Fereydun Adamiyyat and Homa Nateq, eds., *Afkar-e Ejtema'i va Siyasi va Eqtesadi dar Athar-e Montasher-Nashode-ye Dowran-e Qajar* (Tehran: Agah, 1977), 32–43.

19. Adamiyyat, *Taraqqi*, 144–53; Nashat, 148.

20. He served in the foreign service, in Tiflis and Petersburg (1854–1867) and Paris (1867–1870), among other places; he supported some of the secularist ideas of Akhundzade and was influenced by Malkom; and he advocated the adoption of a French-style constitution. See Mehdi Bamdad, *Sharh-e Hal-e Rejal-e Iran dar Qorun-e 12–14 Hejri* (Tehran: Navar, 1968/9), 4:490–93; Nezam al-Islam Kermani, *Tarikh Bidari-ye Iraniyan* (Tehran: Bonyad-e Farhang, 1967/8), 1:177–204; Adamiyyat, *Azadi*, 182–208; Algar, *Malkom*, 140–41.

21. Adamiyyat, *Azadi*, 206; Bakhash 40.

similar call for "public (*melli*) education" is included in a book written by Abu-Taleb Behbahani. He claimed that the source of western strength was its freedom and the precondition of freedom, in turn, was "universal education."[22] Similarly, ʿAli Bakhsh Qajar demanded (1878/9) that the government set up "public schools" in every single town and village.[23] In an article titled "Siyahat-e Modon" (1896/7), the anonymous writer stated that the spread of education was "the first condition for progress" and recommended opening schools for "the poor and weak" sections of the population.[24] ʿAbd al-Rahim Talebzade, known as Talebov,[25] argued that the government had the duty to provide schooling and that parents had the duty to send their children to school. Unlike his colleagues, he specifically pointed to the role of education in promoting social and occupational mobility; education, he said, would create opportunities for "distinguished appointments" and "good matches."[26]

Advocacy of universal education and especially the emphasis on its role as a social equalizer were, however, rare during this period. As a rule, supporters of the new education stressed its importance for the community rather than the individual. Malkom's assertions—in his treatises *Rushnaʾi* (Enlightenment), *Daftar-e Tanzimat*, and *Shaykh va Vazir*—of the benefits of education for society[27] were commonplace in the writings of intellectuals at the time. In the last named book, he wrote: "The strength of states today depends more and more on the knowledge and education of their people. In the past, the power of the Arab empire was based on the qualifications and characteristics of the leaders. But the strength of the French government [today] is the result of the education of the people. In our days, a situation such as

22. Abu-Taleb Behbahani, "Minhaj al-ʿAli," Manuscript, 1877/8, cited in Adamiyyat and Nateq, 99–114. The author left Iran in 1866/7 to live in Egypt. He was acquainted with the reforms in the Ottoman Empire and familiar with the writings of Malkom.

23. Ibid., 76–79.

24. The manuscript is included in Adamiyyat and Nateq, 248–65.

25. Talebov (1834–1910) was a businessman from Azerbayjan who became acquainted with western thinking through Russian translations; he supported constitutionalism, new education, and secularization. Among his more important books and treatises are: *Ketab-e Ahmad* (Istanbul, 1895/6); *Masaʾel al-Hayat* (Tiflis, 1908/9); *Masalek al-Mohsenin* (Cairo, 1907/8); *Azadi va Siyasat* (first published in 1911/2; Tehran: Sahar, 1978/9). For more information about him, see Iraj Afshar, "Talebov," *Yaghma*, (1953/4), 4:214–21; Rashid Yasemi, "Andishe-ye Talebov," *Sokhan*, 4, issue 5; and Afshar's introduction to *Azadi va Siyasat*, 9–23.

26. Talebov, *Ketab-e Ahmad*, 2:4–5.

27. Malkom, *Kolliyyat*, 92–93; Mohit Tabatabaʾi, *Majmuʿe Aʾthar-e Mirza Malkom Khan* (Tehran: Danesh, 1948/9); Malkom, "Daftar-e Tanzimat," Manuscript no. 5154/1, Majlis Library.

existed in the Arab empire [in the early days of Islam] is no longer sufficient. We must now have a state like France and England; and such a kind of state can exist only after providing education for the public at large."

The point was often made that the elites also needed to be educated. Senior appointments should be the reward of cognitive skills rather than the prize of inherited privilege—as was usually the case. Some intellectuals took the arguments a step farther by stressing the necessity of educating political leaders as well. Malkom complained that Iranians tended to confuse the terms intellect ($'aql$) and knowledge ($'ilm$) and preferred "natural intellect" over acquired education. Consequently, "most of our ministers" regarded their intellect, however "defective," as preferable to greater knowledge. What wise Europeans learn at school "with a thousand troubles," Iranian statesmen "expect to absorb in few minutes" while wandering around.[28] Rulers need not necessarily be highly educated themselves, but they must appreciate the importance of education (as Muhammad 'Ali had done in Egypt). Only thus will they know how to appoint competent people to key positions and to develop the educational system.[29]

Since it was the military strength of the West that impressed the Middle East most, it was only natural for the intellectuals to stress education as a means to promote military power. They pointed out that in the early days of Islam, an Arab army could be powerful even when lacking in education; presently, however, the strength of the European armies stemmed from educational and scientific qualifications. This, the author of 'ilm va Jahl argued, made it possible for small countries to defeat much more populous states.[30] In Shaykh va Vazir, Malkom wrote that "in the days of our great Caliphs, the strength of states stemmed from the number of their troops"; but today, in India, "30,000 British rule over 150 m Asians." This was so because "in the past, states fought each other with the strength of their arms, now they fight with the power of science."[31] In Daftar-e Tanzimat he added: "The strength of Europe derives from a thousand sorts of different instruments. Failure to adopt each and any of them will make it impossible to have armies as the Europeans have." The "instru-

---

28. See arguments set forward in Daftar-e Tanzimat, Osul-e Taraqqi, and Neda'-ye 'Edalat, Majlis Library. See also Algar, Malkom, 16.

29. See his Daftar-e Tanzimat and Esteqraz-e Khareji (Foreign Loans): Tabataba'i, 8–10, 191; manuscript no. 3787, Library of Tehran University.

30. Adamiyyat, Taraqqi, 148–49.

31. Malkom, Kolliyyat, 91.

ments" he specified—social, economic, and political—all depended on
education.[32]

The interrelation of education, freedom, and progress became the
mainstay of intellectual argument in the second half of the nineteenth
century. In dozens of treatises, Malkom drove home his view of education as the prerequisite for progress in general and for a constitutional order in particular. In *Shaykh va Vazir*, a dialogue between the
Shaykh (representing religious conservatism) and the *Vazir* (the reformist minister), the latter argues that "there can be no doubt that the
secret of the strength (*qodrat*), welfare (*refah*), and the very survival
(*baqa'*) of nations depends on the light of knowledge," and that "unless
it adopts western education, Iran will fail to equal the achievements
of the West."[33] In his *Neda'-ye 'Edalat* (Call of Justice), he explained
that only the spread of education had enabled the West to establish a
political order based on justice. "Iran," he went on, "is poor, Iran is
wretched, Iran is bankrupt, and all because it lacks constitutional justice
(*'edalat-e qanuni*) and all this stems from its leaders' failure to perceive
the importance of education."[34] In *Osul-e Adamiyyat* (Principles of Humanism), he said "only knowledge" made human life meaningful,[35]
and in *Dastgah-e Divan* (The Divan [i.e., the Court] System), he stated
that the advancement of education was vital for the establishment of
a "new civilization (*tamaddon*)."[36]

In the first issue of his newspaper, *Qanun* (Law),[37] Malkom stressed
once again that "a great deal of Iran's aspirations for progress" depended on education. In issue number 11, he asked: "Who is the
greatest of Iran's kings," and answered: "He who rescues Allah's wor-
shippers from the courtiers' suppression by spreading knowledge and
by establishing a constitution."

Malkom's thinking is not, however, free from contradictions. From
what might be seen as the practice of *taqiyya* (prudential concealment
of faith) he often changed his line of argument "according to the au-

32. Manuscript no. 5154/1, Majlis Library; see also Adamiyyat, *Azadi*, 119–20.
33. Malkom, *Kolliyyat*, 88–95.
34. Manuscript no. 3787, Library of Tehran University.
35. Malkom, *Kolliyyat*, 232.
36. Tabataba'i, 79–80. Similarly in *Esteqraz-e Khareji* (Foreign Loans), 189–91, and in
Rushna'i, a treatise written in 1878/9 and quoted by Nura'i, 103–4.
37. *Qanun* was published in London (forty-one issues in three and a half years)
beginning 20 February 1890. Banned in Iran, it was nevertheless widely read there among
intellectuals, and was popular even at court. See Hajj Mirza Yahya Dowlatabadi, *Tarikh-
e Mo'aser ya Hayat-e Yahya* (Tehran: Ibn Sina, 1957/8), 1:123; Bamdad, 4:149–50. A complete
collection of *Qanun* with an introduction was published recently: Homa Nateq, *Qanun*
(Tehran: Amir Kabir, 1976/7).

dience he was addressing."[38] It was, for example, not sufficiently clear whether he regarded the spread of education as a prerequisite for a constitutional regime or as its outcome.[39] But such inconsistencies—characteristic of many intellectuals of his age and milieu—did not detract from his great, perhaps overriding influence.[40]

Sepahsalar, influenced by the Young Ottomans,[41] was mainly concerned with the establishment of a constitutional order to guarantee political freedom and social justice. To achieve these, however, he held that a European-style education was essential. *'Ilm va Jahl* , attributed to him, stresses that "the key to spiritual and material progress is knowledge, and knowledge alone. In any sphere of life, be it politics . . . the army . . . or the administration . . . one can achieve perfection only by knowledge." Progress depended on it and "nothing important can materialize without knowledge." The pursuit of knowledge was the source of mankind's "distinction, prosperity and superiority."[42] In a report from Istanbul, he wrote: "What Iran needs more than anything else today are men with experience and know-how . . . . All the progress of Europe has come from the work and wisdom of men with foresight and experience . . . . A governor cannot understand his duties without education and a knowledge of world affairs and of history . . . enabling him to study the governments that have attained progress . . . . In short, individuals can by perspicacity transform a small nation into a strong and great one; similarly, it is possible for individuals to destroy a great nation by sheer carelessness."[43]

Mirza Yusef Khan attached similar importance to the spread of education but considered a constitutional regime its prerequisite. Once such a regime existed, education was essential for its perpetuation. In

38. Algar, *Religion*, 189.

39. In *Shaykh va Vazir*, *Neda'-ye 'Edalat*, and *Rushna'i*, he put education first, in *Qanun* the constitution.

40. Zel al-Soltan and Na'ini compared Malkom's contribution to that of Plato and Aristotle; see Zel al-Soltan, *Tarikh-e Godhashte-ye Mas'udi* (Tehran, 1907), 125; and Hajj Pirzade Na'ini, *Safarname* (Tehran, 1964/5), 1:320–21. Nazem al-Islam Kermani equated him with Rousseau and Voltaire, in *Tarikh Bidari-ye Iraniyan*, 121. For similar appraisals, see Hasan Taqizade, *Tarikh Ava'el-e Enqelab-e Mashrutiyyat* (Tehran, 1949/50); Malekzade, 1:225–27.

41. His dispatches from Istanbul reflected many of their ideas. He demanded that his reports be brought to the attention of the heads of state, to "enlighten them" (Adamiyyat, *Taraqqi*, 144–53). But he knew that they were treated "like fiction . . . read once and then forgotten for ever" (letter of 20 June 1869, quoted by Nashat, 35–36).

42. *Mirikh*, 27 February 1879, quoted by Nashat, 144.

43. Letter of 6 August 1866, archive of the Ministry of Foreign Affairs, Tehran, quoted by Nashat, 145.

Yek Kalame, he claimed that "a single word" contained the key to progress: the word "law." However, without education the reign of law would not survive.[44] In a report to the crown prince, Mozaffar al-Din, he made the point—apparently for the first time in Iran—that education was also important for fostering national unity.[45]

At the turn of the century, appeals by intellectuals for the expansion of the new education became more frequent and more insistent. This was mainly the result of the sharpening struggle over a constitution, the growing number of those who had already acquired a modern education, and the ongoing campaign for the establishment of new schools. One of their most vigorous spokesmen was Talebov. In his *Azadi va Siyasat,* he noted that "lack of knowledge and spiritual poverty" were the "enemies of freedom." "Even the clerics must know . . . that safeguarding the domain of Islam is impossible without knowledge."[46] More than any of his colleagues, he emphasized the interrelationship of education and the economy. Like Adam Smith (whose influence is clearly evident in Talebov's writings), he regarded "human potential *(este'dad)*" as "economic wealth" and education as the main means for its cultivation. His educational philosophy, however, was best expressed in *Ketab-e Ahmad* (The Book of Ahmad). This book, apparently inspired by Rousseau's *Emile,* is a dialogue between the author and two fictitious sons, Ahmad and Mahmud (recalling Rousseau's Sophia and Emile). He tells them:

> Should we possess the potential, i.e. knowledge, and understand the meaning of property, we would not squander what we dissipate now. . . . But we don't have potential and we lack education. Why? Because we don't have laws. We don't have [proper] *maktabs,* [new] schools, or teachers, and, other than some mythical books, we have no literature. . . . We have neither motivation nor educators. Therefore we don't possess wealth. . . . [Therefore] any Muslim who is a patriot and loyal to the Shah will admit that if we will [only] have a constitution, we will have education, and [consequently] will possess wealth, order *(nazm)* and independence. But if we ignore these truths, we will be nothing but fools who betray their nation, homeland and religion.[47]

An important supporter of the new schools was Malek al-Motakallemin. Inaugurating the Sadat school (1898), he gave vent to his boundless expectations:

44. Bamdad, 4:490–93; Adamiyyat, *Azadi,* 182–211.
45. The report is given in Kermani, 1:206–11.
46. Talebov, *Azadi va Siyasat,* 111, 113.
47. Talebov, *Ketab-e Ahmad,* 2:80–84, 89–90. See also his *Masa'el al-Hayat,* 60–61, 74–75.

We have gathered here today to lay a cornerstone for the guidance of
thought and . . . to kindle the light of knowledge and virtues, so that
under their intense blaze the dark hearts and spirits of our fellow Iranians
will brighten; so that with their help the flags of knowledge and education
will fly proudly, ignorance will give way to knowledge, and darkness
be replaced by light, and . . . we will all join the caravan of civilization
. . . . Only through knowledge can mankind achieve the highest peaks
of progress; only under its aegis is it possible to establish justice and
bring redemption to the world . . . only through it can freedom and equality be achieved.

Turning to the young students, he went on: "Having come to study
at these 'factories for producing human beings' (*karkhane-ye adam-sazi*),
you ought to know that the destiny of the world, the fate of your
nation, your own future and that of your children— depend on knowledge alone."[48]
The supporters of the constitutional revolution were divided among
themselves in their approach to the new education. One group, among
whom the clerics were the most adamant, acknowledged the importance of education in general terms but regarded the new schooling
system as dangerous to Muslim civilization and to their own status in
the society. The liberal, westernizing intellectuals, by contrast, extolled
it as the principal means of approaching western civilization. Aware
of the power of Islam and the clerics, the constitutionalists tried to
argue that modern education did not necessarily contradict religion.
Only a few, such as Akhundzade, Sepahsalar, and Talebov, advocated
from time to time the separation of education from religion.[49] The most
sophisticated line in arguing for an accommodation was, again, Malkom's. In *Shaykh va Vazir*, the *Shaykh* wonders: "How is it at all possible
to adopt the principles of infidels?" and the *Vazir* replies: "I do not
deny that they are infidels. My only claim is that the strength of Europe
derives from their unique mechanisms. If we wish to gain the same
power, we must adopt in full their mechanisms and instruments. If
we fail to do so, let us not deceive ourselves that we shall ever equal
them . . . . The ulama should either permit us to imitate the principles
of European strength, or bring some squadrons of angels down from
heaven to rescue us from European rule."[50]
But attempts by intellectuals to describe the new education as being
in line with the Islamic precept of the "search of knowledge" (*talab al-
ʿilm*) failed to convince the ulama; neither could they persuaded that

48. Malekzade, 1:152–54.
49. Talebov, *Ketab-e Ahmad*, 2:80–81; Adamiyyat, *Taraqqi*, 152.
50. Malkom, *Kolliyyat*, 89–91.

education was essential for a constitutional regime. In 1906, Abu al-Qasem Khan Naser al-Molk, a statesman educated in Britain, who regarded education as a prerequisite for constitutionalism, wrote to Ayatollah Seyyed Mohammad Tabataba'i to justify such an approach. Elsewhere, he wrote, constitutionalism, "is the origin of happiness (se'adat), nobleness (sherafat), and honor (eftekhar)"; in Iran it may become the "origin of chaos, destruction, suffering, insecurity, and thousands of additional sore evils," because the country lacked "the knowledge and potential" to absorb it and turn it to good use. A constitutional order could not survive in an illiterate society, and progress did not depend on the formal approval of a constitution but on the spread of education. He added passionately: "Is there any doubt that to change the current situation we need educated people? No!!! In the name of Allah, we need educated people. In the name of the Ka'ba, the prophet, religion (din) and the [Shi'i] faith (madhhab), we need educated people. The one and only way toward progress, equality, justice, happiness, sovereignty and pride is through the spread of knowledge and the existence of people who are educated according to the requirements of the times." The civilized states had achieved the "highest degree of strength and wealth," he added, only after first reforming their educational system. The attempt—supported by Tabataba'i and his fellow ulama—to make the constitution precede educational reform contradicted the national interest. "On the Day of Judgement," the Iranian people will say to the ulama that they could have secured "happiness" for Iran "but failed to do so. . . . All you have done was useless . . . since you did not follow the correct path . . . i.e., first to secure us education, according to the requirements of the times, and rescue us from ignorance so that enlightened with education, we would build up our dignity and happiness."[51]

Similar criticism was voiced by Hajj Mohammad 'Ali Sayyah Mahalati. He blamed the ulama as well as the political establishment and the social and economic elites for deliberately keeping the people "ignorant, illiterate, in permanent need and dependent on them."[52] Nonetheless, throughout the period discussed here, the ulama remained the most adamant opponents of the "new education." Even to those ulama

---

51. The letter is quoted in Kermani, 2:214–23.

52. Sayyah was born to a family of clerics and studied at the holy shrines in Iraq. In 1878, he left for eighteen years of travel in Europe, America, and the Far East (hence his nickname Sayyah, i.e., traveller). His memoirs are included in his book Khaterat-e Hajj Sayyah (Tehran: Ibn Sina, 1967/8). The above quotation is from p. 12. For similar views, see Mohammad Reza Fashahi, Gozaresh-e Kutah-e Tahavvolat-e Fekri va Ejtema'i dar Jame'e-ye Feodali-ye Iran (Tehran, 1976), 322–27.

who supported the constitution, the "new education" often remained "tantamount to irreligiosity."[53]

Education and its interconnection with constitutionalism was also stressed in the debates of the *anjomans* (secret societies) which proliferated at that time. Characteristic are the arguments set forth by Al-Riyasateyn Kermani (addressing one of the important *anjomans* of Kerman in 1905): "As long as the people do not have education, they will remain ignorant of their rights, and as long as they do not know their rights, one should not hope for anything from reforms."[54] In another discussion the same year, Shaykh Mohammad Shirazi ("the philosopher") argued that in the prevailing condition of "almost total illiteracy" even if "a constitutional republic" was declared, the people would still "remain the slaves" of the same influential groups (*motenafedhin*). Only education could guarantee them freedom and social justice.[55]

All in all, Iranian intellectuals of the late nineteenth century tended to regard education as a magic cure for all the ills of society and were optimistic, or rather overoptimistic, about the ease with which the educational achievements of the West could be transplanted to Iran.

Intellectuals on Traditional Schooling

With so much depending on education, the intellectuals criticized the traditional religious schooling system as stagnant and incapable of facing up to the challenge of the times. They attacked it mainly on two counts: for the distorted social perceptions on the part of the religious and, often enough, the political establishment that were reflected in the system of traditional education; and for its own inherent demerits. Social traditions valuing lineage above merit; the neglect of educational reform on the part of those in power; and the religious establishment's ideological opposition to the new education—all came in for persistent criticism.

Since it was ancestry rather than competence that determined a person's occupation and status, the elite had little need, and the lower classes little incentive, to see to their children's schooling. Malkom mocked the prevailing practice in his *Dastgah-e Divan*: "One of my sons has extraordinary talents, but he does neither pursue knowledge nor

53. 'Ali Bakhsh Qajar, "Mizan al-Mellal," manuscript, around 1878/9, published in Adamiyyat and Nateq, 76–79.
54. Kermani, 2:13–14.
55. Ibid., 42.

do I encourage him to study. The reason is that in Iran one can be appointed minister even if one has no education; the rank of brigadier-general can be bought for 500 *toman*; and a person can be made commander-in-chief at the age of fifteen. But I, even if I knew seven languages, would still have to be the servant of a vacant-minded illiterate. Even should my son study public administration, it will still be the children of the rich who will become provincial governors."[56]

Indeed, a number of distinguished families had a traditional claim to certain political or administrative appointments, much as certain crafts were traditional in others.[57] *Shaykh va Shukh*—a book similar in title, style, and contents to *Shaykh va Vazir*—refers to the "trading of positions" as a "historical occupation" of Iranians.[58] The sentiment of the critics was brought out by a frequently quoted phrase attributed to Naser al-Din Shah: "I want my courtiers to be illiterate and lacking in understanding and knowledge to the degree that they will not be able to tell whether Brussels is a city or a cabbage."[59] Writing in the tenth issue of *Qanun*, Malkom accused the shah of wishing to keep his subjects "as illiterate as possible" and to "do away with . . . science and the arts." Educated people, he went on, would demand to be treated "like human beings," and that ran counter to the shah's aims.[60] Some critics blamed the great powers instead, who, in their view, thought of the spread of education as endangering their continued exploitation of Iran.[61] But the brunt of the criticism was leveled at the ulama. Here,

56. Tabataba'i, 75–76, 92–93. Similarly in *Shaykh va Vazir* (Malkom, *Kolliyyat*, 92–98).

57. 'Abdollah Mostowfi, *Sharh-e Zendegani-ye man, ya Tarikh-e Ejtema'i va Edari Dowre-ye Qajariye* (Tehran: Tehran Mosavvar, n.d.), 2:329.

58. This unattributed treatise, written in the early 1880s, is quoted in Adamiyyat and Nateq, 144–54. For similar views, see Talebov, *Ketab-e Ahmad*, 2:5–6; Zayn al-'Abedin Maraghe'i, *Siyahat Name-ye Ebrahim Beg* (Cairo, n.d.), 179; Abu-Taleb Behbahani, "Menhaj al-'Ali," Manuscript, 1877/8, as cited in Adamiyyat and Nateq, 99–114.

59. Homayun Khaje-Nuri, *Tarikhche-ye Nim Qarn-e Akhir* (Tehran: Markaz-e Amar, 1966/7), 1957. There were, however, exceptions. Thus, for example, J. Perkins, who taught in the American missionary school in Azerbayjan, quotes a *firman* (issued in 1839) by Mohammad Shah, who, anxious to prove his concern for education, demanded that hospitality be extended to "those learned men . . . [who] teach knowledge to our children." See his book, *A Residence of Eight Years in Persia* (New York: Allen, Morrill & Wardwell, 1843), 397, 404. For Naser al-Din's support of the Dar al-Fonun in its initial stages, see Chapter 2.

60. Adamiyyat and Nateq, 144–54. For similar accusations, see "Tarbiyyat," quoted in Adamiyyat, *Taraqqi*, 144–53; and words of Mirza Yusef Khan, quoted in Kermani, 1:206–11. See also Sayyah, 12; Al-Riyasateyn Kermani (Kermani, 2:42); and Talebov (*Ketab-e Ahmad*, 2:4–5).

61. See the views of Sepahsalar (Sasani, 67–69 and Adamiyyat, *Azadi*, 68–70) and Talebov (*Ketab-e Ahmad*, 2:80–81).

too, Malkom was the most scathing spokesman. In *Nowm va Yaqza*, he made one of his characters say: "Those most hostile to the ordering (*nazm*) of the country, the education and liberty of the people, are the ulama and the fanatic grandees."[62]

The danger the new education posed for the ulama was twofold: for one thing, they would no longer have control over education, to the detriment of both religion and their own status; for another, the *akhunds* (*maktab*, i.e., religious elementary school teachers) stood to lose an important source of income. The arguments put forward by intellectuals to depict reform as compatible with religion had fallen on deaf ears.

Some foreign observers writing early in the nineteenth century had given rather optimistic descriptions of traditional schooling. Sir John Malcolm, for instance, noted: "There are *maktab* schools in every town and city, in which rudiments of Persian and Arabic are taught....This education, [though] slight and superficial . . . has the effect of changing the habits, and of introducing a degree of refinement among those who use it, unknown to their ruder countrymen." Although "often under management of ignorant pedants," he remarked, it was a gratifying sight to watch Persian boys and girls going to school.[63] J. Perkins refers to the "low standard" of the schools but nevertheless adds: "Imperfect as is their education, ... [students] acquire an ease and grace of manners, a propriety of deportment and polish of expression."[64]

For their part, Iranian modernists, who held no such romantic view of the East, could point to three major problem areas in traditional schooling: the curriculum, the method of instruction, and the quality of the teachers.

The *maktabs* and *madreses* (religious schools of higher education) concentrated on teaching the Qur'an, Islam, and some fables in Persian and on good manners. Sciences were not taught. The students were

62. Tabataba'i, 84 (translation by Algar, *Religion*, 189). Similarly, Maraghe'i, 90, 178; Sayyah, 21–26, 88; Talebov, *Ketab-e Ahmad*, 2:80–81; Dowlatabadi, 2:44–46; 180–81; "Tarbiyyat," quoted by Adamiyyat, *Taraqqi*, 152.

63. Malcolm, *History*, 2:422. For more evidence by local and European observers on the state of the educational system throughout the century, see: Mostowfi, 1:219–21; Dowlatabadi, 1:14–16; 'Isa Sadiq, *Yadegar-e 'Omr* (Tehran: Maravi, 1974), 1:13–14, 76–82; Safa, *Madrese*, 731–33; Curzon, 1:493–95; Wills, 337–39; Maraghe'i, 39–47; Perkins, 436–37; Robert G. Watson, *A History of Persia: From the Beginning of the Nineteenth Century to the Year 1858* (London: Smith, Elder, and Co., 1866), 18–19; Ella C. Sykes, *Persia and Its People* (London: Methuen, 1910). On the *Madrese*, see: 'Ali Asghar Hekmat, "Farhang," in *Iranshahr*, 2:1165–1242; Rashid Yasemi, "Daneshju'i," *TT*, 1936/7, 781–91.

64. Perkins, 436. He also emphasized that the missionary schools, too, were attended by some Muslims, including girls (Perkins, 290, 326, 336–37, 404).

not prepared for any useful occupation. The syllabus was totally irrelevant to the country's needs.[65] One graduate of the system wondered
whether the sole intention was to pave the path to paradise, or whether
students were actually supposed "to have any advantage in this world
as well."[66]

The traditional method was rote learning; asking questions was dis-
couraged, and there was no discussion and no attempt at analysis.
Foreign observers noted this with astonishment,[67] local writers with
bitter criticism.[68]

The *maktab* teachers (*akhunds*) were usually lower-ranking *mollas*,
themselves lacking in education and pedagogical training. Malcolm
defined them as "ignorant pedants."[69] In his book of fictitious travels
in Iran, in which he mercilessly exposed the evils of Iranian society,
Hajj Zayn al-'Abedin Maraghe'i describes a meeting with such a
teacher. He had never heard the word "geometry" and did not know
elementary arithmetic: "I asked him to write one thousand two
hundred and thirty-four; he wrote 1000200304." Maraghe'i concluded:
"I realized that he was a true *akhund*."[70] Mehdi Qoli Hedayat wrote of
his own teacher: "May God bless him. He was so illiterate that we,
the students, were correcting his mistakes."[71]

Typical in style and contents of the prevalent criticism is the letter
from Naser al-Molk to Ayatollah Tabataba'i written in 1906. Blaming
the ulama for mismanaging education, he wrote: "We have in Iran
today thousands [sic] of *madreses* . . . but all of them together are not
worth one *dinar* . . . . A gentleman enters the *madrese* at the age of
twenty, hinders other students and wastes the *waqf*'s [endowment's]
money, only to have his corpse carried out at the age of seventy, while
he is still stuck at studying the letter 'M' and his knowledge is not any
greater than on his first day there. Honestly, these *madreses* have created nothing but a band of idlers."[72]

65. See Talebov, *Ketab-e Ahmad*, 1:10–11 and 2:5–7; Naser al-Molk, quoted in Kermani,
2:216–22; Maraghe'i, 46–47; Tabataba'i, 8–10.

66. Dowlatabadi, 1:30.

67. Malcolm, *History*, 2:422; Perkins, 437; Curzon, 1:493–94; Wills, 337–39; Sykes, 61–
64.

68. Dowlatabadi, 1:14–16; Talebov, *Ketab-e Ahmad*, 1:10–11, and 2:5–7; Tabataba'i, 8–
10; Khaje-Nuri, 1973–74; Sadiq, *Yadegar*, 2:13–19 and 76–82; Yasemi, *Daneshju'i*, 786.

69. Malcolm, *History*, 2:422.

70. Maraghe'i, 40 and also 46–47, 178.

71. Mehdi Qoli Hedayat, *Khaterat va Khatarat*, 10.

72. Kermani, 2:216–22. Similar arguments are set out in "Tarbiyyat," quoted in Adamiyyat, *Taraqqi*, 152.

Talebov explained to his son Ahmad why he refused to send him to a *maktab*: "If the *akhund* teaching [your brother] Mahmud had gone through the same teacher training customary in other countries, if he had passed the same exams as they do, if our education system had any resemblance to that of the developed countries . . . I would have allowed you to study at the *maktab*."

And when Ahmad started going to a "new" school, he added:

> [You] see how after studies of only four months in the new school you have gained more knowledge than Mahmud who is attending the old *maktab* for over three years, and you already know English and German. Before the age of nine, the students at the new schools study the history of their nation, the principles of religion, the first elements of geometry and arithmetic, geography, physics, chemistry, literature and several foreign languages. At the age of fifteen, they fully master the science of law and *'ilm-e hayat* (life sciences). But the *tollab* (students of *madrese*), even at the age of seventy, are still stuck in the laws of *taharat* (purification), wondering how to spell that word.[73]

Conclusion

In general terms, as has been seen, Iranian intellectuals, like their counterparts elsewhere in the Middle East, were united in viewing education as the cure for all that was wrong with their country and their people. More particularly, at the end of the period under review, their optimism was fueled by the speedy modernization of Japan. The Japanese victory over Russia (1904–1905) fired the imagination of Muslim intellectuals and gave them confidence in the ability of the East to equal, and eventually outpace, the West. Analyzing Japan's overall progress, they were impressed most of all by the way the Meiji restoration went hand in hand with educational reform.[74] Ignoring what was unique in the Japanese experience, Iranians used it as a paradigm. Malek al-Motakallemin, for example, stated that "only by virtue of education has the old Japanese nation which for thousands of years

73. Talebov, *Ketab-e Ahmad*, 1:10–11 and 2:5–7.
74. For the role of education in Japan's development, see: Kikuchi Dairoku, *Japanese Education* (London, 1909), 68–69; Government of Japan, Ministry of Education, *Japan's Growth and Education* (Tokyo, 1963), 32–33; Herbert Passin, *Society and Education in Japan* (New York: Columbia University Press, 1965); Marius Jansen and Lawrence Stone, "Education and Modernization in Japan and England," *Comparative Studies in Society and History*, 9, no. 2 (1966–67), 208–32.

lived in darkness and deprivation come to enjoy such a prominent position."[75]

Such an approach not only reveals the appreciation these writers had for education, but also attests to their optimism about the ease with which Iran could copy foreign educational systems. This optimism stemmed partly from an assumption that it was much easier to transplant educational systems than political and economic institutions.[76] Education was seen as an entity seemingly isolated from social, economic, and political structures and therefore capable of being shipped out—almost like a crate of industrial products—from developed to underdeveloped countries.[77] Mostafa Khan Afshar, secretary of the mission to Russia in 1829, for instance, was so impressed by the schools there that he advised establishing similar schools in Iran and asserted that it would be perfectly easy to do so.[78] Malkom[79] and Malek al-Motakallemin[80] attested to their underlying sentiment by calling schools "factories for producing human beings." Just as factories "take in raw materials and turn out products," Malkom wrote, so schools "take in ignorant children and turn out engineers and accomplished thinkers." Setting up several such "factories" would enable Iran "to advance by 3000 years in the space of three months."

It seems unlikely that the authors quoted in this chapter took such statements quite literally. Obviously, there is an element of persuasion in their eloquence, whether it was meant to enlist support (on the part of the shah, his courtiers and ministers, the social elites, and, to a much lesser degree, public opinion in general) or to counteract opposition (mainly on the part of the ulama). While knowledge in the traditional sense had always been appreciated in Iranian society, these intellectuals gave it a much broader, modern, and more practical meaning. They did not reject traditional religious knowledge but held that it needed to be complemented by modern, European education if Iran's ills were to be cured.[81] Instead of instilling beliefs and fostering good manners,

75. Malekzade, 1:152–53. Similarly, Malkom's treatises *Rushna'i* and *Osul-e Taraqqi*; Sepahsalar, in Adamiyyat, *Azadi*, 68–72; Zayn al-ʿAbedin Maraghe'i, in his *Siyahat Name-ye Ebrahim Beg*.

76. For similar concepts in other developing countries, see Coleman, *Education and Political Development*, 5.

77. For similar ideas on the part of an Ottoman official, see Lewis, *Modern Turkey*, 126–29.

78. Adamiyyat, *Azadi*, 39–41.

79. Tabataba'i, *Malkom* (from his *Daftar-e Tanzimat*), 8–13. The spelling is from Algar's translation (*Malkom*, 28).

80. Malekzade, 1:152–54.

81. Such distinctions are made, for example, by Jaʿfar Ibn Ishaq, ʿAli Bakhsh Qajar,

schools should prepare their students for productive participation in building a new Iran. Such resolute support of new educational concepts, derived from the first contacts with western thinking and schooling, undoubtedly contributed to the spread of modern education, but at the same time stimulated fierce opposition by the ulama. To a large extent, the establishment of new educational institutions during this period took on the nature of a *Kulturkampf*.

---

and the treatise *Goftogu-ye Yek Mirza ba 'Ilm Ba yek 'Ami-ye Mostahzar*, quoted in Adamiyyat and Nateq, 32–43, 76–79, and 136–44, respectively.

2

Early Experiments

The First Students Abroad

The first attempts to obtain the benefits of western education were made by sending Iranian students to European universities—at about the same time that similar steps were being taken in Egypt and the Ottoman Empire. The first Iranian students left in 1811, making them among the first Middle Eastern students to do so.[1] The beginning, however, was modest and slower than in Egypt (under Muhammad ʿAli) and in the Ottoman Empire (under Mahmud II).[2]

State-sponsored programs for studies abroad were undertaken during three periods. The initial one lasted from 1811 to 1815. The first initiative came up in the course of negotiations between the Iranian government and a British diplomatic mission led by Harford Jones which, among other things, discussed British training for the Iranian army. During the talks, ʿAbbas Mirza asked Jones to take two Iranians to London for studies of "benefit for me, themselves and their coun-

1. The only Middle Eastern students sent earlier were those dispatched by Muhammad ʿAli to Italy in 1809; see Heyworth-Dunne, *An Introduction to the History of Education in Modern Egypt*, 2d ed. (London: Frank Cass, 1968), 105. For a survey of the mutual interests of Iran and the European powers in the dispatch of students, see Mohit Tabatabaʾi, "Tarikhche-ye Eʿzam-e Mohsel be Orupa," *Shafaq-e Sorkh*. The article was published from 6 July through 29 August 1933; see mainly issues of 9 and 10 July. See also Mojtabi Minovi, "Avvalin Karavan-e Maʿrefat," *Yaghma*, 1953/4, 4:182–83.

2. The flow of *tollab* leaving for studies to the holy shrines in Iraq continued, of course, but this subject is beyond the scope of this book.

try."[3] Consequently, in 1811, the first two students left for London: Hajji Baba Afshar, to study medicine, and Mohammad Kazem to study technical draftsmanship. Kazem died there; Afshar returned nine years later as a trained physician. Five others left for London in 1815, following negotiations with a British mission under Colonel William D'Arcy: Mirza Reza Mohandes Bashi (for artillery training), Mirza Ja'far (engineering), another Mirza Ja'far (medicine), Mohammad 'Ali Ahangar (gunsmithing and locksmithing), Mirza Saleh Shirazi (humanities and languages). Four returned after forty-four months and Mirza Ja'far (the medical student) a year later.[4]

The second period ran from 1845 to 1847. It began when, on orders from Mohammad Shah, five students were sent to France in 1845: Hoseyn Qoli Khan and Mirza Zakki (both for military training), Mirza Reza (natural sciences and mining), Mirza Yahya (medicine), and Mohammad 'Ali Aqa (mining). They were rushed home after only three years because of the 1848 revolution in Paris and the death of the shah. Three others studied at government expense in other European countries: Mirza Sadeq (medicine, in Britain), Mohammad Hoseyn Beg Afshar (sugar manufacturing, in Russia) and Abu al-Hasan Naqqash Bashi (technical draftsmanship, in Italy). There may have been a few others, but their records have not been found.[5]

The third period was coincident with the first years of Naser al-Din's reign (1848–1896). In 1856/7 three students, on whom we have no information, were sent to France. Two years later, a group of forty-two students left for France, where they studied from five to eight years. This group stands out not only because of its unprecedented size but also because all its members were graduates of the newly established Dar al-Fonun,[6] (see the following section). A few years earlier, in 1849, Amir Kabir had sent out six Iranian craftsmen for vocational training. These men, commoners as suggested by their names and fields of study, were: 'Abbas Karbala'i (glass blowing, in St. Petersburg), Sadeq Karbala'i (metallurgy, in Moscow), 'Ali Meshhedi (carpentry and wheel making, in Moscow), Aqa 'Abdollah (candle

---

3. See report from Jones to the Foreign Office, 20 April 1812: P.R.O., F.O., 60.

4. Minovi, 181–85, 232, 315–16; Tabataba'i, *Shafaq-e Sorkh*, 7 July 1933.

5. Hoseyn Mahbubi Ardekani, "Dovvomin Karavan-e Ma'refat," *Yaghma*, 1965/6, 10:592–98; Tabataba'i, *Shafaq-e Sorkh*, 20 July 1933.

6. Hoseyn Moradi-Nezhad and Parviz Pazhum-Shari'ati, *Barresi Naqsh va Athar-e Tahsilkardegan-e Kharej az Keshvar dar Jame'e-ye Iran* (Tehran: MTE, 1974), 13, 23–24, 44–55. This survey of the Institute for Social Research of Tehran University concentrates on analyzing the impact of foreign-educated Iranians during the reign of Reza Shah. It also includes data on the previous groups.

making, in St. Petersburg), and Aqa Rahim Esfahani (paper manufacture, in St. Petersburg). Two others, from Kashan, were sent to study the silk industry in Istanbul.[7] Others were dispatched in the second half of the century.

In addition to the state-sponsored groups, some other young people left for studies in Europe privately, mainly in the second half of the century. However, because they belonged to elite families, they were often supported by the government to some extent and chose their field of study on the advice of prominent government figures,[8] or else on the strength of their families' evaluation of the future needs of the country.[9] No such cases are known before the government initiative of 1811. Private students usually left Iran at a much earlier age and spent more time in Europe; examples include Sepahsalar and his brothers, and Malkom.

The fields of study of government-sponsored students were decided for them according to directives from the court, as the need for professional manpower arose. In the early stages, most received military training or else took up subjects useful to the army, such as engineering and mathematics. Medical study, too, was mainly for service in the army. Very few turned to liberal or social sciences (four out of fifty-one for whom such data are available).[10] From among the latter, Shirazi was asked to take up a technical subject as well, but refused, arguing he was ill-suited for such studies.[11] The duration of their studies was influenced by academic considerations (their field of study and the need for preliminary general and linguistic qualifications) as well as by political developments, whether in Iran or in Europe. Usually they spent between five and eight years in Europe. Private students often studied longer and remained abroad for an additional period after graduation.[12] All those sent out by the government returned home

7. Lorentz, 228–29; Fereydun Adamiyyat, *Amir Kabir va Iran*, 2d ed. (Tehran: Amir Kabir, 1955/6), 385.

8. Thus, for example, when Malkom decided to study political science, he is believed to have been following advice given to his father by Amir Kabir (Tabataba'i, *Malkom*, p. ii; Algar, *Malkom*, 16).

9. See a letter of the father of Mehdi Qoli Hedayat Mokhber al-Saltane to his sons in Berlin (1878), listing the fields of study that "currently enjoyed people's interest and respect" (Hedayat's memoirs: *Khaterat va Khatarat*, 32).

10. Moradi-Nezhad and Pazhum-Shari'ati, 24, 56–59.

11. Abu al-Hasan Shirazi, *Safarname*, ed. Mohammad Shahrestani (Tehran: Razun, 1968/9), 47.

12. Tabataba'i, *Shafaq-e Sorkh*, 21 July 1933.

after graduation,[13] one major reason being their sense of alienation in the foreign environment.[14]

Gradually, over time, better-educated students were sent abroad. The first groups had left without knowing a foreign language, sometimes even without fully mastering Persian, and were unprepared for academic study.[15] The graduates of Dar al-Fonun sent out in midcentury, though still at a disadvantage as compared with European university entrants, were much better prepared. As we have seen, the early choice of England soon gave way to a preference for France which was to last well into the twentieth century. French had became the main foreign language at court as well as in Dar al-Fonun, and there was a special admiration for the French military system, not unrelated to the growing tension in relations with Britain.

Almost all the students came from prominent, wealthy families, though not necessarily from the very highest ranks.[16] The lists suggest that most had fathers in senior administrative positions. From among those sent out in 1858/9 for whom details are known, almost all belonged to the social or political elite.[17] As graduates of Dar al-Fonun, they were in any case likely to be upper-class. The same was true of the private students. This practice was so blatant that the French government in 1847 recommended to the Iranian ambassador, Mirza Mohammad ʿAli Khan Shirazi, that twenty children be sent to Paris "from among sons of working people," and not—as was customary—"sons of lords, who were thoroughly spoiled."[18] One Mohammad ʿAli, from an artisan family, was apparently the only student in the group of forty-two to come from a lower-class background.[19] The same was true of the private students.

Two things were characteristic of the careers of graduates after their return from abroad: they rose rather quickly to high positions; and their positions often had little to do with the subject of their studies.

13. Moradi-Nezhad and Pazhum-Shariʿati, 25.

14. This comes out clearly in the memoirs of Shirazi. The possibility of permanent residence abroad was not even considered by him and his colleagues.

15. See, for example, remarks by Major Southerland in his report of 16 July 1812: P.R.O., F.O., 60; also, Minovi, 184.

16. This was also true, by and large, of Egyptian students abroad at that time; see Heyworth-Dunne, 104–6, 157–81.

17. Tabatabaʾi, *Shafaq-e Sorkh*, 27 July 1933. See also: Minovi, 181–85, 232–35, 315–16; Moradi-Nezhad and Pazhum-Shariʿati, 11, 37–38, 53–54; Ardekani, 597–98.

18. Based on the memoirs of the ambassador, *Ruzname-ye Maʾmur-e Iran Dar Faranse*, and quoted by Adamiyyat, *Azadi*, 41–44.

19. Minovi, 432–33.

From among the first six students, we have later information about four: Hajji Baba Afshar became physician to ʿAbbas Mirza and Mohammad Shah and was given the title *Hakim Bashi* (chief doctor); Mirza Reza Mohandes Bashi (engineering) first became chief engineer of the army, then ambassador to the Ottoman court, and finally, in 1858, head of the State Consultative Assembly, the forerunner of the cabinet; Mirza Saleh Shirazi (languages) made a career as a diplomat and as consultant and translator to the shah; and Mirza Jaʿfar Khan (engineering), known by his title *Moshir al-Dowla* (engineering) became a prominent political figure and the first man to head the Consultative Assembly when it was first formed in the late 1850s. The five who studied in Europe from 1845 to 1848 had similar careers: Yahya Khan (medicine) became governor of Yazd and Fars and later minister of justice; Mohammad ʿAli (mining) held senior positions in the Ministry of Foreign Affairs; Mirza Zakki (artillery training) was a translator in Dar al-Fonun and rose to the rank of brigadier-general (*sartip*); Mirza Reza (mining) also became a translator in Dar al-Fonun; and Hoseyn Qoli Khan (infantry training) became a brigadier-general. Of the group of forty-two in 1858/9, we have information about the later careers of nineteen: of the five who had studied mathematics, ʿAbd al-Rasul Khan and Mirza ʿAbbas Khan became brigadier-generals, ʿAbbas Qoli Khan and Mirza Mahmud were appointed to senior administrative positions, and Nezam al-Din Kashani worked as an engineer in the government service. Of the three who had had artillery training, Mohammad Taqi Khan and Mohammad Khan became brigadier-generals (the latter also governor of a province) and Hoseyn Khan a senior administrator. The three infantry trainees were Mahmud Aqa, who became a colonel (*sarhang*); ʿAli Aqa, a colonel and later a provincial governor; and Mohammad ʿAli Aqa, a brigadier-general and later a high official in the civil service. Six had studied medicine: four of them (Shaykh Jalil, Mirza Reza Doktor, Mirza ʿAli Taqi Hakim al-Mamalek, and Mirza ʿAbd al-Wahhab) became court physicians; one (Mirza Aqa Bozorg) a provincial governor; and one (Mirza Hoseyn Khan) a professor at Dar al-Fonun. Mirza Kazem, who had studied natural science, also became a professor there, and ʿAli Akbar Kashani, who had studied draftsmanship, became a court painter.[20]

The data we have probably relate to those graduates who had the most successful careers. Still, it is clear from the information about the first group, and about more than half of the later groups, that study

20. Moradi-Nezhad and Pazhum-Shariʿati, 7–9, 59; Tabatabaʾi, *Shafaq-e Sorkh*, 18, 20, 27 July, 1933; *Vaqayeʿ-e Ettefaqiye*, no. 98 [1851].

abroad led to comparatively important initial appointments and to quicker than usual advancement later on. The advancement of foreign graduates was so rapid that it caused resentment among their less-educated countrymen, who, as Robert Watson wrote, distrusted them and did "all in their power to prevent them from having the opportunity of putting in practice anything they may have learned, and thereby throwing others into the shade."[21] The frequency of government or court appointments for the graduates (notably the physicians) reflected the importance attributed to the new education, and in turn fostered the interest of young people in studies abroad. Clearly, even in this initial stage, study abroad assured the graduates of signal professional and social prestige. It must be borne in mind, however, that given the social background of the students they would have been assured of a fine career in any case.[22] Nevertheless, education—and particularly a European education—became increasingly important, and gradually even upper-class families came to believe that the careers of their sons had to be underpinned with educational qualifications.

It was, however, not only their foreign skills that proved of value to the returning graduates. Appreciation of western science and technology, coupled with curiosity toward these "explorers" of Europe, made them a focus of social attention—at least in their own narrow circles. Back home, people were not much interested in their academic credentials; what mattered even more was that they had had a glimpse of the West and its secrets. As Malkom put it, anyone who had "wandered the streets of Europe for a couple of days" was regarded as "an expert and a source of knowledge."[23] The author of *Shaykh va Shukh* complains that it did not matter how much the graduates had actually learned of western science; they were lionized just for having been to Europe. *Shukh* wondered: "So why whoever walked in the streets of Paris is appointed upon his return to a directorship in a government hospital, referred to as a doctor, owns a stable, . . . builds himself a large house, is granted a title, earns a good salary, [and] obtains decorations?"[24] Consequently, an education abroad, initially undertaken for the sake of qualifications, soon became an important means of securing social prestige as well.

This conclusion is corroborated by the gradually widening gap between the graduate's chosen field and his later occupation. Clearly,

21. Watson, 20; similarly: Mostowfi, 2:222–23.
22. Mostowfi, 2:66; Tabataba'i, *Shafaq-e Sorkh*, 27 July 1933; Ardekani, 595–96.
23. See his *Dastgah-e Divan* (Tabataba'i, *Malkom*, 77–78).
24. *Shaykh va Shukh*: Adamiyyat and Nateq, 144–45. (See Chapter 1, note 58.)

the returning graduate preferred political, diplomatic, or administrative appointments over work in his academic profession. The first six students—mainly because of the personal interest and involvement of ʿAbbas Mirza—were still appointed to positions related to their studies. However, even some of them later abandoned their professions. Hajji Baba Afshar (a physician) and Jaʿfar Khan (an engineer) went into politics and diplomacy. Many of those who left for Europe in 1845–1848 did not complete their studies, which helps explain why most of them served in positions where they could make use of their general education (mainly their knowledge of foreign languages) rather than their specific training. But those sent out by Naser al-Din did complete their studies, yet later proved reluctant to work in their own field. According to a study by the Institute for Social Research of Tehran University, one third of them eventually worked in fields without "*any* connection" with their studies.[25]

This career outcome was usually welcomed by the students and their families. Mirza Asadollah Khan was undoubtedly exceptional in expressing annoyance at such a turn of events. Having studied paper manufacturing and then been assigned to a senior position in the post office, he said: "thanks God, I still have business with paper; although I am not a maker of paper (*kaghaz saz*), I still play with paper (*kaghaz baz*)."[26] However, Hoseyn Qoli Khan was the only one known to have rejected a job offer for such reasons; he had studied military science, and when assigned to supervise development projects in Azerbayjan, he reportedly argued that he was not competent to hold such a job.[27] Typically, students and their families made use of personal ties to secure administrative or political positions. The annalist ʿAbdollah Mostowfi mentions the case of Mirza ʿAbdollah Khan (the son of Amin al-Dowla), who had studied agriculture in France and ended up in the foreign service, under the pretext that his expertise was not required.[28] Already in 1852, the official gazette cautioned that such malpractices limited the contribution specialists were capable of making to the community.[29] But, as we will see, through their involvement in the country's social, political, and economic life, they were still able to contribute significantly to the overall process of modernization.

25. Moradi-Nezhad and Pazhum-Shariʿati, 52–61. Similarly, Minovi, 181–85, 315–17; Tabatabaʾi, *Shafaq-e Sorkh*, 18 July 1933.

26. Tabatabaʾi, *Shafaq-e Sorkh*, 28 July 1933.

27. Ardekani, 569.

28. Mostowfi, 2:66.

29. *Vaqayeʿ-e Ettefaqiye*, issues 452 and 453.

The Earliest Institutions of Higher Education

The first new institution of higher learning in Iran, Dar al-Fonun, was inaugurated on 28 December 1851. Its establishment was the natural outgrowth of the motives and expectations that had led to the dispatch of students to Europe earlier on. Its object, like that of the earlier studies abroad, was to make western technology available to Iranians. Dar al-Fonun was the first educational institution in modern Iran to be set up by the political, rather than the religious, establishment, and the first to teach western (not religious) sciences.[30] That is why its inauguration is often held to mark the beginning of modern education in Iran.

Dar al-Fonun was a polytechnic designed to teach upper-class youngsters western technology and sciences, thereby preparing them for senior appointments in the army and the administration. Its name (meaning Academy of Technology), first mentioned in *Vaqaye'-e Ettefaqiye* (the official gazette) shortly before its opening, best expresses its academic focus. Other names used initially were Madrese-ye Jadid (New School), to distinguish it from the traditional type of schools; *Madrese-ye Nezamiye* (Military School); and *Maktab Khane-ye Padeshahi* (Royal School).[31]

Amir Kabir, who was the initiator and driving force behind Dar al-Fonun, had before him the model of similar schools in Russia (where he had traveled in the 1820s) and the Ottoman Empire (where he spent a long time in the late 1840s). In Russia he was particularly impressed by the technical college at St. Petersburg (founded in 1828); and in Istanbul by the *Maktab 'Ulum Harbiye* (School of Military Sciences, established in 1834) and by the wider educational reform under Rashid Pasha in the 1840s. Dar al-Fonun's name and curriculum were clearly modeled on a comparable school first opened in Istanbul in 1845.[32] The reforms of Muhammad 'Ali, and particularly the establishment of a medical school in Cairo, also influenced Amir Kabir. The idea of founding Dar al-Fonun was first put forward in a report from Amir Kabir on his mission to Russia. Referring to the St. Petersburg college, the mission's secretary, Mostafa Khan Afshar, wrote: "The establishment of

---

30. This needs to be qualified by saying that already in the 1820s, secondary schools were established by missionaries from the West. About half their students in the first years were Muslims. See SSHBA, *Arzyabi-ye Gostaresh-e Amuzesh-e 'Ali-ye Iran*, ed. Mohammad Taqi Tayyeb (Tehran, 1974/5), 29–32.

31. For these names and their use, see Daneshgah-e Gondi Shapur, *Amuzesh dar Iran az 'Ahd-e Bastan ta Emruz* (Ahvaz, 1971/2), 1:58–59.

32. Nashat, 19; Lewis, *Modern Turkey*, 177–78.

such schools in Iran is extremely easy and simple. It is possible to bring from Europe several scientists and establish a school for the children of the notables." The students would study "Iranian sciences under Iranian teachers and European sciences under Europeans."[33]

From Dar al-Fonun Amir Kabir expected to obtain the same benefits as were derived from sending students abroad, without incurring the heavy expenses of travel abroad and, more important, without exposing them to the "negative influences" of a prolonged residence in a foreign country. Unlike many others, he was apprehensive of the political rather than the cultural influence that the stay abroad was likely to have on the young men's thinking.[34] The sums required for training twenty students in Europe, he calculated, would suffice to engage seven foreign instructors capable of teaching 200 students at home.[35] There was also pressure from wealthy families, mainly from the Bazar community, who wanted to give their sons a modern education but were reluctant to send them abroad.[36]

In bringing in the required instructors, he was careful not to engage nationals of countries having strategic interests in Iran (Britain, Russia, and France) and therefore preferred Austrians. Even so, he insisted, by the testimony of one of them, that foreign instructors should refrain "as far as possible from interfering in political affairs."[37] In 1850, Amir Kabir sent Jan Dawud Khan to Austria as a special envoy. With the personal support of Emperor Franz Joseph, he engaged seven instructors. Britain (viewing Austria as being under Russian influence) opposed the Austrian monopoly and brought pressure to bear on the government, at the same time supporting opponents of the school within the country. Consequently, Amir Kabir was forced to hire some Italian and French teachers as well.[38] Ten local teachers were also hired: four of them, graduates of European universities, were to teach modern science; the others, educated in Iran, were to teach Persian, Arabic, geography, and traditional medicine.[39] Since instruction was in Persian, an Iranian translator (usually from among those who had studied

33. See his manuscript, "Safarname-ye Khosrow Mirza," quoted by Adamiyyat, *Azadi*, 39–41.

34. Polak, 1:298; Mostowfi, 1:70; Dowlatabadi, 1:324–28; Makki, 183.

35. Makki, 184.

36. For such arguments, see Dowlatabadi, 1:328.

37. Polak, 1:178. Also: Adamiyyat, *Amir Kabir*, 147–48; Makki, 183–87; Sadiq, *Farhang*, 353.

38. Polak, 1:178; Adamiyyat, *Amir Kabir*, 148–51.

39. Sadiq, *Farhang*, 352; Adamiyyat, *Amir Kabir*, 152–54.

abroad) was assigned to each foreign teacher. In the opening year, the enrollment was 105. The number of students then grew slowly: in 1891, there were 387. (Growth was much more rapid under Reza Shah; when Tehran University opened in 1935, it had 886 students).[40]

In its early years, the school concentrated on military studies. The first class was divided as follows: artillery (twenty-six), infantry (thirty), cavalry (five), engineering (twelve), medicine (twenty), pharmacology (seven), and mining (five). Gradually, greater stress came to be placed on science, technology, and foreign languages. When George Curzon visited the institute in the early 1890s, seventy-five students were taking military subjects; 140, scientific and industrial subjects, ninety-two were language students, and eighty were studying draftsmanship.[41] During the 1850s, courses in English, Russian, drafting, and music began to be offered as well. Students usually enrolled when they were fourteen to sixteen years of age and spent some six to seven years at the school. Tuition was free of charge, and students got free lunches and distinctive uniforms for each of the seven branches, but they had to find their own quarters. Outstanding students were rewarded with very generous prizes.[42]

During the early years, the student body was made up almost exclusively of children of grandees and nobles. Although Amir Kabir was himself of humble origin (his father was a cook), the school was deliberately designed for the elite. In November 1851, its headmaster, Mohammad ʿAli Khan, asked the adjutant-general of the army and the Tehran police chief to publicize the imminent opening of the school, and to send him suitable candidates from among "the sons of the *Khan*s, the notables (*aʿyan*) and aristocrats (*ashraf*)."[43] In the following year, provincial governors-general were asked to suggest "sons of rich families" for enrollment.[44] In fact, throughout the period under discussion, the students came from very distinguished families. Hedayat, whose father and three uncles were in the class of 1851, noted that the students were children of "princes (*shahzadegan*) and *Khan*s."[45] Mirza Mohammad Hasan Khan, Eʿtemad al-Saltane, wrote upon visiting the school that the students were "sons of distinguished princes,

---

40. Elwell-Sutton, 67; Sadiq, *Farhang*, 354–55.
41. Adamiyyat, *Amir Kabir*, 154; Curzon, 1:493–95.
42. Browne (*A Year amongst Persians*, 103–4) observed in 1887–1888 that neither theology nor metaphysics nor Arabic figured in the curriculum.
43. The letter is quoted in Adamiyyat, *Amir Kabir*, 252; Makki, 190.
44. The decree is cited in "Maʿaref," *TT*, 460.
45. Mehdi Qoli Hedayat, 85–86.

of chiefs of the army, of the rich and of leading politicians."[46] Yahya
Dowlatabadi described them as the spoiled "sons of rich people"; to
accustom them to discipline and hard work was like "bringing order
into a flock of desert gazelles." They related to the school as if it was
"a private *maktab* of their parents [and] as if the headmaster and staff
were their nannies and nurses."[47]

The school took a hand in launching its graduates on their careers,
securing them useful initial appointments in the army or the administration of the kind likely to lead to rapid advancement.[48] Coming from
the upper-class background described, they were bound to have a good
career in any event, but graduating from Dar al-Fonun obviously added
to their credentials. More significant: a modern education was gradually
becoming a desirable qualification for young people from the upper
classes, thereby giving it a wider general appeal.

Opposition to Dar al-Fonun, as to modern education in general, came
mainly from the ulama. They opposed the very act of setting up schools
outside their control or influence and resented the teaching of modern
subjects. Aware of their attitude, the founders tried to smooth tempers
by incorporating religious studies into the curriculum and by holding
public prayers at school. But this failed to appease the opponents.
Having failed to prevent its establishment, the ulama appealed to the
shah not to support a school bound to "foster anti-monarchical philosophies," as they put it. Their pressures increased with the spread
of the liberal movement in the Ottoman Empire and the approval of a
constitution there (in 1876) and with the growth of the liberal movement
in Iran (at the end of the century), in which graduates of Dar al-Fonun,
together with the graduates of foreign universities, played a significant
part.[49] In fact, following charges of subversive activities against the
Faramushkhanes (the Free Masons) in the late 1850s, the shah's initially
enthusiastic support of the school gave way to indifference. Even before
Dar al-Fonun opened, the assassination of Amir Kabir had removed
its most vigorous supporter. All in all, the school had its ups and
downs, according to the shah's arbitrary and inconsistent approach to
it. In Hedayat's words, in the early days of the school "Naser al-Din

46. As quoted in Makki, 190–91. See also: Safa, *Madrese*, 736; Sadiq, *Farhang*, 354–55;
"Farhang-e now Chegune Aghaz Shod?" *AP*, 1951/2, 20.

47. Dowlatabadi, 1:327.

48. See the testimony of the following: Mostowfi, 1:86; Dowlatabadi, 1:328–29; Curzon, 1:494–96; Wills, 393. See also words to the same effect by two twentieth-century
ministers of education: Sadiq, Ma'aref, 354; 'Ali Asghar Hekmat, "Ta'limat-e 'Aliye,"
TT, 1936/7, 251–52.

49. Dowlatabadi, 1:327–28.

Shah was unlikely to go out riding without stopping at the school . . . encouraging [students] and granting prizes." But after "that untoward event" (of the Faramushkhane) he "became indifferent to European education."[50] Nevertheless, in its first—and critical—years, Dar al-Fonun had the shah's support. He took a personal interest in it and himself handed the graduates their diplomas and the papers for their first appointments.[51] In a special decree of 1852/3 he also established four classes of honor, with distinctive decorations, for the students.[52] Two decades later, in an attempt to revive the shah's interest in the school, Sepahsalar gave him the following gloomy description of a visit there: "Although they knew I was coming and tried to put on their best appearance, the truth is that I was deeply disappointed by my visit. The only European teacher is M. Richards, the Englishman; the rest . . . come from among the [former] students. The total number of students is supposed to be one hundred and fifty, but I only found seventy-nine [persons] which includes the teachers and their assistants."[53]

In the late seventies the shah's attitude changed once more. E. G. Browne describes the positive interest the shah took in the school, including personal visits and the distribution of prizes "on the most liberal scale."[54]

For half a century, Dar al-Fonun was the only institute for higher learning and, up to the establishment of Tehran University, it remained the most important one. What was its contribution to the making of modern Iran? (1) Most important was the very initiative by the state to set up a school to teach modern sciences in defiance of the ulama. This itself turned it into the cornerstone of modern education. (2) Dar al-Fonun trained relatively large cadres of Iranians, giving them some expertise in their particular field of study and also generally acquainting them with western culture and languages. In the high positions they came to occupy, the graduates contributed significantly to the overall process of change and reform. (3) The graduates in turn promoted modern education, whether by propagating their views or by founding and directing new schools. (4) Dar al-Fonun itself served as a cultural center where public lectures and discussions were held. Its printing press published not only the official newspaper and textbooks but also translations of western literature (for details, see Chapter 3).

50. Mehdi Qoli Hedayat, 75.
51. Mostowfi, 1:86; Dowlatabadi, 1:327–29; Mehdi Qoli Hedayat, 75.
52. The decree is quoted in Piemontese, 471–72.
53. A report from 1872/3, quoted in Nashat, 147.
54. Browne, *A Year amongst Persians*, 104, 112.

Yet the school had a number of deficiencies from the very start, and some of its flaws proved so persistent that they colored modern Iranian education for as long as the royal regime lasted. A major shortcoming was that Dar al-Fonun was placed firmly under government auspices. It owed its existence to a government initiative, the government appointed the administrative and academic staff, drafted the curriculum, selected the entrants, and dealt with the employment of the graduates. This benefited the school as long as establishment figures (such as Amir Kabir, Sepahsalar, and, initially, Naser al-Din Shah) supported it, but proved harmful when those in power turned against it. Such dependence made the school greatly vulnerable to political changes. Obviously, under these circumstances, academic freedom had no chance to develop.[55] Moreover, the official approach fostered the attitude among students that it was "the government's duty" to provide them with "suitable jobs" and nurtured the feeling that they were primarily training to take up administrative appointments.[56] And ironically, the new education still had some of the basic flaws of traditional schooling, such as the preference for learning texts by heart and quoting from the textbooks as opposed to analysis, theoretical discussion, or scientific experiment. Under these conditions, research was, of course, altogether lacking.

Other shortcomings reflected the realities of the time: the fact that the institute was established before the creation of any new elementary schools affected the quality of the education it offered; the foreign professors' ignorance of Persian and the lack of Persian-language textbooks made it difficult for students to benefit fully from their studies; and the lack of qualified local staff led to the appointment of some incompetent teachers.[57] On balance, however, the school contributed significantly to the development of modern education and to the larger process of westernization. Hekmat's conclusion that its graduates were of "the most important service for the advancement of Iran," and Dhabihollah Safa's assertion that they were an "important source for

55. Such deficiencies were pointed out not only by its professors (Polak, 1:302) and scholars (Makki, 185–87; Adamiyyat, *Amir Kabir*, 149–51), but also by experts at the Court Ministry and Ministry of Science in the midtwentieth century, when some of the same problems still existed. See SSHBA, *Amuzesh-e ʿAli*, 43–45; Vezarat-e ʿUlum, MTBRA, *Amar-e Amuzesh-e ʿAli-ye Iran dar Panjah Sal-e Shahanshahi-ye Pahlavi* (Tehran, 1977), 1.

56. See Mehdi Qoli Hedayat, 86; SSHBA, *Amuzesh-e ʿAli*, 44–45.

57. One of the first instructors, Richard Khan, wrote to a friend in France, in 1852: "The son of Madame Yaʿqub [Malkom] was appointed lately to serve as mathematics instructor without any inquiry whether he knew anything at all in this field. Another Armenian, who had studied only two years with priests in Istanbul was appointed teacher of geography and French" (Adamiyyat, *Amir Kabir*, 156; Gondi Shapur, 1:67).

ideological, scientific and literary change," do not seem exaggerated.[58] (For details on their contribution, see Chapter 3.)

If we disregard the military academy founded by Sepahsalar, the next institute of high learning, Madrese-ye 'Ulum-e Siyasi (School of Political Science), was not founded until 1899/1900. The initiative came from Mirza Hasan Khan Moshir al-Molk (the son of the minister of foreign affairs, Mirza Nasrollah Khan Moshir al-Dowla). Hasan Khan had studied at a military academy in Moscow and spent some years in the West in the diplomatic service. He convinced his father to set up a school to train senior staff for the foreign service. Nasrollah Khan responded enthusiastically, viewing the school not only as a training college for professionals but—in an echo of Malkom's terminology— as "a factory for the creation of human beings" likely to contribute to the country's general progress.[59] The school operated under the Ministry of Foreign Affairs until 1928, then under the Ministry of Education, until it was eventually merged into Tehran University in 1935. Its teachers (Iranian and foreign) offered a general education as well as specific training for the foreign service. From the observations of Mostowfi, a student of the first class, it is clear that its students were from the upper classes, mostly sons of prominent public figures and often sons of men themselves in the foreign service.[60]

Several other ministries followed suit in founding schools to provide themselves with expert staff. A school of agriculture was set up in 1900/ 1, a school of arts in 1910, a law school in 1921, and some others after the 1921 coup. They failed to meet the growing need for professional manpower, quantitatively or, even more so, qualitatively. Thus Hedayat went so far as to complain—with much exaggeration—that "for some years now we have had a school of agriculture but to date it has not produced even one graduate who really understands agriculture."[61] Nevertheless, these schools (and particularly the Madrese-ye 'Ulum-e Siyasi) contributed something to the overall modernization of the educational system; and all became building blocks of Tehran University. During the stormy years early in the century, the Madrese-ye 'Ulum-e Siyasi became a center of intellectual activity. In 1907/8, its graduates founded the Sherekat-e Ma'aref (The Association for Education), which organized cultural events and established new schools.[62]

58. Hekmat, "Ta'limat," 251–52; Safa, *Madrese*, 736. Similarly: Mostowfi, 1:86; Mehdi Qoli Hedayat, 94.
59. See his letter to Malkom, quoted in Adamiyyat, *Amir Kabir*, 139.
60. Mostowfi, 2:67–73. See also Dowlatabadi, 1:268.
61. From a lecture in Tehran quoted in his memoirs, 624.
62. Its original name was Anjoman-e Ta'sis-e Makateb-e Melliye (The Council for the

An important feature of these schools was that they were the first to
go beyond imitating the military or narrowly technological features of
western education.

Elementary and Secondary Education

Modern elementary and secondary schools were opened in Iran only
in the 1870s, much later than in Egypt and the Ottoman Empire. Their
establishment was made possible largely through the collaboration between intellectuals and politicians who supported westernization. Most
prominent among the latter were Sepahsalar (in the 1870s) and Mirza
'Ali Khan Amin al-Dowla (at the end of the century), the ministers of
education Ja'far Qoli Khan Nir al-Molk, Mirza Mahmud Khan Ehtesham al-Saltane, and to a degree, Shah Mozaffar al-Din himself. In 1873/
4, Sepahsalar (Moshir al-Dowla) established in Tehran the first public
secondary school, named Moshiriye in his honor. A similar school was
established in Tabriz in the same year, to be followed by military high
schools in Isfahan (1882/3) and Tehran (1884/5).[63]

Public elementary schools were opened only from 1890 onward, first
by Mirza Hasan Roshdiye and later mainly by the Sherekat-e Ma'aref
whose members set up schools and served as their first headmasters.
Ehtesham al-Saltane established the 'Ilmiye school; Dowlatabadi, the
Adab and Sadat schools; Mahmud Khan Miftah al-Molk, the Eftetahiye;
and Firuz Kuhi Montazem al-Dowla the Kheyriye school. Also in 1897/
8, the first school for girls was founded. All in all, in 1918/9—more
than a century after the first contacts with western education—there
were no more than several dozen new elementary schools (with a total
of 24,033 pupils) and few secondary schools (with 2,392 students). Most
of them were private schools.[64] They did not, however, prove sufficiently attractive to many elite families. Mahmud Mahdavi, a professor
at Tehran University, told me that his family refused to allow its children to attend such schools, believing they would "debauch" them.
Instead, many upper-class families hired private tutors.

Foundation of Public Schools); however, owing to the subversive connotations of *An-
joman*, members dropped the initial name. On its activities, see the memoirs of Dowlatabadi, one of its founders (2:300–315). Also see Mostowfi, 2:315–17.

63. Dowlatabadi, 1:177–78; Mostowfi, 1:17–18.

64. In 1924/5 there also were, according to government sources, 22,924 students in
maktabs and 4,979 in *madreses*: SBB, *Bayan-e Amari-ye Tahavvolat-e Ejtema'i va Eqtesadi-ye
Iran dar Dowran-e . . . Pahlavi* (Tehran: Markaz-e Amar, 1976/7), 35–36; Sadiq, *Farhang*,
354–59.

The curriculum and the pedagogical approach differed from one school to another according to the educational philosophy of their founders. It was, as Sadiq (himself a student at such a school) noted, a period of "experimentations with a new education."[65] However, they all were completely different from the traditional system: the contents of the studies went far beyond the curriculum taught by the clerics and included mathematics, science, and foreign languages; the majority of teachers and headmasters were graduates of foreign schools or of Dar al-Fonun and were not dependent on—indeed often hostile to— the religious establishment.

The new elementary schools were vehemently opposed by the ulama (most adamantly by Mirza Hasan Ashtiyani).[66] They claimed that the curricula in these schools were bound to weaken the students' faith, deplored the loss of an important source of income for the *akhunds*, and resented their lack of control. There were, in addition, two more reasons why their opposition to the new elementary schools was much more vehement than their resentment of Dar al-Fonun or of the dispatch of students to Europe. One was that, unlike the other initiatives, which involved limited numbers of students, elementary schools were seen as the first step toward a sweeping change that threatened to embrace the entire population eventually; the other was that the opening of elementary schools (unlike Dar al-Fonun, for example) resulted in the closing down of many *maktabs*. For the ulama, therefore, opposition was no more than the defense of their traditional privileges and functions, not to say their beliefs. Just as the extension of *'urf* jurisdiction restricted their judicial power, the new schools were an intrusion into a traditional domain of theirs—one hitherto exclusively their own.[67]

The struggle over modern education consequently acquired the nature of an acute cultural conflict. The ulama pressured the government to refrain from supporting the new schools, threatened their headmasters and staff, and brought pressure to bear on the students and their families.[68] Roshdiye suffered *takfir*, and his school (the Roshdiye, in Tabriz) was destroyed by a mob of *tollab*. Under threats against his life, he was twice compelled to seek sanctuary in Meshhed. His father had warned him that by founding new schools "you will provoke the

65. Sadiq, *Farhang*, 359.
66. Malekzade, 1:154.
67. Algar, *Religion*, 224. *'Urf* jurisdiction is secular law embodied in royal decrees administered by government-appointed lay judges, as opposed to *shari'a* (religious) law administered by ulama.
68. Dowlatabadi, 1:262–79, 307–9; "Ma'aref," *TT*, 20–22.

envy of the owners of *maktabs*. They will organize against you . . . blame you as an infidel, publish manifestoes against you . . . and depict you and your supporters as faithless."[69] His prophecies came true.

Instructors and students of new schools have given vivid description of such hostility. Dowlatabadi (headmaster of four schools) reported threats against his life by the ulama. ʿAli Javaher Kalam spoke of incitement against the new schools in the mosques, resulting in some cases of arson. Sadiq related that although the headmaster of his school (the Kemaliye) invited Ulama to participate in preparing the curriculum, and organized public Qurʾan examinations in their presence, they continued to inflame tempers against the school. In the lanes leading to the school, hostile manifestos were displayed and stones thrown at students and teachers.[70]

The clerics also tried to bias the shah against the new education. In a treatise submitted to the shah in 1897/8, Aqa Seyyed Hoseyn Musavi argued that the new schools strove not only to undermine the foundation of Islam but also to promote new political philosophies likely to threaten the political system.[71] Such argument intensified with the spread of the constitutional movement. In 1903/4, Shaykh Mohammad Najafi arranged for a *fatva* (religious decree) to be issued by four *mojtaheds* from Najaf, urging the shah to forbid the founding of new schools. Being informed of the matter by one of their men in the telegraph office, the supporters of modern education persuaded the shah to reject it and to request the ulama not to interfere in educational matters.[72]

As with higher education, some of the flaws of the *maktabs* and their methods persisted in the new elementary education. The curriculum was not geared to the country's needs; the pupils—as Hedayat complained—learned "only a few faulty words" and turned into "a burden on the state budget."[73] Dependence on the encouragement, or otherwise, of the politicians caused tremors in the educational system. Although some of the founders of new schools wanted to attract middle- and even lower-class entrants, in fact the students were almost all

69. Dowlatabadi, 1:180–84; "Roshdiye Pir-e Maʿaref," *AP*, 1944/5, 543–46; Malekzade, 1:150.

70. Dowlatabadi, 1:180–84; Sadiq, *Yadegar*, 1:15–16; the memoirs of Javaher Kalam are included in documents 5101–7 in the archives of the Court Ministry (Darbar-e Shahanshahi, MAM). I wish to convey my gratitude to the staff of the archives for their valuable support.

71. Quoted by Adamiyyat, *Ideolozhi*, 203–4.

72. Dowlatabadi, 1:238–43.

73. Mehdi Qoli Hedayat, 624.

from the upper classes,[74] and the education of girls was almost totally neglected.

Nonetheless, the advocates of the new education overcame clerical opposition. Once the crucial early years had passed, the expansion of the new school system—and the concomitant closure of the *maktabs*— became irreversible. It is for that reason that the major breakthrough in the history of education can be placed in this period. Founded mostly with the support of foreign or Dar al-Fonun graduates, the new schools in turn supplied entrants to institutes of higher learning who were far better qualified than their predecessors.

Conclusion

The dispatch of students abroad, and the establishment of Dar al-Fonun and the new elementary schools, signify two major innovations: for the first time, there was a deliberate, even methodical attempt to learn from the West; and, for the first time, the state assumed responsibility for education, dislodging the religious establishment from its former monopoly. Both innovations would remain major features of the educational system until the 1979 Islamic Revolution. This was true even though the Iranian approach was, at least initially, narrowly functional and technological, aiming primarily at that part of European education likely to be useful in promoting Iranian military strength. The social prestige that came to be attached to the new education, gradually made it an important prerequisite for a successful career and thereby further encouraged its expansion.

The new educated class played a central role in the nineteenth-century reforms and in the liberal movement leading to the Constitutional Revolution. Although too weak to mobilize mass support for their new ideologies, they were successful first in influencing individual politicians to carry out reforms, and then in turning the socioeconomic elites against the regime. All in all, the graduates of Dar al-Fonun and of universities abroad contributed considerably to the growing intellectual enlightenment.[75] Weak as they were, they introduced new notions and contributed to the knowledge of western thought and to the creation of a new class of intellectuals. More specifically, in the hectic years of the late nineteenth century, they provided the ideology sup-

---

74. Dowlatabadi, 1:197, 219–20; "Ma'aref," *TT*, 463; *AP*, "Farhang," 21.

75. Ann K. Lambton, "The Impact of the West on Persia," *International Affairs*, 33 (January 1957), 16.

porting the opposition to the tobacco concession and, even more so, advancing the Constitutional Revolution. Considering the small numbers of their students, the new educational institutions had an astonishingly disproportionate influence on the spread of liberal thought and the modernization process in general.[76]

Yet opposition to modern education continued throughout this period. It revolved around two principal arguments. One was the view of the ulama that the western impact on education—and through education, on the community—was harmful to Iran in general and to Islam in particular. They accused the European powers of wishing to turn the students away from Islam in order to place them under their own influence, and thus to advance their imperialist interests in Iran.[77] (The European powers fed this argument by openly competing for teaching positions in Iran and for hosting Iranian students abroad.) A second, more specific argument—here it is difficult to differentiate between pertinent concern and doctrinaire opposition—questioned the contribution to society of the new education, in particular of studies abroad. According to this argument, the graduates did not contribute much to the advancement of Iran because most of them ended up in administrative positions.[78]

Even some supporters of the new education expressed disappointment both with the limited number of students and with the narrow scope of their contribution to society. Malkom wrote: "Send a thousand student to Europe, not in order for each of them to marry two or three wives, as has hitherto been the case, but for them all to be locked up in colleges for ten years, so that a third of them die from overwork and the rest make something of themselves."[79] More bitterly critical, the author of *Shaykh va Shukh* accused graduates returning from abroad of being "exhibitionists" (*zaher parast*) who had studied parrotlike and were only interested in securing high positions; moreover, they had become subservient to foreigners, had forgotten their native culture and customs "even before arriving in Europe" yet had achieved no more than a "superficial" understanding of the West.[80] Some went so

76. See similar evaluations by: Adamiyyat, *Azadi*, 38; Farman Farmayam, 126; John Lorentz, "The Impact of Western Education on Nineteenth and Early Twentieth Century Iran" (forthcoming).

77. For such arguments, see: Tabataba'i, *Shafaq-e Sorkh*, 20 and 28 July 1933; Minovi, 236–37.

78. Such arguments were put forward by: 'Abd al-Razeq Donboli, *Ma'aser Soltaniye* (Tabriz, 1825/6), 115; Mostowfi, 2:125.

79. Letter quoted in Adamiyyat, *Azadi*, 152. Translation by Algar, *Malkom*, 135.

80. Adamiyyat and Nateq, 144–54.

far as to speak of the "alienation" of returning graduates. Majd al-Molk called them "chameleons" for whose sake "the state had to incur considerable losses," but who had learned "only two things: . . . to be contemptuous of the people and to dishonor the nation."[81]

Yet all its quantitative and qualitative limitations notwithstanding, the nineteenth-century new education became the cornerstone of twentieth-century education. True, the functional expectations underlying the dispatch of the first students abroad and, later, the founding of Dar al-Fonun never fully materialized. But in a manner neither planned nor foreseen by its initiators, the educational reform became significant to the overall advancement of Iran. The following description by a leading intellectual, overly picturesque though it may be, does convey a truth. He compared modern education to the spreading of seeds in uncultivated soil; the land had not been fertilized or irrigated, weeds and stones had not been removed. Some of the seeds therefore fell on spots where they could not germinate. But a few fell on fruitful soil and yielded the crop of progress.[82]

81. Majd al-Molk, *Resale-ye Majdiye* (Tehran, 1942), as quoted in B. Alavi, "Critical Writings on the Renewal of Iran," in Edmond Bosworth and Carole Hilleband, eds., *Qajar Iran: Political, Social and Cultural Change: 1800–1925* (Edinburgh: Edinburgh University Press, 1983), 245.

82. Minovi, 181.

3

The Educated Class
as a Motor for Change

As noted earlier, the recipients of a modern education did not usually
work in the field they had studied, and Browne's observation that until
his time none of them had "made a reputation for original research"[1]
was undoubtedly correct. But the fact that many had moved into politics, the administration, or the army, coupled with the social prestige
that now went with being western-educated, rendered them all the
more capable of promoting the overall modernization of Iran. They
had experienced western realities at first hand; they had been exposed
to the spirit—revolutionary and nationalist—of nineteenth-century Europe and were struck by the idea of freedom.

The most important single testimony to the influence of Europe
on the first students to go there is the travel book of Mirza Saleh
Shirazi, who studied in London from 1815 to 1819. Shirazi was exceptional not only for insisting on studying humanities but also for
becoming the earliest author of a Middle Eastern student's auto-
biography. Alongside many trivial or commonplace passages, it attests to the depth of the European experience and its imprint on a
young man's thinking and behavior. He gives a lengthy description
of London, of the history of England, of daily life there, the opera,
theater, and press, class differences, and relations between the
sexes, as well as many details of the education of the Iranian students and their relations with their hosts. He enlarges on his

1. E. G. Browne, *A History of Persian Literature in Modern Times* (Cambridge: Cambridge
University Press, 1924), 4:441.

impressions of the political system, the liberties of the individual, the supremacy of law, the limits of royal authority, and the power of parliament (319–25), the concept of freedom (207), religion and the state (292–98), and the educational system.

The notion of political freedom so captivates Shirazi that he refers to England as the "Realm of Freedom" (*velayat-e azadi*) and coins new words to describe it. He calls Parliament *mashvarat khane* ("house of consultation"), the House of Lords *Khane-ye Khanin* ("house of nobles") and the House of Commons *Khane-ye Vakil-e va Ro'aya* ("house of representatives and the people"). With much amazement he relates how the regent (George IV) wished to build a new street (to be called after him) but failed because a shopkeeper refused to sell his shop. "Even all the army," he writes, could not force him to sell against his will, nor could the regent cause him "financial or physical harm." Even more illuminating is his remark that such *azadi* did not contradict *entezam* (public order). All citizens—from the poorest to richest—were subject to the same law and enjoyed the same liberties. It was this, he concludes, that turned Britain—formerly beset by "wild" and criminal subjects, much like "the Arab kingdom"—into "the best country on earth" (207). He was similarly impressed with the British people's sense of justice and was amazed when a golden watch he had mislaid in a coffeeshop was returned to him by a waiter the following day (369–70).

Referring to the principle of habeas corpus, he explains how nobody could be punished unless found guilty under the law (326). He depicts the political system, speaks of the separation of powers, and gives a vivid description of the electoral process. He tries to make it comprehensible to his readers that the people elected their representatives freely and thus became responsible for their own destiny, that members of Parliament enjoy unlimited freedom, and that their decisions—being the will of the people—had sovereign force (290–325). "If necessary," he exclaims, "Parliament can even change the religion" (325). But, at this stage at least he did not advocate imitating the West. In his words: "the principles of government and the law of England are exclusive [*makhsus*] to England itself" (p. 319).

Another subject that catches his attention is religion. He notes that, unlike Islam, Christianity is mainly a religion of conscience rather than practice (292–98). This leads him to conclude that the ulama are an obstacle to the progress of Muslim societies. Returning to Iran via Istanbul, he gives vent to the anticlerical convictions he came to hold while in London: he makes mention of the reforms instituted by Sultan Selim III and comes out against the "forces of reaction" that had thwarted them. Making a plea for ending the involvement of the ulama in politics, he adds:

> As long as . . . the *mollas* continue to interfere in the affairs of the Ottoman government, . . . [it] will never achieve progress. Sultan Selim wished to introduce a European order of things (*nezam*) in Istanbul. But the *mollas*, out of pure jealousy, considered it contradictory to religious law and, from their own particular motives, foiled him. Similarly, the Sultan wanted to introduce European sciences in Istanbul but they, out of envy, would not let him rescue even some of the people from ignorance and foolishness (*hemaqat*). In fact, any government the *mollas* interfere with . . . will never achieve progress (427).

Shirazi's was not the first Persian book to describe the European political system. Two others—by ʿAbd al-Latif Jazaʾeri (1798) and Mirza Abu-Taleb Khan (1804)—had appeared earlier.[2] The latter, of which a translation was published in London in 1810, apparently served as a model for Shirazi.[3] But if not the first *author*, Shirazi was the first *student*—from anywhere in the Middle East—to set out his impressions of the West for the benefit of his countrymen. The importance of Shirazi's book (as well as of Abu-Taleb's) lies not in its details, but in the generally positive image of the West that he conveys. Shirazi (much more than Abu Taleb) not only holds up the political institutions of the West as a model but also praises European "good manners," the calm temper of the British people, the "healthy weather and food," the clean streets, and the medical services. He does not advocate the adoption of western ways, as other Iranians would do later. But because he addresses descriptions to a society largely isolated from the West and traditionally considering the non-Muslim world its inferior, his record, even though descriptive rather than admonitory, is a harbinger of change.

On their return, Shirazi and people like him developed something of a double standard. Shirazi made that point in so many words when

2. ʿAbd al-Latif Jazaʾeri [Musavi Shostari], *Tufat al-ʿAlam* (the copy used here was published in Bombay in 1846); Mirza Abu-Taleb Khan ibn Mohammad Esfahani, *Masir Talebi ya Safarname-ye Mirza Abu-Taleb Khan*, better known as *Masir Talebi fi Bilad al-Faranji* (the references that follow are from the edition by Ketabha-ye Jibi, Tehran, 1973/4). Talebi, who resided in India, lived in Europe from 1799 to 1803.

3. There are many similarities between the above-mentioned passages by Shirazi and those in *Masir Talebi*, concerning, among other topics, the Parliament (pp. 91, 239–59), freedom (231–36), equality (232), the press (195, 212), Freemasonry (151–55), descriptions of London (184–92, 208–13) and of the colleges of Oxford (115–16). Shirazi made no reference to Talebi's writings, but it is unlikely that he was not familiar with them.

he wrote of his arrival at Istanbul: "Now that we have re-entered the realm of Islam we must [again] act according to our religion." Still in Istanbul, he therefore asked another graduate who had married a British lady while in London not to visit him with his wife (403–4). Yet while in Europe, and not without some hesitation, Shirazi and his friends adopted western dress and some western customs. The Russian traveler Count Saltykov-Shchedrin recalls visiting, in 1840, the house of Hajji Baba Afshar (the first Iranian to study abroad). Much to his amazement, he was allowed to meet the women and young girls of the household in the living room.[4] Similarly, Joseph Arthur de Gobineau mentions an Iranian graduate of Saint-Cyr (1845–1848), named Hoseyn Qoli Khan, who kept wearing a French uniform even back home and remained a passionate reader of French novels. Gobineau goes on to relate that Qoli Khan refused to take off his shoes in the presence of the shah, as was customary, claiming: "This is not military [behavior].... You have sent me to France to learn what is appropriate for soldiers and I [did so]... down to the most minute details. Consequently, I will not agree to depart from it."[5] The accuracy of the story is very doubtful. After all, even foreign ambassadors removed their shoes for an audience with the shah,[6] and it seems unlikely that a young man would challenge the shah in such way. Nevertheless, the fact that such conduct could be attributed to an Iranian recipient of a foreign education attests to new norms of behavior. Qoli Khan apparently went far beyond the usual reactions of returning graduates. "His hatred of Islam," Gobineau attests, "had no limit. He saw in this religion the... mark of Arab oppression of his country." He recommended cleansing the Persian language of all Arabic words and idioms. "All in all, he saw neither rescue nor salvation for his homeland except through the return—as completely as possible—to its most ancient past ... [to] the religion and philosophy of its most remote ancestors."[7] Although secularist views were occasionally expressed late in the century, such thinking, undoubtedly reflecting the intellectual ferment of France during Qoli Khan's stay there, were highly unusual in the Shi'i Iran of his time.

The graduates were the driving force behind the first newspapers (in midcentury) and behind the expansion of the press in the following

4. This was so exceptional that Saltykov thanked Afshar especially for giving him an opportunity to get to know them (Saltykov-Shchedrin, 121–25).

5. Joseph Arthur de Gobineau, *Religion et philosophies dans l'Asie central* (Paris: Gallimard, 1933), 124.

6. Ardekani, 596; Morier, *Haji Baba*, 481–82.

7. Gobineau, 124–25.

decades. They launched and published the most important newspapers and were both their main writers and their principal readers. Shirazi had become interested in the press while studying in London and brought a printing press with him which he used to print, in 1837/8, the first Iranian newspaper, *Kaghadh-e Akhbar*. The title of the first issue was *Ruzname-ye Akhbar-e Vaqaye'-e Ettefaqiye* (Diary of Current Events). Ten and seven years earlier, respectively, the first official gazettes had been published in Cairo and Istanbul, with similar names. Though Shirazi's paper appeared irregularly, and did not last for more than two years, it eventually led to the publication of *Vaqaye'-e Ettefaqiye* in 1851, by the printing house of Dar al-Fonun. The latter, though also coming out irregularly, lasted until the Constitutional Revolution. In line with the traditional chronicles (and much like the Cairo and Istanbul gazettes), it was a cumbersome compilation of brief news mainly of the shah's personal doings. Later official or semiofficial papers— such as *Iran*, *Sharaf* (Honor) and *Ettela'* (Information)—still concentrated on praising the shah, covering his hunting expeditions and describing the gifts presented to him by the people. They did, however, include some interesting articles of an educational and literary nature,[8] and a modest amount of foreign news was gradually inserted. But by and large, Browne was right to dismiss them as "worthless" and "colorless."[9] Among those writing for the first papers were graduates of European studies, such as Shirazi, Mirza Reza Mohandes, and Mirza Reza Afshar.[10]

Even more important were the newspapers published abroad by Iranian expatriates, beginning in the 1870s. Unlike the press inside Iran, they were not subject to supervision or censorship, genuinely reflected political developments, and took a stand for reform and, above all, for a constitution. The most significant was undoubtedly Malkom's *Qanun*. Others were *Akhtar* (Star), first published in Istanbul in 1876; *Habl ul-Matin* (The Strong Cord), published in Calcutta (1893); *Thoraya* (Star) and *Parvaresh* (Nurture), published in Cairo (in the 1890s).[11] Many more were published on the eve of the Constitutional Revolution, bringing the number up to ninety. Altogether, Browne lists 371 news-

---

8. Jan Rypka et al., *History of Iranian Literature* (Dordrecht: Reidel, 1968), 338.

9. Edward G. Browne, *The Persian Revolution of 1905–9* (London: Frank Cass, 1966), 143, and *Literature*, 4:469.

10. Adamiyyat, *Amir Kabir*, 159–62; Tabataba'i, *Shafaq-e Sorkh*, 21 July 1933.

11. On these newspapers and their political significance for the modernization of Iran, see: Bamdad, 4:149–50; Kermani, 2:221; Dowlatabadi, 1:123; Fashahi, 264–76.

papers published until the start of the revolution.[12] Some of them, Browne notes, were of "a very high order, and afford[ed] examples of a prose style, forcible, nervous, and concise, hitherto almost unknown." Provoked by an article in the *Times* (2 July 1908) calling the Iranian press "mischievous" and "dangerous," Browne writes: "At its best the free Persian Press reached a very high level, and at its worst it was superior to certain French, English and American papers."[13] This may be somewhat exaggerated, but clearly the Persian press abroad, on the eve of the revolution, was rich in the number of publications and their contents, and proved highly influential.[14]

Similarly, graduates of foreign studies or of Dar al-Fonun contributed to the publication of the first scientific periodicals to appear in Persian. First was *Ruzname-ye 'Ilmiye-ye Dowlat-e 'Aliye Iran* (Scientific Gazette of the Sublime State of Iran), published by Dar al-Fonun itself since 1863/4. In 1902/3, a magazine called *Ganjine-ye Fonun* (Treasury of Arts) was founded in Tabriz by Browne and three "friends of learning and culture."[15]

Another avenue for changing the climate of political and literary opinions was translation and original critical writing; both owed a great deal to the new graduates. The first translations were published in the first half of the century. Most prominent among the early translators was Mirza Reza Mohandes (who had studied in Paris). Supported by 'Abbas Mirza, he translated (in 1829/30) Voltaire's essays on Peter the Great and Charles XII of Sweden and later Edward Gibbon's *Decline and Fall of the Roman Empire*.[16] But these remained isolated instances. Greater numbers of translations and original books did not begin to appear until the second half of the nineteenth century. The new trend began with the establishment of Dar al-Fonun and its printing house and the employment there of foreign instructors and translators. The first publications were scientific and technical works published by European and Iranian teachers, to be used as textbooks in their classes. Since most Iranian graduates had studied in France, the influence of French culture and literature was dominant. Browne's "partial and

12. E. G. Browne, *The Press and Poetry of Modern Persia* (Cambridge: Cambridge University Press, 1914), 27–153.

13. Browne, *Revolution*, 127–28. Lists of two dozen papers are given there and on p. 143.

14. Amin al-Dowla wrote of *Qanun* that it had become the "center of conversation at every meeting" (Amin al-Dowla, 148).

15. Browne, *Press*, 14.

16. *Vaqaye'-e Ettefaqiye*, no. 98 (1851); Ardekani, 595; Fashahi, 254–55.

incomplete" catalog of Persian books published before the Constitutional Revolution lists 162 titles, sixty-five of them by teachers of the college. There were eighty-eight military textbooks, some language textbooks, medical handbooks, four biographies of Muslim leaders, ten travelogs of the West, translations of European classics (including Defoe's *Robinson Crusoe*, Molière's plays, Dumas' *Three Musketeers*, Verne's *Around the World in Eighty Days*, and—of most significance, politically speaking—Morier's *Hajji Baba of Isfahan*), ten histories of Iran (including Malcolm's), and over twenty translations of works on western history: biographies of Napoleon, Nicholas I, Frederick the Great, William I, and Louis XV, and short histories of Rome, Athens, France, Russia, and Germany. The shah had in fact commissioned some of these translations to glorify the monarchy, but by inadvertently causing Iranian readers to contrast their shahs with the most famous kings of Europe, and the poverty of Iran with the prosperity of Europe, their publication contributed in some measure to the weakening of the Qajar monarchy.[17]

In the last quarter of the century, there appeared many original books of political and social criticism. Most influential were the books by Talebov (mainly *Ketab-e Ahmad*), Maraghe'i (*Safarname-ye Ebrahim Beg*), Mostashar al-Dowla (*Yek Kalame*), some of the treatises of Malkom (mentioned earlier), and those of Mirza Hasan Khan Eʿtemad al-Saltane (who had studied at Dar al-Fonun and later in France).

It is not altogether certain whether Eʿtemad al-Saltane actually wrote or translated all the books appearing under his name, or whether he had some of them written by "men of learning whom he collected from every quarter" at the Ministry of the Press which he headed. But all of them clearly reflected his views.[18] Among his most important books are the *Salnames* (Yearbooks), *Hojjat al-Saʿadat* (The Proof of Happiness), *Mir'at al-Boldan* (Mirror of the Lands), *Matlaʿat al-Shams* (The Rising of the Sun), *Al-Maʿather va al-Athar* (Monuments and Achievements), *Name-ye Daneshvaran* (The Book of the Learned), and translations of

17. Browne, *Press*, 154–66; Abrahamian, 57–58; H. Kamshad, *Modern Persian Prose Literature* (Cambridge: Cambridge University Press, 1966), 27–28; Adamiyyat and Nateq, 76.

18. According to Browne (*Press*, 156), al-Saltane "himself was devoid of any profound knowledge or scholarship and only caused these works to be written under his supervision . . . afterward causing their writings to be published in his own name." Mahmud Katira'i, in his article "Eʿtemad al-Saltane: Scholar or Illiterate," argues, on the contrary, that he was in fact a scholar: the article, first published in *Nagin*, is included in Eʿtemad al-Saltane's book *Khalase* which Katira'i edited (Tehran: Tahuri, 1969), 225–32.

Molière's *Le Medecin malgre lui* and the *Memoirs of Mademoiselle de Montpensier.*[19]

His sharp criticism of the current mismanagement of Iranian affairs came out most clearly in his book *Asrar-e Enhetat-e Iran* (The Secrets of the Decline of Iran), better known as *Khalase* (Ecstasy), written in 1892/3. Like Maraghe'i in *Ebrahim Beg* and Talebov in *Ketab-e Ahmad*, E'temad al-Saltane adopted a loose fictional framework—a poetical dream—to voice his criticism. But whereas the others put criticism in the mouths of fictitious characters, he made them confess their crimes "in the presence" of the great figures—legendary or historical—of the past. Questioned by the founders of the Achaemenian, Sassanian, Safavi, and Qajar dynasties, eleven nineteenth-century chancellors were called upon to admit their part in the destruction of Iran. Reviewing the Qajar period through their actions, he blamed them (most particularly Sepahsalar and Amin al-Dowla and through them Naser al-Din Shah) for all the misfortunes of Iran: they were incompetent; they had preferred their personal interests over that of the state; they were brutal and greedy and practiced deception; they engaged in nepotism and bribery; and, most disgracefully, they had sold the country to foreigners. Some eight years later, Malek al-Motakallemin, Jamal al-Din Esfahani, and others jointly wrote a similar book: *Ro'ya-ye Sadeqe* (True Dreams).[20] They, in turn, made the dignitaries, clerics, and governors account for their sinful deeds at the Last Judgment. Among the many charges against the ulama, the authors stressed their opposition to the new education.

More and more frequently, the graduates returning from abroad felt an urge to make their newfound views public. Although they were no more than "inexperienced youngsters," Hedayat wrote, "each holds under his arms a thesis (*resale*) about the French Revolution and wishes to play the role of Robespierre or Danton . . . . They are extremely enthusiastic and fiery."[21] They thought of themselves "as the new apostles," spreading the message of reason, science, liberty, and progress.[22] This is not to say that they all had the same perception of western civilization or wanted to imitate it in every respect. But they were all

19. A list of his publications is given in Mohammad Nura'i's introduction to the first edition of *Asrar-e Enhetat-e Iran* (Meshhed: Zavvar, 1945), v.

20. For the circumstances of the composition of *Ro'ya-ye Sadeqe* see Katira'i's appendix to *Khalase*, pp. 203–5; and Alavi, 243–54.

21. Mehdi Qoli Hedayat, 150.

22. Mangol Bayat-Philipp, *Mysticism and Dissent: Socioreligious Thought in Qajar Iran* (Syracuse: Syracuse University Press, 1982), 134.

impressed by what they had seen and wanted to borrow some of it. Hedayat, for example, though greatly impressed by the ideas of freedom and fraternity of the French Revolution, still regarded a republic as "a school without a headmaster."[23] On balance, there is undoubtedly much truth in Gobineau's observation that those returning from Europe "understood everything in a special way, which is not our way at all .... Their native ideas were fundamentally changed but not at all in a European sense.... [They] brought back European ideas that have been Asianized."[24] One such "special way" was that, with only a few exceptions, they sought an accommodation between western thinking and Islam.

In the last quarter of the century, their urge to publish was complemented by a growing desire to read. The reading public fed on political treatises, periodicals, and newspapers. Banned publications were smuggled into the country and read avidly, not just in the closed circles to which they were primarily addressed, and even circulated at the court. On the eve of the Constitutional Revolution, some newspapers printed a few thousands copies of each issue, and these were passed from reader to reader.[25] Browne noted at the time that the "popular journals, written in comparatively simple language," were widely read. Undoubtedly with some exaggeration, he added: "Everyone seems to read a paper now."[26] The same was true of the critical treatises. *Ro'ya-ye Sadeqe*, for example, appeared "in thousands of copies and [was] sent to all parts of Iran."[27] Iranians, with their long tradition of admiring verbal skill, marveled at the new idiomatic style and popular language of such books as *Ketab-e Ahmad, Ebrahim Beg, Shaykh va Vazir, Khalase* and *Ro'ya-ye Sadeqe*. The revival of drama, poetry, and fiction likewise profited greatly from the writings of the recipients of the new education. As Kamshad put it: "The intricate tales and excitements of this new literature were so fascinating...that families used to gather to hear them read aloud."[28]

But granting all that, it still remained true that the intellectuals' ability to approach the public at large, let alone attract them to their cause, was severely limited. Despite the relative growth of the reading public, Hedayat was right in remarking: "Of books we have enough; what we

23. Mehdi Qoli Hedayat, 21.
24. Gobineau, 125–26.
25. Browne, *Press*, 25–26.
26. Browne, *Revolution*, 143.
27. Quoted from Mehdi Malekzade in Katira'i's appendix to *Khalase*, 203.
28. Kamshad, 28.

lack are readers . . . . The customers are illiterate."[29] And, in fact, when it came to the point of mobilizing mass support for the tobacco revolt and the Constitutional Revolution, it was the Ulama, not the intellectuals, who were the driving force. The great contribution of the latter was their growing hold over the views of the upper classes and parts of the political establishment—not over the masses. But they gained some influence over the religious establishment as well and thus made it possible for intellectuals and ulama to cooperate in the great upheavals at the turn of the century.[30] When political change was finally in the offing and revolutionary forces were searching for an ideology to unite the utterly divergent components of their camp, it was the intellectuals who imposed their own ideology as the cohesive element: constitutionalism and nationalism were their contributions, and the wording of the constitution of 1906 carries their imprint. In the 1970s, their fellow intellectuals could not claim as much.

29. See the introduction to Mehdi Qoli Hedayat's book, iii.

30. An interesting episode in this regard is cited by Browne (*Press*, 24). He relates the story of a wealthy man who subscribed to nearly 500 copies a year of *Habl ul-Matin* and arranged for them to be sent free of charge to clerics and *tollab* at the holy shrines of Najaf and Karbala. According to Browne: "This great service rendered by him to the enlightment of the ulama and their political awakening greatly conduced to the circulation of newspapers in spiritual circles and societies."

4

The Constitutional Regime

The period discussed in this chapter—from the ratification of the constitution in 1906 to Reza Khan's coup in 1921—is one of transition, from the reign of the Qajars to that of the Pahlavis. The Constitutional Revolution considerably weakened the Qajar regime. So did the ensuing economic crisis stemming from the prolonged throes of the revolution, from mismanagement by the Qajars, and from growing foreign interference in and exploitation of the country. Combined, these brought about what the then American financial adviser in Iran, Morgan W. Shuster, called "The Strangling of Persia."[1] The country's embroilment in World War I added to the already pressing social and economic distress. Domestic instability prevailed.

This was, however, also an era of relative liberalism, an interlude between two periods of autocracy. In a manner that was to become a recurrent theme in modern Iranian history, the intellectuals took advantage of the weakening of central authority to promote their reform programs. But these intervals of slackening control were too short, and too beset with instability, social tension, and economic upheaval, to allow reforms to be firmly launched. True, supporters of educational reform could well be content when the constitution was eventually approved—after all, many of them had long regarded a constitutional regime as a guarantee for the advancement of education. But as in many other fields, their high expectations fell prey to the chaotic circumstances of their time.

1. Thus the title of Shuster's book (London, 1912).

The Initial Expansion of Primary and Secondary Education

In line with the tendency already prevalent before the revolution, advocates of educational reform attached overriding importance to elementary education. The early stage of education—more than the later ones—was, they held, a prerequisite for a durable constitutional regime and an essential condition for building a modern nation-state, for social and economic progress, and, of course, for expanding and improving higher education. The educational legislation of the period reflects such thinking.

The first educational laws of the period laid down the broad guidelines for a school system in keeping with the ideals held by the intellectuals. Already the Supplementary Constitutional Law of 1907 established the legal basis for education to be free, and for schools to be removed from clerical control—two major tenets in the reformist creed. It guaranteed the freedom of "acquisition of and instruction in all sciences, arts and crafts" (article 18); laid down that the "establishment of schools . . . and the [implementation of] compulsory education are to be regulated by the Ministry of Science and Arts"; and placed "all schools and colleges . . . under the supreme control and supervision of [that] ministry" (article 19).[2] The Administrative Law of the Ministry of Education of 1910 made the minister responsible for providing compulsory elementary education as well as for the promotion of secondary and higher education (article 2).[3]

The Fundamental Law of Education of 1911 and the Majlis debate preceding it set forth with greater force and clarity the conceptual framework of the educational system.[4] Both the debate and the law dealt with elementary education only. Special stress was laid on how to bring the children of lower-class parents into the schools and how to make educational programs uniform throughout the country. All Majlis speakers came out for compulsory education, many holding it up as a means to achieve greater social and political justice. In line with the optimistic mood prevalent during the years of the revolution, but in total disregard of the reality of widespread illiteracy, the law specified that each

2. *Majmu'e-ye Qavanin*, Majlis-e Shura-ye Melli (Tehran: Ketabkhane-ye Majlis; hereafter *MQ*), terms 1 and 2, 18. Each Majlis was initially elected for a term of two years and later for four years.

3. Ibid., 24–32.

4. For the text of the law, see ibid., 348–49; for the discussion in the House, see Majlis-e Shura-ye Melli, *Modhakerat-e Majlis-e Shura-ye Melli* (Tehran: Ketabkhane-ye Majlis; hereafter *MM*), term 2, 200–206.

village or urban quarter must have a school (article 19), and that public schools should primarily serve the poor (article 25). Wealthy families from towns were to be made responsible for the upkeep of urban schools, rural landlords for village schools (articles 22–24).

With regard to the introduction of a countrywide uniform curriculum, there were two opposing views in the House. One group (represented best by Mo'tamen al-Molk, Vakil al-Tojjar, and Asadollah Mirza) argued that uniformity would provide a cohesive element and contribute to national unity; and that it would advance the level of education (among other things by having fewer textbooks to write and print). They added that the massive internal migration then in progress made such a step mandatory. The other group (led by Vakil al-Molk and Hasan Taqizade) claimed that the proposed article contradicted the principle of educational freedom which the law had recognized. Eventually, they argued, uniformity would do damage to the quality of schooling and curtail scholarly achievement. In a compromise solution, the law as passed laid down that schools must offer a uniform compulsory program but were free to add to it (articles 4–5). This applied also to private schools, which were now placed under the supervision of the Ministry of Education as well (article 12). Two other articles of the law are noteworthy: article 17 made it mandatory for the ministry to include Islamic studies in the curriculum and empowered it to withdraw textbooks conflicting with the religion; and article 18 stipulated that public employment was open only to those who had graduated from school with satisfactory grades on the final examinations.

Later in 1911, the Majlis passed a law establishing five elementary schools in Tehran as an "initial effort for the implementation of compulsory and free elementary education."[5] In the debate, members stressed once again the importance of bringing education to the lower classes and of encouraging it in the provinces rather than in Tehran. 'Ali Khan and Zaka' al-Molk demanded that half the school places be reserved for entrants of lower-class origin. Others, supported by Hajji Aqa, demanded that all places should go to them. Another view, put forward by Baha' al-Molk, was that education must be free for everybody, without "discriminating against the rich." Some deputies (Hajj Seyyed Asadollah, Behjat, Mo'azzez al-Molk, and Hajj Seyyed Ebrahim) opposed giving the provinces higher priority than Tehran. The version that became law specified that half the students would be

5. *MQ*, terms 1 and 2, 322–23. The debate in the Majlis: *MM*, term 2, 1602–5, 1635–39.

exempt from tuition fees (article 2) and that fees collected from the rest were to be earmarked for setting up new schools. In response to pressure from provincial deputies, the Majlis decided to open four new schools in provincial cities (one each in Shiraz, Meshhed, Tabriz, and Kerman).

Another law, approved in 1921, provided for the formation of a Supreme Council of Education—a public body to help the Ministry of Education formulate educational policies. Among its functions were: planning for the improvement of education, for the implementation of compulsory education, and for the establishment of vocational (agricultural and technical) schools; and laying down criteria for opening new schools, engaging teachers, sending students abroad, and evolving standards for evaluating their diplomas.[6]

Clearly, Majlis legislation—in particular the stress on compulsory education—reflected the aspirations of the liberals rather than the capabilities of the educational system. The formal power of the law notwithstanding, realities precluded immediate change. This seems to explain why the conservatives, including the many clerics in the House, were not too vehement in their opposition.[7] Nevertheless, the laws listed here were significant. First, the new laws delineated the educational system in a manner that—despite various later amendments— remained valid until the Islamic Revolution; second, the adoption of the principle of free and compulsory education led directly to the law of 1943 which provided for its actual application; similarly, the emphasis on education reaching lower-class and provincial children foreshadowed the practice of later years; and lastly, the laws did lay the foundation for a uniform school system throughout the country.

Studies Abroad

Following the revolution, the demand for academic education abroad grew quickly. But here, too, expectation and realities were rather far apart. The Majlis supported the dispatch of students to the West. So did the shah, who now recognized the growing demand for higher education and acknowledged the lack of facilities to meet it at home. Moreover, elite-group families, impressed by the current regard for

6. *MQ*, terms 3 and 4, 75–79.
7. On the social composition of the Majlis, see the valuable survey by Zahra Shaji'i, *Nemayandegan-e Majlis-e Shura-ye Melli dar 21 Dowre-ye Qanungodhari: Motale'e az Nazar-e Jame'e-Shenasi Siyasi* (Tehran: MTE, 1965).

education and the success of graduates of western universities, and possibly fearing social change following the revolution, thought more than before of higher education as an important means of upholding their status. The expansion of the administration and the current social and economic reform plans also augmented the demand for academically qualified staff.[8] Sadiq and ʿAli Akbar Siyasi—two leading educationalists of the twentieth century who were among the students sent to Europe in 1911—told me of the importance of these factors. They added that a European education was then viewed by many families as an important (additional) means of securing social prestige and economic well-being for their younger members.[9] Yet the number of Iranian students in the West remained small. According to Tabataʾi, there were only six Iranian university students and eleven high school students in Europe in 1911, most of them sons of "key figures."[10] If there were students Tabatabaʾi was unaware of, their numbers were minimal.

A 1911 law provided for the immediate dispatch of thirty students to Europe at government expense, to be followed by other groups of twenty in each of the four following years. But because of severe budgetary problems, only the first group actually left. Even their dispatch became possible only after Shuster intervened.[11] A few more students later went to Europe at the expense of their families. The outbreak of World War I caused a sharp drop and even led to the recall of some students before their graduation.[12] But by 1918, the number had risen again and there were some 500 Iranians (both university and high school students) in the West, most of them financed by their families.[13]

The only organized government-sponsored group was thus the one of 1911. Half a century had passed since the last such group had been

8. Sadiq, *Yadegar*, 1:90–95; Tabatabaʾi, *Shafaq-e Sorkh*, 4 August 1933.

9. Sadiq served several times as minister of education and chancellor of Tehran University in the early 1940s, was director of the Tehran Teachers Seminar, and a senator since the 1960s. He wrote many books on education. (Details on his studies in the West are given in this section and in Chapter 6.) During 1975–1977, with characteristic generosity, Sadiq gave me many interviews and supplied me with valuable insights.

Siyasi was minister of education in the 1940s, chancellor of Tehran University (1942–1954), and dean of its humanities faculty (1941–1961). He was active in the opposition movement of the 1950s and 1970s. Interviews with him were held in Tehran in February and April 1977 and in London in August 1982.

10. Tabatabaʾi, *Shafaq-e Sorkh*, 6 and 7 August 1933.

11. An interview with Sadiq, included in the archives of the Darbar-e Shahanshahi, *Markaz-e Asnad va Madarek*, Tehran (hereafter MAM) as document 5100.

12. Sadiq, *Yadegar*, 1:96–99.

13. Arasteh, 40.

put together. The information available attests to the importance attached to it by the Majlis, the government, the students themselves, and their families. Unlike the preference for military studies in the nineteenth century, education and science were favored by most of the students of 1911. Some Majlis members (such as Mo'azzez al-Molk and Hajj Seyyed Ebrahim) still preferred military training (arguing that the "life of the nation depends on the army"), but most speakers in the debate (including the chairmen of the education and finance committees) demanded priority for pedagogy. In the version eventually passed, the law assigned fifteen students to study education; seven to military sciences; two each to agriculture, road engineering, and technology; one to study public administration; and one to chemistry.[14] Clearly, study abroad, which had hitherto been considered a tool for military advancement, was now viewed as an instrument for educational reform. By and large, the division of fields was adhered to, but most of the students of pedagogy took up science rather than the humanities.

In contrast to the past, Majlis members (most forcefully Hajj Shaykh al-Ra'is and Soleyman Mirza) now insisted that preference be given to students from a lower-class and/or provincial background. The rich, they argued, could send their sons abroad in any case. They carried the day, and, for the first time, the law spelled out criteria for the selection of candidates: all must be from poor families (*foqara'*), bachelors, and between fifteen and thirty years of age, and all had to pass competitive government examinations to show that they possessed the necessary academic qualifications.[15] About 150 candidates competed for the thirty scholarships, another indication of the growing demand for higher education.[16]

Yet these provisions again reflected the gap between the liberal ideas of some Majlis members and the stark realities of the country: if *foqara'* candidates could be found at all, they were unlikely to have had the education enabling them to pass the examinations. The upshot was that—as in the past—most recipients of scholarships were upper-class or upper middle-class sons. Looking at a group photograph of the 1911 students with Sadiq, I asked him about their backgrounds: none, he said, could be classed as poor; most were the sons of Qajar princes,

14. For the text of the law, see *MQ*, terms 1 and 2, 603–4; for the debate, see *MM*, term 2, 826–30.

15. *Ruzname-ye Rasmi-ye Dowlat-e Iran*, issue no. 22, 1911/2.

16. Moradi-Nezhad and Pazhum-Shari'ati, 15. Sadiq and Siyasi, however, mentioned 200 candidates; see interviews with Sadiq, document 5100, MAM; and Siyasi, *Majale Daneshkade-ye Adabiyyat va 'Ulum-e Ensani*, 23 (nos. 93–94), 1–44.

courtiers, ministers, high officials, and prominent Bazar merchants. Only a few students would have been hard put to go abroad at their families' expense.

In the careers of the returnees, the patterns of the past continued to prevail. Although they were sent out in a more orderly fashion, their initial appointments were arranged by the students or their relatives in direct "deals" with prominent government figures intended to give them a "decent" start. This was confirmed by Sadiq and Siyasi in my interviews with them. Sadiq, for example, turned to Prime Minister Vothuq al-Dowla and obtained an appointment as supervisor of the new schools in Tehran. As a rule, graduates were appointed to prominent positions in government service, resulting in frequent tensions between them and their veteran colleagues.[17] Their head start gave them the opportunity to rise to the top: ʿAbdollah Riyazi became Majlis speaker; Esmaʿil Marʾat, Sadiq, and Siyasi served as ministers of education; ʿAli Riyazi was minister of war, and Bahnam Zaman deputy minister of war; and Gholam ʿAli Sheybani became Tehran's police chief. All those who had taken up military subjects rose to senior command positions in the armed forces. Many from among the group as a whole later taught at Tehran University. Obviously, as in the past, their prestige and status was due not only to their scholarly credentials but also to the fact that most of them had been of elite background, and that they had been abroad. Echoing Malkom's observation in an earlier period, Tabatabaʾi said of the 1911 group: "There was no yardstick to define who was, or was not, an expert in his chosen field. It was sufficient for someone to disclose that a certain man had been in Europe and had acquired his education there for his professional qualifications to be accepted."[18]

Thus, although the law had assigned students their fields of study, there was still no close correlation between the subjects taken up and subsequent occupation. There was, however, a measure of approximation. For example, of those who had studied pedagogy, not one became a schoolteacher, but most eventually taught at Tehran University or worked in the Ministry of Education (or both). Much like the situation in the preceding century, the main contribution of the graduates was in promoting the overall trend toward modernization.

Apprehensions of negative cultural influences persisted and may have been reinforced by the lessons of the past. During the debate on the law in the Majlis, for example, Eftekhar al-Vaʿezin and Shaykh al-

17. Sadiq, *Yadegar*, 1:192–94. For previous rivalries, see Chapter 2.
18. Tabatabaʾi, *Shafaq-e Sorkh*, 4 August 1933.

Ra'is pointed out that study abroad might hurt the religious belief of the students and their national consciousness.[19] In an address to the students about to leave for France, the shah said: "The reason that we send you from a monarchy to study in a republic is that we want you to find inspiration, and take your model from the French sense of patriotism. You should learn from them love of the motherland . . . . I hope that [you,] my children, will return and serve Iran equipped with two important qualifications: first, patriotism (*hobb-e vatan*), sense of duty and consciousness (*vazife-shenasi*); and second, expertise in the field of science assigned to you."[20]

In my interviews with Sadiq and Siyasi, they stressed that, for all their progress at the university, it was the impact of the western world-view and of the concepts of freedom and democracy that became the really lasting influence of their sojourn abroad. Sadiq discussed their appeal at length and wrote: "Such influences caused significant changes in my character, manners and spirit, [an outcome] considerably more weighty than that reflected in the formal diploma." He pinpointed the difference between the French educational system and the new schools in Iran: in the *kemaliye*, he said, he had been taught to recite "nice phrases"; in Paris he was trained "to think": "The most important thing I have learned in the Versailles seminary was to think . . . . There was no topic raised which did not require thinking; again and again they stressed that there was no limitation to or restriction on thought and that each and every person is free to say and write whatever he wishes . . . . In the classrooms of the Kemaliye and Dar al-Fonun, the only thing the teachers expected from the students was to recite precisely what they had taught him . . . thereby fostering memory only . . . [in France] they trained us . . . in logical thinking."[21]

In the long run, such experiences could contribute more to the emergence of modern Iran than the professional qualifications.

Medical Training

Having far-reaching impact on the modernization of higher education, the Medical Law (*Qanun-e Tababat*) of 1911, made the practice of medicine conditional on acquiring modern medical training.[22] It became

19. *MM*, term 2, 827–29.
20. The text of the shah's speech is included in Mehdi Qoli Hedayat, 490.
21. Sadiq, *Yadegar*, 1:76–82, 118–20.
22. For the text of the law, see *MQ*, terms 1 and 2, 312–15.

a precedent for similar laws under Reza Shah restricting the practice of law, and the teaching and other professions, to graduates of modern universities (see Chapter 5). Until then, of course, both lawyers and schoolteachers were mostly men of the religious establishment who had received a traditional religious education. The new laws threatened their hold over these professions and paved the road for the modernization of education.

The medical law was nothing short of revolutionary. Medicine had traditionally been taught by an apprenticeship system, whether by an individual doctor or at a hospital. However, the new law faced two major obstacles: first, throughout the country there were only a few western-trained physicians and not a proper medical school; and second, there was fierce opposition by those practicing traditional medicine, now reduced to fighting for their livelihood. Furthermore, many people still trusted traditional medicine and were skeptical about the new doctors.

Acknowledging realities, the law took a gradualist approach: in the provinces, the traditional doctors were allowed to continue; in Tehran, they could do so only if they had practiced for at least ten years (and thus—as Lesan al-Hokama' and Zaka' al-Molk put it—proved that their treatment was not harmful); those in Tehran practicing for more than five but less than ten years would be required to take a government examination within three years. In the Majlis, some deputies (among them Dr. Amin Khan, Behjat, Mo'azzez al-Molk, and Shaykh al-Ra'is) had demanded that the same rigid conditions apply throughout the country. Otherwise, they argued, unqualified practitioners from Tehran would "go to the provinces and there engage in murder." Others (Dr. Reza Khan, Dr. 'Ali Khan, Entezam al-Hokama', Lesan al-Hokama', and Zaka' al-Molk) insisted on more flexible conditions for the provinces, arguing that the lack of physicians there made such an approach imperative; that in Tehran doctors could seek specialization; and that in the capital, they had access to new drugs liable to be harmful if used improperly.[23]

Important as it was, the law was premature and its implementation quite impossible at the time.[24] Two supplementary laws under Reza Shah (in 1927 and 1928) extended its provisions to the country as a whole, but even then it had no immediate results.[25] However, the

23. *MM*, term 2, 1576–80.

24. Sadiq, then chief of the education bureau in the province of Gilan, testified to such difficulties (*Yadegar*, 2:64–65).

25. *MQ*, term 6, 30–32 and term 7, 237–38.

principles of the law gradually came to be accepted. Although some traditional practitioners still enjoy some respect even today (mainly in tribal and rural areas), the concept of modern education won out. Ahead of their time as the laws were, they gave an important impetus not only to medical education but to modern education in general.

Conclusion

The widely held expectation that the Constitutional Revolution would lead to immediate advances in education did not materialize. Not that ideas and plans were lacking; but prevailing circumstances proved stronger. In retrospect, leading Iranian educationalists were critical of such "failures." Dowlatabadi described the "gloomy situation" of the school system following the ratification of the constitution and concluded that the Constitutional Revolution had not contributed significantly the advancement of education.[26] Sadiq regarded these failures as a threat to "the future of Iranian constitutionalism."[27] *Ta'lim va Tarbiyyat*, the organ of the Ministry of Education, wrote that it had failed to discern a "specific and significant contribution" of the constitution to the field of education.[28] As we have seen, such criticism applied the yardstick of expectations rather than that of realities.

In fact, the constitutional period registered some important achievements. The overall objectives of the educational system were defined and incorporated in legislation. These objectives were free and compulsory education, a uniform educational system opening the schools to children from the lower classes and from the provinces, and making certain occupations conditional on an appropriate modern education. Also in this period, the foundations of the Ministry of Education were laid. The keen interest of the Majlis in educational matters, in particular the speeches of some of the provincial delegates, helped draw attention to the educational requirements of the outlying districts. But translating principles into practical action was another thing altogether. The Pahlavis later tried—in their own way—to implement some of the ideas of the early years of the century; others were put forward over and over again by the opposition whenever the Pahlavis' government authority seemed to be weakening at the center.

26. Dowlatabadi, 2:207–10.
27. Sadiq, *Farhang*, 364–66.
28. "Ma'aref," *TT*, 530.

PART TWO

Education under Reza Shah

The two decades from the coup that brought Reza Khan to power in February 1921 to his abdication and exile in September 1941 were a period of (comparative) political stability, authoritarian rule, and intensive modernization. As such, they contrasted sharply with the instability and economic depression immediately preceding them and with the ensuing deterioration during World War II.

Sporadic attempts at reform had failed to halt the Qajar decline over the years. The dynasty never recovered from the blows of the Constitutional Revolution. Ahmad Shah (1909–1925)—the last of his line—and his governments were too weak to run the country effectively. Neither was the newly formed Majlis capable of assuming a role of political leadership.

This unstable situation was rendered incomparably worse by World War I, its antecedents, and its aftermath. Iran's location at the crossroads of southwest Asia had prompted involvement by the superpowers throughout the nineteenth century. With the outbreak of the war, the country became a veritable cockpit of world events. The weakening of domestic rule and the alliance between Russia and Britain—the powers immediately interested in Iran—made it much easier for both to implement their schemes. The discovery of oil in Iran added a new dimension (particularly after 1913, when the British navy converted from coal to oil). So did the fact that wartime developments made Iran the highway for western supplies to Russia. (Already in August 1907, Russia and Britain had signed an agreement dividing Iran into zones of influence.) In spite of its declared neutrality, Iran was swept into the maelstrom of the war. British troops entered the south, Russians the north, Ottoman forces the northwest, and German agents were active in the south. When the war was over, the foreign powers remained reluctant to withdraw their troops. The Anglo-Persian treaty of 1919 was to formalize British control and would have made southern Iran virtually a British protectorate. A cause for much Iranian resentment, its ratification was still being negotiated on the eve of the 1921 coup. Postrevolutionary Russia, for its part, regardless of its declared stand against everything czarist, continued to support separatist movements in the north. All this had a devastating effect on the country and stimulated nationalist feeling and xenophobia.

The shah and his government were incapable of stemming the tide. The Majlis was dispersed shortly after the outbreak of the war, and a new one (the fourth) did not convene until 1921. During the critical wartime and immediate postwar years, therefore, it did not meet at all. Nor did the armed forces present an alternative national leadership. The main forces were the Gendarmerie and the Cossak Brigade under Swedish and Russian influence, respectively. The army had disintegrated. A political vacuum had formed, beckoning, as it were, for a new leader.

In Iran's ethnically heterogeneous society, a combination of social tensions, economic distress, and weak government has always engendered fragmentation. Foreign "encouragement" often exacerbated this fragmentation. On the eve of the 1921 coup, the main separatist movements were in Gilan and Azerbayjan. Both enjoyed Bolshevik support. There were also uprisings in Kurdistan, Lorestan, Khuzestan, and Fars, where some tribes established quasi-autonomous zones. The country was on the brink of disintegration. At the same time, the forces that had cooperated in the Constitutional Revolution (the ulama, the Bazar merchants, the landlords, the tribal chiefs, and the intellectuals) fell apart. Once there was a constitution, their ad-hoc alliance during the revolution gave way to the inherent conflict of interests.

As the war compounded economic difficulties, thousands of villages were deserted by their inhabitants; agricultural products needed to feed the population were instead shipped to the allies; many died of malnourishment; inflation grew fast; and civil servants as well as soldiers were not paid for months on end.[1] Donald N. Wilber did not exaggerate when he wrote: "As 1920 drew to its close Iran seemed to be upon the

---

1. On the economic problems on the eve of the war, see the book by Shuster, who served as financial consultant in Iran in 1911–1912. For postwar problems, see the evidence of Millspaugh, who led an American financial mission to Iran in 1922 and again in 1943–1945: A. C. Millspaugh, *The Financial and Economic Situation of Persia: 1926* (New York, 1926); idem, *Americans in Iran* (Washington, D.C.: Brookings Institution, 1946), 1–19.

verge of collapse, about to disintegrate into a number of separate parts
.... Hunger, poverty, insecurity, despair and apathy reigned."[2]
The ground was thus prepared for a radical change. It came through
cooperation between the vigorous commander of the Cossak Brigade,
Reza Khan, and the intellectual and politician Seyyed Ziya al-Din Tabataba'i. On 21 February 1921, the two took control of the government.
At first, they were able to overcome the pull of their different backgrounds, ideologies, and character; gradually, however, they drifted
apart and Reza established his personal dominance. In 1925, he became
shah, the first of the Pahlavi dynasty.[3]

As shah, Reza soon concentrated all real power in his own hands.[4]
Neither the cabinet nor the Majlis challenged his authority. The election
of Majlis members was made subject to the shah's approval, and the
nominees had to agree in advance to approve government decisions.
To quote Dowlatabadi, "Even the existence of several independent-
minded members did not have any significance. [They] were unable to
voice criticism, even on minute issues, and had no choice but to remain
silent and be shamed in the face of their conscience."[5] Even admirers
spoke of the shah as "a benevolent autocrat" or a "wise dictator."[6]

Reza did not come to power because he possessed a coherent ideology or a specific plan of action. Rather, his emergence was the outcome of the failure of an earlier ideological movement, namely, the
constitutional movement. In contrast to many leading figures in that
movement, the shah was a man of action, not of words, who viewed
action as sufficient justification for his rule. He never summed up his
worldview.[7] Neither did he master Persian.[8] Nevertheless, by analyzing

2. Donald N. Wilber, *Riza Shah Pahlavi: The Resurrection and Reconstruction of Iran* (New
York: Exposition, 1975), 17. For details on the wartime and immediate postwar situation,
see: Pahlavi, *Mission*, 34–41; Amin Banani, *The Modernization of Iran: 1921–1941* (Stanford:
Stanford University Press, 1961), 28–38; Averi, 211–31; Hasan Arfa, *Under Five Shahs*
(London: John Murray, 1966), 81–112; Muhammad Asad Bey, *Reza Shah* (London: Hutchinson, 1938), 47–54; Percy Sykes, "Persia and the Great War," *JRCAS*, 9 (1921), 175–87;
Reader Bullard, "Persia in the Two World Wars," *JRCAS*, 50 (1962), 6–20.
   3. Five Majlis members opposed Reza. Among them were two leading educationalists,
Dowlatabadi and Hasan Taqizade, whose views will be discussed in the next chapter.
   4. On this concentration of power and its effect on policy decision, see the evidence
of two of his ministers of education: 'Ali Asghar Hekmat, *Si Khatere az 'Asr-e Farakhande-
ye Pahlavi* (Tehran: Pars, 1976), 388–93; interview of Isma'il Mar'at, *AP*, 1944/5, 201–4.
Similarly, Sadiq, *Yadegar*, 2:175–76.
   5. Dowlatabadi, 4:403–6. (Dowlatabadi was one of the shah's most adamant opponents.)
   6. Arfa, 280; Rosita Forbes, *Conflict: Angora to Afghanistan* (London: Cassell, 1931),
181.
   7. Thus one cannot speak of "Pahlavism," as one can of "Kemalism" in Turkey. For

his policies, his brief speeches and interviews, and the writings of his courtiers, one comes to the conclusion that, over and above his personal ambition to rule, he had three broader goals: nationalism, secularization, and westernization.

Reza Khan viewed national consciousness and loyalty to the state as the cohesive bond of Iranian society. To achieve the goal of nationalism, he had to overcome two other sets of much stronger loyalties: the subnational loyalty to local, tribal, or ethnic communities and to social units; and the supranational loyalty to Islam. Nationalism and patriotism (*mihan-parasti* and *vatan-parasti*), he held, were the means for building an integrative, strong, independent, and prosperous national entity. A sine qua non for nation building was, in his view, the breaking of the clerical power base. It is possible to argue—as some scholars have done[9]—that Reza was anticlerical rather than anti-Islamic. But such a distinction is alien to Islam, which rejects the separateness of the temporal and the spiritual. In the traditional view, in wishing to diminish the power of the religious establishment, the shah was aiming to reduce the power of Islam. Finally, Reza Shah aspired to make Iran into a nation-state in the modern, western mode. He believed that progress depended on the adoption by Iran of western technological achievements and on the selective borrowing of some western cultural values and social, economic, and political institutions. For all three goals, a modern educational system was, in the shah's view, a primary, indeed a vital, requirement.

---

criticism of the lack of an ideology, see Mohammad Taqi Bahar, *Tarikh-e Mokhtasar-e Ahzab-e Siyasi-ye Iran: Enqeraz-e Qajariye* (Tehran, 1942), 247–53; and Banani, 44–45.

8. According to his son, Reza had not attended school but gained a basic acquaintance with Persian while in the Brigade: VD, *Majmu'e-ye Ta'lifat, Notqha, Payamha, Mosahebeha va Bayanat . . . Mohammad Reza Shah* (Tehran: VD, 1975–1978), 1:194. These volumes, published by the Court Ministry, contain most of Mohammad Reza Shah's lectures and messages from his childhood up to 1975. See also his book, *Mission*, 6–38. Mostowfi (3:323) claimed that even when an officer of the Brigade, Reza misspelled simple words. For data about his background and worldview, see: Wilber, 3–15; Banani, 29–41; Asad Bey, 47–73; Pahlavi, *Mission*, 29–44; and interviews of Mohammad Reza Shah with the Indian journalist R. K. Karanjia, in Karanjia, *The Mind of a Monarch* (London: Allen and Unwin, 1977), 30–42.

9. Vida Garousian (Riyazi-Dawoudi), "The Ulema and Secularization in Contemporary Iran" (Ph.D. diss., Southern Illinois University, 1974), 46–47. Such a distinction was made by Reza Shah himself. See, for example, his words at a reception for Majlis members, 1 December 1936, as quoted in 'Abd al-Reza Sadiqi-pur, *Yadegar-e 'Omr* (Tehran: Javidan, 1964), 164.

5

Aims and Dilemmas

The shah, the country's leading educationalists, and its politicians were united in their appreciation of education and in their conviction that it could produce rapid advances in the nation. Reza's views in this respect—much like those of Muhammad ʿAli a century before him—were based not on a study of educational theories but on a soldier's instinct. Educationalists and other intellectuals for their part argued from theoretical premises, whether western or Islamic (or both), as well as from their own experience (mostly acquired in Europe). The politicians may have had their own convictions but acted mainly from a desire to show support for the shah and make his views their own.

The regime being what it was, the shah's personal interest shaped educational policy in all its essentials. Even a consistent opponent like Dowlatabadi extolled the shah's "belief [in] and appreciation" for education which, he wrote, were an inspiration for all advocates of educational advance.[1] His ministers of education and leading educationalists,[2] and historians of the period [3] have all stressed Reza's support of education. His approach was, nevertheless, utilitarian: he considered education as primarily a means to advance his policies, valuable only if it contributed to the stability and progress of the state and to the social adaptation of the individual in it.

1. Dowlatabadi, 4:263.
2. Hekmat, *Khatere*, 35–37, 51–55, 136–37, 206–7; interview with Esmaʿil Marʾat, *AP*, 1944/5, 201–4; Sadiq, Sadiqi, and Siyasi in interviews with the author.
3. See, for example, Wilber, 261; Arfa, 290–91.

Accordingly, society, rather than the young person to be educated, was at the center of the shah's thought. Education was to integrate the individual into society, not to develop his particular personality. The gap between these two approaches runs through much of modern educational theory in the West. One side viewed "man" and his individuality as the object of education, the other sought to form the "citizen," loyal to his nation and his state.[4] Reza's instincts settled the matter as far as he was concerned: citizens must be totally subordinate to the state; and education was nothing if it was not the means to create loyal citizens.[5] The *vatan* or *mihan* (motherland), the *mellat* or *qowm* (nation), and the concept of nation-state in general, were the highest values: education was there to inspire students to serve them.[6]

The shah took many opportunities to state his view. In 1928, for example, he told students about to be sent to Europe that they were to be trained "to serve the motherland," and that upon their return they should regard such service as the supreme ideal.[7] In 1935, he told students at a teachers training college to educate children to place the state's interests above their own.[8] The crown prince, adopting his father's views, also repeatedly emphasized the same point.[9] During his father's reign, he stressed on numerous occasions the formula of triple loyalty to *Khoda* (God), shah and *mihan* as mandatory for all Iranians and as the goal of education.[10] He held similar views during his own reign.

Loyalty to the state and the ruler was, in consequence, promoted through the curriculum, mainly in the teaching of history, geography and social sciences. Textbooks exalted the notion of "good citizenship," which included loyalty to the monarch.[11] This notion stood out most clearly, however, in the program for adult education, which revolved around themes calculated to elicit loyalty to the *vatan* and shah.[12]

4. John Dewey, *Democracy and Education: An Introduction to the Philosophy of Education* (New York: Macmillan, 1942), 106–16; J. L. Talmon, *The Origins of Totalitarian Democracy* (London: Secker and Warburg, 1952), 240–47.

5. For such aims of the shah, see: Sadiq, *Yadegar*, 2:81–88.

6. Ibid., 157–59.

7. Daneshgah-e Gondi Shapur, *Amuzesh dar Iran az 'Ahd-e Bastan ta Emruz* (Ahvaz, 1971/2), 2:18–22.

8. 'Ali Javaher Kalam, one of the students, quoted part of the speech in his memoirs (MAM, document 5106). Similarly, *AP*, 1935/6, 449–51.

9. For example, on his return from studies in Switzerland in 1936, and in addresses to students in 1936, 1937, and 1938.

10. Pahlavi, *Ta'lifat*, 2:940; MAM, document 3252; Sadiq, *Yadegar*, 2:339–40; *AP*, 1937/8, 566–67.

11. VAP, *Gozaresh-e Mostanad dar bare-ye Amuzesh va Parvaresh*. The report is in document 284 in MAM.

12. Government of Iran, Ministry of Education, *Adult Education* (Tehran, 1938), 5–6 as quoted in Banani, 104–5. See also words to this effect by the head of the Department

The shah's approach was supported by many politicians, education-alists, and intellectuals,[13] but there were dissident views as well. Some intellectuals—following the example of their predecessors from the period of the Constitutional Revolution—openly negated the prevalent approach. Aligned with liberal western thought, they believed that education existed mainly to foster free individuals. Their most forceful representative was Hasan Taqizade. In a Majlis session in May 1928, he went so far as to present the spread of education as a means to prevent errors or abuses on the part of the rulers. Education meant insistence on individual rights, participation in politics, and even the possibility of the people changing the regime.[14] He developed these thoughts further in an article titled "Social Development and the Methods of Its Achievement in our Country," in which he stressed that, for the sake of social and political development, the schools should promote freedom of thought and expression.[15] Similar views were expressed by Majlis member Mo'adel[16] and the educationalists A. Vahid and M. Shajare.[17] Such expressions were, however, few and far between, and their influence on the educational system was negligible.

Nationalism

Education for the sake of transmitting "national values," patriotism, and knowledge of one's country was a relatively new phenomenon—dating in Europe from the late eighteenth or early nineteenth century. Earlier western educational systems, though likely to emphasize the distinctive characteristics of a particular society, would usually incor-

---

for Adult Education in the ministry: Hoseyn Farhudi, "Amuzesh-e Salmandan: Mobareze ba bi-Savadi" *AP*, (1939/40), 9–10:21–23.

13. For example, Sadiq, *Modern Persia*, 84–85; idem, "Vaza'ef-e Jadid Nesbat be Ta'lim va Trabiyyat-e Dokhtaran," *Mehr*, 1925/6, 974. In a Majlis speech, Minister of Education Hekmat pointed to the fostering of national consciousness as the "most exalted aim" of his ministry, and Majlis members Ruhi and Kashef expressed similar views (*MM*, term 9, 932–33 and 1045–46, respectively).

14. *MM*, term 7, 4391.

15. Hasan Taqizade, "Roshd-e Ejtema'i va Vasa'el-e Hosul-e an dar Mamlekat-e ma," *TT*, 1927/8, 372–88. He repeated such views in a lecture at the American school in Hamadan which is included in the collection of his articles, *Maqalat*, vol. 3: *Zaban va Farhang, Ta'lim va Tarbiyyat* (Tehran: Opset, 1972/3), 152–57. See also his article "'Avamel Mohem dar Taraqqi Ejtema'i" in the same volume, 209–15; and "Ta'lim-e Ebteda'i ya Ta'lim-e 'Ali," *Ayande*, 1925/6, 181.

16. *MM*, term 9, 1042–43.

17. A. Vahid, "'Ulum va Awqaf," *Armaghan*, 1926/7, 273–74; M. Shajare, "Ravesh Novin dar Tarbiyyat-e Emruz," *Mehr*, 1936/7, 5:38–40.

porate them in more general worldview. "National education" in the stricter sense of the word developed along with national liberation movements (as in Poland, Czechoslovakia, and the Balkans) or with national unification (as in Germany and Italy). Between the two world wars, the role of education in nation building became widely acknowledged.[18] In the Middle East, the notion can be traced back to the appearance of national ideologies there, late in the nineteenth century. Until then, education aimed at inculcating moral precepts and fostering loyalty to Islam as a whole, rather than to ethnic, linguistic, or political units within it.[19] The most salient Middle Eastern example of harnessing the educational system to the cause of nationalism was that of Turkey[20]—which became a major influence on Reza Shah.

Reza Shah thought of education as the most potent force for Iran's cohesion as a nation, a force simultaneously capable of blunting supranational loyalties to Islam and blurring subnational ethnic and local loyalties. The schools were to promote patriotism (*mihan-parasti*), loyalty to the nation, national unity (*vahdat-e melli*), and national independence (*esteqlal-e melli*). He sensed that the display, or use, of force could consolidate his authority in the short run only; in the long run, education alone was able to bring the constituent elements of Iranian society together and create a hub for Iranians to rally around.[21] Already in 1921, proclamations issued by Reza and Tabataba'i set forth such views. One by Tabataba'i said: "It is essential for the character, the spiritual foundations and the feelings of our young people to be developed and advanced by means of a national-patriotic education, so that our . . . sons [will be] willing to sacrifice their lives for the motherland."[22] Foreign advisers in the Ministry of Education took a similar line. For example, a report for the ministry prepared by the French expert André Hess in 1925 stated that a countrywide, uniform educational system would achieve "identity and unity in the citizens'

18. Among numerous books on this topic, see, for example: Edward H. Reisner, *Nationalism and Education* (New York: Macmillan, 1922); Alfred Cobban, *Dictatorship* (London: Macmillan, 1938).

19. Szyliowicz, 40–47; Jean-Jacques Waadenburg, *Les universités dans le monde arabe actuel* (Paris: Mouton, 1966), 35.

20. See Andreas M. Kazamias, *Education and the Quest for Modernity in Turkey* (Chicago: University of Chicago Press, 1966), 220–23.

21. For such perceptions on the part of Reza, see: Pahlavi, *Mission*, 242; interview with his son, included in Karanjia, 36–37; 'Isa Sadiq, *Chehel Goftar* (Tehran: Dehkhoda, 1973/4), 165–75.

22. The proclamation, issued on 26 February 1921, is cited in: Mostowfi, 3:218–19; Dowlatabadi, 4:235–36; Ahmad Mehran, *Iran und dem Weg zur Diktatur-Militarisiezung und Widerstand, 1919–1925* (n.p.: SOAK, 1972), 191–95.

minds." Hess added: "Schools develop people's mind and implant in them a sense of patriotism . . . [and] devotion to national responsibility."[23] And indeed, the formation of a centralized and unified schooling system throughout the country was taken in hand early on.[24] Already in 1922, the government formed the Supreme Council of Education (Shura-ye ʿAli-ye Amuzesh) and charged it with outlining a unified education policy. In 1925, the Department of Public Education (Edare-ye Amuzesh-e ʿOmumi) was formed in the Ministry of Education to supervise its implementation.[25]

In the mid-1920s, a uniform syllabus was prepared for elementary and secondary schools (for boys and girls) and was made mandatory for all schools. The graduates of all elementary schools (having completed sixth grade), intermediate schools (ninth grade), and high schools (twelfth grade) were required to take final examinations set by the ministry. Private schools were subordinated to the ministry and obliged to follow the official program.[26] In 1928, a decree compelled all foreign schools to use the official syllabus up to the fourth grade, and use Persian as the only language of instruction. In the upper grades, they were required to complete the Persian language and literature syllabus as well as the official teaching program in Arabic and in the history and geography of Iran (but they could establish their own syllabi for other subjects). In 1937, the government nationalized all foreign elementary schools, and in 1939, the secondary schools as well.[27]

Another important step was the introduction, in 1928, of standard textbooks for all regions. In 1939, a new, modified series of textbooks were published for all subjects in all elementary and secondary grades. This was of great academic value, for until then there had been no government supervision of textbooks; they were published as commercial ventures and filled with mistakes and distortions. Besides, the new books were tailored to fit the regime's needs.[28] They emphasized the customary elements of a national education: language, literature, history, and geography, as well as music and folklore.[29] To counteract

23. André Hess, "Raport-e Monsieur André Hess dar bab-e Tashkilat-e Taʿlim dar Iran," *TT*, 1925/6, 2:20.

24. Such a tendency stemmed naturally from the French example on which the Iranian education was modeled. See Sadiq, *Modern Persia*, 45–50.

25. *MQ*, term 7, 65–67; Banani, 91–92; Sadiq, *Modern Persia*, 49–50; Ali Alaghmand, "The Public School Teacher in Iran: Social Origin, Status and Career Orientation" (Ph.D. diss., to Southern Illinois University, 1973), 41–42.

26. Sadiq, *Yadegar*, 2:51–55; Banani, 92; Arasteh, 76–77.

27. *TT*, 1927/8, 106–7; Sadiq, *Yadegar*, 2:327; Hekmat, *Khatere*, 242–43.

28. Sadiq, *Modern Persia*, 53; Banani, 94–95.

29. For such elements of national education, see I. L. Kandel, "Nationalism," in

the country's ethnic and linguistic pluralism, special emphasis was put on the knowledge of Persian. Teachers were enjoined to use only the correct standard pronunciation in class and to avoid local dialect. The teaching of pre-Islamic history, mainly of the Achaemenid period, was stressed. Instruction in geography attempted to make students see Iran as a unified *vatan* and to stress the bonds linking its various regions. Literature, especially poetry, and Iranian art were likewise emphasized. Physical education and paramilitary training—typical of nationalist education—were also promoted.[30]

The interrelationship of education and national consciousness came out most strongly in the adult education project undertaken in 1936. It was modeled on ninteenth-century projects that had gone along with the national reawakening in Europe. Later, in the interwar period, two such programs in neighboring countries attracted special attention in Iran: one in the Soviet Union (in 1919), the other in Turkey (in the late 1920s). The latter, whose link with the fostering of nationalism was most conspicuous, and with which Reza had personally become acquainted during his visit to Turkey, directly influenced the Iranian project.

The idea of adult education dated back to the time of the Constitutional Revolution but had not been acted upon then. In 1926, the minister of education, Mohammad Tadayyon, drew up an appropriate program. The Supreme Council of Education approved it, but once again it was not implemented.[31] In 1936, the then ministers of education (Hekmat) and finance (ʿAli Akbar Davar) again raised the idea. A special committee chaired by Hoseyn Farhudi (later to head the Adult Education Department in the Ministry of Education) finalized regulations and had them approved by the minister. Under the scheme, as of September 1936 adult classes were to be inaugurated in all public schools; they were to be held three evenings a week in two shifts, and no tuition was to be charged.[32] In the first year, 1936/7, there were some 1,500 classes (operating in two shifts each), with 93,371 students. In 1937/8, there were 1,700 classes with 124,233 students, and in 1938/ 9, 1,720 classes with 137,703 students.[33]

G. Z. F. Bereday and J. A. Lauwerys, eds., *The Yearbook of Education, 1957* (London: University of London, Institute of Education, 1957), 130–42.

30. Sadiq, *Modern Persia*, 79–80; A. A. Hekmat, "Iran: Modernization and Expansion," in *The Yearbook of Education, 1949*, 463; Banani, 108–9; Arasteh, 105–13; Alaghmand, 42.

31. *TT*, 1926/7, 218–22; Banani, 103.

32. Hekmat, *Khatere*, 377–84; Ministry of Education, *Adult Education*, 4–12 in Banani, 103–6.

33. For their age groups and occupations, see: Farhudi, 17–28; Ministry of Education, *Adult Education*, 4–8 in Banani, 103–6.

The success of the elementary adult education led to the opening, in 1937, of twenty-two secondary schools for adults.[34] The desire to use this project as a lever for promoting national consciousness and good citizenship was embodied in the regulations and emphasized by Farhudi.[35] It was also evident in the curriculum. Out of ninety-six hours of study in the first year, thirty-one were allocated to the history and geography of Iran, to Persian poetry, and to civics. In the second year, fifty-six hours were assigned to these subjects.[36] Textbooks included appeals to patriotism and promoted the historical (mostly pre-Islamic) heritage of Iran. In addition, numerous extracurricular lectures were organized, also clearly aimed at indoctrinating the students along the same lines.[37]

For the same purposes, the Ministry of Education formed in 1937 the Department of Public Enlightenment with the declared aim of providing "moral education" (*tarbiyyat-e ma'navi*) for the wide public. It held lectures, distributed numerous publications, and organized exhibitions and concerts—all intended to strengthen national pride and patriotism. Lectures dealt with Iranian history, literature, social sciences, and "modernism, patriotism and the loyalty to the sovereign and the remarkable improvement achieved in the country in recent years." In its first year, the organization held 700 public lectures attended by 181,250 people.[38] In October 1940, at the shah's request, the government formed the Department for Publications and Information, which, according to its director, Sadiq, had similar goals.[39]

In 1935, the government initiated a series of further measures to stimulate identification with the pre-Islamic heritage, mainly poetry, archaeology, and art. The Ministry of Education encouraged and financed the relevant research. In partial emulation of Kemal Ataturk's policy, Reza instructed the newly formed Academy for the Persian Language (farhangestan) to "cleanse" the language of Arabic loan words and to find "pure" Persian words to replace them.

At the same time, an archaeological museum and Academy of Arts were established.[40] Much was also made of poetry written in the Islamic

34. Banani, 105.
35. Farhudi, 21–23; Ministry of Education, *Adult Education*, 20–21 in Banani, 105.
36. Ministry of Education, *Adult Eduction*, 5–6 in Banani, 104.
37. Among the topics emphasized in the textbooks were: the structure of Iranian society and of the state; the importance of agriculture and industry for the advancement of the motherland; the importance of fulfilling one's civic duties; the rule of law; and the importance of solidarity with one's fellow citizens (*ham-vatan*): Farhudi, 22; Ministry of Education, *Adult Education*, 20–21 in Banani, 105.
38. Ministry of Education, *Adult Education*, 8–10 in Banani, 106.
39. Sadiq, *Yadegar*, 2:343–50; similarly in an interview with the author.
40. Sadiq, *Yadegar*, 2:201–33; Banani, 98.

period, inasmuch as it reflected, or was currently interpreted as reflecting, a sense of national distinctiveness and pride. New editions were printed; poetry was given prominence in the school curriculum; and the graves of the great poets—Ferdowsi, Saʿdi, Hafez, and ʿOmar Khayyam—were turned into imposing mausoleums and became veritable pilgrim sites. In 1935, the government marked Ferdowsi's one thousandth birthday by special ceremonies.[41] Because of the traditional Iranian admiration for poetry, all of this appeared to have great significance.

Reza Shah also perceived an interconnection between the spread of education and the lessening of Iran's dependence on foreign countries—another link between education and nationalism. Minister of Education Hekmat, for instance, stressed that "small countries" like Iran could "face up to the grasping aspirations (*matameʿ*) of the superpowers" only by virtue of spreading education.[42] Majlis representatives Dashti and Tehrani also spoke of education as a "barrier against the infiltration of foreign influence and the penetration of foreign interests." Political and economic independence, they claimed, depended on education.[43]

The linkage between education and the reduced dependence on foreign experts was even more obvious. The employment of such experts had grown rapidly since the turn of the century. On the eve of Reza's accession there were, among others, Belgian advisers in the customs service; Americans directed the country's finances as well as its postal and telegraph services; Frenchmen were employed in the Ministry of the Interior, the health services, and the judiciary; and Swedish experts worked in the Gendarmerie. Foreign advisers were also employed in the school system. The shah himself was well aware of the interconnection. He told an interviewer: "For too long my countrymen have relied on others. I want to teach them their own value, so that they may be independent in mind and action."[44]

Secularization

Before we examine the interrelationship of education and secularization, it is important to clarify the term "secularization" in its appli-

41. Hekmat, *Khatere*, 51–55; Sadiq, *Yadegar*, 2:201–33; Wilber, 163–65.
42. Hekmat, "Taʿlimat," 260.
43. *MM*, term 9, 934–40.
44. Forbes, 184–85. For similar references to Reza's approach, see the memoirs of Javaher Kalam, MAM, documents 5106, 5107; Wilber, 233, 257.

cation to the domain of Islam, as distinct from its connotations in Christian countries.

In Europe, the struggle between temporal and spiritual authority (and their eventual separation in the modern state) are part and parcel of the course of history. In Islam, such a separation is totally irrelevant to traditional thinking on the nature of the polity, and altogether unacceptable to the men of religion. In essence, rather than being a creed and a set of rituals, Islam lays down for its adherents norms of behavior and guidelines for a life-style in *all* spheres of life. "Secularization" cannot be a matter limited to the issue of religion and the state, or of religion versus science. It necessarily extends to the entirety of man's action, conduct, and thought. To challenge tradition, or any of its elements, means, perforce, challenging Islam itself. As Niyazi Berkes noted, in Islam "religion and state were believed to be fused together; the state was conceived as the embodiment of religion, and religion as the essence of the state."[45]

In Muslim society, therefore, any change in the traditional life-style, and the removal of any sphere of activity from clerical influence, come under the heading of "secularization." In practical terms, this has often meant restricting the power and authority of the clerics. But dislodging clerics from their traditional hold over education and the administration of justice signified more than a mere diminution of the activities of the religious establishment; through the schools and courts it opened up many other areas of life to the winds of change. Moreover, it deprived many clerics in the educational and judicial system of their livelihood.

A trend toward secularization had become evident in the Muslim Middle East mainly since the second half of the nineteenth century: in Egypt (during the reign of Isma'il); and in Iran (toward the end of the rule of Naser al-Din) and in the Ottoman Empire (mainly under the Young Turks). In the twentieth century, it reached its peak in Turkey under Ataturk. But compared with Ataturk's policies, Reza's were no more than half-measures. In Turkey, beginning in 1924, the *madreses* were closed down and religious studies in public schools discontinued; the Latin script was adopted in 1928 and Arabic removed from the high school curriculum in 1929. None of these steps were taken in Iran. Indeed, resistance to them would have been much fiercer there than in Turkey. In Shi'i Iran, religious sentiment was always stronger than in Sunni Turkey; ties between the individual believer and the leading clerics were much closer, and the religious establishment was much

45. Niyazi Berkes, *The Development of Secularism in Turkey* (Montreal: McGill, 1964), 3–8.

more independent and powerful and already had a record of forceful opposition to the ruler. Moreover, Turkey had maintained close contacts with the West for a much longer period. Finally, the trauma of the loss of the empire during the war and later of the Greek invasion created what J. Talmon has called that "break in historic continuity," which facilitated the emergence of totalitarian movements and the acceptance of new ideas.[46] In Iran, the harsh realities notwithstanding, no similar break occurred.

Reza was not concerned with conducting an ideological campaign against Islam but with fully establishing his monopoly of power. This implied reducing the influence of the ulama in all spheres of life and confining them to matters of faith and ritual. In fact, he wanted religion to take a place similar to that customary in the Christian West at the time. To achieve this goal, the shah once again pinned his hopes on education: he could reduce the power base of the religious establishment by removing education (and the courts) from its scope; and he could make education a conduit for the spread of new ideas in society. He believed that the influence of the ulama was largely based on the ignorance of people at large. In his *Travelbook to Mazanderan*, which he often used to mock the ulama, he relates that when he was prime minister he met someone who presented himself as a *Shaykh ul-Islam*. When he asked him about his religious education, the latter answered: "Throughout Iran, a primary condition for being a *Shaykh ul-Islam*, is ignorance. Therefore I, who cannot read or write, am more a *Shaykh ul-Islam* than any [real] *Shaykh ul-Islam*." He added that the ulama, even though illiterate themselves, still managed to turn popular ignorance to their own advantage.[47]

Reza Shah knew the extent of clerical power very well and correctly assessed that the clerics would challenge his reforms. Although he managed to maintain cordial relations with them as long as he was prime minister, he realized the sharpness of the imminent confrontation. He would not forget that, in 1924, clerical opposition had forced him to reverse a decision to set up a republic. (The clerics feared the antireligious connotation of a republican regime for which they took Ataturk's to be the model.) Such a realization reinforced his resolve to launch a comprehensive educational effort.[48]

Liberals viewed the accession of Reza as a good omen for seculari-

---

46. J. Talmon, *Political Messinanism: The Romantic Phase* (New York: Praeger, 1960), 24–26.

47. VD, *Reza Shah Pahlavi: Safarname-ye Mazanderan* (Tehran, 1976), 54–55.

48. Sadiq, *Yadegar*, 2:163–65.

zation. A leading figure among them was 'Abdollah Razi, editor of *Rastakhiz* (Resurrection), a periodical rallying secularist intellectuals around it. Writing on the eve of Reza's coronation, Razi published an article suggesting that Iran's root problem was not its military or political weakness but rather the power of the ulama. He appealed to the shah to correct that situation by "taking away their means of livelihood."[49] In another article the unnamed author claimed that all corruption in Iran stemmed from the ulama and called for "education and action" to counteract them.[50]

To achieve its goals in this respect, the regime took action to bring down the number of *maktab* and *madrese* students, while expanding the new education and reducing the number of classes in Islamic studies in the new schools. It was a two-pronged approach, intended to make the young generation less strongly attached to Islam and to counteract the influence of the *akhunds*, the *maktab* teachers who derived their livelihood from religious instruction and played an important role as intermediaries between the people at large and the religious establishment. Special efforts were made to cut down the number of *tollab*, the reservoir of future religious functionaries. This was reflected in the conscription laws. The new law of June 1925 did not cancel the exemption of *tollab* from army services,[51] but—unlike past practice—the government began to make sure that only "real *tollab*" would benefit from it. Army and police officers carried out frequent inspections and enlisted many whom they did not consider "genuine," even if their teachers attested to the contrary. This caused much resentment in *madrese* circles, reaching a peak in the summer of 1927, when Ayatollah Hajj Aqa Nurollah from Isfahan called for an ulama protest meeting in Qom.[52] The minister of education, Hekmat, explained that under the old law "any illiterate *akhund* or idle vagrant youngster who wanted to shirk conscription through guile and dissimulation could bear an 'amama (turban), call himself a *taleb* or *modarres* and find refuge in one of the places where ulama were gathering."[53] Finally, in 1938, the Majlis

49. See his article "Owza'-ye Iran va Rah-e Nejat-e An," *Rastakhiz*, September 1925, 34–35; Banani, 51. (This periodical should not be confused with the daily of the same name, first published in 1975.)

50. *Rastakhiz*, September 1925, 2–3; Banani, 51.

51. For the clauses of the new law, see *MQ*, term 5, 217–22.

52. Although the pretext for the meeting was to protest against the conscription law, it was used to denounce the entire "anti-Islamic" policy of the regime. Participants condemned increased drinking and the use of record players in clubs. See the evidence of Court Minister 'Abd al-Hoseyn Taymur-Tash who was sent by the shah to meet the organizers of the protest, as cited by Hekmat, *Khatere*, 206–7.

53. Ibid.

Table 1. Students in *maktabs* and *madreses* as compared with public schools, in selected years between 1924/5 and 1946/7

Year	Students in public elementary and secondary schools		*Maktab* students		*Tollab*	
	No.	%	No.	%	No.	%
1924/5	59,339	46.6	22,929	63.8	4,879	88.2
1929/30	127,546	100.0	35,931	100.0	5,532	100.0
1935/6	193,271	151.5	60,008	167.0	4,004	72.4
1936/7	231,119	181.2	55,645	154.9	2,935	53.1
1939/40	290,118	227.5	54,069	150.5	2,373	42.9
1940/1	314,173	246.3	51,922	144.5	1,341	22.2
1941/2	315,355	247.2	37,289	103.8	784	14.2
1944/5	323,891	253.9	27,012	75.2	1,299	23.5
1946/7	327,509	256.8	22,087	61.5	3,057	55.3

Sources: Figures computed by the author, based on: SBB/MA, *Dowran-e Pahlavi* (Tehran: Markaz-e Amar, 2535 [1976/7]), 35–55; VAP, *Gozaresh-e Amuzesh*, document 284 in *MAM*; Khaje-Nuri, 1955–2050.

revoked the exemption altogether with regard to initial training and service, leaving it in force only for reserve call-ups (article 62).[54] All in all, the new policies caused a drastic decrease in the number of the *tollab*, though after the fall of Reza Shah the *madreses* largely regained their focal role and prestige.

The changeover from the traditional to the new education, which had begun late in the nineteenth century, was now significantly accelerated, with the concomitant decline in the number of *maktab* students. Unlike the previous period, however, the government now deliberately worked to limit the *maktabs* and to subordinate them to the Ministry of Education. The most forceful indication of this policy was the set of regulations, approved in 1924 by the Supreme Council for Education, laying down for the first time conditions (both pedagogical and sanitary) for opening new *maktabs*. It also required owners of such schools (*maktab-dars*), who were usually teachers or headmasters as well, to meet certain academic and sanitary standards. Henceforth, new *maktabs* could be opened only with the approval of the minister of education.[55] Unlike the *madrese*, which emerged after the fall of Reza Shah, the *maktabs* continued their decline toward near-extinction.

Table 1 compares the percentage growth or decline of *maktab* and *madrese* students with public school attendance in selected year between

54. *MQ*, term 9, 275–76, 352–56.
55. Sadiq, *Modern Persia*, 61–62.

1924/5 and 1946/7. (The years after Reza's abdication have been included to establish continuity.) Since the data are based on government sources, it is possible that public school figures are overstated and the *maktab* and *madrese* figures fall short of reality. Nevertheless, they are now generally accepted by scholars[56] and certainly reflect the general trend. They show a constant growth in public education and illustrate the uneven but eventually very steep downward course of the *maktabs*, as well as the gradual and partial recovery of the *madreses* after the shah's resignation. Remarkably enough, having lost the *maktabs* as their recruiting ground, the *madreses* eventually succeeded in attracting graduates of the new schools.

Reza Shah not only worked against the traditional school system but also took action to limit Islamic studies in the new schools. Although the government did not follow the Turkish example of banning religious instruction in the public schools, it did significantly reduce the number of classroom hours devoted to Islam and Arabic; instead, classes on natural sciences (in high schools), music, and painting were added.[57] (In adult education courses, the Qur'an was taught in Persian, clerical opposition notwithstanding.[58]) However, a modicum of religious instruction was retained, and there was no explicit cultural campaign against religion in the public schools. The new education did indeed promote secularization but refrained from directly challenging Islam.

A related development occurred meanwhile in the legal profession.[59] Following the adoption of new penal, civil, and commercial codes, which ended the validity of *Shar'i* (religious) law in these fields, a modern legal education—rather than religious training—became a prerequisite for practicing law. In 1923, Reza established a law school[60] which was to become the nucleus of Tehran University's Faculty of Law. Aware of the danger to themselves, the clerics vehemently opposed this school and even caused a temporary halt in its operation. In 1925, it resumed activities in a special ceremony attended by the

56. See, for example, Akhavi, 187–89; *Iranshahr*, 2:1268–1308.
57. From 1930/31, the teaching of Arabic was abolished altogether in elementary schools.
58. Sadiq, *Modern Persia*, 55–74; Banani, 92–95.
59. For the significance, until then, of the religious court system in Islamic society, see H. A. R. Gibb and Herold Bowen, *Islamic Society and the West* (London: Oxford Universtiy Press, 1963), 5:114–38. On the judicial reforms of Ataturk, see Lewis, *Modern Turkey*, 266–69; and Berkes, 467–72. On the judicial reforms of Reza Shah, see Banani, 68–84.
60. Hekmat, *Khatere*, 184–85.

shah. Mir-Taheri, then a student there, wrote later that this was a warning to its opponents, signaling the shah's personal support of the school.[61] Early in 1927, the Ministry of Justice was disbanded, resuming its operations after a few months with many "new faces": the former clerics among its officials had been replaced by lawyers, many of them educated in the West.[62] In March 1932, the Majlis took the process a step farther by enacting a law requiring the registration of all deeds and similar legal documents by the state courts. Until then, this had been a matter for the *Shar'i* courts and, together with the registration of marriages and divorces, had been an important source of revenues for many clerics. Consequently, many *Shar'i* court officials were forced to seek other employment—as had been the case with the *akhunds*.[63] Another law, of December 1936, made it mandatory for judges to hold university degrees.[64] (As we have seen, a parallel development occurred in the medical profession.)

All in all, given popular devotion to religion and the strength of the Shi'i establishment, secularization in the school system and through it in other areas of life, was a considerable achievement. But much of the hope for making education a lever for secularization necessarily depended on its expansion to include most, if not all, of the school-age population. The fact that at that time education still remained the privilege of a tiny minority precluded such results. More important, the religious devotion even of the graduates of the new schools remained very much alive. Sadiq, who had gone to a modern elementary school and later studied in Paris, London, and New York, wrote that most of the graduates of his school in Tehran, and most of his fellow students abroad, remained firm in their emotional attachment to Islam.[65] Secularization efforts notwithstanding, the inherent strength of the Shi'i sentiments in Iran made it possible for Islam to remain Iran's one cohesive element even under Reza Shah. The religious revival following his abdication bears witness to this.

Westernization

In the domain of Islam, secularization subsumed westernization. The latter is being discussed separately only to bring out more fully the

61. See his memoirs, included as document 3248 in MAM.

62. Zahra Shaji'i, *Vezarat va Vaziran dar Iran* (Tehran: MTE, 1976), 131–49, 203–21.

63. For the text of the law, see *MQ*, term 9, 90–132; also, Banani, 72–73.

64. *MQ*, term 10, 98–100. Practicing judges with no degrees were required to take special examinations and were limited in their career prospects.

65. Author's interview with Sadiq, Tehran, June 1977; Sadiq, *Yadegar*, 1:67–68.

regime's eagerness to adopt western ideas and a western life-style and to stress the role it assigned to education in this context.

The shah and his courtiers perceived a twofold connection: (1) the expansion of the new school system as such, the growth of the school population (including girls), and the launching of new branches of schooling (i.e., vocational schools and universities) were seen as bringing the country closer to western ways; (2) the new material taught in schools was intended to give an added impetus to westernization. Similar trends had already existed towards the end of the Qajar period; now they became the ideal of a powerful and authoritative regime. Intellectuals, including some with an ulama family background, supported them as a matter of course. Most influential among them were Taqizade, Ahmad Kasravi, Hoseyn Kazemzade, ʿAli Dashti, Mostafa ʿAdl, and Sadiq. Also as a matter of course, opposition came mainly from the ulama, who, unlike many of their Sunni counterparts elsewhere, resisted reform altogether. The Turkish religious establishment, for instance, actively supported the Ottoman *Tanzimat* reforms during the reign of Selim III and Mahmud II (though some nonestablishment ulama did not).[66] Shiʿi ulama, by and large, despite their frequent political collaboration with liberal intellectuals (such as during the Constitutional Revolution or later in the first stages of the Islamic Revolution), rejected westernization as a "conspiracy" to weaken Islam.

The tendency toward westernizations was prevalent in all aspects of Reza's educational policy. Its goals were the adoption of western sciences and technology, a cautiously selective adoption of some western cultural values, and the borrowing of western social and economic structures.

Westernization was pivotal to the dispatch of students to Europe. Reza told them that the purpose of sending them abroad at public expense was not only for them to acquire *ʿilm*, but also to acquaint them with western culture.[67] In his address to students sent out in 1930 he said that if it was only a matter of their receiving instruction, "we could have engaged foreign instructors" to teach in Iran. "Our chief aim . . . [he went on] is that you should receive a moral education, for we note that western countries have acquired a high standing as a result of their thorough moral education." Turning to the minister of education, he added: "You should take care to select the countries which pay proper attention to moral (*maʿnavi*) education and . . . send

66. Uriel Heyd, "The Ottoman *ʿUlamaʾ* and Westernization in the Time of Selim III and Mahmud II," in Uriel Heyd, ed., *Scripta Hierosolymitana*, vol. 9: *Studies in Islamic History and Civilization* (Jerusalem: Magnes, 1961), 63–96.
67. See his speech to students going abroad in 1929, in Gondi Shapur, *Amuzesh*, 2:18.

the students there. Certain foreign countries are poor in this respect. Insofar as scientific instruction is concerned, all are alike but some are exceedingly strong and advanced in moral education."[68]

In Reza's view, students should bring back from the West, among other things, a sense of patriotism and loyalty to the nation-state modeled on Europe. In a speech to the first group he sent out to Europe, in 1928, he said it might be thought strange for monarchical Iran to send students to republican France. The reason was that they were to acquire the "French sense of patriotism and keep it deep in [their] hearts."[69]

Yet there remained an underlying ambivalence. As the shah put it in 1930:

> It would be much better to educate them here in the country where they are going to live, and with whose progress they must inevitably be concerned. But we do not yet have the necessary machinery. . . . I hope the young men we send to France and Italy will realize that civilization is different for every country. I don't want to turn the Persian into a bad copy of a European. That is not necessary, for he has [a] mighty tradition behind him. I want to make out of my countrymen the best possible Persians. They need not be particularly Western or particularly Eastern. Each country has a mold of its own, which should be developed and improved till it turns out a citizen who is not a replica of anything else, but an individual sure of himself and proud of his nationality.[70]

The same dilemma, of wanting to assimilate western cultural values but fearing the loss of Iranian identity, was clearly articulated by Prime Minister ʿAli Forughi at the inauguration of Tehran University. He said that interaction between civilizations (*tamaddon*) was necessary for their advancement, and that introversion and isolationism would unescapably lead to degeneration. Interaction with western culture was therefore essential, but it must not prejudice Iran's unique culture or national identity. It was this equilibrium that the university was intended to uphold.[71] (For the contribution of the university to westernization, see Chapter 7.) Next to the university, the new vocational schools were a primary means for introducing western technology.

A special goal of educational policy was to encourage girls to go to school at all levels (and thus eventually to change the overall status of women). Under the traditional system, the number of girls in school

68. Ibid, 2:20–22; Wilber, 135.
69. *Ettelaʿat*, 9 October, 1928.
70. Forbes, 185.
71. Hekmat, *Khatere*, 26–28.

had been very small indeed. Although technically a woman could become a *majtahed* (entitled to use her own *ejtehad*), none was recognized as *marjaʿ-e taqlid*.[72] In the Ottoman Empire, schools for girls had been established during the *Tanzimat* period, and in the 1910s the first girls were admitted to universities. Ataturk further encouraged education for girls, and coeducation in elementary schools was introduced in 1927.[73] In Egypt, girls' schools were opened during the reign of Ismaʿil, but attendance remained low.[74] In Iran, the first nonmissionary girls' schools were opened during the Constitutional Revolution (such as Namus in 1907 and the Ecole Franco-Persane in 1908), and women *anjomans* were active in expanding education for girls.[75] In private *maktabs*, boys and girls often studied together even earlier.[76] On balance, however, as observers and scholars noted, education for women on the eve of the period under discussion was extremely limited.[77] Girls were not admitted to institutes of higher learning until 1935, and in the same year elementary schools became coeducational. (See the figures on education for girls given in Table 2.)

Intellectuals and educationalists who favored the expansion of education for girls viewed the accession of Reza as a golden opportunity and sought to convince the shah and his courtiers of its importance. On 17 September 1923, the first issue of *Name-ye Javanan* carried an article in support of girls' education. It was vehemently criticized by the ulama, and the editor, Ebrahim Khaje-Nuri, was detained and sentenced to three years in prison for supporting girls' education as well as the unveiling of women.[78] Sadiq stated in September 1925 that education for girls was an important duty (*vazife*) of the government,

72. Ayatollah Kazem Shariʿatmadari stressed that only a man can be recognized as *marjaʿ-e taqlid* (*Resale-ye Towzih al-Masaʾel* [Qom, 1974/5], 9). See also Michael M. J. Fischer, "On Changing the Concept and Position of Persian Women," in Lois Beck and Nikki Keddie, eds., *Women in the Muslim World* (Cambridge: Harvard University Press, 1979), 189–215.

73. Szyliowicz, 301–4.

74. Ibid., 130.

75. Missionary girls' schools had already been established in 1874, and the first two Muslim girls graduated in 1891: see Mongol Bayat-Philipp, "Women and Revolution in Iran, 1905–11," in Beck and Keddie, 295–308.

76. Mostowfi, 3:102.

77. Clara C. Rice, *Persian Women and Their Ways* (Philadelphia, 1923); Yahya Nuri, *Hoquq-e Zan dar Islam va Jehan* (Tehran, 1974/5); Mohammad Hoseyn Tabatabaʾi, "Zan dar Iran," *Maktab-e Tashayyoʿ*, (1959/60), 3:7–30 as cited in Fischer, "Persian Women," 189–215.

78. Owing to the shah's intervention, he was able to spend this period in a hospital (Sadiq, *Yadegar*, 2:300–305).

likely to launch Iran "on the path of westernization and progress."[79] In numerous lectures in the 1920s, Taqizade, too, supported the expansion of women's education as a means to better the status of women and bring progress to the country as a whole.[80]

Reza Shah himself saw a direct link between education for girls, the status of women, and the westernization process. The turning point in his policy was his 1934 visit to Turkey, where he was impressed by the expansion of girls' education. To his ambassador in Istanbul, Mostashar al-Dowla, he said that it was essential for Iran to imitate the Turks and advance education for girls.[81] He underscored the link between education and the evolution of women's status in January 1936, when he decided to mark the abolishing of the veil with a ceremony at the training college for women teachers. Students, teachers, and Ministry of Education officials as well as the empress, the princesses, and the shah all took part in the ceremony, at which every woman appeared unveiled. In his speech, the shah stressed the vitality of expanding girls' education. So did the president of the Women's Club (Kanun-e Banuvan), Hajar Tarbiyyat.[82] Later the same day, the shah added that "because of our women's custom to wear the veil, due to their ignorance and illiteracy, the Europeans have always taunted and despised us." Discarding the veil and educating women, he claimed, would change that.[83]

A few months earlier, girls had for the first time been admitted to the Tehran seminar for high school teachers (Daneshsara-ye ʿAli). Sadiq, then the director of the school, told me in an interview that he knew he would have the shah's backing in enrolling them. Their admission encountered fierce clerical opposition. To their threats against him, he replied: "the time when the ulama decided which way this country was moving has gone forever." Assessing the situation forty years later, he concluded that only the support of the shah had made it possible to overcome clerical opposition. He added that the first three girls at the seminar were from distinguished families who had spent several years abroad, a fact which had its imprint on their daughters' "dress, behavior and thinking."[84] Tehran University did not admit its first female students until five years later, in 1940/41.

79. Sadiq, *Amuzesh-e Banuvan*, 974–76, and *Modern Persia*, 115–16.

80. Taqizade, *Maqalat*, 3:146–48, 159–66.

81. Sadiq, *Yadegar*, 2:300–305.

82. MAM, document 5106; *AP*, 1935/6, 449–51, 517.

83. Hekmat, *Khatere*, 88–97.

84. Similarly, Sadiq, *Yadegar*, 2:309–10. This is also mentioned by Hekmat (*Khatere*, 89–100), who was then the minister of education.

An important contribution to the spread of education for girls (and to the improvement of women's status in general) was made by the Kanun-e Banuvan, whose establishment was initiated by the shah upon his return from Turkey. It was formed by Hekmat, the minister of education, around a nucleus of educated women in the ministry headed by Sadeqe Dowlatbadi (wife of Yahya Dowlatabadi), Fateme Sayyah, and Hajar Tarbiyyat.[85] It worked hard to propagate women's education. In a lecture in November 1935, attended by the prime minister, the minister of education, many army officers, and Majlis members (in itself a tribute to this forum), Tarbiyyat said that a country in which half of the population was doomed to illiteracy would never progress. Education, she said, should train women to be "good housekeepers, good mothers and useful citizens, capable of contributing to the progress of our dear nation." In order for them to educate the young generation, women must be educated themselves. The authorities should give priority to the education of women, because "women need physical and mental health more than men."[86]

However, some of the supporters of girls' education still retained the traditional view that the place of woman was in the household. This attitude can be seen in a statement by Majlis deputy ʿAli Dashti. In a Majlis speech in February 1934, he called for the expansion of girls' education, but said their studies should be "in line with the tasks they are supposed to perform in society": "We must ask . . . why do we send girls to school? The answer is: [to enable them] to take better care of their children, be better housekeepers and possess knowledge to pass on to their children. . . . Why do girls have to study mathematics or geometry? . . . We should teach them cooking and sewing instead."[87] Similarly, Majlis member Tehrani held that education should train girls "for family life," so that men would feel "pleased, comfortable and happy when returning home from work."[88] Hekmat, by contrast, opposed the implied notion of creating two different and separate educational goals. His ministry's task, as he saw it, was to train women for important posts in education, the health services, and elsewhere.[89]

85. Hekmat, *Khatere*, 89.

86. *AP*, 1935/6, 231–40. She repeated such views in a lecture to (women) teachers after a visit to Germany (*AP*, 1936/7, 864–72).

87. *MM*, term 9, 941. He expressed similar views in his article "Andishe'i dar Atraf-e Taʿlimat-e Ejbari," *Mehr*, 1933/4, 930–36. See also words of Dr. Malekzade: *MM*, term 10, 492–93; term 11, 567–68. See also Sadiq, *Amuzesh-e Banuvan*, 975–76; article by Tabataba'i, in *Shafaq-e Sorkh*, 29 February 1933; and speech of Moʿadel in *MM*, term 9, 1043.

88. *MM*, term 9, 1044–45.

89. Ibid., term 10, 493–94.

Table 2. Expansion of elementary and secondary education according to sex, in selected years between 1922/3 and 1941/2

Year	Total no. of students	Girls		Boys	
		No.	% of students	No.	% of students
1922/3	44,819	7,592	16.9	37,227	83.1
1926/7	60,337	18,084	30.0	42,253	70.0
1930/1	137,504	31,477	22.9	106,027	77.1
1934/5	183,204	45,542	24.9	137,662	75.1
1941/2	315,355	88,195	28.0	227,160	72.0

Sources: The table was prepared by the author on the basis of data from: SBB/MA, *Dowran-e Pahlavi,* 33–55; VAP, *Gozaresh-e Amuzesh,* document 284 in *MAM;* Khaje-Nuri, 1955–2050.

But such views—often supported by Kanun-e Banuvan—were exceptional at the time. In fact some, though not quite all, girls' schools offered a curriculum that enabled their graduates to move on to university, but also taught what was termed "practical education" (housekeeping and the like).[90]

Enrollments at elementary and secondary schools rose even faster for girls than for boys. This is evident from Table 2, which shows the number of boys and girls at school between 1922/3 and 1941/2. The number of girls among the student body rose from 16.9 percent in 1922/3 to 28.0 percent in 1941/2. During these years, the aggregate school population grew by 7 times, but while the population of boys rose by 6.1 times, that of girls grew by 11.6 times, i.e., almost twice as fast. True, the campaign for women's rights in the mid-1930s did not produce drastic change in women's education, yet the fact that their share in the school population rose to 28 percent must be regarded as an important achievement.

Options and Dilemmas

Contemporary Iranian discussion of the new education revolved around a number of difficult questions: To what degree is education a matter of teaching and learning (*amuzesh* or *ta'lim*), and to what extent is it its business to impart values, ideas, and "culture" (*parvaresh* or *tarbiyyat*)? Is quantity or quality more important? Should priority be given to vocational or academic studies, to elementary or to higher schools? Should education be directed at the elite or the masses? An

90. For the schools' program, see Sadiq, *Modern Persia,* 55–82.

analysis of opposing views on these questions, and of the policy choices eventually made, leads to a better understanding of Iranian expectations from education and the actual contribution it made to the advancement of its aims.

Amuzesh or *Parvaresh*

Much of the educational philosophy underlying public debate at the time revolves around the precise connotations of *amuzesh* and *parvaresh*.[91] The etymological meaning of *amuzesh* and *ta'lim* is the conveying of knowledge (*'ilm* and *ma'lumat*). Hence the nouns *amuzegar* or *mo'allem* (teacher). *Parvaresh* and *tarbiyyat* originally meant to nurture and make grow. Gradually, *parvaresh* came to mean the fostering and cherishing of habits, ideas, and values. In keeping with the prescriptive definitions of "education," its function was to pass on the country's cultural heritage from one generation to the next.[92]

The shah, his courtiers, the educationalists, and the liberal intellectuals all thought of *parvaresh* as the chief goal of education. Proper (*sahih*) *parvaresh*, they believed, would help the regime realize its aims. Whatever some of the liberals may have thought, the shah's own concept was plainly totalitarian: the purpose of education was not only to provide *'ilm* but also to impart to the citizen attitudes likely to be useful to the regime, to convince them of the wisdom and justice of the existing leadership and render them willing to sacrifice their lives for its cause. The philosophy of education, and issues of the state's moral right to place the stamp of such an education on its citizens, were no concern of his. His confidence that he was leading the nation along the right path was sufficient.[93] Accordingly, schools were to inculcate "self-evident" values and simple principles, not to encourage critical thinking likely to undermine the student's faith in the justice of the regime. Education was seen as a combination of indoctrination (imparting views) and censorship (withholding harmful information).

The intellectuals, though on the whole inclined toward democracy rather than totalitarianism, also placed *parvaresh* above *amuzesh*. But in

91. In the efforts to cleanse the Persian language of Arabic words, the terms *amuzesh* and *parvaresh* replaced, respectively, *ta'lim* and *tarbiyyat*.

92. Education included what John Dewey defined as communicating to the people what they must have in common in order to form a community, as well as the function of character building which Locke held to be the most fundamental part of education. See Dewey, *Democracy and Education*, 4–6; J. Locke, *Some Thoughts Concerning Education* (London: Cambridge University Press, 1889), 50.

93. See words to this effect in Pahlavi, *Ta'lifat*, 2:2084.

their view, education should not uphold a fixed set of values and ideals, but rather convey the skills to cope with constant change. Like their western counterparts, they opposed the imposition of values and ideas, advocating, instead, logical understanding and free choice by the individual. Inasmuch as values were to be taught, they were to be of a formal, rather than a substantive, character, such as respect for the right of others and freedom of conscience. However, these differences, basic though they were, were not clearly articulated during the period under review. Most intellectuals preferred to present their arguments so as to make them appear to be in line with the shah's.[94] Dashti came close to the shah's position when he argued that

> the aim of the elementary schools is, first and foremost, to educate our children to be religious and pious, though not in the same way that their ancestors had perceived God .... Schools must mold the conscience of our youngsters [and] teach them patriotism so that they will be ready to sacrifice themselves gladly for their community and the *vatan*, will be aware of their nation's glorious past and have enough national pride to meet any foreign encroachment with indignation and resentment (*motahayyej*). Elementary schools must inculcate in children a sense of duty and respect for the law and for the state's high authorities.[95]

Sadiq, in making proposals for changes in the educational system (in the concluding chapter of his doctoral thesis presented to Columbia University in 1931), stressed that education "must create national solidarity through appreciation of common culture and the spiritual heritage ... of the nation's past," and train the youngsters to become "good citizens of modern Persia."[96]

In practice, however, the schools placed the main emphasis on cognitive achievements, i.e., on *amuzesh* rather than *parvaresh*. This was in large measure a holdover from the traditional schools which had conveyed great masses of information and relied on memory rather than understanding. The fact that, as in most totalitarian regimes, schools preferred transfer of information and strict examinations worked in the same direction. Students absorbed, and tried to mem-

---

94. For the preferences of *parvaresh* over *amuzesh*, see: Hekmat, in *MM*, term 9, 934, 941; Mirza Ahmad Khan Badr Basir al-Dowla, "Ta'lim Gheyr az Tarbiyyat Ast," *TT*, 1925/6, 8–9:12–23, 10:8–10, 11–12:8–12 (Badr was minister of education in 1918/9 and 1926); Hasan Taqizade, "Mavad Mofide dar Ta'lim va Tarbiyyat 'Omumi: Che Chizha be Vasile Madares-e Ebteda'i va Ta'limat-e Ejbari Bayad ... Amukht?" *AP*, 1934/5, 585–89.

95. Dashti, *Ta'limat-e Ejbari*, 935–36.

96. Sadiq, *Modern Persia*, 84–85.

orize, a vast amount of data and thought of schooling mainly as preparation for the governmental examinations. *Amuzesh* thus eventually won out over *parvaresh*.

Quality versus Quantity

Limited budgets and the scarcity of qualified teaching staffs made it necessary to consider whether to work at raising the level of teaching at existing schools while slowly adding schools, or to launch into a rapid expansion of the school system. This controversy spilled over into the public debate on compulsory education, first advocated during the Constitutional Revolution and declared an official policy under Reza.[97]

In light of the basic deficiencies of the educational system, many viewed its rapid expansion as impracticable, or even undesirable. The monthly *Mehr*, keen on finding new ways to advance education, held a public debate on the question: "What is the easiest way of implementing of compulsory elementary education?" The leading educationalists who contributed articles—Siyasi, Sadiq, E'tesamzade, Fateh, Sa'id Nafisi, and 'A. Dashti—all agreed on this issue. Their first objective was to do away with the method based on memorizing great amounts of mostly irrelevant information and underemphasizing analysis and understanding. All referred to the lack of qualified teachers, and all deplored the fact that education was almost entirely academic, with graduates fit only for administrative occupations.[98]

Responding to this debate, Dashti wrote another article ("Reflections Concerning Compulsory Education"), stressing the hazards of implementing compulsory education. True, he wrote, education was the basis of economic, social, and national advances, but "schools in themselves do not solve any problem. They are useful only if they help to remove the deficiencies of [the existing] society and to create a new one." As long as the schools were not capable of achieving this goal, the expansion of education was useless. He concluded: "We want schools to produce educated carpenters, educated farmers, craftsmen and . . . merchants, we do not want them to deprive us of carpenters, farmers, craftsmen and merchants by turning them into parasites and useless idlers."[99]

97. *MM*, term 6, 2499.
98. "Sahltarin Rah-e Ejra'-ye Ta'limat-e Ebteda'i, 'Omumi va Ejbari Chist,?" *Mehr*, 1933/4, 321–28, 415–16, 497–502, 561–67.
99. Dashti, *Ta'limat-e Ejbari*, 930–36.

Tabataba'i, writing in *Shafaq-e Sorkh,* took a similarly line. If all Iranians were to pass through the existing schools, he asserted, there would be "crowds of semi-illiterates" swarming into the cities demanding "easy work with good pay." Presently, he went on, the schools in Iran rendered their graduates unsuitable for productive employment by accustoming them to "idleness and egoism."[100] Sa'id Nafisi, too, claimed that the existing schools were eliminating the working class and supplying nothing but clerks.[101] Vahid complained that the educational system did not impart an appreciation of manual work. Thus education tended to turn people away from their traditional occupation but did not train them for anything else. If all young people graduated from such schools, Iran would end up as a strange place where nobody was skilled to do anything other than work in a government office.[102] All agreed that the expansion of the present school system would be harmful to the country.

In support of these views, a Majlis member quoted from a fourth-grade textbook in use at the time. It contained the story of two brothers, Naser and Mansur, the first studious and diligent, the other a dropout. Naser becomes "director-general in a government office . . . sits behind a large desk . . . and has an easy, comfortable and respected job." Mansur ends up as a servant in a government office. The moral was clear.[103] More and more, students and their parents came to regard the diploma rather than the acquisition of knowledge as the end of education. And the diploma was primarily an instrument for obtaining a "respected" post in the public administration. Logically, then, it was the government's duty to provide employment for the graduates or, alternatively, to find them a place at the university. The very phrasing of the high school diploma confirmed this: it was issued, the text read, to allow the graduate to "take advantage of the legal privileges (*mazaya-ye qanuni*) accompanying it." Gholam Hoseyn Sadiqi claimed that students believed that by obtaining the diploma they had fulfilled their part of the bargain and that now it was up to the government to keep its part.

This being so, many educationalists preferred to work for the improvement of education prior to its expansion. But, unmindful of

100. *Shafaq-e Sorkh,* 29 August 1933.

101. *Mehr,* the debate on *Ta'limat-e Ejbari,* 321–22.

102. Vahid, "'Ulum va Awqaf," 273–82. Similarly Majlis members Kamali and Mo'ayyed Ahmadi, *MM,* term 6, 2830, 3137.

103. Ahmadi, who mentioned this story twice in the Majlis, said that this concept was so deeply rooted that even Mansur ended up as a government employee: *MM,* term 13, 2830, 3137.

the inherent contradiction, they continued to urge the implementation of compulsory education. In actual fact, not much was done during this period to improve the quality of schooling. The main effort went into expanding education and into bending it to the benefit of the regime.

Academic or Vocational Education

As the preceding discussion implies, there was broad agreement to give priority to vocational over strictly academic education. And it was mainly technical backwardness which educational reforms had been initially meant to correct. Reza Shah himself thought of manual work as an important value and was a resolute supporter of vocational education. A senior manager in the Anglo-Iranian Oil Company, for example, who was present when the shah paid a visit to the vocational school the company had established for the children of the local workers, remarked on Reza's enthusiasm when observing the students with their tools and machines.[104] In 1940, when all foreign-operated schools were taken over by the Ministry of Education and foreign teachers were asked to leave the country, the sole exception was made in favor of the Irano-German Industrial School (established in Tehran in 1922).[105]

The shah's support of vocational education, upheld even when it clashed with his generally xenophobic sentiment, tallied with the advice of foreign advisers. In their 1925 report to the Ministry of Education, the French scholars Parnou and Hess recommended giving priority to vocational education, mainly at the high school level.[106] Dr. A. Stronach, then headmaster of a vocational school in Tehran, took the same view,[107] as did many local educationalists, among them Sadiq, Nafisi, and Vahid.[108]

Actual policy followed this overall line. The ministries of industry, roads, war, agriculture, health, communication, finance, and mines each set up various vocational schools and technical colleges with the immediate purpose of training qualified staff for their respective departments. The first nondepartmental polytechnical school was founded in 1922. From 1923 on, every concession to a foreign company

---

104. Hekmat, *Khatere*, 277.

105. Gondi Shapur, *Amuzesh*, 2:8; Banani, 97–98.

106. So also in another report by Hess the same year: Hess, 13–21.

107. A. Estronach [Stronach], "Ta'limat-e Fanni," *TT*, 1925/6, 1:8–12.

108. Sadiq, *Yadegar*, 2:118–19; Vahid "'Ulum va Awqaf," 273–74; and passages by Nafisi in *Mehr*, "Ta'limat-e Ejbari," 321–22.

was made conditional on its providing professional instruction for Iranian workers and students.[109] To attract more students, vocational
schools canceled tuition fees, beginning in 1926.[110] Yet their standards
remained low, and they developed at a much slower pace than the
academic schools (see Table 11, Chapter 10).

The main reason for this poor performance was the traditional perception that education was "meant" to free its recipients from manual
work, not train them for it. "Vocational education" seemed a contradiction in terms: manual work was taught in workshops and out in
the fields; schools were there to escape from it. In encouraging the
demand for schooling, the educational system unwittingly strengthened such conceptions.

Elementary versus Higher Education

Which level of education was to be given priority? Clearly, the spread
of nationalism, secularization, westernization, and loyalty to the regime
was best served by the expansion of elementary schools. But it was
difficult to judge what level of education contributed most to economic
growth.[111] Later studies opt for a shift from elementary to secondary
education only when the former has come to embrace some 10 percent
of the total population.[112] If this is accepted, then from the point of
view of economic advantage, too, elementary schools ought to have
had priority under Reza.

In fact, the shah and the educationalists of his time supported giving
priority to elementary education, though they often had different reasons for doing so. Reza Shah stated: "We must, first and foremost,
teach our workers and farmers to read and write"; only then was it
time to move on to higher education.[113] Hekmat and Esma'il Mar'at,

109. *MQ*, term 4, 163–64, 177.
110. *TT*, 1926/7, 139–42; an explanation of the decision by the minister of education
appears in *MM*, term 4, 2502.
111. For various later assessments, see Harbison and Myeres, 23–48; H. Correa, *The
Economics of Human Resources*, as quoted by Jan Tinchergen, "Educational Assessment,"
in UNESCO, *Educational Planning*, 173–74; Neil J. Smelser and Seymour M. Lipset, eds.,
Social Structure and Mobility in Economic Development (Chicago: Aldine, 1966), 32; Szyliowicz, 7.
112. Alexander Paeslee, "Education's Role in Development," *Economic Development
and Culture Change*, 17 (1968), 293–318.
113. Hekmat, *Khatere*, 290–91; General Hasan Arfa', a close associate of the shah,
confirms this in Arfa, 290.

the two ministers of education,[114] as well as many Majlis members[115] took the same line.

The most prominent advocate of such a policy was Taqizade. In an article written in 1925, he listed the main arguments for giving priority to elementary education:

A. The greatness of nations, Taqizade wrote, did not depend on individual leaders or a restricted elite of "messengers of God" possessing higher education, but rather on the "qualifications, education and social, political and national level" of the entire population. Muhammad 'Ali, Mahmud II and 'Abdul-Hamid failed because of the lack of mass education; the Japanese succeeded because they developed it. He concluded: "Illiterate people are a dam obstructing an intelligent leader."

B. "Real" progress depended on the active participation of the people in social, political and economic life; and this in turn depended on comprehensive elementary education.

C. Priority for higher education was socially unjust. It meant that the majority of people would remain "blind" (illiterate) while a tiny minority would "have eyes" (elementary education) as well as "binoculars" (higher education).

D. Improved and expanded elementary education was the prerequisite of a proper higher education. Developing higher education against the background of almost total illiteracy was as helpful as "training mining experts on board a sinking ship."[116]

In a lecture at the American school for girls, he summarized his views by saying that "progress, civilization, independence, . . . salvation, freedom and nationalism" all depended on elementary education.[117]

It is true that there were dissenting views, like those of Sadiq and Majlis member Malekzade, who were alert to the difficulties of a rapid expansion in the number of elementary schools and acknowledged the pressing need for skilled manpower (including teachers for elementary schools), and who therefore tended to prefer higher education. But such views were clearly exceptional.

Actual developments again contradicted ideological preferences. Although some important initiatives were in fact taken to promote elementary education, higher education had effective priority. The major

114. See their views, respectively, in *MM*, term 9, 942 and term 11, 566.
115. See speeches by Dashti and Mo'adel, respectively, in *MM*, term 9, 940–41, 1040–42.
116. Taqizade, *Ta'limat-e Ebteda'i*, 180–81.
117. Taqizade, *Maqalat*, 150.

educational projects—the dispatch of students abroad, the foundation of Tehran University, and the expansion of teachers' seminars—had to do with higher education. Such a policy was dictated by the growing demand for skilled labor to implement the regime's reform programs and to man the expanding bureaucracy. Consequently, the growth of higher education was more rapid than that of elementary education. The number of students in new elementary schools grew from 43,055 in 1922/3 to 287,244 in 1940/1 (i.e., it increased 6.7 times). The number of students in new high schools rose from 3,000 in 1924/5 to 26,929 in 1940/1 (i.e., nine times), and the number of students at the college or university level from 301 in 1925/6 to 3,367 in 1940/1 (i.e., 11.1 times).[118] (To the final figures must be added the number of students at foreign universities.)

Mass or Elite Education

The priority awarded to elementary education attests to the government's desire to open the schools to children of the lower classes. Arguing from their functional approach to education, Iranian intellectuals saw in the spread of schooling to the poor the means for bridging social gaps, whether between classes or between urban and rural society, or the capital and the provinces, or even between young men and women. Soon after the 1921 coup, the prime minister's manifesto stated that education must not be restricted to "oppressive elites": everybody, including the village population, should enjoy "the enlightenment of education."[119] Throughout the period under review, this theme ran through the declarations of politicians and intellectuals. Moreover, many, expressed hope that higher education, too, would be open to the underprivileged.

This approach was best illustrated in the Majlis debate on two laws designed to advance these aims: the law establishing education grants to low-income earners (October 1927); and the law providing financial support for needy students in institutes of higher education (December 1929). Ehteshamzade, who tabled the first law, urged the government to open the way for poor students at all levels of education. Yasani argued that education at all levels should be "free of charge and open to all" and called for the opening of secondary schools in the villages. Dashti seconded them. The minister of education opposed free secondary education, arguing that since most secondary students were from rich families, waiving tuition fees meant subsidizing the wealthy.

118. Khaje-Nuri, 1975–1976; SSHBA, *Amuzesh-e 'Ali,* 64.
119. Dowlatabadi, 4:235–36; Mostowfi, 3:218–19.

Instead, he suggested that fees, at both the elementary and secondary level, should be waived only for the needy. Aqa Seyyed Ya'qub supported him.[120] In the debate on the second law, many members (Malekzade, Taheri, Kazeruni, Ehteshamzade, and the deputy minister of education, Farrokh) demanded to make it possible for children of low-income groups to go to elementary and secondary schools.[121] Other members insisted on the expansion of education in the provinces and censured the government for concentrating its efforts in Tehran.[122] Hekmat admitted that such a disparity did exist, but attributed it to the difficulty of finding teachers to work in the provinces, rather than to a lack of goodwill at his ministry.[123]

In practical terms, the most important step was the government decree of 16 May 1927, declaring that education at all public schools was to be free for the impecunious. In addition, in places where private schools were operating, the public schools were to admit *only* the children of low-income groups.[124] Regulations approved in 1927 laid down that tuition would be charged only if the parents could afford it. In addition, high school tuition was to be free for outstanding students in the top 10 percent of each elementary school, as well as for orphans, children of teachers with ten years of service, and children of physically handicapped parents. College education was to be free for the best 5 percent of high school graduates, for orphans of teachers, and for children of the handicapped.[125] In reality, however, inasmuch as these regulations were implemented at all, they served only to widen and perpetuate the social gaps: they sanctioned two separate educational systems (with different standards)—one for the poor and another, with higher standards, for the rich.

It is quite impossible to discern to what degree such measures did in fact draw lower-class children into the educational system. In 1936, Minister of Education Hekmat pointed out with a measure of satisfac-

120. *MM*, term 6, 2494–2503.
121. Ibid., term 7, 1289–1303, 1307–11, 1339–48. For the text of the law, see *MQ*, term 7, 231–34.
122. See, for example, Malekzade's words: *MM*, term 7, 1172; term 10, 493; term 11, 569.
123. Ibid., term 9, 1174.
124. *TT*, 1926/7, 168. Already on 4 December 1923 a committee formed by the minister of education decided to impose a special tax on "the rich and the notables" and to deduct between 1 and 10 percent of government employees' salaries to finance the expansion of education (Gondi Shapur, *Amuzesh*, 2:6). Just prior to the 1921 coup, a special tax was levied on rice in Gilan province to finance education (Sadiq, *Yadegar*, 2:196–204). All in all, these measures did not have significant results.
125. *TT*, 1927/8, 142.

tion that more youngsters than in the past were arriving in the capital for secondary and higher education.[126] But those who did so faced tremendous problems, as ʿAli Eqbali (from Hamadan) testifies in his memoirs.[127] There were no dormitories; travel was expensive (and often dangerous); and living expenses in Tehran were high. Moreover, the Tehran University entrance examinations and the examinations to select candidates for study abroad were held only in Tehran. All this put higher education beyond the reach of the poor, even assuming that, despite their weak elementary and secondary education, they were able to qualify for university studies. On balance, only very few students from a lower-class background made their way into the schools. Numerous declarations were made, and some laws passed and decrees issued, but in practical terms not much was done. Education in villages (where 65 percent of the Iranians lived at the end of period reviewed) remained almost as restricted as before; so did education in provincial towns. This was partly due to the lack of facilities and the failure of simple people to demand better ones, and partly due to elite opposition to mass education. Siyasi, for example, stressed that the merchants and landowners, viewing education as a challenge to their status in society, opposed its expansion. The ulama, who had opposed the new education as such, did not encourage people to send their children to schools that they thought to be a danger to Islam.

The Further Expansion of Elementary and Secondary Education

What can the statistics tell us about the spread of schooling from 1922 to 1941? Table 3 examines the number of students as a percentage of the population over this period; it shows no more than a modest growth. It would have been more informative to compare student figures with the overall number of people in the corresponding age group, but such data were not available for the entire period. Owing to the decrease in infant mortality during this period, there was a gradual growth in the percentage of young people in the total population, but this cannot have changed the overall picture much.[128]

Despite these reservations, the table gives several important point-

126. Hekmat, *Amuzesh-e ʿAli*, 359.
127. MAM, document 4692.
128. The population data are based on estimates of the Statistical Bureau (*Markaz-e Amar*); data on the students, on official statistics of the Ministry of Education.

Table 3. Growth of elementary and secondary schools as compared with that of the population, in selected years between 1922/3 and 1940/1

Year	Estimated population (in thousands)	No. of students in public elementary and secondary schools	No. of students as % of total population
1922/3	9,500	44,819	0.47
1926/7	10,900	60,337	0.55
1931/2	11,000	138,567	1.26
1936/7	12,000	231,119	1.93
1940/1	13,000	314,173	2.41

Sources: Computed by the author from data included in: Khaje-Nuri, 1955–2050; MAM, document 284; SBB/MA, *Dowran-e Pahlavi,* 18–55.

ers. In 1922/3, only 0.47 percent of the population studied in elementary and secondary schools (*maktab* and *madrese* students excluded); in 1940/1, that figure was 2.41 percent. In these eighteen years, the number of students had grown sevenfold, the population 1.4 times. The rate of the growth, however, was not uniform throughout the period. In the first four years, the student body grew only by 34.4 percent (an average of 8.6 percent a year). In the following five years, it accelerated to an average growth of 25.9 percent yearly. Then it slowed down again: between 1931/2 and 1936/7, to 13.3 percent a year; and from then to 1940/1, to 9 percent. All in all, growth was considerable given the situation at that time, but it still fell short of the regime's expectations. Moreover, after the relatively rapid growth following the initial consolidation of the regime, its momentum was curbed: the average growth at the end of the period was similar to that at its inception. This slowdown was not due to a lack of demand for education or to diminishing goodwill on the part of the government, but rather to a shortage of teachers, insufficient budgets, and demographic problems.

The severe shortage of skilled teachers was directly related to the decline in social prestige of the teaching profession. This decline had already begun under the Qajars, but accelerated between the two world wars. Urbanization and industrialization, the social and economic reforms, and the resultant expansion of the bureaucracy opened new, more prestigious employment opportunities for the educated class. A teacher's income was much lower than that of a civil servant with the same educational qualifications. The assertion by Don Adams and Robert M. Bjork that in developing countries the educated class searching for occupations with prestige, status, and income look down on teaching is certainly applicable to Iran.[129] A vicious circle was set up: less tal-

129. Adams and Bjork, 123–24, 134.

ented high school graduates choose teaching; to accommodate them, the profession lowered entrance qualifications for teachers' seminars; in consequence, the prestige of the profession was further hurt; and so on. The common perception was that anyone who could read and write was qualified to teach and that only those who had failed to secure a more appropriate position would turn to teaching. The social barrier preventing more women from going into the profession was another obstacle.[130]

Insufficient budgets slowed down the construction of schools and the acquisition of teaching aids.[131] The country's overall economic difficulties kept allocations for education at a low level: throughout the period, they averaged no more than 4 percent of the total budget, and much of that went to higher education. (By comparison, defense expenditures accounted for 33 percent of the annual budget.)[132]

As in other developing countries, the high rate of population growth militated against the expansion of education. Moreover, the population was spread out over vast areas, many of them but sparsely settled. The majority lived in rural or tribal areas. The rural population was scattered over 50,000 villages, most of them too small to sustain a school of their own. In addition, in the countryside children were still considered part of the family's labor force, and parents were reluctant to send them to school. Moreover, the elite groups had no incentive to encourage rural education, and the clerics had no wish to do so.

Conclusion

As we have seen, Reza Shah viewed the educational system not merely as an instrument for supplying the cadres he needed for his

130. On the low prestige of teachers as one reason that graduates did not join the profession, see: Sadiq, *Yadegar*, 2:248–49; speeches in the Majlis by Taqizade and Reza Afshar, *MM*, term 4, 4397, 4401 (the latter claimed that in Iran teachers were "not even considered human beings"); remarks by Shaykh Hadi Taheri, *MM*, term 7, 1290–91; Hekmat, *MM*, term 11, 932–34, 940; Tabataba'i-Diba, *MM*, term 11, 1284–90; Mirza'i, *MM*, term 11, 1179–80; Vahid, 275–76; 'Ali Mohammad 'Ameri, "Shakhsiyyat-e Mo'allem," *AP*, 1940/41, 6–7:33–34; Badr, *ibid*, 10:9–10 and 11–12:8–12; E'tesamzade, in the debate on compulsory education, *Mehr*, 415–16; Siyasi, *Mehr*, 501–2.

131. See report by Hess, 14–15.

132. M. H. Farrokh-Pars, "The Budgets of Iran, 1930–1959: An Analysis of Their Financial and Economic Impact" (Ph.D. diss., New York University, 1960), 64–111; Ali Muhammad Kardan, *L'organisation scolaire en Iran* (Geneva, 1957), 125–26; Banani, 108. For the impact of this on the development of education, see: Sadiq, *Modern Persia*, 107–8; 'Ameri, 13; Seyyed Ahmad Kasravi, "Bayad az Gozashte Anche nik ast Bardasht va Anche bad ast Baz Godhasht," *AP*, 1934/5, 136–38.

modernizing policies, but equally as a tool for mobilizing broad support for the regime and its policies. His son, writing with a great deal of empathy, had this to say of him:

> Reza Shah did more for Persian education than to construct buildings, train teachers, and send people abroad for study. *He transformed the whole spirit and philosophy of our educational system.* As he saw it, education must first of all serve to create the patriotic devotion.... He understood that the country's genuine Westernization and modernization required much more than factories and paved streets; of far greater importance were changes in the basic Persian culture and psychology.... *He was energetically reshaping our thinking and action to meet the challenge of the present and the future.*[133]

Precisely the points praised by Mohammad Reza were singled out by foreign observers as Reza Shah's gravest failure. The American Overseas Consultants Incorporated, evaluating Iran's educational system, reported in 1949:

> *The principal point of weakness in the educational structure of Iran is its educational philosophy.* The existing school system has been relatively successful in accomplishing the apparent aims of its founders three quarters of a century ago, which were to produce a distinguished intellectual elite and to establish an instrument by which the thoughts and actions of the common people might be efficiently manipulated. The existing system is anachronistic and unsatisfactory because of a changed social philosophy rather than because of technical failure of the schools.... The nation's educational system has failed to meet the needs of modern Iran.
> The educational philosophy, and the technical details of the school system, are largely a copy of the traditional French system—characterized by extreme centralization of administration, authoritarian mythology, theoretical rather than practical studies, stereotyped and overloaded curricula, and a policy of eliminating rather than salvaging students who do not meet the arbitrary and rather artificial standards of academic excellency.[134]

A similar observation—with a very condescending tone—was made by Arthur Milspaugh, the American financial consultant: "We should approach the educational part of the plan [for the reconstruction of Iran]

133. Pahlavi, *Mission*, 242 (emphasis added).

134. Overseas Consultants, Inc., *Report on the Seven-Year Development Plan for the Plan Organization of the Imperial Government of Iran* (New York, 1949), 1:20 and 2:82–84. (emphasis added). The head of the group's unit for education, Robert King Hall, repeated this assessment in the article "Seven Year Plan in Iran," *The Yearbook of Education, 1954*, 285.

with the knowledge that the Persians need fundamental and many-sided rehabilitation. . . . What the situation calls for primarily is not formal schooling. *The prime need is for emotional adjustment and moral regeneration. The country requires a thorough physical and spiritual cleansing.*[135]

Both the positive and negative evaluations had their subjective element. Mohammad Reza stated frankly that he had inherited the general philosophy of education from his father[136] and could not do otherwise than praise it. For their part, the foreign observers thought completely in terms of their own cultural values.

To what degree, then, did the educational system fulfill the shah's avowed expectations? The Overseas Consultants seem to overrate its accomplishments, even when one allows for their reservations. People's "thoughts and actions" were being less "efficiently manipulated" than they imply. Westernization and patriotism had failed to reach deep into the masses (certainly not among the ethnic minorities), and above all: religious sentiment continued to eclipse all other loyalties. The power base of the religious establishment had not been significantly curtailed. This was not solely a policy failure but also had to do with the still limited scope of education, which prevented new ideas from reaching the mass of devoted Muslims. Even more important reasons for the modest success of the new educational system stemmed from the shah's modus operandi: in his reforms, he endeavored not to destroy old institutions and values, but rather to build the new alongside the old. Unlike Ataturk, Reza did not abolish the monarchy or move the seat of government. The same approach governed his educational policy. His failure to launch more thoroughgoing reforms and to step beyond the narrow scope of the new education precluded greater success.

Yet there were some significant long-term achievements: the infrastructure for a national school system was put into place; the traditional elementary schools were almost totally eliminated; and the concept of the new education—the vision of intellectuals a generation or two earlier—finally won out. Although the popular attachment to Islam remained strong, clerical control of education was terminated; and finally, for the first time the government put forward explicit educational policies and planned practical steps to carry them out.

135. Millspaugh, 249 (emphasis added).
136. Pahlavi, *Mission*, 242.

6

Iranian Students Abroad

Until the foundation of Tehran University in 1935, the government was compelled to meet its growing need for professionals by encouraging study abroad; after 1935, by contrast, it preferred to promote study in Tehran, and the number of students abroad decreased significantly.

Altogether, in the interwar years, some 1,500 Iranians went to study in the West.[1] In the first decade or so after World War I, they numbered only a few—about seventy.[2] Between 1928 and 1933, 640 students were sent abroad under the provisions of a law first issued in May 1928 and subsequently amended twice, in 1929 and 1932. The government defrayed the cost of their tuition and upkeep, specified the subjects they were to study, and saw to their suitable employment on their return. Simultaneously, different ministries (mainly the Ministry of War and the Ministry of Roads) determined what specific skills they needed and sent out students to acquire this specialized training. The first of these were dispatched by the Ministry of War in 1922, under a special law passed in June 1922. In the next decade, a total of 261 students left under the same law.[3] To supply the necessary personnel for the construction of the Trans-Iranian Railway, the Ministry of Roads sent out another sixty-nine students between 1929 and 1932, under laws issued in 1925 and 1930.[4] Another category was that of students who went

1. Elwell-Sutton, 138. (Students leaving for Middle Eastern countries such as Beirut and Istanbul are not included.)
2. See official figures of the Ministry of Education cited in Gondi Shapur, 2:5.
3. *MQ*, term 4, 325; Sadiq, *Yadegar*, 1:294–95.
4. *MQ*, term 7, 228–31; *Shafaq-e Sorkh*, 13 August 1933.

abroad on their own initiative and at their own expense. These included many who had been sent abroad under the law of 1911 and who now returned to western universities for advanced studies. On the eve of the inauguration of Tehran University, there were fewer than 500 Iranian students in the West.[5]

By and large, the debate surrounding the dispatch of students touched on themes already discussed earlier in the century and even in the nineteenth century, such as attracting poorer and provincial students, selecting appropriate fields of study, the possible "bad" influences of the West, and so on.

In the period between the foundation of Tehran University and the abdication of the shah in 1941, the government severely limited the dispatch of students abroad. The number of those leaving privately also declined considerably.

Objectives and Plans

We have seen how study abroad fitted in with Reza Shah's overall views of education as an agent of westernization, secularization, and the promotion of patriotism.[6] Patriotism, of course, was synonymous with loyalty to the shah and with resolute support of his aims. Two of the students sent out during this period, Gholam Hoseyn Sadiqi and Mahmud Mahdavi, told me that it was obvious to them and their colleagues that upon their return they were supposed to give active proof of their loyalty to the regime. Another student of that period, ʿAli Eqbali, wrote in his memoirs that the students understood that they had been sent out as a token of the shah's goodwill and that, in return, they were expected to serve the country and its ruler.[7] (When it became clear to the shah that study abroad did not necessarily achieve that aim, the whole project was called off.)

In the same spirit, the shah insisted on sending the crown prince to study at a European school. General Hasan Arfaʿ, who met with the shah at the time of his son's departure, heard him say: "It is very hard for me to part with my beloved son, but one must think of the country.

---

5. According to the yearbook of the Ministry of Education (*Salname-ye Ehsaʾi, 1932/3,* 101–3), 445 Iranian students were in the West in 1932. According to the 1935/6 yearbook, 400 students were there in 1935. See also Arasteh, 41; *Shafaq-e Sorkh,* 28 August 1933.

6. For expressions by the shah in this regard, see his speeches to students delivered in 1929 and 1930 (Gondi Shapur, 2:18 and 22, respectively). See also his views quoted in Forbes, 181–87; Wilber, 135; *Ettelaʿat,* 9 October 1928.

7. MAM, document 4692.

Iran needs educated and enlightened rulers; we, the old and ignorant must go."[8]

The largest organized group of Iranian students ever to be sent abroad were the 640 dispatched under the law of 22 May 1928. That law required the government to finance a hundred Iranian students each year; laid down that their subjects of study were to be decided by the government, with at least 35 percent of them to be trained as teachers (article 1); that candidates would be selected by competitive examinations, suitable for applicants with twelve years of schooling; that upon their return they would be assigned jobs by the government for at least as long as they had studied abroad (article 2); in contrast with the 1911 law, but in line with the tradition established more than a century ago, the law required the government to employ the graduates in accordance with their field of expertise (article 3). In contrast with past practice, the law stipulated that government supervisors (*sarparasts*) would accompany the students (article 4).[9] In an amendment passed on 27 June 1929, the Majlis empowered the Ministry of Education to apply the law also to Iranians already studying in Europe but lacking means to continue toward graduation, provided that their number would not exceed 20 percent of the total yearly quota.[10] On 30 April 1932, the House again amended the law to include such students in the United States as well.[11]

In the Majlis debates on the law and its amendments, the House was almost unanimous in acknowledging the importance of the project. Many deputies, such as Rafi', Taqizade, Aqa Seyyed Ya'qub, and Davar, viewed it as the principal means for achieving progress, for creating a new generation of "virtuous" (*fazel*) Iranians, and for securing Iran's independence. Taqizade labeled the 1928 law "the most important . . . the Majlis has legislated since its formation." The minister of justice, Davar, called it the country's "most significant investment." All speakers stressed its importance for both *amuzesh* and *parvaresh*.[12]

At the same time, public statements made it clear that the authorities were keenly aware of the possible "negative influences" of study abroad. This was true of the shah himself: while he encouraged candidates to study and—selectively—absorb some elements of western culture, he also warned them to reject "harmful" influences and pre-

---

8. Arfa, 226.
9. *MQ*, term 6, 120–23.
10. Ibid., term 7, 228.
11. Ibid., term 8, 464.
12. *MM*, term 6, 4389–91; term 7, 896; and term 8, 1199. For the debate on the concepts of *amuzesh* and *parvaresh*, see Chapter 5.

serve their own identity and national pride.[13] In practice, however, such a selective absorption was quite impossible. The experience of a century—as reflected first in the memoirs of Shirazi and much later in those of Sadiq—showed that the impact of the West on the students often exceeded the government's aims. In 1926, Mirza ʿAbbas Eqbal, then a student at the Sorbonne, wrote that his Iranian colleagues were losing their attachment to their country and their national pride. He expressed concern that upon their return they would do their country more harm than good. To prevent such bad influence, he proposed to send out supervisors along with the students, like the imams who had accompanied the Egyptian students abroad under Muhammad ʿAli.[14]

A few Majlis deputies questioned the advisability of sending students to Europe altogether. Among them were Mirza Abu-Taleb Shirvani, Mirza Mohammad ʿAli Khan Bamdad, ʿAtaʾollah Ruhi, and Rafiʿ, they claimed in 1928 that the "atmosphere and the conditions" in Europe were such that "our students . . . do not learn much, yet their character is spoiled." Shirvani said that 75 percent of the graduates fail to live up to expectations and, all things considered, caused more damage than good to their society. Reza Firuzabadi and Aqa Seyyed Yaʿqub and others took similar views but stopped short of advising to drop the project.[15] In the 1929 debate, Ruhi spoke once more of the danger of students acquiring bad habits abroad and weakening in their faith and their patriotism. Davar replied that he had studied in the West himself yet was no less of a patriot "than anyone else in the House."[16]

The presence of the supervisors sent out under the 1928 law was strongly felt by the students. Mahdavi and Sadiqi told me that supervision was close, both with regard to their academic record and the way they spent their free time. The supervisors met with them regularly and paid out their monthly allowances. Supervisors were also sent out with the young men studying on behalf of the various ministries.[17]

The question of enabling children of low-income earners to study abroad was raised frequently. In the 1928 debate, some deputies, among them Taqizade, Dashti, Firuzabadi, Yaʿqub, and Davar, all known for their more liberal views, urged that when applicants had similar qualifications, preference be given to poor students. They argued that the rich would send their children abroad even without government grants; and that lower-class students were likely to con-

13. See the shah's statement as cited by the student Eqbali in MAM, document 4692.
14. ʿAbbas Eqbal, "Eʿzam Mohsel be Paris," *TT*, 1926/7, 182–84, 233.
15. *MM*, term 6, 4443–58.
16. Ibid., term 7, 1198–1200.
17. *MQ*, term 7, 228–39.

tribute more to society after their return by taking up "useful" occupations whereas the rich would usually join the family business or seek government office for the sake of prestige only.[18] In articles written in 1926 and 1928, Taqizade spoke of the money of the poorest taxpayers being used to finance the study of rich boys. Upper-class parents in any case thought of study abroad as no more than a good investment rendering high returns for the following forty years, he said.[19]

Spokesmen for the Majlis committees on education and finance countered by saying that it was difficult to set clear standards of wealth or poverty and that a hundred vacancies per year were sufficient to meet all demands.[20] Eventually, as noted above, the amendments of the law only opened the way for "students lacking financial ability" who were already studying in Europe and the United States, but said nothing about including poor applicants in the original selection. Supporting the amendment, Mirza Mahmud Khan claimed that it was unjust for the government to send more rich students to Europe while others already studying there needed help. Mirza ʿAli Kazeruni, on the other hand, doubted whether anyone already abroad really needed help. Opponents of the amendment viewed it as a means to allow rich students who had left before 1928 to benefit from the new law. Majlis member Firuzabadi called on his "rich and honorable colleagues" to reject the proposed amendment by which they wished only to benefit their own children and those of their relatives.[21]

Although the available data do not allow us to draw firm conclusions, it was most unlikely that there were poor students in the West who had gone out with insufficient means and now needed help to complete their studies. Sadiqi and Mahdavi could not recall any impecunious student who eventually benefited from the amendments. One can only conclude that well-to-do students who had left before the 1928 law now wanted to be eligible for grants under it. Some of them must have belonged to families influential enough to talk the government into proposing the amendments.

But Sadiqi and Mahdavi confirmed that not all of the candidates approved under the law belonged to elite families. Both used the term "upper middle-class and above" to define their social origin. Yet there were a few who could not otherwise have paid for study abroad. ʿAli Eqbali, for example, wrote that he could not have studied in Paris had

18. *MM*, term 6, 4394–98, 4413–17, 4463–64.
19. Taqizade, "Tasavvorat dar Bab-e Eʿzam-e Mohsel be Orupa," *Shafaq-e Sorkh*, 1 March 1928. Taqizade, *Amuzesh-e Ebtedaʾi ya ʿAli*, 186–87.
20. *MM*, term 6, 4413–17.
21. Ibid., term 7, 895, 898–900.

it not been for the 1928 program.[22] The survey of the Institute for Social Research at Tehran University supports these conclusions. It examined the occupation of the fathers of 176 (out of 640) students and found that: 32.7 percent were high-ranking officials, 16.8 percent were businessmen, 13.3 percent professionals, 11.7 percent landlords; 7.1 percent had professions not requiring higher education (such as builders, wholesalers, shopkeepers), 5.7 percent were clerics, 4.1 percent politicians, and 3.6 percent served in the armed forces. (Another 5 percent did not answer the survey.) The survey concluded that most students were from an upper-class background, but in some cases the families could not have financed their studies themselves.[23] These results largely bear out Taqizade's claim that on the whole the project helped perpetuate the position of the upper strata rather than provide a channel for social mobility.

There was not a single women among the students sent abroad under the 1928 program (neither were there women at any local institution for higher learning at the time). A proposal by Niya'i Nuri in 1929 to allow women to benefit from the new law—presumably to apply it to certain girls already studying in the West—was rejected by the Majlis.[24] In 1933, there were some fifty Iranian girls at European high schools and universities, but most of them were not Muslims.[25]

During the debates on the laws, much was also said about the need to include students from the outlying provinces in these groups. It was believed that this would help close social gaps and—since removing differences between the center and the periphery was considered a hallmark of a modern society[26]—contribute to the country's modernization. Majlis members who supported the inclusion of students from the provinces maintained that the proposed laws put the latter at a disadvantage. For one thing, the competitive examinations were held only in the capital. For another, the law stipulated that high school graduates were to be preferred over those who had had private tuition. (In 1928, provincial high schools existed only in Isfahan, Rasht, and Tabriz.) Furthermore, the Tehran schools had in fact a higher standard, giving their

22. See his memoirs in MAM, document 4692.

23. Moradi-Nezhad and Pazhum-Shari'ati, 20. Of the 176 students asked, eighteen gave two occupations and one gave three. According to the authors of the survey, the 176 comprised nearly all those sent out under the 1928 law who were still alive and living in Iran when the survey was conducted in the mid-1970s (v–vi).

24. MM, term 7, 901.

25. Tabataba'i in Shafaq-e Sorkh, 20 August 1933.

26. S. N. Eisenstadt, Social Differentiation and Stratification [in Hebrew] (Jerusalem: Magnes Press, 1978), 105–6.

graduates a built-in advantage in the competitive examinations. There-fore, these members argued, a quota should be set for provincial stu-dents. (Taqizade put it as high as 80 percent.)[27] Once again, the deputy minister of education argued that such clauses were not needed, since there was enough room for everyone.[28] And once again, the Majlis re-jected a proposal, that could have contributed, at least minimally, to opening higher education to wider groups of the population.

The upshot was that only a few dozen of the 640 students came from small cities. Their difficulties ranged from finding transportation to Tehran to take the examinations, to academic problems stemming from the lower quality of schooling in the provinces.[29] The above survey of the Institute for Social Research included the following findings about 176 students: 59.1 percent were born in Tehran; 21 percent in the next eight largest cities; and 18.2 percent elsewhere. Another 1.7 percent were born abroad.[30] It must be remembered, however, that urbani-zation being as rapid as it was, many native provincials may have moved to Tehran long before their departure for Europe. More signif-icant, many applicants from the provinces did not return there upon graduation but chose to reside in the capital, where they had better career opportunities. Thus not only did the project fail to contribute to bridging the gap between center and periphery, it actually removed some local high school graduates from the provinces.

Correlating the fields of study with the requirements of the country was a major concern of the government. Some Majlis deputies de-manded that the law lay down quotas for various subjects, similar to the 1911 law. Their main emphasis was on teacher training, both be-cause of the severe lack of teachers and because, unlike other profes-sionals, teachers could not be imported.[31] The shah himself attached great importance to teacher training. Even after being disappointed with the project—one of the motives for setting up Tehran University—he still let twenty students per year be sent out for that purpose.[32]

27. *MM*, term 6, words of Taqizade (p. 4393), Dashti (4398), Afshar (4400–4401), ʿAdl (4403, 4415), and Malekzade (4417). See also Taqizade's article in *Shafaq-e Sorkh*, 1 March 1928.

28. *MM*, term 6, 4401.

29. An assessment of the number of provincial students and an account of their difficulties are given in the memoirs of Eqbali, a student from Hamadan, in MAM, document 4692.

30. Moradi-Nezhad and Pazhum-Shariʿati, 18.

31. Mirza Abu-Taleb Shirvani demanded that all applicants become teachers; others wanted half their number to train as teachers. See *MM*, term 6, statements by Shirvani (4386–87), Taqizade (4390–93), Aqa Seyyed Yaʿqub (4404–5), and Rafiʿ (4389).

32. Hekmat, *Khatere*, 69–70.

Taking into consideration the pressing need for other skills as well as the low popularity of teaching as a profession,[33] the law set a quota of 35 precent (as against 50 percent in 1911). Although the Majlis did not vote for quotas for other fields, the government decided to allot 24 percent of the available places to medicine; 21 percent to engineering; 7 percent to agriculture; 5 percent to law; 5 percent to finance and administration; and 3 percent to chemistry.[34] In practice, however, this division was not adhered to. The Ministry of Education reported later that of the 408 students sent out between 1928 and 1931, only 25 percent were trained as teachers.[35] The survey of 176 students by the Institute for Social Research shows that 27.3 percent studied medicine; 25.6 percent chemistry, physics, and/or mathematics; 19.9 percent engineering; 19.9 percent arts and social sciences; and 7.3 percent agriculture. (The survey counted teacher trainees as belonging to one of the above categories.)[36] The apparent contradiction between these findings stems from the fact that the ministry's report spoke of their fields of study and of the government's expectation as to their future employment, whereas the survey registered their actual occupation forty years later. A student sent out to study chemistry in order to teach that subject on his return may not actually have gone into teaching. Moreover, the amendment including students already abroad and studying subjects of their own choice further decreased the number of those training to be teachers. The newly included students were mostly upper-class sons who studied subjects they expected to profit from.[37]

The system of allotting fields of study was based on the assumption that graduates would eventually work in their fields. To ensure that this was done, the law laid down that the government would provide graduates with jobs for a period commensurate with the length of their studies. Should the authorities fail to offer them an adequate position within six months of their return, they would be free to make their own arrangements. But even then, during the first four years, the government could call them back to a job of its choice (article 3 of the 1928 law). The Majlis was divided on this issue. Dashti, Mohammad Taqi Bahar, Bamdad, and Ya'qub viewed these clauses as contradicting the principles of freedom. The latter two proposed that the government should be permitted, but not obliged, to find jobs for graduates. But

33. For such considerations, see *MM*, term 6, 4389, 4401.
34. Moradi-Nezhad and Pazhum-Shari'ati, 26.
35. *Shafaq-e Sorkh*, 11 and 15 August 1933.
36. Moradi-Nezhad and Pazhum-Shari'ati, 27.
37. *Shafaq-e Sorkh*, 15 August 1933.

their proposals were rejected.[38] Again, in practice, graduates often did not end up in occupations where they used the expertise acquired abroad, but the feeling persisted that the government owed them a "respectable" position.

As already mentioned, decisions about where to send candidates took into account the academic facilities and cultural background of the prospective host countries. Because of these considerations, but equally because the Iranian educational system was modeled on the French one and French was the main foreign language taught in Iran, the majority of students went to France (just as had been the case earlier on). However, there was a gradual increase in the number of students going to England, Germany, and, later, to the United States. From among the overall figure of the 640 mentioned earlier, 75.2 percent studied in France. But year-by-year figures show a decline of the share of France from 90.1 percent in 1928 to 65.4 percent in 1933. England attracted 3.6 percent in 1928, 12.3 percent in 1933. Its overall share for the 640 was 11.6 percent. Of particular importance was the increase in number of students going to Germany, which was to become the major center for student activity against the regime. Germany's share rose from 6.3 percent in 1928 to 11.5 percent in 1933. During these years, Iranian students also "discovered" the United States: none of those sent out in 1928 studied there, but in 1933, 6.9 percent did. The percentages for the United States rose significantly after World War II (see Chapter 10).

To what degree did this project and the Iranian institutions for higher learning meet the country's demands? Statistics of secondary school graduates are likely to be misleading, since many young people qualified without attending school: some (like Eqbali) because there was no school close enough to attend (this was the case mainly in the provinces); others (like Mahdavi) because rich families were reluctant to send their children to public schools, fearing the "moral damage" that would occur there.[39] Thus a greater discrepancy existed between qualified entrance candidates and the number of available places than would appear from the statistics. In some years, there were even more vacancies for higher education than there were high school graduates: in 1928/9, for example, there were 148 graduates and 160 vacancies.[40] Between 1928 and 1933, there were 1,531 high school graduates, and

38. *MM*, term 6, 4389, 4398–99, 4406–13, 4427–32; term 7, 897.
39. Mahdavi told me that, for this reason, his family would not have considered sending him to such a school. For the prevalent attitude among families in the elite group, see also the memoirs of Eqbali (MAM, document 4692) and Sadiq (*Yadegar*, 2:94).
40. Khaje-Nuri, 2013; *Shafaq-e Sorkh*, 16 August 1933.

a similar total of places in local institutions and in the project for state-financed study abroad. More revealing of the supply and demand are the figures for the competitive examinations for study abroad. In 1928, 250 candidates competed for 111 places; in 1929, 366 competed for 98 places; and in 1930, 246 for 97.[41] But some of the unsuccessful candidates as well as other high school graduates were admitted to institutes for higher learning in Iran, so that almost all properly qualified applicants seem to have been able to find their way to higher learning. The rest could still get prestigious jobs in the administration. This balance was, however, not the result of an advance in higher education, but rather of the backwardness of secondary education (see Chapter 9). Higher education remained limited in numbers and confined to a small group of well-to-do families.

The Contribution of Returning Graduates

No other group of people contributed so much to the development of the country in the period discussed as did the returning academics. Many modernization projects depended on their skills: the foundation of the university, the judicial and administrative reforms, the attempts at industrialization, and the improvement of transportation (including the construction of the trans-Iranian railway). Not only did they help in the implementation of such programs, but they also advocated modernizing policies as such and became active in politics—particularly after the abdication of the shah.

Many from among the 1928–1933 group went on to graduate schools, often during their first stay abroad. In this they differed from earlier groups. To illustrate: of the 176 graduates surveyed by the Institute for Social Research, 69.4 percent obtained Ph.D. or M.D. degrees. (Of the medical graduates, 41.7 percent completed their specialization before returning home.) The duration of their stay in Europe was longer than their predecessors': of the 176, only 6.2 percent stayed abroad for less than five years; 10.2 percent remained over ten years; the rest stayed between five and ten years.[42]

In career terms, the graduates were offered comparatively prominent initial positions and enjoyed rapid promotion. Since prestigious positions were mainly to be had in the administration and since they were given a choice of various administrative appointments, their obligation

41. Gondi Shapur, 2:16, 20.
42. Moradi-Nezhad and Pazhum-Shari'ati, 17, 28–30.

to work for the government for as many years as they had been abroad at government expense was no hardship. Since it was customary to hold more than one job, some continued to work in their family business alongside their government position.[43] Given the practices of nepotism and favoritism in Iranian society, family connections played a significant role in appointments and promotions—often more so than academic qualifications.

Since most of the graduates returned on the eve of, or immediately after, the inauguration of Tehran University, it was only natural that many of them joined its faculty. Another large group took up administrative appointments. Many did both. The above-mentioned survey shows that 52.2 percent of the 176 graduates were appointed to the civil service, the municipalities, or government-owned firms; 31.8 percent were on the staff of the university; 12.5 percent taught at the Tehran Teachers Seminar or other schools; only 1.2 percent went into the professions. (Another 2.3 percent did not answer the question on the survey about occupation.) The survey shows a high correlation between the field of study and the graduates' initial occupation: in 92.6 percent of the cases it spoke of a "high correlation."[44] This may, however, be somewhat misleading because it is not entirely clear how long they remained in their initial occupations. Nor is it clear exactly how the correlation was determined. For example, a student of agriculture holding an administrative position in the Ministry of Agriculture was listed under "high correlation." Similarly, when teachers intended under the law to teach at high schools joined the faculty of the university, they were still marked as having achieved "high correlation." Obviously, the correlation between the intention of the legislators and the actual long-term employment of the returnees was somewhat lower than the survey had reported.

Be that as it may, the graduates certainly made fine careers for themselves. Many of them held two positions, often of a very different character. This was customary in many Middle Eastern countries and was at least partly due to the growing demand for university graduates. Though often detrimental from a professional standpoint, holding two positions nevertheless helped give the graduates a wider scope for their influence. Combining a university teaching post with prominent administrative or political office—as was often the case—added to their prestige and, consequently, to popular appreciation for education. When the Institute for Social Research conducted its survey, all of the

43. Interviews with Sadiqi and Mahdavi.
44. Moradi-Nezhad and Pazhum-Shari'ati, 70.

176 included in it were already over the age of sixty, yet only 25.6 percent held just a single position, 53.9 percent had two "full-time" jobs, 18.2 percent had three, and 2.3 percent even four or five "full-time" positions.[45]

What were the occupational fields of the returnees? The above survey provides data for 418 out of the total of 569 graduates (176 had answered the questionnaire, the data for another 242 were gathered by the staff of the institute). Since some gave more than one occupation, 742 occupations were listed altogether. They divided as follows: education, 274; administration, 183; the professions (excluding university teaching), 143; politics, 80; industry, 40; writing, 12; others, 10.[46] Most occupied top positions in their field.

Of the 274 engaged in teaching, most were at Tehran University. Five of them held the office of chancellor at one time or another, three had been vice-chancellors, eight deans, and another 193 senior professors. Four were principals of high schools, and fifteen were high school teachers. Of the 176 who had answered the questionnaire, fifty-six had joined the university immediately after returning. The authoritarian nature of the regime notwithstanding, it was this group, together with their predecessors from the previous period, who shaped the character of the university, and in fact the essence of Iranian higher education. Siyasi, a professor at the university since its inception and its president between 1942 and 1954, told me that without this group the university could not have functioned at all in its early years. He added that they helped cast it in the mold of a western university and supported him in his attempts to secure its independence (see Chapter 13). Sadiq, one of its planners and among the first faculty members, said that the existence of the cadre of returning graduates underlay the decision to establish the university. By contrast, and very much contrary to the intentions of the project's initiators, their direct contribution to elementary and secondary education was marginal.

Politics was another area in which graduates returning from abroad became highly active. Eighty of the 418 covered by the survey held political and diplomatic positions, often the most prominent ones: at various times, thirty-two were ministers, four deputy prime ministers, eighteen deputy ministers, thirty-one were Majlis members (including one speaker), four were senators, and nine ambassadors. In the administration, too, graduates held high office: twenty-three were directors-general of ministries, one was a mayor, four were provincial governors,

45. Ibid., 71–73.
46. Ibid., 73.

thirty-six chairmen or members of boards of government companies, two directors of museums, three directors of banks, and ninety-eight held other high civil service posts.[47] Given the prevalent belief that education opened the way to administrative positions, it was only natural that 44 percent of the 418 held such posts. Their rapid advancement only proved the accuracy of such notions. From their elevated posts, they also played a leading role in the administrative reforms implemented by the two Pahlavi shahs.

Another 143 held positions according to their qualifications: ninety-three were physicians, forty engineers, and ten judges. Unlike in the past, the physicians were no longer mainly employed in the army (fifty-three maintained a private practice, often alongside other jobs). They contributed to the progress of medicine by establishing hospitals, developing public health services, and bringing the beginnings of modern medicine to outlying areas. Whereas in the past the public had been suspicious of the "new" medicine and its practitioners, this attitude now began to change. Similarly, western-trained jurists contributed greatly to the establishment of the new judicial system. The secularization of the legal system could not have been carried out without them. The forty engineers and another forty graduates who had gone into industry (thirty-six became factory managers) made their mark in construction, transportation, and the new industries.[48]

Publishing was another major field for the returning academics. Four became editors of periodicals, five were journalists, one an editor of a daily newspaper, and two became translators. No fewer than 76.7 percent of the 418 graduates published books and/or articles.[49] Of great significance for higher education were the many textbooks written or translated by them. Although much criticism was leveled at their writing textbooks instead of engaging in original research, they were nevertheless the first to launch the massive publishing of academic books in Persian. Even more important in the overall context of modernization were their contributions to nonscientific periodicals and newspapers. Some wrote for opposition newspapers (mainly abroad) or published periodicals supporting westernization in Iran. Owing to the nature of Reza's regime, this was not a widespread practice in the period under review. But after 1941, when the media temporarily enjoyed much freedom, they expressed novel and liberal ideas in the many journals and newspapers then being published.

---

47. Ibid., 75–77.
48. For a list of dozens of factories established by them, see ibid., 95–101.
49. Moradi-Nezhad and Pazhum-Shari'ati, 78, 102–5.

The remaining ten included four businessmen, three contractors, two agronomists, and—a western-inspired innovation—the manager of a modern theater. The fact that only two were engaged in agronomy is striking and may reflect the relatively strong emphasis at that time on industry rather than agriculture. Also, agronomy was likely to involve manual work or assignments away from the urban centers. However, in an agricultural country like Iran, this numerical proportion attested to the failure of the quota system, let alone of the government's attempts to channel graduates into the employment it had planned for them.[50]

At the start of their careers, returning graduates were appointed to prominent positions (even better than those held by the graduates of institutions of higher learning in Iran), and they were promoted rapidly. This practice was so conspicuous that it caused resentment on the part of older, and less well educated, personnel. One of the students answering the above survey, for example, wrote in his comments: "Although the shah . . . stressed that the best use should be made of the educated youngsters, the environment in the administration was suffocating. They [the veteran bureaucrats] accused us of lacking experience, and they were in fact right. We did not have what they thought of as experience."[51] Others had similar complaints.[52]

No less important than their professional skills was the way they worked for the introduction of new ideas. In doing so, they were helped by their salient careers, but also by the high social standing that now attached to having graduated abroad. Their company was being sought, and they came to be considered desirable husbands.[53] Unlike earlier returnees, whose impact was mainly ideological, these graduates, who had spent a long time abroad, had made changes in their daily lives as well: their choice of dress and cutlery, the furniture and plumbing in their houses. In upper-class circles, it became fashionable to imitate their life-style.

Sadiq's memoirs give us some insight into an Iranian student's experience in the West and its imprint. True, Sadiq had an exceptionally rich experience, having studied in London and Paris (1911–1915) as well as in New York (1930–1931, for his Ph.D.). Yet what he writes no

50. As noted above, the government assigned a quota of 7 percent for agricultural studies; and an appropriate number (thirteen out of the 176 surveyed) indeed took up agronomy, but only two out of 418 pursued it as a career.

51. Moradi-Nezhad and Pazhum-Shari'ati, 86.

52. MAM, document 4692.

53. Thus Sadiq, Sadiqi, and Mahdavi in my interviews with them; Eqbali in MAM, document 4692; Hekmat, *Khatere*, 80–83.

doubt reflects the perceptions of many. Speaking of the impact of his stay in the United States on his "spirit, thought and character," and his personal conduct, he writes:

> First, the shackles of tradition (*sonnat*) and of the past were removed from my hands and ankles. Before traveling to the USA, all customs, habits, practices, laws, institutions, regulations, programs etc. seemed to me unchangeable.... In the USA, I learned that... traditions can be changed and they were created in the first place for the utility and progress of society. [If they]... do not benefit the community, it is possible to adapt them to the needs of a [different] time and place.
>
> Second,... I perceived the meaning and essence of democracy.... My stay in America taught me that equality is not confined to legal matters or to the way the Majlis is elected, but must apply to all spheres of life....
>
> Fourth, the emphasize in the USA on social education and moral training... influenced me greatly.... They convinced me of the necessity for imitating and utilizing the moral and educational methods of the USA.
>
> Fifth, my belief in the future and my optimism were strengthened since I had myself witnessed that success in life depends on faith, qualifications and perseverance.[54]

Given the prominent positions he held subsequently (minister of education, chancellor of Tehran University, director of the Tehran Teachers Seminar, senator, and author), it is clear that his experience marked not only his own chosen road but also influenced that of others as well.

Ever since Iranians first left to study in Europe, freedom was what impressed them the most. This was particularly true under Reza Shah, because of the stark contrast between the western democracies and the shah's autocratic rule. Yet for all their excitement over actual contact with a democratic regime, most students did not think it possible, or even essential, to adopt democracy in Iran. Perhaps they were not unaware of the fact that the existing social order served their particular interests. Consequently, they did not seek change in Iran and as a rule refrained from political struggle. Upon their return, they usually adapted again to the old realities and were co-opted into the system. A smaller group would have wished to apply new political ideals, but acknowledged the strength of the existing regime and did not fight for their aims. Some among them, while still abroad, held meetings to discuss democratization. Most of these students later became profes-

54. Sadiq, *Yadegar*, 2:24–28.

sors at Tehran University, and their main concern was to safeguard its independence. They remained generally inactive under Reza, but became vocal and active at the time of his fall and went on to become the nucleus of the liberal movement of the first years under his successor. Some of them remained active (at least intermittently) in opposition movements right up to the Islamic Revolution. A third, still smaller group, influenced mainly by Marxism, turned to active opposition, but like their colleagues in the past, they had to act mainly from abroad, fearing the crushing strength of the regime at home. Unlike earlier groups, however, they organized themselves into established political movements. And whereas earlier opposition groups had demanded freedom while (for the most part) acknowledging the legitimacy of the regime, the opposition forces under Reza worked against the regime itself.

Opposition activity on the part of educated Iranians sympathetic to Marxism can be traced back to the closing year of World War I.[55] Ervand Abrahamian identifies fourteen people as the "leadership personalities of the early Communist Movements." All were well educated: all of them had completed high school, two were graduates of Dar al-Fonun, and five were university graduates (three of whom had studied at Moscow University).[56] With the consolidation of Reza Shah's rule, opposition elements were forced to concentrate their activities abroad, mostly in Germany. Being expatriates in turn led them to emphasize Marxist indoctrination of the intelligentsia rather than training their people for immediate action, which did not seem a practical proposition.[57] In 1926, Iranian students in Germany established the Iranian Republican Revolutionary Committee. It engaged in antishah propaganda and demonstrations against him (such as the protests held on the occasion of the visit of the court minister, Taymur-Tash, to Germany in September 1928).[58] In 1929, the Iranian Communist party was formed in Germany and began publishing its organ *Setare-ye Sorkh* (The Red Star) there. Many copies were smuggled into Iran. In 1930, a congress of dissident students in Europe convened in Cologne, demanded the release of all political prisoners, called for the establishment of a re-

55. For the beginnings of the Communist party in Iran and the role of the educated class in it, see Sepher Zabih, *The Communist Party in Iran* (Berkeley: University of California Press, 1966), 1–64; George Lenczowski, "The Communist Movement in Iran," *The Middle East Journal*, 1 (January 1947), 29–45; Abrahamian, 102–65.

56. Abrahamian, 132–33.

57. Zabih, 64.

58. On the party and its activity, see Ahmad Mahrad, *Die Deutsch-Persischen Beziehungen von 1918–1933* (Bern, 1974), 329–31.

public, and denounced Reza Shah as a "tool of British imperialism."[59] In 1931, the Action Committee of Republican Iranians, composed mainly of students, organized a conference in Cologne in which the possibility of taking action against the shah's regime was discussed. It sent liberal and leftist newspapers in Europe a pamphlet titled "Protest gegen den Terror des Reza Khan Pahlavi in Persien," which spoke of the shah as an oppressor and murderer.[60] Also in 1931, a group of students in Munich came together with some members of the Iranian Communist party to publish a new periodical named *Paykar* (Combat), which included articles denouncing the suppressive regime in Iran, the torture of political prisoners, the lack of freedom, and the shah's dependence on Britain. Simultaneously, *Paykar* stressed Russia's support of the Iranian people. Official Iranian pressure on the German government led to some restrictions, but the new trend continued nonetheless, with university graduates and students at its center.[61]

Gradually, the Communist movement organized in Europe infiltrated into Iran, despite the measures taken by the regime. The activists were mainly young academics returning from abroad. The founder of the movement was Dr. Taqi Arani, who had studied medicine in Berlin and returned to Iran in the early 1930s to teach at Tehran University. Other activists included Dr. Reza Radmanesh, who had studied physics in Paris and returned to Iran in 1935; Bozorg ʿAlavi, a writer, Dr. Morteza Yazdi and Dr. Mohammad Bahrami, both physicians (all three were graduates of Berlin University); and Iraj Eskandari, who had studied law at the University of Grenoble. Their first step was to set up an organization called Kanun-e Javanan (Youth Organization), which they made into an instrument for propagating Communist ideology. The secret police watched them closely and soon exposed their activities. A police report submitted early in 1937 to the minister of education, Hekmat, showed that twenty-five out of fifty activists were university graduates. (No details were available on another three also listed by the police.) All fifty-three were tried and sentenced to long prison terms. When the allies entered Iran during World War II, the activists were released (except for Arani, who had died in prison) and became the nucleus of the Tudeh party.[62]

The fact that academics (some of whom had studied at government

59. Abrahamian, 154.

60. The text of the pamphlet is cited in Mahrad, 341.

61. A. Basir, "Barkhi Moshakhkhasat-e Sabak-e Arani dar Tarvij-e Afkar-e Marksisti dar Iran," *Donya* (1958), 2, no. 4: 94–100.

62. Hekmat, *Khatere*, 213–28; Zabih, 65–66. For the list of the fifty-three, their education, occupations, and class origin, see Abrahamian, 158–61.

expense) should turn against him greatly disappointed the shah. Following the trial of the fifty-three, he told the cabinet: "Look at this group of young people whom we sent abroad with a heart full of hope, and whom we supported for years, so that they would return to their homeland and serve it. Now that they are back . . . they brought us Bolshevism in their saddlebags."[63] Already in 1933, Tabataba'i had pointed to the emergence of such opposition activity among Iranians studying abroad and had suggested putting an end to study programs abroad. Instead, he argued, a university ought to be established in Iran.[64] The shah and his ministers of education had already entertained such an idea. In 1935 that link became in fact one of the principal reasons for the foundation of Tehran University.

63. Hekmat, *Khatere*, 227–28.
64. *Shafaq-e Sorkh*, 22, 25, 27, 28 August 1933. For a similar statement by Ruhi, also in 1933, see Chapter 7.

7

The Founding of
Tehran University

Tehran University was officially inaugurated on 4 February 1935 and immediately raised great expectations for the overall advancement of education. Like universities in other developing countries, it had been created from above rather than grown by an organic process. People in developing countries tended to believe that the ideologies and structure of western universities largely explained the achievements of the West and, hence, that imitating them would produce similar progress in their own countries. They failed to see that the emergence of western universities was not the cause of progress but to a large degree the result of the social conditions of their growth.[1] In Flexner's words, "a university, like all other human institutions . . . is not outside, but inside the general social fabric of a given era . . . . [It is] an expression of the age, as well as an influence operating upon both the present and future."[2] But Iran shared the optimistic approach typical of educational thought in the developing states. It was firmly believed that the foundation of the university would, by itself, start to propel Iran toward the achievements of the West.

But the system of higher education in the West was not uniform. Britain had its two elite universities, concerned with character molding and an elitist way of life as much as with the acquisition of knowledge,

1. Joseph Ben-David and Abraham Zloczower, "Universities and Academic Systems in Modern Societies," *European Journal of Sociology*, 3 (1962), 45–84.
2. A. Flexner, *Universities: American, English, German* (New York: Cornell University Press, 1955), 3.

alongside other colleges conceived primarily as professional schools preparing students for middle-class careers. In the United States, the federal system as well as the comparatively open and mobile nature of the society prevented the emergence of a similar hierarchy. In France, as in Russia, higher education was under a great deal of bureaucratic control, consistent with the centralized nature of government as a whole. In Germany, since the early nineteenth century, and up to the advent of the Nazi regime, there was no centralized control of the universities and no single dominant educational philosophy governing its educational system. Lively competition between individual campuses made for rapid innovation.[3] All in all, the structure and aims of the western university systems were the product of historical circumstances in each individual country, rather than the other way round. As such, none of these systems quite fitted developing countries.

Background

Earlier modern institutions of higher learning in Iran had in the course of time become prestigious high schools, such as Dar Al-Fonun, or had remained colleges for specialized training that turned out graduates needed by the ministries to which they were attached. This was true of the School of Political Science (attached to the Foreign Ministry) and of the schools of medicine and agriculture. The founders of Tehran University wanted to go beyond that and to set up a campus including all branches of knowledge, active in research as much as in teaching.

The earliest thoughts on the advisability of founding a western-style university were voiced in the late 1920s by educationalists such as Siyasi, Hekmat, and Sadiq who had themselves studied in the West.[4] However, no practical steps were taken until the shah himself came to regard a university as vital for his vision of a new Iran and for his reform projects. Moreover, projects for study abroad had failed to provide the required manpower. Demand by the elites for higher education for their children kept growing. Furthermore, bringing together the various existing institutes for higher learning into a single administrative and academic unit fitted the prevalent tendency toward centralization. Finally, as we have seen, sending students abroad had proved politically risky. The last point determined the shah's decision, or at least its timing.

3. For a comparative analysis of university systems, see Ben-David and Zloczower.
4. *MM*, term 7, 4386; also interviews with Siyasi and Sadiq.

On 31 March 1931, the court minister, Taymur-Tash, wrote to Sadiq (then working on a doctoral dissertation on Iranian education at Columbia University) asking him to inquire "in case the Government itself decides to establish a dar al-fonun with departments for pedagogy, medicine, and road engineering in Tehran, how many professors would be needed, what mechanisms will be required and what expenditure would be involved."[5] Sadiq considered the letter an invitation to outline a university scheme and proceeded to do so, with the help of American experts. But he came to the conclusion that because of the weakness of elementary and secondary education, the lack of academic staff, and the lack of a research infrastructure, the establishment of a university was not advisable at that time. His American advisers, Dr. Carter (head of medical studies at the Rockefeller Foundation) and his deputy, Dr. Robert Lambert, had specifically come out against opening a medical school in Tehran. Medical study abroad was, in their view, preferable (they particularly recommended the American University of Beirut). Nonetheless, Sadiq drew up an outline, assuming that in turning to him the court had wanted a plan, not an argument of pros and cons. The shah's resolution, in his view, did not follow from an assessment of the strengths and weaknesses of education in Iran, but was a political decision.[6]

On 6 June 1931, Sadiq submitted his plan to Taymur-Tash. He detailed the recommended number of students in each of the three departments, assessed the costs, listed the equipment needed, and made recommendations for the length of the course of study in each branch and for the standards for admitting students and engaging professors. He wrote: "The university will strive, as its first priority, to train the leaders (*pishvayan*) and heads of the nation (*ro'asa-ye qowm*) and as second priority, to engage in research."[7] At the time, it remained moot whether by leadership training he meant that children of the nobility should be prepared for their future tasks, or whether young people with a gift for leadership should be trained for it regardless of their social background. Some fifty years later, he told me that it was the latter approach he had had in mind. But because—by his own testimony—he was holding up England as a model, and because successful candidates at that time were bound to come from upper-class families, it was the first approach that he was more likely to follow.

5. A letter by the court minister to Sadiq, no. 1/1753. A copy was given to me by Sadiq.

6. Sadiq, *Yadegar*, 2:19–21. He emphasized this point more explicitly in an interview with the author.

7. Sadiq, *Yadegar*, 2:22–24.

Upon his return to Iran early in 1932, Sadiq was summoned to a meeting with Taymur-Tash, who told him: "His Majesty liked the plan that you submitted for the foundation of [a new] dar al-fonun and has commanded that you yourself will implement it. An order in this regard has been given to the minister of education." The latter, Yahya Qaragozlu (E'temad al-Saltane), consequently appointed Sadiq to head the Tehran Teachers Seminar with the intention of turning it into "the nucleus of the dar al-fonun."[8] In the spring of 1932, Sadiq drafted a law for the creation of the university but continued to think that the circumstances were unsuitable for going ahead. He said: "At that time, there was not a single person in the Ministry of Education who had any idea how a university should be organized and run." At the end of the year, the plan was dropped—not, however, because of such arguments, but because Taymur-Tash and Qaragozlu, who both supported the idea of founding a university, had lost their posts.[9]

As often before in the history of the "new education," changes in government entailed changes in policy. The new minister of education, Hekmat, whose relations with Sadiq were tense, ignored the whole issue, and the shah, for reasons that are not clear today, lost interest. In his memoirs, Hekmat let it be understood that he was unaware of Sadiq's plan, though this is hard to believe. His version is that the idea was first raised at a cabinet meeting in February 1934, at which the development of Tehran was on the agenda. Hekmat, by his own account, pointed out to the shah that despite its overall progress and "unlike all big cities of the world," Tehran "lacks a specific building for a university." The shah replied: "Very well, build one." Within a month the plans were ready,[10] and on 13 March 1934 Hekmat presented to the Majlis a law for the establishment of a university. Asserting that it "was inspired by the shah's will and his interest in the issue," he argued for its rapid approval.[11] The Majlis debated and approved only ten of its twenty-one articles; there was no discussion on the others, and no vote on the law as a whole. But the government and the shah now evidently wanted to move fast and seem to have taken the view that the entire law had come into effect.[12]

It was in the language of this law that the Persian *daneshgah* (literally: place of knowledge) was first used for "university" in an official text. "Faculty" was rendered as *daneshkade*. Taymur-Tash had still used *dar*

8. Ibid., 86–92.
9. Ibid., 173–74.
10. Hekmat, *Khatere*, 332–35. See also his memoirs in document 3249 in MAM.
11. *MM*, term 9, 1071–72.
12. Ibid., 1171–84, 1211–16.

al-fonun; later, both Sadiq and Hekmat used the French *université*. Finally, in his presentation of the law to the Majlis, Hekmat spoke of "université, i.e., *daneshgah*."[13] The terminology is not insignificant. Names like *dar al-ʿulum* and *jameʿe* were deliberately avoided because of their traditional religious connotations. *Dar al-fonun,* on the other hand, had too narrow a meaning, implying the teaching of science and technology only. *Daneshgah* came closest to conveying the idea of a western-style university.

Tehran University may not have been the shah's own original idea, but without his personal support it would not have been established at that time. When Taymur-Tash (in his letter to Sadiq) and Hekmat (in his Majlis speech) linked Reza's name with the initiative, they were probably just following the requirements of the times. The available evidence suggests, however, that once the project was launched, the shah became deeply involved in all stages. He himself, for example, decided the location and the size of the campus. With the foresight typical of him, and against the advice of some of his ministers, he gave instructions to allocate to the campus a site large enough to accommodate its future expansion, such as he envisioned it.[14] He often visited the construction site to check on the rate of progress and told Gudard, the French engineer in charge, to expedite the building work because "we are in real rush [to complete] this project."[15] Finally, a day before the inauguration of the university, when the minister of education inquired at court whether the shah would attend the ceremony even if the then inclement weather was to continue, the shah replied: "Even if stones fall from the sky, I will be there."[16]

At the time of its establishment, the university still lacked a sufficient academic infrastructure as well as a clear operating scheme. Some public figures, like the minister of justice, Davar, and Majlis deputy Mirza ʿAbd al-ʿAli Mirzaʾi, suggested to postpone its opening and to concentrate first on improving pre-university schooling.[17] But the decision to go ahead regardless was to a large extent politically motivated. Precisely what were these political considerations?

An analysis of the deliberations surrounding the founding of the university reveals, once more, the attitude—not only of the shah and his successive governments but also of the intellectuals—that higher

13. Both terms had already been used by Sadiq in his preliminary plans in 1932 (Sadiq, *Yadegar,* 2:173).
14. Hekmat, *Khatere,* 334; Wilber, 163–64.
15. See testimony of Javaher Kalam, Gudard's translator, in document 5106 in MAM.
16. Hekmat words in: *Khatere,* 338; MAM, document 3249.
17. *MM,* term 8, 1199; term 9, 1180.

learning was the cure-all for the country's ills. Like their predecessors, they thought of education as a commodity easily transferable from one country to another and with an immediate impact on the importing country. Moreover, a university was conceived as a symbol of progress as well as status.

At the inauguration ceremony, the shah and Mehdi Qoli Khan emphasized the university's potential contribution to the advancement of Iran.[18] During the Majlis discussion of the university law, the same attitude came through even more vividly. Tabataba'i called it "one of the most important steps . . . taken by this government"; Malekzade termed it a major initiative "for the advancement of the country"; Mirza'i (who had originally advised postponement) went so far as to label it "one of the most important laws" ever approved by the House.[19] Yet they differed in their specific approaches. Some, Hekmat most prominent among them, held that its primary function was to train skilled manpower.[20] Others, like Hajj Seyyed Nasrollah Taqavi (the dean of the school of theology), spoke of it as a nucleus for cultural advance.[21] At this stage at least, nothing was said of its role in bridging social gaps. The dominant view, it turned out, was that of Hekmat. The university would scale down, if not altogether abolish, the need for foreign experts and for sending students abroad. At that time, it had already become conventional wisdom that study abroad was costly, numerically insufficient, and politically perilous. As Ruhi put it in the Majlis in 1932: "With the huge sums of money we spend on students abroad we could establish an excellent university in Iran, allowing more students to study [and to do so] according to our own customs and national traditions."[22] When he repeated similar views in the 1934 Majlis debate, Hekmat, Tehrani, and Tabataba'i all seconded him.[23] (Somewhat similar arguments were used to support the creation of Dar al-Fonun, a century earlier.)

Yet ties with western centers of scholarship were not to be severed altogether. Prime Minister ʿAli Foroughi made it clear that Iranian students would continue to attend western universities. Even among western nations, he said, there was a constant exchange of students and scholars. "Today there is no single center of science . . . each endeavors to learn from the experience of others . . . . We have not yet reached

18. Gondi Shapur, 2:32–33; Wilber, 163–64; Hekmat, *Khatere*, 341.
19. *MM*, term 9, 1171, 1179.
20. Hekmat, *Khatere*, 341.
21. *AP*, 1934/5, 174–75.
22. *MM*, term 8, 1198.
23. Ibid., term 9, 933–36, 1171–75.

the stage to be satisfied [with Iran's scientific level] and we still need to go, see and learn from others."[24]

The issue of the university's academic independence was a central one in the public debate. The government spoke publicly in favor of its autonomy, but at the same time worked to make sure it would be able to bend the university to its will. This reflected the government's desire, on the one hand, to initiate western academic patterns, while keeping up the existing modus operandi of the regime, on the other.[25] Some advocates of academic autonomy failed to perceive its real meaning. Tabataba'i spoke for the university's independence but at the same time urged the Ministry of Education to supervise the curriculum and the textbooks.[26] Even the university law referred to the institution as "an independent legal entity" enjoying administrative and financial independence, while being "under the direct responsibility (*mas'uliyyat*)" and "supervision (*nezarat*)" of the Ministry of Education (both clauses in article 7). All in all, however, the law gave the university considerable autonomy, and still left room for ministerial intervention. The power to engage and promote academic staff, to admit students, and to elect the president and deans was the prerogative of the school. But, the language of the law notwithstanding, the nature of the regime dictated considerable limitations. In actual fact, throughout the reign of Reza Shah, the university did not have even that degree of independence which the law had granted it. (For details, see Chapter 13.)

Under the law, the university initially was to have six faculties: political science and law, arts, theology, science, medicine, and engineering. This composition reflected not only current needs but also the prior existence of institutes of higher learning, now to be integrated into the university. Reza himself attached the greatest importance to the fields of engineering, medicine, and pedagogy. Only these had been listed in Taymur-Tash's letter to Sadiq. The shah gave instructions to give preference to constructing the engineering and medicine buildings.[27] Of special significance was the decision to incorporate theological studies in the university. Following the decline of the *maktab* and the *madrese*, this was meant to open a channel for "bureaucratizing" the body of the ulama—a concept hitherto altogether alien to Shi'i Islam, though common in Sunni countries. Already a decade earlier,

24. Ibid., term 9, 1175.

25. See words to this effect in Sadiq, *Yadegar*, 2:173. He was even more explicitly critical on this point in an interview with the author forty years later.

26. See his speeches in *MM*, term 9, 1171 and 1214.

27. MAM, document 5106, memoirs of Javaher Kalam; Hekmat, *Khatere*, 344–46.

Ataturk had taken a similar step by making the Medrese Suleymaniye the Faculty of Divinity of Istanbul University.[28] The Iranian ulama considered the Tehran faculty one more threat to Islam and to their own status and opposed it vigorously.[29]

The supporters of the "new education" like their predecessors in the late nineteenth century, tried to convince themselves and others that there was no contradiction between religion and the spread of science. But unlike their predecessors, they had the support of a powerful shah who himself endorsed secularization. The power of the religious establishment to challenge his policies was by now extremely limited. Their charges that the university was a danger to religion were vehemently rejected by the prime minister and the minister of education. In the Majlis debate, both emphasized that the government's policy was to integrate western science with the values of Islam, not to harm religion.[30]

The Early Years (1935–1941)

The period from the founding of the university to the abdication of the shah in 1941 is too short for us to draw definite conclusions on its workings, let alone its broader contribution. An assessment of its first years must therefore remain tentative.

The first point to make is that Tehran University was not an entirely new institute: in some respects, its establishment was no more than an administrative and academic integration of existing bodies. Only the faculties of engineering and theology were innovations. Its first challenge was therefore to set up an infrastructure suitable for a campus embracing various fields of study, and develop teaching and (much less so) research in each of them. Next was the struggle for academic autonomy. Without at least a measure of independence from the state, it would not be able to establish itself as a center of influence in its own right. But there was no getting away from the fact that when all was said and done, the university was not independent but was under the thumb of the government, just as its constituent parts had earlier been controlled by their ministries. This gained the university much initial support from official quarters which it would not otherwise have enjoyed, but also exposed it to the harsh winds of each political change.

28. Lewis, *Modern Turkey*, 408.
29. See memoirs of Hekmat in document 3249 in MAM.
30. *MM*, term 9, 1178–79.

Table 4. Number of students attending Tehran University between 1934/5 and 1940/1

Year	Total no. of students	Agriculture	Arts	Theology	Medicine	Law	Engineering	Veterinary
1934/5	1,043	44	152	—	407	388	52	—
1935/6	1,550	70	390	91	436	421	142	—
1936/7	1,776	115	433	127	423	449	162	67
1937/8	1,787	127	411	130	444	421	188	66
1938/9	1,882	119	378	142	456	537	186	64
1939/40	2,113	91	575	155	473	534	217	68
1940/41	2,023	95	483	166	467	530	224	58

Source: SBB/MA, *Dowran-e Pahlavi,* 25–28.

In the last analysis, the university was run by the Ministry of Education much as the high schools were.

The numerical growth of the campus from 1934/5 till 1940/41 is summarized in Table 4. Of the 1,043 original students, most were from the old colleges. By the end of the period, their number almost doubled. Naturally, the most rapid growth was in the first years, before outgoing graduates began balancing the intake. The first three years therefore accounted for 70.3 percent of the overall growth. From then on, the rate of increase slowed down, and after the outbreak of World War II there was even a small decline, owing to wartime difficulties.

A comparison of academic choices shows a preponderance of medical students, reflecting both government encouragement and growing popular demand. Their numbers kept growing in absolute terms, but their share of the total dropped from the initial 39 percent to 23.1 percent in 1940/41. Unlike the medical school, the school of engineering was an altogether new venture. In 1934/5, its share was only 5 percent, but it grew to 11.1 percent in 1940/41. Of the three major fields in which the government was most interested—medicine, engineering, and pedagogy—the last was a total failure. Its incorporation in the university had been expected to raise the prestige of the teaching profession. But the students, hitherto at the Tehran Teachers Seminar but now at the Faculty of Arts (and later partly at the Faculty of Science), came to feel that they were now qualifying for careers other than teaching and chose them instead. As a result, the teachers seminar was eventually reestablished as a separate entity in 1955.[31]

What was the social background of the student population during these years? Official statistics and university publications are silent on

31. For an official report of the seminar, see MAM, document 4694.

this question. The personal files of the students mention only their place of birth and the high school they graduated from. The parents' income, occupation, or educational level is not given. The only useful data are the student's name (which may point to his being related to one of the prominent families) and his place of birth.[32]

A survey of the files of engineering students reveals that out of 131 graduates during 1937/8–1940/41, sixty-eight (51.9 percent) were natives of Tehran and eighty-one students (61.8 percent) had completed their high school there. Most of them presumably lived in the capital. Yet only 3.7 percent of Iran's total population then lived in Tehran. Another 3.7 percent of the total population lived in the other three cities that had high schools at the time (Tabriz, Isfahan, and Rasht), but 28.2 percent of the graduates finished high school there, and 21.4 percent were born in one of the three cities. Only 26.7 percent of the graduates were born in the rest of the country, where 92.6 percent of the population were living. Since the situation in other faculties was by and large similar, it is fair to conclude that at that juncture higher education was almost entirely a matter for residents of a few large cities whose population did not exceed 10 percent of the total.

More information about the social background of the students can be gathered from the impressions of their teachers. In my interviews with four of these teachers—Sadiq, Siyasi, Sadiqi, and Mahdavi—they defined "almost all" students as upper-class. Sadiqi, one of Iran's most prominent sociologists, told me that this could be clearly inferred from their clothes, manners, and accents. Sadiq added that despite the government's decision, prior to the inauguration of the school, to aid needy students, the university remained throughout this period exclusively for "the children of the rich."

The teaching staff was composed mostly of graduates of western universities. Iranian-educated faculty usually taught subjects such theology, Arabic, Iranian history and geography, or Persian literature. Some foreigners were also engaged, mainly for the schools of medicine and engineering. It is important to note that the teaching body grew more rapidly than the student population: from 121 in the university's first year to 566 in 1939/40.[33] A professorial appointment conferred much social prestige and resulted in offers of additional part-time or full-time jobs which were taken up often enough.

No significant research activity developed at this early stage. Even

---

32. I wish to thank the university authorities for making it possible for me to study the student files.
33. Khaje-Nuri, 2034.

though a tradition of inquiry and investigation had exist in the *madreses*, scientific research in the western sense was unknown at the colleges brought together to form the university. Moreover, research equipment was scarce, and libraries were poor. Also, research was not, at that time, made a condition for academic advancement, and in any case the multiple positions held by most professors would not have left them time for it.

In many ways, the university inherited some of the methods of traditional education. Formal lectures and the memorizing of the teaching materials prevailed over discussion and analysis. Even in medicine and engineering, study was mostly theoretical. It was these deficiencies that Sadiq had in mind when, in 1941, he concluded a lecture by saying that with regard to methods and contents of university teaching, "the intentions we all had did not materialize."[34]

Conclusion

Tehran University was created by a political decision, at a time when the overall state of Iranian education was not ready for it. Government tutelage had made its establishment possible but also accounted for some of its flaws. Dependence on the government limited academic freedom and stunted intellectual activity. The old traditions of Iranian education continued to leave their mark, at least in part, and militated against the development of research. The inspiration of western university education was felt, but only became dominant after the fall of Reza Shah.

In the years of the university under Reza, it became abundantly clear that its fundamental problem was the uncritical borrowing from western theories and methods without any real attempt to sift out and adapt that which might suit the country's unique circumstances. With this in mind, Banani wrote: "Such intellectual short-sightedness, coupled with the attendant vices of exclusiveness, jealousy, social and personal rivalries, and political ambitions, prevented the university from attaining a high academic standing."[35] Similarly, Joseph Szyliowicz concluded that Tehran University "possessed all the deficiencies of a French university and none of its strengths."[36] But its main weakness—even in these early years—was its failure to turn itself into a center of

34. *AP*, 1941/2, 5–6:xi–xii.
35. Banani, 100.
36. Szyliowicz, 241.

creative intellectual activity. In Reza Shah's view, intellectuals were no more than professionals fit to replace foreign experts yet pliable enough to toe the official line.[37] Some political student activity did occur occasionally[38] and a group of professors did meet to discuss politics (see Chapter 13), but all things considered, the university became that center of conformism which the shah expected it to be and to which be turned for ideological legitimization, propagandist support, and statements of flattery and ingratiation. Yet the concomitant quantitative expansion of higher education and the growth in the number of graduates were significant both professionally and politically. It was under Reza Shah that the intelligentsia in the words of Abrahamian, "developed into a significant modern middle class whose members not only held common attitudes toward social, economic and political modernization, but also shared similar educational, occupational, and economic background."[39] Its disparate groupings came to form a social class, and this class played an important role in the conflicts following the abdication of Reza Shah (see Part Three).

37. See Reza Arasteh, "The Role of Intellectuals in Administrative and Social Change in Modern Iran," *International Review of Education*, 9 (1963/4), 331.

38. Thus, for example, three hundred students of the Tehran Teachers Seminar protested in 1936 against a government proposal that would have obliged them to work in public schools after their graduation. In 1937, the law students boycotted their classes in protest against the lavish sums spent on preparing the university for the visit of the crown prince: Abrahamian, 155.

39. Abrahamian, 145–46.

PART THREE

Education under
Mohammad Reza Shah

The thirty-seven years of Mohammad Reza Shah's reign (1941–1979)[1] were one long struggle for power. Starting out as a figurehead under the thumbs of local power groups and of the superpowers, he went on to make himself an absolute monarch, as Zonis put it, "more powerful than . . . any previous Iranian ruler,"[2] only to lose throne and country in a signal collapse.

In terms of his political stature, three periods stand out: the era of weakness, from his ascension to the throne until the downfall of Mohammad Mosaddeq in 1953; the period of consolidation, from 1953 to the triumph over the opposition in 1963; and the years of the "White Revolution" (*Enqelab-e Sefid*).[3] The latter saw the shah at the height of his powers until, in 1977, a new opposition arose, led by Ayatollah Ruhollah Khomeyni, and rapidly brought about the final collapse of 1979.

Yet even the periods of gathering strength were interspersed with challenges to the shah's authority. At first, the collapse of Reza Shah's rule encouraged his old opponents to try and reassert themselves against his young (twenty-one-year-old) and untried successor. This was true of the elite groups Reza had suppressed (leading clerics, Bazar merchants, landlords, tribal chiefs, and members of the Qajar aristoc-

---

1. He died in 1980—in exile.
2. Marvin Zonis, *The Political Elite of Iran* (Princeton: Princeton University Press, 1971), 18.
3. "White"—that is, bloodless.

racy) as well as of the ethnic minorities (mainly the Kurds and the Azeri Turks). At the same time, intellectuals, liberals, and nationalists thought of the weakness of the shah's early reign and of the presence of the superpowers as an opportunity for themselves. There was a sense of slackening control. Mohammad Reza, inexperienced and with no significant power base of his own, seemed incapable of taking his dreaded father's place. Some thirty years later, he was to say: "You can just imagine a regime based on the prestige of my father tumbling down, the country going to pieces under the occupation by foreign troops, the resurgence of the feudal system, some of the tribal chieftains going back to their almost autonomous regime, the creation of imperialist colonies, the resurgence of the mullahs and their black reaction, and the breakdown of law and order."[4]

It was only after the evacuation of the foreign troops in 1946 that the shah was able to launch a purposeful drive for consolidation. By 1949, he felt confident enough to outline comprehensive plans for social and economic reconstruction, to present the first Seven-Year Plan, and to begin speaking of liberalization and reform (mainly agrarian reform).

The popular expectations he raised in doing so were destined to remain unfulfilled, but his promises sufficed to antagonize the elite groups. The shah's growing power united them against him: the landlords resented talks of land reform; the Bazaris were disgruntled by growing economic regimentation (witness the Seven-Year Plan); the ulama resented his westernizing and secularizing policies; the tribal chiefs were, as always, apprehensive of any sign of greater control from the center; and the intellectuals were antagonized by the retreat from the comparative liberalization of the preceding years. The pro-Moscow Tudeh party joined forces with them. This was the basis for Mosaddeq's Jebhe-ye Melli (National Front) which, between 1951 and 1953, deprived the shah of much of his power and eventually forced him into a short exile.

On his return, he had, as he put it, to start the struggle for power all over again.[5] The army, which had returned him to the throne, was now strengthened, in part at least as a safeguard against internal opponents. At the same time, the shah sought the support of veteran

---

4. Karanjia, 62. For more details on the internal situation, see the shah's descriptions: Pahlavi, *Mission*, 59–81; Karanjia, 60–72; for other Iranian witnesses, see: Arfa, 297–330; Sadiq, *Yadegar*, 3:48–49; Ramesh Sanghvi, *Aryamehr the Shah of Iran: A Political Biography* (London: Transorient, 1968), 57–135; also: Averi, 342–67; Bullard, 13–18; Millspaugh, *Americans in Persia*, 20–62; Leonard Binder, *Iran: Political Development in Changing Society* (Los Angeles: University of California Press, 1962), 66–68.

5. Pahlavi, *Tamaddon-e Bozorg* (Tehran: Ketabkhane-ye Pahlavi, 1977/8), 81.

politicians, of liberals disillusioned with the Mosaddeq experience, and of the merchant class, making appropriate promises to each group. By 1957, he had regained enough strength to appoint the first prime minister personally loyal to him (Manuchehr Eqbal), to authorize a measure of political activity, and to have his closest friend, Asadollah 'Alam, form a "loyal opposition" in the shape of the Mardom (People's) party. Significantly, the SAVAK (the State Intelligence and Security Organization) was formed the same year.

Over the following years, further reform measures, a gradual secularization process, and growing government and foreign involvement in the economy, coupled with suppressive measures, combined to bring into being a new coalition of opposition forces. Its religious component now came to be led by Khomeyni, who regarded the entire reform program as anti-Islamic and as an imperialist plot. Most of its liberal and national elements had come together in the Nehzat-e Moqavemat-e Melli (National Resistance Movement) under Karim Sanjabi, Shapur Bakhtyar, and Daryush Foruhar, and in the Nehzat-e Azadi (Freedom Movement) led by Mehdi Bazargan and Ayatollah Mahmud Taleqani. It posed a serious challenge for the shah between 1960 and 1963.

Harsh measures followed. Some opposition leaders, such as Bazargan and Taleqani, were arrested; others, like Bakhtyar, went into exile; still others remained in the country but ceased their activities; and the remainder were absorbed into the establishment. The takeover of Tehran University's campus by the military was one of these measures (see Chapter 13 for details). Similar strong-arm methods were applied against landlords and Bazaris. The clerics were dealt with in a similar fashion: Khomeyni was detained in 1963 and exiled in 1964.

From then on, and until 1977, political stability prevailed and the shah's rule became altogether autocratic. By 1963, according to the shah, "after many vicissitudes, I was in a position to act."[6] It was now that he launched the White Revolution. The reforms undertaken under that name have contributed significantly to the emergence of a new Iran. Yet their scope, their pace, their brutal enforcement, and perhaps most of all the rapid change they produced elicited mounting popular resentment. As often before in modern Iranian history, the four main skeins in the pre-1979 revolutionary fabric were autocratic rule, secularization, foreign influence, and social and economic tension.

Looking back over the ebb and flow of periods of strength and of weakness, one sees a negative correlation between the shah's power

6. Idem, *The White Revolution* (Tehran: Kayhan, 1967?), 16.

and the processes of democratization and liberalization: the stronger the shah, the more forcefully liberties were put down; in times of weakness, by contrast, the liberals were able to make some gains, but the circumstances proved unfavorable to implement their vision. The ensuing period of royal reassertion then nullified whatever advance had occurred in the interval. This pattern applied to educational reform as much as to any other area.

The overall ups and downs of the regime are well reflected on a smaller scale by the rate of turnover in staff at the Ministry of Education (as at most other ministries, for that matter). Between 1941 and 1947, Sadiq was appointed five times to this post, never holding it for more than five months on end. Similarly, in the last four months of the shah's rule, four ministers of education held office. Both Sadiq and Siyasi claimed that during each tenure the government was changed before they were able to formulate policy; when they next returned to office, they found new staff and new plans with which they disagreed.[7] Many liberal and reformist ideas were therefore being floated by politicians and educationalists without ever reaching the stage of implementation. The educational policies that did take effect were mainly those laid down by the shah at the times when he was free to act.

At such times, the shah concentrated his attention on the White Revolution or the "Revolution of the Shah and the People" (*Enqelab-e Shah va Mardom*) as he preferred to call it in the 1970s. This was a program he had initiated to propel Iran to the level of "the most advanced countries of the world" before the turn of the century. After its ratification in a referendum on 26 January 1963, its principles underlay Iran's "political, social and economic policies."[8] To its implementation, the shah directed most of the country's resources.

Elements of the scheme had existed in the shah's thinking long before,[9] and some reform steps had been decreed earlier on. But it was only now that reform was placed in a clear ideological framework, that its philosophy was spelled out and a timetable laid down for its implementation. And it was only now that the program was backed by the political strength required to carry it forward.

The White Revolution was a multidimensional undertaking: it was intended to bridge social gaps and establish a just society; to make use of oil revenues to give Iran a modern economy; and to be a national

---

7. This was also emphasized by Siyasi in a Majlis speech in 1948, at a time when he was minister of education: *MM*, term 15, 2573.

8. Pahlavi, *Revolution*, 1.

9. In his own words, he had entertained such ideas "for long years" (Pahlavi, *Tamaddon*, 94–95).

revolution, bringing about national unity (*vahdat*) and independence (*esteqlal*). Its final aim was the "Great Civilization" (*Tamaddon-e Bozorg*), a vague ideal of reviving Iran's glorious past and of making it once again a leading force in human history.[10] It was meant to combine Iranian national culture with the material achievements of western science and technology.[11] It was, the shah wrote, "essentially an Iranian revolution, compatible with the spirit and tradition of the Iranian people," but utilizing "all the experiences of others" and open "to introduce new thinking whenever necessary."[12] It included "dogmatic, unalterable principles" alongside "pragmatic guidelines."[13] Among the former, the shah stressed loyalty to the "monarchical order" (*nezam-e shahanshahi*); fidelity to Islam; national unity, independence, and territorial integrity; and attachment to democracy.[14] The pragmatic principles were reflected in the nineteen articles of the revolutionary program.[15] Three of them dealt with education: the creation of the "literacy corps" (article 6), educational reform (12), and free schooling at all levels of education (15). At the core of the White Revolution was land reform legislation. Other main points, either contained in the original six principles or in the articles added later, included the nationalization of forests and water resources, administrative reform, the transformation of industrial workers into shareholders, electoral reform, formation of a "health corps" and a "reconstruction corps," antiprofiteering and anticorruption campaigns, and social insurance.

A closer analysis reveals internal contradictions. In spite of his assertion that the revolution was based on national values, its overriding target was modernization and its model were the developed western societies. But in the shah's mind, the advancement of the state, the glorification of his rule, and the consolidation of his dynasty were one indivisible whole. Consequently, as in other monolithic systems, the shah's social and economic policies became totally subordinated to political considerations.[16] Whittling down the power bases of the tra-

10. For the shah's delineation of his aims, see his books *Revolution*, 24; *Tamaddon*, 250.

11. See, for example, the shah's interview with Varenne in *Kayhan*, 20 November 1976.

12. Pahlavi, *Revolution*, 22.

13. E. A. Bayne, *Persian Kingship in Transition* (New York: American Universities Field Staff, 1968), 101–2.

14. Pahlavi, *Revolution*, 1–24.

15. Upon its approval, the program included six articles. Thirteen others were added as follows: six (articles 7 to 12) up to October 1967; five (articles 13 to 17) between August and December 1975; and the remaining two in August 1977.

16. For such considerations in similar political systems, see S. N. Eisenstadt, "Patterns of Stratification in Middle Eastern Societies—Comparative Notes on the Question of

ditional elites and enlisting mass support for his own rule were therefore essential. Religious loyalty had to be placed at the service of national loyalty.

Previous phases of the modernization process in the Middle East had not achieved profound changes in the social and political stratification,[17] because the traditional power groups had consistently impeded modernization and circumscribed power at the center. They still posed a challenge to the shah as well. Hence the need, in his own words, to replace the "old archaic order" by a "new order."[18] New elites, owing their existence and advancement to the shah alone, were needed. The place of the landlords, the ulama, the Bazar merchants, and the nomadic tribes (who should be disarmed and settled) was to be taken by a new industrial and agro-industrial, commercial, administrative, and military upper class—all bound in loyalty to the shah. Prominent clerics were to be enlisted to give religious legitimization to his rule and his policies, intellectuals to explain them and rally public support. The army and the SAVAK were further built up to provide additional support for the political system.

The shah did want progress, most particularly in agriculture and education. But he firmly believed that reforms could only succeed through initiatives from above. He often declared that if Iran needed a revolution, he wanted to lead it himself.[19] An alliance between the throne and the people would further neutralize the old elites and prevent the rise of a popular opposition.[20] Political development and popular participation, however, could well be postponed until after the completion of the reforms.[21]

Differentiation and Convergence on Modern Societies," *Hamizrah Hehadash* [Hebrew], 26 (1976), 172, 178. On the primacy of political consideration in the shah's decision making, see Norman Jacobs, *The Sociology of Development: Iran as an Asian Case Study* (New York: Praeger, 1966), 416–19.

17. Eisenstadt, "Stratification," 178; Morroe Berger, "The Middle Class in the Arab World," in Walter Z. Laqueur, ed., *The Middle East in Transition: Studies in Contemporary History* (New York: 1968), 67–71; James A. Bill, "Class Analysis and Dialectics of Modernization in the Middle East," *IJMES*, 3 (1972), 417–34; Nikki Keddie, "The Iranian Power Structure and Social Change 1800–1969, An Overview," *IJMES*, 2 (1971), 3–20.

18. Pahlavi, *Revolution*, 14.

19. Idem, *Ta'lifat*, 2:1976–79.

20. Idem, *Tamaddon*, 2–15; and interviews in *Kayhan*, 20 November and 8 December 1976.

21. The gap between modernization and political development has been stressed by Samuel P. Huntington. He asserts that modernization (as seen in Asia, Africa, and Latin America) did not necessarily result in political development. On the contrary, "rapid

But the alliance with the people proved hollow. The "Revolution of the Shah and the People" remained the shah's alone. Of his first years on the throne, he said: "I witnessed the fate of my country not from the inside but from above, isolated and alone."[22] He might well have said that of the closing period of his reign, too.

An important means of promoting his policies was the channeling of religious sentiment so as to reinforce national loyalty. He spoke of the "sanctity" of the homeland (*vatan*), explained his "mission" in religious terms, and made use of Islamic traditions to legitimize his reforms.[23] Yet at the same time he promoted secularization, worked to separate state and religion, and wished to restrict clerics to matters of faith and ritual. The "Great Civilization" was to be based on ancient Iranian culture and western science, not on Islam. The religious establishment, he held, was a barrier to modernization and national integration and a permanent threat to the monarchy.

As his power increased, his references to Islam became rarer. In proclaiming the White Revolution in 1963, the shah had demanded total loyalty to God (*khoda*), Shah, and Homeland (*mihan*). Though alien to the spirit of Islam, this still left some room for religion. Twelve years later, when he formed the Rastakhiz (Resurrection) party, he declared that loyalty was due to the monarchical order, the constitution, and the White Revolution.[24] God no longer figured in the list. Yet he reaffirmed his faith in Islam[25] and continued to use religious terms to describe his mission—sometimes even using terms offending the pure religious feelings of the believers: "I was convinced that God had ordained me to do certain things for the service of my nation.... I considered myself as an agent of the will of God."[26] And again: "My reign has saved the country ... because God was on my side."[27]

Despite the wide scope of the White Revolution program, the shah pushed for rapid implementation. For one thing, he wanted to see it

---

modernization ... produced not political development but political decay" (Huntington, "Political Development and Political Decay," *World Politics*, 17 [1964/5], 386–430).

22. Pahlavi, *Revolution*, 8.

23. Ibid., 16, 103–6. In 1976, he told Varrene that basing the revolution on Islam had encouraged popular support for it (*Kayhan*, 14 November 1976).

24. *Ettela'at*, 3 March 1975.

25. Pahlavi, *Mission*, 54–58. Similarly in interviews in *Kayhan*, 7 November 1976; Karanjia, 56; and in an interview with Oriana Falacci in *New Republic*, 1 December 1973, 15–21.

26. Pahlavi, *Revolution*, 16.

27. *New Republic*, 1 December 1973, 15–21.

completed in his lifetime; for another, he feared that the pace of prog
ress in the industrial countries would make it impossible to bridge the
gap later on. And last, he realized that the program must be carried
out before oil revenue gave out.[28]

This sense of time running short was one reason that the shah set
aside his declared adherence to democracy and liberty[29] and preferred
totalitarian methods instead: he acted on the principle that ends sanc
tified means. "Advice and guidance and recourse to ordinary parlia
mentary methods were not enough," he wrote in 1966.[30] Enforcement
and the suppression of any sign of opposition were therefore necessary
In the mid-1970s, he conceded that contrary to his intentions the rev
olution had not been "white" and that "blood was shed in its course."[31]

Many of the White Revolution reform programs were not well
thought out, inadequately prepared, and not suited to the Iranian real
ities. Oftentimes prestige and quantity were more important than qual
ity and sober usefulness. Timetables were unrealistically tight. The
primacy of political considerations vitiated results. All this was as true
of the educational reforms as of any other field.

All in all, the fact that the reform programs were a priori subordinated
to political considerations and compacted into a tight unrealistic time
table significantly influenced the nature of the reforms and their ulti
mate results. The educational reforms were no exception.

---

28. According to Iranian statistics at that time, if production continued at the 197
rate, oil reserves would run out before the turn of the century. The shah's apprehension
in this regard were expressed in interviews in *Kayhan*, 25 October and 16 December 1976
In an interview with Varrene he said that "in twenty or thirty years" the population
would number about sixty-five million and "we will have no oil." If Iran did not mod
ernize fast, it would face grave problems (*Kayhan*, 20 November 1976).

29. See his books *Mission*, 161–94; *Revolution*, 1–24; *Tamaddon*, 291–99.

30. Pahlavi, *Revolution*, 12.

31. *KI*, 26 September 1976; *Kayhan*, 5 November 1976.

8

The "Blessings" of Education

The shah, his cabinet ministers, the intellectuals, and the education-alists often had differing, sometimes widely divergent, concepts of the essence and aims of educational reform, but they—as well as broad sections of the public at large—were united in the belief that education was the magic wand for producing the results they desired for themselves and for their country. Such overoptimism was common to many developing countries and, as has been noted, had emerged in Iran before. But it was most strongly marked in the second half of Mohammad Reza's reign. Individuals expected education to aid them personally in climbing the social ladder; the government, and perhaps even more so the intellectuals (in particular the educationalists), believed it would place the entire nation on a new footing.

The Shah's View

Mohammad Reza Shah himself fully shared that belief.[1] Three out of the nineteen articles of his White Revolution dealt with the "educational revolution" (*enqelab-e amuzeshi*; see Chapters 9, 10 and 11). In his view, education was not merely an instrument for the modernization of Iran but also a means for enlisting popular support and consolidating the monarchy. It was this, he conceded, which dictated the

---

1. Pahlavi, *Ta'lifat*, 2:2075.

essence and rhythm of the educational reforms.[2] In his mind, imparting character values, fostering new loyalties, and teaching "useful skills" were all part and parcel of education. Character formation (*tarbiyyat* or *parvaresh*) took prominence over instruction (*ta'lim* or *amuzesh*); but *tarbiyyat* must be subordinated to the regime's philosophy, while *ta'lim* must serve to train the manpower it needed. Like his father, he was not concerned with philosophical questions about the moral right of the state to instill in its citizens a set of values laid down from above. Having set himself an ideal—that of the "Great Civilization"—he wished to use education to bring it about.[3] Under his direction, he believed, education was sure to fulfill all his expectations.[4] He was fond of quoting studies pointing to the impact of education on children at a tender age and was convinced that education must come to include children "from the mother's breast to the university."[5] Later, referring to UNESCO studies on the influence of early nutrition on child development, he revised that to read "from the womb." Consequently, in 1975, he added article 16 to the program of the White Revolution; this article dealt with providing nutrition for infants and pregnant women.[6]

The shah stated his views on education right from the start. Only one month after ascending the throne, he said in a speech that only education could steer the "national ship" (*kashti-ye vatan*) toward the "shore of progress. (*sahel-e taraqqi*), happiness (*se'adat*), and progress (*pishraft*)."[7] Years later, with the consistency characteristic of his views and statements in this respect, he spoke of education as the best "national investment."[8] More specifically, he held that education was a prime agent for developing national consciousness and safeguarding

2. Ibid., 2:2084.

3. Gondi Shapur, 2:172; Pahlavi, *Ta'lifat*, 2:1692.

4. For an example of such optimism, see Pahlavi, *Ta'lifat*, 4:3024–30.

5. This was declared to be the framework of the Educational Revolution at the first educational conference in Gochsar, 1967: *Konferans-e Gochsar*, MAM, document 4714, p. 8. For such definition by the shah, see V'U, *Sevvomin Konferans-e Arzyabi-ye Enqelab-e Amuzeshi, Ramsar 1970*, 10; idem, *Chaharomin Konferans-e Arzyabi-ye Enqelab-e Amuzeshi, Ramsar 1971*, 2. On the annual conferences on education, see Chapter 10.

6. *Kayhan*, 24 December 1975. The importance of this extension of the educational reform was emphasized by Dr. Rahnama (the first minister of science and higher education) as far back as 1964. See Majid Rahnama, *Amuzesh dar Khedmat-e Ensan* (Tehran: Amir Kabir, 1971?), 1:63, 72, 77; 2:104–5.

7. Speech of 26 October 1941, quoted by Gondi Shapur, 2:71–72; similarly Pahlavi, *Ta'lifat*, 2:902; and his speech of 16 August 1954: Gondi Shapur, 2:124–25.

8. Pahlavi, *Ta'lifat*, 4:3024–30, 3592–96, 3621, 3725, 4332–36; idem, *Mission*, 171–86; Gondi Shapur, 2:127.

national unity. National unity would in turn lead to political and economic independence. To make this possible, all his subjects should have comparable schooling, all should have a knowledge of the country's cultural heritage and history, and all—including the linguistic minorities—should be taught Persian.[9] In regarding the spread of "the spirit of patriotism" (*ruh-e mihan parasti*) as the "holy duty" (*vazife-ye moqaddas*) of education,[10] Mohammad Reza was greatly influenced by his father, but he made such thoughts his own and emphasized them throughout his reign, most firmly during periods of political strength.[11]

The shah's tendency to equate education and patriotism was brought to bear on the annual education conferences held from 1968 on. Already at the first one, which laid down the framework of educational reform, the resolutions stated explicitly that the schools—including the universities—must make the preservation and spread of national culture one of their main targets.[12] The third (1970) resolved that in the modern world, which had abandoned "moral and spiritual values ... in the process of splendid technological progress," Iranian education must "make special efforts for the preservation, renewal and glorification of the national cultural heritage."[13] The fifth conference (1972) went a step farther and made it the schools' "national mission (*resalat*) and responsibility (*mas'uliyyat*)" to work for "strengthening attachment to the nation and ... national pride."[14] In 1973, the shah told the conference that education must foster an "atmosphere of patriotism." Taking its cue from him, the conference passed resolutions outlining plans to turn schools into "bases for patriotism."[15]

To the shah, national loyalty meant loyalty to the monarchy as an

9. Pahlavi, *Tamaddon*, 136–50, and *Ta'lifat*, 5:4484–85; interview with the Indian paper *Blitz* (22 May 1966) as cited in: Ramesh Sanghvi, *Aryamehr the Shah of Iran: A Political Biography* (London: Transorient, 1968), 314.

10. Pahlavi, *Ta'lifat*, 2:939–43. He expressed similar views when visiting Dar al-Fonun (22 December 1938) and Tehran University (29 December 1937); see *Ta'lifat*, 2:940, 944–45.

11. Ibid., 3:2134, 2154; Gondi Shapur, 2:104–5, 114–15.

12. V'U, *Konferans-e Enqelab-e Amuzeshi, Ramsar 1968*, clauses 13 and 14 of the resolutions: V'U/MTBRA.

13. *KAEA, 1970*, articles 7 and 19 of the resolutions.

14. V'U, *Panjomin Konferans-e Arzyabi-ye Enqelab-e Amuzeshi, Ramsar 1972*, articles 1 and 5 of the resolutions: V'U, secretariat of the educational conference.

15. V'U, *Sheshomin Konferans-e Arzyabi-ye Enqelab-e Amuzeshi, Ramsar 1973*, the shah's speech on pp. 5–9, and articles 34–37 of the resolutions: V'U, secretariat of the educational conference. For similar themes in 1974 and 1975, see V'U, *Haftomin Konferans-e Arzyabi-ye Enqelab-e Amuzeshi, Ramsar 1974*, mainly article 4 of the resolutions; V'U, *Hashtomin Konferans-e Arzyabi-ye Enqelab-e Amuzeshi, Ramsar 1975*, articles 1 and 2 of the resolutions: V'U, secretariat of the educational conference.

institution and to him personally. Already as crown prince he asked teachers at the Tehran Teachers Seminar to foster in their students "the spirit of devotion to God (*Khoda-parasti*), love of the shah (*Shah-dusti*), and patriotism"—as an unseparable triad.[16] This theme came through most explicitly almost forty years later, in 1975, when he established the Rastakhiz party. That year's educational conference addressed itself to "Teaching the Principles and Meaning of Rastakhiz" and resolved that it was the aim of the schools to teach the young generation "the philosophy of the Iranian revolution" so as to prepare them to become "more competent servants (*khedmatgozaran-e shayeste-tar*) of the shahanshah and the homeland." For this purpose, it recommended:

(1) "The foundations of Iranian nationalism, the development of Iranian culture, the principles and ideology of the Rastakhiz party...and the philosophy of the [White] Revolution" should be stressed at all levels of education. The Ministries of Education and Science, the universities, as well as all other schools must revise their syllabuses and textbook accordingly, for the change to take effect as of the 1977/8 academic year.

(2) "The teaching of the principles of the Rastakhiz [party]...should also be emphasized in the extracurricular activities of educational institutions."[17]

The schools were thus to become recruiting grounds for a new educated class that would combine the cognitive skills the country needed for its modernization with utter loyalty to, and identification with, the regime. Its members would eventually form a new elite certain to become another pillar of support for his rule.[18] At the same time, the people at large would be grateful for the schooling increasingly available to them, in addition to absorbing the contents the shah had infused it with. Popular support would thus stem from logic and conscious choice, underpinned by material gain, mainly from the agrarian reform. Thus, he believed, would the perpetuation of the regime be ensured.[19]

16. Pahlavi, *Ta'lifat*, 2:941–43 (from a speech on 20 January 1938).

17. *KAEA, 1975*, pp. 4–5.

18. For these aims of the shah, see Pahlavi, *Ta'lifat*, 2:2134, 2154. For his methods of recruiting elite support, see Zonis, *Elite*, 80–117, 134–98.

19. Pahlavi, *Revolution*, 111; MAM, document 330, pp. 1–3, 9; Ramesh Sanghvi, Clifford German, and David Missen, *The Revolution of the Shah and People: The Literacy Corps* (London: Transorient, 1967), 23.

The View of Educationalists

In contrast to the shah, the intellectuals—particularly the professional educationalists—saw the general goal of education as man rather than state, individual rather than nation. But it should be noted that the intellectuals' specific views about education differed widely, and the following discussion attempts only to address the views most widely accepted by them. Another caveat is that many of those about to be mentioned, though opposed to the shah's policies, worked at one time or another for, or within, the existing political system. It is therefore often hard, if not impossible, to distinguish their innermost convictions from the views they expressed in paying lip service to the shah. Sometimes they proffered arguments they knew to be acceptable to the shah with the intention of obtaining results totally different from what he had in mind. Thus, for example, in an attempt to gain the shah's support for compulsory education, Siyasi stressed the role of education in fostering popular support for the regime—a view totally incompatible with his own ideas on education or on the nature of Pahlavi rule. Or again, Siyasi, Sadiq, and Kazem Vadi'i (the latter deputy minister of education from 1974 to 1977) claimed that they had agreed to serve in the Ministry of Education despite their disapproval of the shah's educational philosophy, in order to be able to influence the course of educational reform in the direction of their own beliefs.[20]

These reservations notwithstanding, one can point to some basic differences between the shah's views on the essence and function of education and those of the mainstream educationalists. Both linked the progress of the state and the well-being of the individuals, but against the shah's utilitarian-totalitarian approach, many intellectuals—most of them graduates of western universities—took their stand on tenets of liberalism. Whereas the shah proclaimed the state to be the supreme value, they tended to sanctify the individual. True, they too viewed education as ultimately serving society, but not by imposing beliefs on the individual, but rather by the latter's own logical choice. In the nature of things, the intellectuals stated their views more explicitly in periods when the shah was politically weak, and more guardedly, or not at all, when he was strong.

A keynote was sounded by Sadiq only a month after the shah's accession. In the past, he said, "responsibility rested with one who gave orders"; today "we are free." He went on:

20. Unless stated otherwise, all references to their views are based on the author's interviews with them.

If until yesterday we have only trained our children to be obedient and fulfill commands, as from now we must educate them . . . to be loyal to the will of society . . . . Today we are duty-bound to raise the children of this land to derive the utmost benefit from freedom; to be familiar with their rights; to be aware of their duties; to be able to distinguish between freedom and anarchy; not to surrender to oppression and decay; to act according to the law and the command of their conscience; and—in sum—to be citizens worthy of living in a free country.[21]

His later speeches reflect the correlation between the vigor of his liberal views and the weakness of the regime, and vice versa.[22]

On entering office, Siyasi (who soon replaced Sadiq) as the minister of education spoke of education as a lever for consolidating democracy, implementing social justice, and achieving progress. When presenting the law for compulsory education to the Majlis (29 December 1942), he said that in "developed (*motaraqqi*) and civilized (*motamadden*) states which enjoy freedom" governments consider schooling as a step toward political freedom and social justice.[23] During the debate he added:

A preliminary condition for a democratic regime is general and compulsory education. If we wish to have democratic rule, we must implement this principle . . . . A democratic reign is based on its members being aware of their rights and duties . . . . [For this, they must] be able to read and write and have some knowledge of the geography and history of their country . . . . One of the reasons for the existence of dictatorship is lack of knowledge and illiteracy and the peoples' ignorance of their rights . . . . [In the past] periods of . . . strength always occurred under the leadership . . . [of] dictators. Upon their downfall, the country became weak . . . . It is not appropriate any more to continue along these lines. People must govern their own affairs and become themselves the source of their progress and happiness . . . . And this is possible [only by] advancing education.[24]

Although Siyasi held such views throughout the period under review, he put them forward unequivocally and publicly only at times when the shah's position was weak—mainly in the early 1940s when Siyasi was minister of education, in the early 1950s when he was chan-

21. Radio Tehran, 23 October 1941, cited in *AP*, 1941/2, 5–6: xviii–xxiii. For similar views in his memoirs, see *Yadegar*, 3:1–233.
22. A collection of forty of his speeches appeared in book form under the title *Chehel Goftar*. Compare his speeches of 1966 (*Chehel Goftar*, 7–9), 1967 (10–15), and 1970 (313–18) with his speech of 1948 (192–202).
23. *MM*, term 13, 1943.
24. Ibid., 2742–43.

cellor of Tehran University, and again since 1978.[25] At these times, many others came forward to express similar views. One of the most prominent to do so in the 1950s and early 1960 was Dr. Mohammad Derakhshesh.[26]

In periods when the shah's position was strong, such opinions were still heard, but they were worded cautiously to avoid any appearance of criticizing the regime. There were many general references to education being capable of furthering liberty, equality, and the good of the individual—not just the good of the state. Examples are provided by the writings of Dr. Mohammad Masha'ekhi,[27] Dr. Majid Rahnama,[28] and Shapur Rasekh.[29] They and many others[30] held that individuals as well as the nation as a whole would benefit from exercising freedom of thought rather than by having the views of the regime imposed on them.[31] But when they found the shah's position to be strong, they played down their differences with him and searched for a common denominator. They were, after all, in complete agreement with him

25. See, for example, his views cited in *Kayhan*, 20 August 1978.

26. Derakhshesh became head of the teachers' organization in the early 1960s, when he also served for a brief period as minister of education. For his views as expressed in 1953 and 1978, see Mohammad Derakhshesh, "Aya Tahsilat-e Dabirestani va Daneshgahi Bayad Hamegani Bashad?" *AP*, 1953/4, 9:10–13; *Ettela'at*, 30 August 1978. The author's interview with him took place in Paris in August 1982 and in Washington, D.C., in April 1988.

27. Masha'ekhi held prominent positions in the Ministry of Education from the 1950s. From 1973 onward, he was head of the Tehran Teachers Seminar. See his articles: "Hadaf-e Ta'limat-e Ejtema'i," *AP*, 1956/7, 792–94; "Manzur az Tajdid Nazar dar Barname-ye Dowre-ye Avval-e Dabirestanha Che Bude Ast?" *AP*, 1956/7, 771–75; "Hadaf-e Ta'limat-e Motavasete dar Iran," *AP*, 1964/5, 9:1–17; "Ba'zi az Masa'el va Moshkelat-e Javanan-e Iran dar Dowre-ye Motavasete," *AP*, 1960/70, 8:1–5; "Mafhum-e Amuzesh-e Motavasete," *Nashriye Daneshkade-ye 'Ulum-e Tarbiyyati*, 3: no. 2 (Winter 1973), 6–11.

28. Rahnama was one of the leading intellectuals during the years of the White Revolution. He was the first minister of science and higher education (1967–1971); see Rahnama, 1:57–63, 79–80.

29. Rasekh was deputy minister of the Plan and Budget Organization (1974–1977). His views are stated in his book *Ta'lim va Tarbiyyat dar Jehan-e Emruz* (Tehran: Amir Kabir, 1970), 37–38.

30. For example: Ma'sume 'Alame, "Lozum Taqviyyat-e Faza'el-e Akhlaqi dar Madares," *AP*, 1951/2, 4:30–32; 'Ali Abadi, "Ta'limat-e 'Aliye va Rah-e Eslah-e An," *AP*, 1949/50, 3:6–11; 'Ali Barzegar, *Siyasat-e 'Ilmi va Nowsazi-ye Ejtema'i* (Tehran: MTBRA, 1976), 28–32; Hadi Sharifi, "Hadaf va Falsafe-ye Amuzesh-e Motavasete," *Nashriye Daneshkade-ye 'Ulum-e Tarbiyyati*, 3 (Winter 1973), 13–24.

31. Abadi, 6–11; Masha'ekhi, *Amuzesh Ejtema'i*, 792–99; Derakhshesh, *Amuzesh Motavasete*, 10–13; 'Alame, 30–32; Sadiq, *Chehel Goftar*, 31–32; 'Aliqoli Behmanbaz, "Ta'limat-e Ejbari," *AP*, 1948/9, 1:12–15; 'Abbas Shaji'i, "Az Amuzesh Che Mikhahim?" *AP*, 1952/3, 3:460–62.

about the crucial role of education as such, whatever specific view one might take.

The Popular View

Appreciation of education is a common feature among the lower strata of developing countries. They think of it, first and foremost, as a kind of magic to release their children from the vicious circle of poverty and backwardness in which they themselves are caught.[32] Theirs is an "undiscriminating faith" in the power of education to automatically confer status and prestige, not only upon the child but also upon the family.[33] In Iran, a highly developed motivation for acquiring education had been rooted in past traditions. In addition, it was now being encouraged by scholars (foreign and native) and by the shah. The upshot was that most people viewed education as the best, and often enough the only, chance to rescue children from the fate of their elders.

In my travels in different regions of the country (mainly in Lorestan, Kurdistan, Fars, Mazanderan, Gilan, and Isfahan), I was impressed by the fact that education was held in high regard even in the most remote regions. The most striking example I came across was the small village of Razun in Lorestan. The village had no running water, no electricity, no sanitation, not even a public *hamam* (bath house). Yet when I asked the villagers what they needed most, they had only one answer: "The only thing we really need is a school. Only that can assure our children a better life than ours." The lower urban class had a similar attitude.[34] As in other developing countries, the only exceptions were the nomadic tribal

32. For a striking example from rural Punjab, see Hanson and Brembeck, 1–14.

33. William J. Plutt, "Conflicts in Educational Planning," in Coleman, ed., *Education and Political Development*, 566. Compare also: Michel Debeauvais, "Education in Former French Africa," in the same volume, 89; C. D. Taiwo, "Planning Science Education" and Kosonike Thomas, "Training of Scientists and Technologists in Developing Countries," (unpublished papers presented to the Rehovot Conference on Science and Education in Developing States, 18–26 August 1969), 1–2. For a similar approach in other developing countries, see Bert F. Hoselitz, "Investment in Education and Its Political Impact," in Coleman, *Education and Political Development*, 220.

34. In a survey conducted in 1969 among 141 heads of families studying at a UNESCO project in Iran, 40 percent said the reason they had decided to study was to secure themselves a better life; only 12 percent said they studied to secure a better income (Derk Kinnane, "Iran: Bringing Literacy and Work Skills Together," *Panorama* [Magazine of the International Labour Organization, Geneva], 49 [1971], 19, 21).

groups,[35] who, in my meetings with them showed no evidence of a similar regard for education. Government efforts to encourage education among them had had little success.[36]

In somewhat more specific terms, the popular view was that the schools had two tasks: to form the students' character, and to prepare them for "respected" employment. The first meant teaching them morals and values (mainly religious) as well as good manners; the second meant rescuing them from manual labor by training them for office work. In the popular view, education was meant not to train better farmers or urban workers capable of advancing agriculture or industry, but to release students from ever having to engage in such fields.[37]

In many respects, the urban middle classes and the elite shared this attitude. The former saw education, in particular a university education, as the best means towards upward social and economic mobility, eventually enabling them to join the elites. For the upper classes, education became an even more essential means of preserving their elite status. In time, they sought more advanced degrees and a more exclusive education (preferably at prestigious universities in the West). In this way they could still stay a jump ahead of the middle classes.[38] Even those who kept opposing the new education—namely the clerics and the landlords—did so from an (often exaggerated) appreciation of its power.

The combined impact of such attitudes was to generate a fast-growing demand for education which in turn led to its rapid expansion, mainly at the pre-university level. It also produced graduates who had higher expectations for employment, which the regime found extremely hard to meet.

35. Debeauvais, 89.

36. For such efforts, see: Arasteh, 18–19; *KI*, 15, 22 January 1969, 8 July 1970, 26 January 1971.

37. On the connection between education and the escape from agriculture in developing countries, see Hoselits, 547–48; Debeauvais, 89. For a warning in 1963 by the minister of education, Parviz Khanlari, in this regard, see "Hal va Ayande-ye Farhang-e ma," *AP*, 1962/3, 12:14–16.

38. Zonis, *Elite*, 163–76.

9
Pre-University Education

The development of higher education under Mohammad Reza Shah cannot be followed without first taking a close look at elementary and secondary education during his reign, from the 1940s to the 1970s.

The most rapid expansion of the pre-university educational system occurred during the years of White Revolution when the shah was firmly in control, and therefore largely reflects his personal direction (as well as the improved economic situation). While popular expectations were centered on higher education, the shah's emphasis was on elementary and secondary education, whose broader numerical base served his goals better. This led to a certain conflict of interests. Moreover, there was the challenge of how to expand education further and, at the same time, raise the quality of teaching and adjust schooling to meet the newly emerging needs of society. This chapter deals with the regime's attempts to meet these challenges, and presents statistics on the number of students moving through the educational system, beginning with entry into the elementary schools and up to university admission.

Elementary Education

The Compulsory Education Law (1943)

The concept of compulsory education, under a law to that effect, had come to the fore in western Europe mainly in the nineteenth

172

century.[1] It stemmed from the political philosophy of that time and from a changed perception of the social functions of education: no longer the privilege of the few, but the right and duty of all. In the Middle East, compulsory education laws were first enacted after World War I: in Egypt in 1925; in Turkey in 1926; in Iraq not until 1940.[2] Here, too, the law reflected changing political and social thought, without much regard for the administrative and professional capability to provide education for all.

In Iran, the idea dated back to the eve of the Constitutional Revolution. (For its inclusion in the 1906 constitution and for the Fundamental Law of Education of 1911, see Chapter 4.) But it required the reassertion of liberal thinking and the weakness of the central government during World War II to move from the enunciation of a principle to the actual passage of a law. As had been the case in 1906, the 1943 legislation was initiated not by the shah but by the liberal movements, more precisely by a group of intellectuals (mostly on the staff of Tehran University) who had themselves studied in the West. The driving force was Siyasi; others in the group were Mas'ud Kayhan, Sa'id Malek, and Sa'id Nafisi. According to Siyasi, the group has discussed such a law back in the 1930s but had not regarded it feasible under Reza Shah. The change of regime gave them their opportunity. With his appointment as minister of education in 1942, Siyasi went to work.

The law was approved on 28 June 1943. It stated that six years of universal, free, and compulsory schooling were to be introduced throughout the country over the following ten years. (During the first five years, the Ministry of Education was entitled to limit compulsory education to a four-year course.) Appropriate school buildings would be designated in each district, and parents failing to send their children to school would be severely punished. Further clauses of the law provided for the establishment of teachers seminars for graduates of the fifth grade of the compulsory schools.[3]

Siyasi, who suspected that he would not be in office for long, feared that he might be replaced by a minister likely to obstruct the implemen-

---

1. The first such law was enacted in Scotland as early as 1560. Some minor German states followed in the seventeenth century and France in 1690. Effective implementation, however, dates from the nineteenth century.

2. Roderic D. Mathews and Matta Akrawi, *Education in the Arab Countries of the Near East* (Washington, D.C.: American Council of Education, 1949), 20–21, 128–29, 340–41; UNESCO, *Compulsory Education in the Arab World* (Paris, 1954), 22, 25; Szyliowicz, 181–83, 208; Helen Miller Davis, *Constitutions, Electoral Laws, Treaties of States in the Middle East* (New York: Amis Press, 1970), 27, 153.

3. For the text of the law, see MQ, term 13, 53–58.

tation of the law. He therefore prepared ministerial guidelines for its implementation and had the Majlis approve them (although the approval of operative ministerial directives by the House was not mandatory).[4] Siyasi did in fact lose his post after a few months, but became minister of education once again in 1948. On 2 December of that year he gained Majlis approval for a supplementary law obliging the ministry to allocate in each of the ten years from 1948/9 to 1958/9 no less than 80 percent of its total budget to implementation of the 1943 law. The supplement also stipulated that local councils would finance schools under their jurisdictions, that landlords would have to participate by means of a special levy in the establishment of village schools, and that the government was to provide special incentives for the teaching profession.[5]

The new political realities and Siyasi's personal commitment combined to push the legislation through. Sadiq, who had been Mohammad Reza's first minister of education, supported the idea in principle but thought that in light of the actual condition of the educational system the law came too soon. Siyasi disputed that, and even in 1977, when the law had still been carried out only in part, he told me that if he had had his way it could have been implemented in the first ten years allowed by the law.

Supporters of the compulsory education law in the Majlis spoke of education as the single most important factor in promoting both the well-being of the individual and the progress of the country. This was most forcefully argued in the speeches of Rahnama, Hashemi, Ruhi, Mo'ayyed Ahmadi, Adham, Anvar, Hadheqi, Dashti, Afshar, Farhudi, Ganje'i, 'Adl Vothqa al-Islami, and Emami Aheri.[6]

Such views on the role of education led Siyasi and his colleagues to demand first of all the development of elementary education. In a

4. Text in *MQ*, term 13, 326–46. Unless stated otherwise, the views of Siyasi and Sadiq cited here were expressed in interviews I held with them.

5. *MM*, term 15, 2570–71.

6. Ibid., term 13, 2737, 2749–53, 2797–99, 3044–49, 3057–61, 3075, 3111, 3117–18, 3127–28, 3137. Similar views were expressed in the House after the approval of the law: *MM*, term 14, 1156–57, 1184–87; term 15, 2622, 2635, 2685–88. Arguing from the point of view of social justice, some deputies suggested a gradual implementation—beginning with the outlying provinces; or advocated free education only for the lower classes: *MM*, term 13, 3045, 3137 (Mo'ayyed Ahmadi), 3057–58, 3137 (Tabataba'i), 3061, 3127–28 (Anvar), 2757 (Sakenyan); term 14, 1184–86 ('Adl Vothqa al-Islami). Numerous articles published between 1941 and 1946 made similar points, for example: Lotf'ali Suratgar, "Ahmiyyat-e Amuzesh va Parvaresh-e 'Omumi va Ejbari," *AP*, 1943/4, 1–3:1–10; 'Abbas Shuqi, "Chera be Madrese Miravim?" *AP*, 1944/5, 65–67; Rabi' Badi'i, "Tarbiyyat va Tahiyye Mo'allem," ibid., 156–58; 'Amele Baradaran, "'Ilm va Ma'refat va Ahmiyyat-e an dar Zendegi," ibid., 512–14.

speech over Radio Tehran on 18 August 1943, Siyasi appealed to Majlis members and the public in general to bring pressure to bear on the government in this regard. Governments, he claimed, tended to emphasize higher education, since the inauguration of colleges and universities was marked by "festive ceremonies," whereas the establishment of elementary schools provided no occasion to be "exhibitionist."[7] (In 1977, he was to add that higher education had priority in order to satisfy the elite groups who tended to view the expansion of popular education as a threat to their status.) Back in the 1940s, however, this point was explicitly and publicly made only by Dr. Reza Radmanesh (from the Tudeh party), who told the Majlis that public interest dictated giving preference to elementary education because universities were open "only to the children of the rich."[8]

The desire for rapid expansion as measured against the limited facilities then available once again raised the issue of quantity versus quality. Like many earlier intellectuals, Siyasi believed in quantity. With the recent wartime food shortages in mind, he said the question of whether to give a tiny minority a "perfect education" or provide "minimal education" to all was like asking whether to give white bread to a few and let the others starve or supply coarse bread to all.[9]

Opposition to the law came mainly from the elites. The ulama, always resentful of modern education, were at that time busy trying to regain the position of strength they had had before Reza Shah. Landlords and heads of guilds probably feared that the law would deprive them of the economic benefits of child labor. But whereas the initial upper-class resistance in the West ended in the nineteenth century,[10] in Iran it persisted. For the most part, however, it was not made explicit or expressed publicly. Rather, behind-the-scenes pressure was brought to bear on the court and the Majlis to prevent the passage of the law. Siyasi was threatened and "advised" to withdraw the draft.[11] He said the shah had told him that Majlis deputies representing elite groups had tried to convince him to withhold his support, arguing that the spread of education was bound to expose the country to Communist

7. For the text of the address, see *AP*, 1943/4, 1–3:iii–iv.

8. *MM*, term 14, 1186–87.

9. Ibid., term 13, 2743–44, 3085–86. Cf. Chapter 5 for a similar preference by Taqizade.

10. For similar conflicts in the West, see the views of Bowles, Gintis, Levitas, and Katz in this regard as given in Hurn, 32, 66–70.

11. Siyasi made this statement in an interview with me. Similarly in an interview of his with *Majale Daneshkade-ye Adabiyyat va 'Ulum-e Ensani*, 93–94 (1976/7), 16–17. For the opposition of the "ruling elites" to the law, see also Lotfi'ali Suratgar's talk on Radio Tehran cited in *AP*, 1943/4, 1–3:5–7.

influence and liable to threaten the regime and endanger Iran's territorial integrity. Siyasi replied that, on the contrary, education under government control would hold down such tendencies and make for greater loyalty to the regime and the country.

The shah's own view does not emerge with sufficient clarity from the available evidence. On taking power he declared his support for universal education and took some (mainly symbolic) steps to promote education for the underprivileged.[12] Yet according to Siyasi, he later allowed himself to be influenced by the opponents of the law and tried to postpone its enactment. But, whether from his basic sympathy with it or from political weakness, he failed to delay it. This did not prevent him from saying in the 1970s: "In 1943, I *forced* the *Majlis* to pass a law providing for free compulsory education."[13]

In the Majlis, criticism of the law turned mainly on two arguments—whether proffered sincerely or as an indirect means of torpedoing the project is hard to say. One claimed that since the principle of compulsory education had already been incorporated in the constitution and because its implementation was currently impossible, the law was unnecessary.[14] The other asserted that the present deficiencies of the school system should first be removed.[15] Against them, supporters of the law, headed by Siyasi and the chairmen of the education and budget committees (Hashemi and Amir Taymur), argued that despite the clause in the constitution, only the projected law could make the implementation of universal education mandatory; furthermore, to suspend legislation until all the defects of educational system were removed was tantamount to "postponing it forever."[16] Eventually, the law was passed; but thirty-five years later, at the end of Mohammad Reza Shah's reign, it had still only been partially carried out.

When it became the government's turn to take up the law and carry it out, a curious inversion occurred, made possible by a deliberate misinterpretation of its text on the part of the administrators. The law had called for gradual implementation, that is, as schools

---

12. See his decree of 29 September 1941 (a week after his accession), waiving tuition fees for the underprivileged (Gondi Shapur, 2:68). See also the memoirs of Sadiq (*Yadegar*, 3:41–134).

13. Karanjia, 164 (emphasis added).

14. See the views of Majlis members Tabataba'i, Rezvi, Sangyan, Naraqi, and Majd Ziya'i: *MM*, term 13, 2738–40, 2746–51, 3044, 3048, 3127–28; term 14, 1157–62.

15. See the views of Majlis members Tabataba'i, Rezvi, and Malekzade: *MM*, term 13, 2738–40, 2746, 2753, 2799–2800, 2829.

16. *MM*, term 13, 2743–44, 2751, 2757, 2749, 2800–2802, 2807–9, 3042.

became available in district after district, so local parents were to assume the responsibility of sending their children to school. But the government acted on the assumption that the clause obliging it to provide classrooms, teachers, textbooks, and so forth, was in fact no more than a *recommendation*, while the duty of parents to send children to school continued to be thought of as an unconditional legal obligation. In principle, the onus was thus shifted from the administration to the parents, in complete disregard of the intentions of the Majlis.

In practice, the following routine was adopted: from time to time, the government declared that facilities for compulsory education had been provided in one particular district and a royal *firman* (decree) then proclaimed them to exist there. The first such *firman* was issued in April 1949 for the towns of Astara and Qazvin. Three more *firmans*, in 1950, 1951, and 1956, listed another sixty-one towns. After 1971, however, they became much more frequent and included some of the large cities: Kerman, Semnan, and Zanjan in 1971; Bandar Pahlavi, Ahvaz, Abadan, Meshhed, Zahedan, and Sanandaj in 1972; Shemiran (north of Tehran), Kashan, Hamadan, Isfahan, and Shiraz in 1973. In some large cities, compulsory education had still not been specifically declared by the time the shah's rule came to an end.[17] Available information is insufficient to determine what percentage of the total school-age population in the country was found in the districts declared to have compulsory education. What is certain is that even there, attendance was far from being complete.

When the pre-university educational system was restructured into elementary (grades one to five), intermediary (grades six to eight), and secondary (grades nine to twelve) schools in 1971/2, the Majlis amended the 1943 law. The amendment, passed on 4 May 1972, extended compulsory education to the intermediary schools, but stipulated that this clause would only take effect "after completion of the implementation of the first phase [i.e., the first five grades] throughout the country."[18] There was no timetable for the conclusion, or even the inception, of implementing the extension. In fact, it was carried out comparatively quickly. Attendance at intermediary schools was made free but—because of the above qualification—not compulsory, and for obvious reasons they sprang up in regions where elementary schools already existed. Ironically, the actual effect of the amendment was to reduce

17. MAM, documents 301, 321, 409–11.
18. Ibid., document 320.

compulsory education from six to five years in most parts of the country.

Rural Education and the Literacy Corps

The implementation of compulsory education was slow everywhere, but much more so in the rural and tribal areas. In 1961/2, according to official statistics, 46.6 percent of all children between six and ten attended school—not an impressive figure considering almost two decades had passed since enactment of the 1943 law. But out of the total school population, only 39 percent came from the rural or tribal regions where some 65 percent of the overall population were then living. At the inception of the White Revolution in 1962/3, 74 percent of the children of appropriate age were going to school in urban areas, but only 24 percent elsewhere. In the same year, only 7,000 out of more than 50,000 villages had schools. In particularly remote districts (urban and rural alike) the proportion was even lower. For example: only 16 percent of the school-age children attended school in the province of Kurdistan and 20 percent in Baluchestan in 1962/3.[19]

The shah therefore concluded that "no basic solution to the country's educational problems was possible by ordinary methods" and that for rapid advancement "revolutionary and unusual means" were essential.[20] The plan he designed in 1962 was to form a Literacy Corps (Sepah-e Danesh; literally: "Army of Knowledge") composed of high school graduates who, instead of performing their regular military service, would go out to teach in the villages. The Majlis approved two laws regulating the structure of the corps, and in January 1963 the plan was presented as the fifth article of the White Revolution. The Literacy Corps' Law of 26 October 1962, with a supplement of 3 December 1962, stipulated that members of the corps would receive four months of military and pedagogic training and then be assigned to teaching positions in remote regions; that the number of teacher-soldiers and their training schedule would be decided upon jointly by the Ministry of Education and the Ministry of War; and that those with a satisfactory record of service would later be offered employment as regular teachers (on terms equal to that of graduates of teachers seminars).[21] To en-

19. Ibid., document 330; Pahlavi, *Revolution*, 106–10; idem, *Tamaddon*, 136–39.
20. Pahlavi, *Revolution*, 109.
21. MAM, document 765; ʿAbbas Khaqani, *Barresi Tahavvolat-e Amuzesh va Parvaresh-e Iran* (Tehran: MTBRA, 1973), 42–44, 526–27.

courage education for girls in the villages, the Majlis—with the shah's encouragement—approved on 5 July 1968 the Law for Women's Social Service (*Khadamat-e Ejtema'i-ye Zanan*) setting up a similar Literacy Corps for women teachers.[22] (Men served two years, women eighteen months.)

In thus promoting rural education, the shah had a threefold aim: to improve the quality of village life, raise productivity, and create a sense of greater social justice—in short: advance modernization; propagate the philosophy of the White Revolution; and foster loyalty to it and to himself. In addressing the first group of teachers going out to the villages on 22 December 1962, the shah told them that in eradicating illiteracy they were pursuing a "sacred aim" and were paving the road toward a better life for the rural population.[23] In *The White Revolution* he wrote that the teachers brought "not just part of the revolution [i.e., education] . . . but the whole of it" to the villages.[24] In a report from the Ministry of Education to the Court Ministry the corps was termed a "vanguard soldier (*sarbaz-e pishro*) of the revolution" who explained its aims to the population and presented it "with its actual results." Teaching was only part—and not the most important part—of its work. A major task, according to the report, was to "enlighten" the villagers and acquaint them with the achievements of the regime;[25] in short, to serve as a kind of resident government agent. Furthermore, the corps was to be a link between urban and rural young people. And finally it was a means of providing employment for the growing number of high school graduates unable to gain admission to a university.[26]

In addition to teaching school, the girls recruited into the Literary Corps were to teach the rural girls and their mothers better home economics and thereby promote modernization. The very recruitment of girls into a branch of the army was also, in the eyes of the shah, a major contribution to secularization and toward improving the status of women.[27]

---

22. MAM, document 330; *Ettela'at*, 11 and 26 November 1967, 6 July 1968. The first women went out on 15 April 1969: *Ettela'at*, 12, 13, and 15 April 1969.

23. MAM, document 330.

24. Pahlavi, *Revolution*, 111.

25. MAM, document 330. See also Sanghvi, German, and Missen, 23.

26. Sanghvi, German, and Missen, 14.

27. For the fierce clerical opposition to this initiative, see "Khomeyni va Jonbesh-e Esteqlal" (unpublished collection of Khomeyni's speeches, clandestinely distributed in Iran in 1973), 56–60 (from a speech in 1970). Aware of such reactions, the shah preferred to present the projects as an initiative of a women's organization (headed by his sister, Ashraf); see *Ettela'at*, 16 and 17 April and 5, 6, and 31 July 1968. In keeping with this

The accomplishments of the Literary Corps, as reflected in the official statistics, were impressive. According to them, a total of 166,949 men and 33,642 women had served in the corps by the end of 1977. In that year 24,346 Literacy Corps members were teaching in the villages (in addition to 63,206 regular teachers employed by the Ministry of Education, many of them former corps recruits). At the end of the shah's reign there were a total of 33,500 schools in approximately 30,000 villages (as against 7,930 schools in about 7,000 villages in 1962/3). Despite a percentage decrease in the rural population, the share of rural and tribal students in the total elementary school population went up to 52 percent. And 74.4 percent of all rural and tribal children between the ages of six and ten were reported to be attending school. No less important was the fact that every second corps teacher remained in the profession, continuing in the employ of the Ministry of Education and adding significantly to the supply of, albeit not fully qualified, teachers.[28]

Even if the (possibly exaggerated) statistics are accepted as valid, the following basic deficiencies posed severe problems for this kind of schooling: poorly prepared teachers, schools with appallingly high student-teacher ratios, a high drop-out rate for students, and ill-defined educational goals.

The concept of the Literacy Corps stemmed from a conscious preference for quantity over quality. Like Taqizade, Siyasi, and other educationalists, the shah concluded that under the circumstances a rapid expansion was essential, even at the expense of quality. He wrote: "Incompletely prepared teachers can help our children incomparably more than no teachers at all."[29] Obviously, four months of teacher training (with a third of the time spent on military training) was insufficient to turn out competent teachers. Furthermore, the corps had to make do with mediocre high school graduates (the better ones went on to colleges or universities). This being so, personal motivation ac-

---

line, Mrs. Farah-rou Parsay was appointed minister of education in 1968 (becoming the first female minister in Iran). In September 1979, she was executed by order of Khomeyni's revolutionary courts.

In a lecture in Qom in 1963, Khomeyni criticized the corps as a whole and asserted that since the current educational system was intended to serve imperialism, any expansion of education was damaging ("Khomeyni va Jonbesh-e Esteqlal," 19–12). For more details on opposition by the ulama and for the opinion that the corps threatened to do away with the remnants of traditional education in remote areas, see Akhavi, 98–99.

28. MAM, document 330; Pahlavi, *Tamaddon*, 136–39; and figures supplied to the author by the general headquarters of the Literacy Corps in Tehran.

29. Pahlavi, *Mission*, 251.

counted for a great deal. One supervisor of the Literacy Corps in the Shiraz region told me late in 1976 that highly motivated corps members "accomplish miracles" but that many were "totally indifferent" to their mission, "wandering around frustrated," and causing more harm than good.[30] Another drawback was the fact that on completion of their period of service, many teachers—mainly the women—left their posts, sometimes even in midterm.

It is possible to divide the village school into three main categories. The first category included schools in large villages where corps teachers taught alongside regular teachers, offering a full curriculum for grades one to five. These were similar to schools in the smaller towns. The second category comprised medium-size schools, at which fewer than five teachers had to cope with five grades. At Razun (in Lorestan), for example, one teacher taught the second and fourth grades together. When he finished teaching part of a lesson to one grade, he gave the pupils assignments to keep them busy while he addressed the other grade. Another teacher applied the same system to the third and fifth grades. In some schools, classes were taught in two shifts. Most villages had schools that fell into the third category, where there was only one teacher (sometimes two) who divided pupils into "beginners" and "advanced." The graduates of schools in the second and third categories—that is, the majority of rural students—did not reach an academic level that would have allowed them to move on to intermediate schools.

The most striking feature that emerged from observing the student population in these schools was the extremely high drop-out rate, particularly from the "advanced" grades (i.e., the third grade and above) and especially among girls. According to data on 1,035 schools at which women were teaching in December 1975, the number of students was as follows: first grade, 78,067; second, 56,478; third, 38,299; fourth, 28,573; and fifth, 24,671. In 1975, for example, the largest number of students dropped out between the second and the third grades: only 45 percent of those who had been in the second grade in December 1974 were still at school a year later. A visitor could plainly observe that each class was smaller than the grade below it and could notice at a glance that this was particularly true of the girls. In the same 1,035 schools (where, because of the presence of women teachers, the per-

---

30. An official of the Literacy Corps women's training center in Fars made this same point in an interview with me. Such criticism was also voiced publicly shortly before the fall of the shah; see, for example, an article by Habib Chini in *Ettela'at*, 21 September 1978.

centage of girls was well above the average), girls numbered 51.6 percent in the first grade; 46.7 percent in the second; 40.8 percent in the third; 37.9 percent in the fourth; and 31.0 percent in the fifth. (Figures are for December 1975).[31]

The high drop-out rate resulted from the notion—still prevalent in rural areas—that children were a "work force" to be used for the benefit of their families. Yet more parents were becoming willing to allow children a few years at school before setting them to work at the "late" age of nine or ten. But most parents thought it improper to leave "mature" girls (i.e., those above the age of nine or ten) at school. Among those attending schools, there was frequent absenteeism (mainly for the purpose of helping with seasonal farm work).

The main aim of schooling was to produce better farmers and more loyal citizens. Preparing them for continuing education was clearly not a major educational goal. This being so, it was odd that agricultural training did not form part of the curriculum. Already in 1942, Dr. T. B. Alan, an American expert on rural education who had been invited to advise the Ministry of Education, recommended more and better agricultural training. He argued that rural education must reflect "the needs of the village," be compatible with the local life-style, and avoid "lofty words which carry no practical meaning."[32] But the Literary Corps did not take its cue from such thinking: teaching remained centered on moral precepts and on theory. And the attitude of the parents in rural areas might well have defeated any attempt to offer agricultural training. To them, after all, education meant escape from manual work: either temporarily (until the children were "too old" to stay away from work in the fields) or permanently (in the hope that education would lead to a desk job). Training for agriculture, they believed, would come by working on the farm. For them, education and manual work were a contradiction in terms.

The extracurricular activities of the corps were no less important to the regime than teaching schools. Teachers held adult education classes[33] and (unlike in the schools) gave courses on agriculture for

31. Based on data supplied to me by the headquarters of the Women's Literacy Corps.

32. His recommendations are included in his article: T. B. Alan, "Barresi dar Bare-ye Amuzesh va Parvaresh-e Rusta'i," *AP*, 1944/5, 205–11, 271–75, 319–24. Compare an article by Majlis deputy Ahmad Rezvi, "Amuzesh-e Fanni," ibid., 181–83.

33. According to data supplied to me by sources in the corps, a total of about 767,000 men and women participated in such classes between 1963 and 1977. At the end of 1977, 59,000 people were enrolled in adult classes. The recruitment of women into the corps was followed by a significant increase in the number of adult women students, up to almost half of the total in 1977. The corps also helped construct mosques, *hamams* (public

adults and on hygiene and home economics (mainly for women). Women teachers also advised the village women on family planning.

Most important, in the eyes of the court and government, was the corps members' contribution to promoting "loyalty to the Shah and the Revolution." The military framework in which they functioned helped in this regard. Their own training included specific classes on the principles of the White Revolution, and courses on history, geography, literature, and social science were used to drive home the same points. The fact that the farmers respected the teachers (because they were educated and had given help to the villages) made it easy for the latter to pass on the indoctrination they had undergone themselves. Pictures of the shah and other members of the royal family, and the slogans of the White Revolution, decorated each classroom. The first page of a typical textbook had the picture of the shah, the second of the empress, the third of the crown prince, and the fourth that of Princess Ashraf. The text was drafted to convey loyalty to the shah and admiration for his philosophy. (For the use of textbooks by the Islamic regime, see the Epilogue.) In ethnic minority areas (such as Kurdistan and Lorestan) teachers were instructed to emphasize the teaching of the Persian language as a means of promoting national unity. Nonetheless, in isolated cases, teachers relied on the remoteness of their stations to vent criticism of the regime.[34]

It is of course difficult to ascertain the degree to which such measures succeeded. As a rule, the rural population was not significantly active in the revolutionary process of the late 1970s. But those farmers who had migrated to the cities became an important power base of the opposition. All in all, it seems that the project helped in modernizing the rural areas, to a degree, but failed to recruit significant support for the shah.

The Scope of Compulsory Education
Is Widened (1974)

Thirty years after the passage of the compulsory education law and a decade after the start of the White Revolution, even official statistics— exaggerated as they often were—showed that over one-third of all children between the ages of six and ten (and over half the girls) were

---

baths), purification rooms, wells, and local bridges (*Kayhan*, 26 January 1978). More on these activities, in Pahlavi, *Revolution*, 110–12; idem, *Tamaddon*, 136–50.

34. I witnessed an instance of this kind at the village of Razun, in Lorestan.

not going to school.[35] Despite the growth in absolute numbers and the increase in school attendance as a percentage of the relevant age group, the overall population growth was so rapid that during the first ten years of the White Revolution the number of illiterates increased by two million. Even in purely quantitative terms, the educational system had failed.[36] This, as well as the opportunity offered by the recent steep rise in oil revenue, led the shah to reaffirm the compulsory law and simultaneously extend its scope. In a *firman* to Prime Minister Amir 'Abbas Hoveyda dated 20 February 1974, he spoke of his "wish to secure the well-being and progress of our children," mentioned that "we now have the means," and ordered the government to take the following steps, as of September 1974:

1. To provide free and compulsory education for all children from kindergarten through intermediate school (i.e. aged five to fourteen), and at the same time to improve the quality of instruction for these age groups.
2. To provide each child with a free daily school meal.
3. To prepare plans for the use of television for educational programs.
4. To report to him, within a month, on the progress made.[37]

In compliance with the *firman*, the government tabled the Law for Securing the Means and Facilities for Education. It was approved by the Majlis on 21 July 1974, and its passage reflected the political realities of the time: unlike in 1943, there was no public debate and no opposition. On some points, the text even exceeded the shah's expressed intentions. It required education to be free and compulsory from kindergarten through intermediate schools, and obliged parents to register their children in any region where the government provided such facilities. Instruction at vocational high schools was to be free, and attendance at other high schools was to be free for those agreeing to work for the government upon graduation—one year of work for every year of free education.[38] On 10 December 1975, the law's clauses were incorporated in the White Revolution program as article 15.

35. MAM, document 301; SBB/MA, *Dowran-e Pahlavi*, 29–51.

36. The relevant statistics were summed up in 1975 in a report prepared for the shah by Dr. Mohammad Baheri, deputy court minister and head of the Royal Institute for Research on Eduction; see SSHBA, *Gozaresh be Pishgah-e Mobarak-e A'lahazrat . . . . Dar Hastomin Konferans-e Enqelab-e Amuzeshi* (Ramsar, 1975). A copy of the report was given to me by a senior associate of SSHBA, who told me in late 1975 that the educational system had failed to meet the quantitative expectations placed in it.

37. MAM, document 695.

38. Ibid., document 314.

Mindful of the shah's personal interest in the matter, the Ministry of Education worked hard to carry out the law. The minister, Hushang Sharifi, sent out circulars to the ministry's provincial bureaus warning that any deviation or negligence would be considered a contravention of the shah's wishes and would be punished severely. He ordered them to check the population register to make sure that all children were in fact being registered for school.[39] Within a few months, the ministry prepared detailed directives and approved appropriate budgets. Priority was given to the school meal program. Lists of recommended foods were sent out, stating the calories they contained, and beginning in September 1974 meals were actually provided, a fact much publicized by the media.[40] Other circulars laid down regulations to compensate private intermediate schools for waiving tuition fees.[41] On 10 July 1974, the government approved regulations for free tuition in vocational schools; on 20 July, for free university tuition, and on 28 September for free instruction in other high schools.

Within three years, the rising opposition against the shah and his regime had reached proportions seriously obstructing the government's administrative work. An accurate assessment of the effects of the 1974 law is therefore difficult to arrive at. But the Ministry of Education now came out with impressive figures on the growth of education.

Overall Quantitative Results

Elementary education grew by leaps and bounds during Mohammad Reza's reign. Table 5 shows that between 1941/2 and 1978/9 the number of students grew eighteenfold: from a modest 286,598 to 5.2 million (this despite the fact that, in 1971/2, elementary education was reduced from six grades to only five). Although official figures of this kind are bound to be somewhat misleading (for instance, not quite all the registered pupils actually attended school), the general trend was indisputably impressive. According to the same sources 87 percent of children between the ages of six and ten went to school in 1978/9.

To what extent did the above-mentioned measures influence the rate

39. See letters nos. 3000/B from 16 April 1974; 6000/B from 8 August; 2750/Judicial Bureau from 22 September 1974. Copies of the letters from Ministry of Education files were given to the author by ministry staff.

40. Letters to the heads of provincial bureaus: 6000/B, 8 August 1974; 15454/B, 20 December 1974; 16350/B, 1 January 1975.

41. Letters, 3000/B, 16 April 1974; 4000/B, 2 June; 2750/Judicial Bureau, 22 September 1974.

Table 5. Students at elementary
schools, in selected years between
1941/2 and 1977/8* (1941/2 = 100%)

Year	No. of students	Index
1941/2	286,598	100
1946/7	293,724	102.5
1953/4	730,793	255.0
1956/7	816,501	284.9
1961/2	1,436,169	501.1
1966/7	2,565,918	895.3
1970/1	3,444,362	1201.8
1975/6	4,124,803	1439.2
1976/7	4,939,800	1723.6
1978**	5,200,000	1814.4

Source: SBB/MA, *Dowran-e Pahlavi* (Tehran: Markaz-e Amar, 2535 [1976/7]), 35–48;
Khaqani, 126.
*Until 1971/2 the duration of elementary
education was six years, from then on, five.
**Estimate, according to *Iran Almanac,
1978,* 440–43.

of expansion? The Literacy Corps clearly accelerated the process. In
the first five years of its operation (to 1966/7) the number of students
grew by 78.8 percent (an average of 15.8 percent a year). The impact
of the two laws for compulsory education is more difficult to determine.
As long as World War II lasted (i.e., for the first three years, after the
original law), there was no significant growth, but from 1946/7 to 1953/
4 there was an average annual increase of 20.1 percent. This was not
necessarily the result of the law but stemmed more likely from greater
public awareness of the importance of education, promoted by liberals
in the early 1940s. Beginning with the late 1960s, there was constant
and rapid growth, with some additional acceleration following the 1974
initiative (19.8 percent from 1975/6 to 1976/7 alone).

After almost a century of struggle for the new education, there thus
occurred a quantum leap. The *maktab* system came to a virtual end.
And as elementary education expanded, it produced an avalanche of
secondary school entrants.

Secondary Education

The Road to University Admission

Throughout the history of modern education in Iran, the secondary
schools (*madrese-ye motavasete* or, more recently, *dabirestan*) were its

weakest part. The struggle for priority was fought between elementary and higher education, at most times ignoring secondary education. As its Persian name implied, it was seen as no more than a link in the chain leading from elementary to higher education, with no defined aim of its own—a means (*vasete*) for securing a desk job or gaining university admission.

The earliest secondary schools of Iran's new education had set out to imitate the European humanistic gymnasium of the nineteenth century. Founded on the ideals of W. von Humboldt in Germany and the educational reforms of F. Guizot and R. Cousinet in France, it offered an intensive humanistic and general education intended to train students to think for themselves, express themselves clearly, and develop good taste. When Iran turned to imitate this model late in the nineteenth century, it had already come under criticism in Europe and was beginning to undergo important changes. The new role of science and the democratization of the social and political life both left their mark.[42] But Iranian education remained loyal to the original concept: in fact, this suited the Iranian educational tradition of stressing moral character and good manners rather than preparing students for a professional career.

Its perception of its own aim as no more than a transition stage and its emphasis on purely formal qualifications (the *diplom*, or high school graduation certificate) were the main deficiencies of secondary education. The *diplom* was the only yardstick for evaluating the graduate and measuring his "contribution" to society. As Norman Jacobs put it: "By the sole virtue of being educated, he was considered as productive as any member of any occupational grouping."[43] The *diplom* became a commodity in great demand, most particularly because it conferred certain "privileges" on the recipient. Graduates insisted on holding the government to its implied promises.

The concepts underlying secondary education were consistently criticized by educationalists and politicians. Majlis member Mo'ayyed Ahmadi, for instance, asserted in 1943 that schooling geared to the acquisition of administrative posts might well result in the "total demolishment of the state." Deputies 'Abduh and Tabataba'i, the edu-

---

42. On the development of the humanistic gymnasium in Europe and the criticism it eventually encountered, see N. L. Bossing, *Principles of Secondary Education* (New York, 1947); W. M. Saybor, *Modern Secondary Education* (New York, 1959).

43. Jacobs, 153–58. Similar views are in: *KI*, 7 August 1968, 18 July 1970, 30 December 1971; *Ettela'at*, 2 September 1971. For the support of such concepts from within the school, see Chapter 5.

cationalists Sadiq and Shuqi, and many others made similar points.[44] Criticism intensified in the 1960s, with the shah himself setting the tone. On the eve of the White Revolution, he spoke out against the "wasteful concept" that proclaimed the holder of a "piece of paper called *diplom*" to be a "positive and productive" element in society. This conjured up the danger of secondary schools becoming "*diplom* factories" likely to turn out functionally illiterate and useless gradu- ates.[45] Returning to the theme in 1968, he called it "a crime" that "anyone, whether capable or not, like an automaton, receives a *diplom* . . . goes on . . . to an university . . . [and] ends up sitting behind a desk."[46] Some educationalists spoke of the *diplom* as having become an ornament (*zaynat*) or an "insurance policy" or a "certificate of own- ership."[47] Experts like Masha'ekhi, Ahmad Qasemi, Sharifi, Sadiq, Vadi'i, and Rahnama demanded a "qualitative revolution" (*enqelab-e keyfi*).[48] All of this was to no avail. The quality of teaching declined; the content of schooling remained unchanged.

The lower standards of the teaching profession resulted partly from the stronger attraction of economic or administrative employment in an expanding market for both; and partly from the social tradition militating against women, particularly married women, working out- side the home. The upshot was that in the mid-1970s, according to Ministry of Education figures, at least two-thirds of the high schools teachers were not properly qualified—by the ministry's own criteria.[49]

The material being taught continued to have little relevance to the reality of students' lives or the country's needs. Like their counterpart

44. *MM*, term 13, 2830, 3137 (Mo'ayyed Ahmadi); term 15, 2623 ('Abduh); term 13, 2737–41, 2767–68 (Tabataba'i); *AP*, 1944/5, 65–67 (Sadiq and Shuqi).

45. Pahlavi, *Ta'lifat*, 4:2997–3000 (from a speech of 19 December 1962); similarly in idem, *Mission*, 238–58.

46. *KI*, 7 August 1968; also *KI*, 30 December 1971.

47. Masha'ekhi, *Hadaf*, 1–17; Ahmad Qasemi, "Moshkel-e Ta'limat-e Motavasete-ra Chegune Bayad Hal Kard?" *AP*, 1965/6, 50–57. Recommendations included to change such attitudes were also included in the resolutions of the annual conferences on edu- cation: *KAEA, 1969*, article 25; *KAEA, 1975*, article 34.

48. Masha'ekhi, *Amuzesh Ejtema'i*, 792–94, *Dowre Rahnama'i*, 771–75, "Hadaf," 1–11, "Moshkelat," 1–5, and "Mafhum," 6–11; Sharifi, 13–24; Sadiq, *Chehel Goftar*, 236–52, and a speech in the Senate quoted in *KI*, 9 May 1970; Kazem Vadi'i, "Enqelab-e Keyfi dar Amuzesh va Parvaresh-e Iran," *AP*, 1975/6, 1–6 and "Nezam-e Jadid-e Amuzesh-e Motavasete-ye Iran," ibid., 7–33; Rahnama, 1:57–80.

49. Fifty-three percent of the high school teachers had the proper qualifications in 1964/5, after which there was a progressive drop: to 48.9 percent in 1967/8, to 35 percent in 1969/70, and to slightly over 30 percent in 1976/7. See Rahnama, 1:122–25; *KI*, 18 June 1968, 24 August 1966, 29 July 1970; *Ettela'at*, 31 October 1971. The data for 1976/7 were given to the author by Kazem Vadi'i, then deputy minister of education.

in other Muslim states of the Middle East, students by and large studied by memorizing.[50] Independent thought and analytical capability were not developed. Referring to the early 1960s, Jacobs used extremely critical language in speaking of the basic deficiencies of the secondary schools:

> The educational system may be said to be well adapted to preparing the students to live and work effectively in their society, and as such . . . [it] may be said to be successful. It only is a failure if, it is argued, its role is to *change* and not *to adapt* to the occupational environment that the student enters. For the system incubates the "educated man" who primarily, although not exclusively, is a political animal, who is a good memorizer, who speaks well, but not correctly, who is quick to copy and serve those in authority, who tends to talk rather than to act, who hates to make decisions, who is not utilitarian, who is not objective, who cannot operate effectively in a critical environment, who does not necessarily understand what he accepts, who cannot analyze his responsibilities, . . . finally, who basically is insecure and consequently, unproductive—in brief, an individual who is the very antithesis of the kind of educated or sophisticated individual required to participate in, let alone create and develop, a rational, self-guarding economic system.[51]

In substance, the shah as well as some educationalists made much the same points, though in less caustic style.[52]

If contemporary theorists described "modern man" in terms of open-mindedness, a less dogmatic outlook, readiness for new experiences, acceptance of innovation and change, creative thinking, orientation toward the present and future rather than the past, and trust in science and technology,[53] then secondary education did little to develop a modern Iranian. A survey among industrial managers in Iran found that "the more educated a manager, the less dogmatic he is. [But]

50. A survey by MTE of those who had taken the examinations for university admission in 1968/9 revealed that most candidates had prepared themselves by memorizing the material (64 percent of them said that they had memorized the material "while walking"); see Morteza Kotubi, *Masa'el Marbut be Amuzesh-e Motavasete dar Iran* (Tehran: MTE, 1969), 2:48. In this survey, 8,075 questionnaires were distributed among candidates for medical schools and 6,000 among candidates for the humanities; 1,270 of the former and 245 of the latter replied.

51. Jacobs, 159.

52. Pahlavi, *Mission*, 238–65; Masha'ekhi, "Hadaf," 1–17; idem, *Amuzesh Ejtema'i*, 792–94; idem, "Mafhum," 1–5; Sharifi, 13–24; Vadi'i, "Enqelab-e Keyfi," 1–6; idem, "Amuzesh-e Motavasete," 7–33.

53. Compare Alex Inkeles, "Modernization of Man," in M. Weiner, ed., *Modernization: The Dynamics of Growth* (New York: Basic Books, 1966), 151–63; and Milton Rokeach, *The Open Mind and Close Mind* (New York: Basic Books, 1960), 71–72.

managers who were educated in the west are less dogmatic than those educated in Iran."[54]

An efficient managerial class, such as the developing economy would have required, was unlikely to emerge from the Iranian secondary schools. This point was made by ʿAlinaqi ʿAlikhani (minister of economy between 1968 and 1971, then chancellor of Tehran University until 1974), Rasekh (deputy minister for the Plan and Budget Organization), Farrokh Aminzade (head of the manpower division in the Plan and Budget Organization), as well as Vadiʿi in observations they made in 1976. They all argued that unless the essence, aim, and methods of education were changed, high school graduates were bound to be an economic burden rather than contribute to economic development.[55]

How well did the secondary schools do in their declared intention of preparing their graduates for university entrance? All the veteran professors interviewed asserted that there was definitely a continual decline in the academic level of the freshmen in their departments, mainly since the early 1960s. Faculty members may tend to make such claims everywhere and at all times, but the correlation between rapid expansion of the elementary and secondary schools and declining standards cannot be ignored. Professors were critical both of the knowledge students brought with them from high school and of the study habits they had acquired there. Sadiq, for instance, stated that he had to "lower the level of instruction year by year." Eventually, the universities would turn into high schools: "What I teach today [he said in 1968] fits graduates of elementary rather than secondary schools."[56] Senator Matin Daftari, himself a Tehran University professor, said that even those who passed the entrance examinations had to spend a year or two "making up for the weakness of their high school training."[57] (On the implications this had for higher education, see Chapter 10.)

With these declining standards in mind, many experts—mainly in the last decade of the shah's rule—questioned the advisability of continued secondary school expansion. Sadiq, Vadiʿi, and Mashaʾekhi and even the Royal Institute for Research on Education recommended curbing it, cautiously warning of the potentially grave political repercussions of producing growing numbers of high school graduates whose

54. Reza Vaqefi, "A Micro-Analysis Approach to Modernization Process: A Case Study of Modernity And Traditional Conflict," *IJMES*, 12 (September 1980), 181–97.

55. See, for example, a statement by ʿAlikhani cited in *Ettelaʿat*, 24 April 1969. Similarly *KI*, 9 July 1968, 22 January 1969, 11 August 1970.

56. From a Senate speech, 8 May 1968, as quoted in *Ettelaʿat*, 9 May 1968.

57. From a Senate speech, 24 June 1967, as cited in ibid., 25, 27 June 1967.

Table 6. Growth of elementary and secondary education in comparison with population growth, in selected years between 1941/2 and 1977/8

Year	Estimated population (in thousands)	Total no. of elementary and secondary students	No. of students as % of population
1941/2	12,833	315,355	2.46
1946/7	14,159	327,509	2.31
1951/2	16,237	834,434	5.14
1956/7	18,955	961,619	5.07
1961/2	22,372	1,733,986	7.75
1966/7	25,789	3,009,669	11.67
1971/2	30,020	4,729,760	15.75
1975/6	33,375	6,114,170	18.32
1977/8	36,000	7,701,000	21.39

Sources: Computed from SBB/MA, *Dowran-e Pahlavi*, 16–17; Khaqani, 126; *Iran Almanac, 1978*, 440–43. Population data based on: Julian Bharier, *Economic Development in Iran 1900–1970* (London: Oxford University Press, 1971), 26–27; *Iran Almanac, 1978*.

great expectation must, perforce, remain unfulfilled.[58] In 1972, the International Labour Organization advised the government to restrict secondary education "as much as possible" and warned of the consequences (mainly increased unemployment and its political effects) should it fail to do so.[59]

Yet despite the warnings, advice, and actual educational deficiencies, this rapid expansion continued. Table 6 displays the rate of change in absolute figures as well as compared with the growth of population. The upturn of the rate of growth after the beginning of the White Revolution stands out clearly. During the shah's reign as a whole, the population grew 2.8 times larger, the total of elementary and secondary students 24.4 times larger. As Table 7 demonstrates, the spread of education was even faster in Iran than in Turkey or Egypt. While on the eve of the White Revolution Iran lagged behind them, by the mid-1970s it had outpaced both. Even more impressive was the growth in education for girls. From an initial position quite a ways behind, Iran outdid Egypt and nearly caught up with Turkey, where, by regional standards, female education was particularly advanced.

Having previously lagged behind elementary and higher education, secondary education now moved ahead of both. Table 8 shows that

58. SSHBA, *Gostaresh-e Amuzesh-e ʿAli*, 5–7, 107–26; Sadiq, *Chehel Goftar*, 13 (from a lecture to the two houses of Parliament, 24 October 1967); Mashaʾekhi, "Hadaf," 1–17; Vadiʾi, "'Obur az Bohran-e Matbuʿ Amuzesh va Parvaresh," *AP*, 1975/6, 34–40.

59. International Labour Organization (ILO), *Employment and Income Policies of Iran* (Lausanne, 1973), 63–77.

Table 7. Percentage of children of elementary-
and secondary-school age in schools in Iran,
Egypt, and Turkey in 1960 and 1975

Year	Sex	Iran*	Egypt	Turkey
1960	Total	29	43	46
	Boys	39	54	56
	Girls	18	32	35
1975**	Total	70	58	66
	Boys	87	72	76
	Girls	53	44	55

Sources: Computed from UNESCO, *Statistical Yearbook,
1977* (Paris, 1977), 128–76.
*In Iran the data for 1960 relate to the age range from
seven to eighteen, and for 1975 from six to sixteen; in
Turkey the age ranges are six to sixteen and seven to
seventeen, respectively; in Egypt data for both years relate to ages 6–17.
**The data for Turkey relate to 1960 and 1974.

between 1941/2 and 1970/1 (before the intermediate schools were introduced) the number of high school students grew 36.7 times larger;
from 1970/1 to 1978/9, it grew by another 2.37 times. Table 9 compares
the growth of elementary and secondary education between 1941/2 and
1970/1 (with university expansion added for the sake of further comparison). It shows that while the increase for elementary education was
twelvefold, that for secondary education was more than 36-fold. Only
in the early 1960s, when the Literacy Corps was first formed, did
elementary education grow faster. Whereas in 1941/2 secondary stu-

Table 8. Growth of
secondary education in
selected years between
1941/2 and 1978/9

Year	No. of students
1941/2	28,757
1946/7	33,785
1953/4	103,641
1956/7	145,118
1961/2	297,493
1966/7	443,751
1970/71	1,056,857
1975/6	1,989,367
1978/9	2,501,118

Sources: SBB/MA, *Dowran-e
Pahlavi,* 41–44; Khaqani, 249; *Iran
Almanac, 1978,* 440–43.

Table 9. Comparative index of growth of elementary, secondary, and higher education between 1941/2 and 1970/1

Year	Elementary school students	Secondary school students	University students*
1941/2	100.0	100.0	100.0
1946/7	102.5	117.5	237.6
1953/4	255.0	360.4	533.9
1956/7	284.9	504.6	621.6
1961/2	501.1	1039.5	1169.3
1966/7	895.3	1543.1	1509.6
1970/1	1201.8	3675.1	2600.7

Sources: Computed from data in: Khaqani, 126, 248; SBB/MA, *Dowran-e Pahlavi*, 38–39.
*Figures include only university students; students in other institutes for higher learning are listed in Table 14.

dents constituted 10.3 percent of the total population in elementary and secondary schools, they accounted for no less than 30.7 percent in 1970/1. The number of girls at secondary schools grew even faster: in 1941/2, girls accounted for 21.6 percent of all high school students, in 1970/1 for 33 percent, and in 1978/9 for 38.5 percent. (In elementary schools, the percentage of girls grew from 28.6 percent in 1940/1 to 40 percent in 1978/9.)[60]

Geographically speaking, all regions participated in the growth of pre-university education, despite a certain persistent differential between rural and urban areas. For example, the share of secondary school students in rural areas grew from 8.4 percent in 1962/3 to 13 percent in 1971/2—that is, even faster than the overall expansion.[61] Table 10 compares the percentage of the elementary and secondary students in each of the provinces in 1973/4 with the share of that province in Iran's total population. It shows that the more industrialized provinces, which include large urban concentrations, had a higher than proportional share of students, mainly in the high schools. Tehran, for instance, had 20.6 percent of the population, but 27.9 percent of elementary and 33.3 percent of secondary students. Khuzestan, Fars, and Gilan had above-average student populations. By contrast, the more deprived provinces with a large rural population had below-average student figures. Thus East Azerbayjan, with 9.5 percent of the population, had 6.7 percent of the elementary and only 5.2 percent of the secondary students. Similar figures were obtained for Kurdistan, Sistan and Baluchestan, Hormuzadegan, Chaharmahal and Bakhtyari,

60. Khaqani, 126, 248; *Iran Almanac, 1978*, 440–43.
61. Khaqani, 250–51.

Table 10. Breakdown by province of students at elementary and secondary schools in
1973/4 as compared with the provincial population (1976 survey)

Province	Provincial population as % of total population	% of Provincial students At elementary schools	% of Provincial students At secondary schools
Tehran (Central)	20.6	27.9	33.3
Gilan	4.7	5.6	6.4
Mazanderan	7.1	8.0	7.1
East Azerbayjan	9.5	6.7	5.2
West Azerbayjan	4.2	3.6	3.2
Kermanshah	3.0	2.7	2.7
Khuzestan	6.5	7.9	9.2
Fars	6.0	6.7	6.6
Kerman	3.2	2.9	2.8
Khorasan	9.7	7.3	7.0
Isfahan	5.8	6.4	5.6
Sistan & Baluchestan	1.9	1.3	1.1
Kurdistan	2.3	1.3	1.0
Hamadan	3.2	2.5	1.8
Chaharmahal & Bakhtyari	1.2	1.0	0.5
Lorestan	2.7	2.1	1.9
Ilam	0.7	0.4	0.3
Bushehr	1.0	0.9	0.7
Zanjan	1.8	0.9	0.6
Yazd	1.1	1.2	1.1
Hormuzadegan	1.4	1.3	0.6
Kahguliye & Boyed Ahmadi	0.7	0.6	0.4
Semnan	1.7	0.8	0.9
Total	100%	100%	100%

Source: Computed from data in: SBB/MA, *Dowran-e Pahlavi*, 48 (number of students); *Iran Almanac,
1978*, 410 (population survey of 1976).

Zanjan, Ilam, and Semnan. Yet, considering the earlier backwardness
of education in these provinces and given that under Reza Shah secondary education had been limited to only a major few cities, there
had clearly been rapid development of secondary education in all provinces. This was an important trend both with regard to the development of higher education and with regard to the overall process of
modernization.

Apart from the somewhat diminishing quantitative differential, was
there a meaningful qualitative differential between the cities and the
countryside? In fact, a considerable disparity was noticed in this regard
between different provinces and between urban and rural areas within
the same province, as well as between rich and poor quarters of the
same city. Tehran's prestigious private schools (e.g., Elborz, Hadaf,
Reza Shah) had a considerable advantage over the public schools of

Tehran's popular southern quarters as far as school buildings, teaching equipment, and the standard of teacher education were concerned. Since private education generally had higher standards, its availability in the larger cities gave them an advantage over smaller urban areas. In the five largest cities, between a quarter to one half of the total students went to private schools in 1973/4: in Shiraz, 51.3 percent; in Tehran, 35.2 percent; in Meshhed, 32.2 percent; in Isfahan, 31.0 percent; and in Tabriz, 24.6 percent. In small towns (with populations of 50,000 to 60,000) the proportion of children in private schools averaged 5 to 6 percent; and many towns of that size had no private schools at all. In still smaller towns, and in the villages, such schools hardly existed at all.[62] This gave children in the large cities a headstart toward university admission.

Revision of the School Structure

Rapid expansion, and the attendant shortcomings, necessitated a fundamental reform of the school system. Most important in this regard was the restructuring of pre-university education, undertaken in 1971/2. Before the restructuring, there had been two school periods of six years each, a structure similar to the French model. Then in 1957, on the advice of American consultants, secondary education was divided into two halves, comparable to the American system of junior and senior high school. The aim was to allow greater specialization at the upper level.[63] But even this step did not prove satisfactory. By the late 1960s, the Ministry of Education came to regard the whole system as "old-fashioned."[64] The minister of education, Mrs. Farah-rou Parsay, said in 1969 that the school structure was "very antiquated . . . [and] in no way capable of serving our present needs."[65]

Reform programs had been discussed in the ministry as far back as the late 1950s. In an article in 1956, and again in 1965, Masha'ekhi had recommended a three-tiered structure, with the intermediate level designed to test the student's aptitudes and thus make it possible to direct him or her toward a suitable future career, whether at school or at work.[66] His principle was adopted in 1966 (but not implemented until

---

62. VAP, *Amar Amuzesh va Parvaresh, 1352* (Tehran, 1974), 176–89.

63. For details, see Sadiq, *Farhang*, 473–76; Masha'ekhi, "Hadaf," 1–17; Arasteh, 94–95.

64. VAP, Edare-ye Kol Amuzesh-e Rahnama'i-ye Tahsili, *Dowre-ye Rahnama'i-ye Tahsili: 'Ellal va Jehat-e Ejra'-ye An* (Tehran, 1970), 11–12.

65. *KI*, 26 August 1969.

66. Masha'ekhi, "Ta'limat-e Ejtema'i," 792–94 and "Hadaf," 1–17.

1971/2). The three tiers were as follows: elementary school (five years), intermediate school (three years), and high school (four years).[67] Highest importance was attached to the intermediate schools, where the student's aptitudes and preferences were to be discerned.[68] According to his or her record at that level, the student would move on to an academic high school, a vocational high school, or a short course of vocational training. The latter—an innovation launched in conjunction with the redivision of schools—ran from six to twenty-four months; some of the training was to be taken after completing elementary school, some after intermediate school. "Senior" high schools were divided into two types: theoretical and vocational. A limited number of graduates from vocational schools would go on to technical colleges. In its last year, the academic high school offered a measure of specialization to fit the student's future study and career plans.

If its potential had been fully developed, the new educational structure might have proved advantageous for both the individual (in cultivating his or her natural talents) and the government (in directing students according to the new needs of the economy).[69] It might also have helped relieve the pressure of applicants on the universities. But its persistent defects prevented it from doing so. One problem was the lack of skilled teachers and educational counselors. Under the new system, Parsay stated, parents entrusted "the destiny of their children" to the schools; therefore the staff must be fully qualified.[70] But in fact most of the teachers at intermediate schools were from elementary schools or the Literacy Corps and had taken no more than a short preparatory summer course to qualify for intermediate teaching. (Corps teachers needed to have a total of five years of teaching experience.)[71]

The main failure of the new structure, however, was over the matter

67. For full details, see VAP, *Dowre-ye Rahnama'i.*

68. To make a telling judgment of students' aptitudes and preferences, the intermediate schools offered a wide choice of courses. Over three years, the intermediate school syllabus comprised: religion and Qur'an, nine hours; languages and literature, fourteen; chemistry, physics and biology, fifteen; mathematics, fifteen; technology, twelve; Arabic, two; history, geography, social science and the White Revolution, nine; a foreign language, twelve; physical education, six; and arts, six hours (VAP, *Dowre-ye Rahnama'i*; *Ettela'at*, 8 December 1969, 22 November 1970).

69. For the shah's words to that effect, see *Ettela'at*, 23 September 1967, 23 September 1969.

70. Ibid., 26 July, 23 September 1971.

71. For critical views, see Sadiq, *Ettela'at*, 10 January 1971; Majlis deputy 'Ali Ashgar Riyazi, *KI*, 22 December 1971; the educator Badr al-Din in an article in *Ettela'at*, 30 January 1969; Vadi'i, "Amuzesh-e Motavasete," 7–33. Similarly: *Ettela'at*, 8 December 1969, 7 January 1970, 22 November 1970, and *Kayhan*, 7 September 1976.

of future specialization. The minister of education had expected that 40 percent of intermediate school graduates would move on to vocational schools[72] (compared with about 3 percent before its inception). Had this occurred, it would certainly have eased the pressure on the universities and done wonders for vocational schooling. The appearance of more upper-classes children in vocational schools would have given these schools a great deal more prestige. But in a country with a social stratification as strict as Iran's, this was too difficult to accomplish. By and large (to borrow Dewey's words), rather than "develop capacity to the point of competency," the prevalent practice generally remained "to fit individuals in advance" for occupations in keeping with "the wealth or social status of parents."[73] Here was the main challenge—and ultimately the failure—of the Iranian experience.

Well-to-do parents were opposed to having their children go into vocational training and used their influence to prevent this from happening. Teachers and headmasters as well as high ministry officials admitted being under such pressures. But in most cases pressure was not even necessary. Intermediate schools clearly fell into two groups—prestigious, and less so—even though officially no such division was recognized. Prestige schools would not admit students unlikely (in their judgment) to measure up to their standards.[74] The rest had to go to the other schools, and these provided the bulk of vocational trainees. Moreover, despite a decision that all intermediate schools must be public, the ministry was compelled right from the beginning—partly in response to public demand, partly for lack of facilities of its own—to allow private intermediate schools to operate.[75] (For similar considerations forcing the Islamic regime to allow private schooling, see the Epilogue.) These private schools charged high tuition fees,[76] usually

72. VAP, *Dowre-ye Rahnama'i*, 4–7; *Ettela'at*, 30 November 1969, 26 July and 31 December 1971.

73. Dewey, *Democracy and Education*, 139–40.

74. Regulations required registration in schools closest to the areas of residence, but many schools turned away unwanted candidates by claiming they had no vacancies. Then they went on to enroll the entrants they were interested in. This practice was common in the 1970s and was often criticized by the media.

75. *Ettela'at*, 25 March, 25 August, 20 September 1971. In the first year of the program, 11.4 percent of the total of 259,635 students were at private schools. In urban centers, the percentage was higher: e.g., 27.2 percent in Tehran in 1973/4 (VAP, *Amar Amuzesh*, 1973/4, 154).

76. In 1971/2, tuition in public schools cost 1,000 Riyals, in private school between 9,000 and 17,000 Riyals (at the time: 70 Riyals = $1): *Ettela'at*, 15 July, 26 August, 20 September 1971. A cartoon in *Ettela'at* (25 August 1971) showed a headmaster telling parents that at his school both students and tuition fees were "outstanding" (*momtaz*).

accepted only middle- and upper-class children, and almost invariably sent them on to academic high schools. In this way, the restructuring, undertaken to advance social mobility, eventually helped perpetuate existing social gaps.

Soon enough it became clear that the intermediate schools were a failure. The harshest criticism was vented at the ninth Conference on Education in September 1976. Its committee on pre-university education stated that, just like its predecessor, the new system served as a mere supplier of university entrants. Professor 'Abbas Safavyan, chancellor of the National (Melli) University and member of the committee on education and employment, told the conference that "all the problems of the educational system . . . stem from the new structure" which failed to answer to "the realities" of the country. By claiming that students would move forward according to their talents, the Ministry of Education had "deceived the children and their parents" because in actual fact it lacked "any means of diagnosing [their] qualifications."[77] At the same time, Professor Vadi'i (then deputy minister of education in charge of educational planning) was already preparing a different program, but the regime collapsed before anything could be done about it.[78]

The Failure of Vocational Education

It was a major aim of the educational system under Mohammad Reza Shah to improve and expand vocational education (both technological and agricultural) so as to supply the skilled manpower needed for the state's reform programs. As in other Muslim countries of the Middle East, this area had remained the weakest link in the chain of educational institutions modeled on western systems. The traditions and perceptions militating against it have been referred to above.

In the 1970s, vocational training (*amuzesh-e fanni va herfe'i*) was offered at four different levels: at intermediate schools (*amuzeshgah-e herfe'i*); at high schools (*honarestan-e herfe'i*) turning out "second-level technicians" (*teknisyan daraje do*); through a two-year course for high school graduates leading to a degree called "high diploma" (*fowq-e diplom*, a degree higher than the high school graduation certificate but lower than any university degree) and to the status of senior technician (*teknisyan 'ali*);

77. *Kayhan*, 4 and 7 September 1976.
78. In an interview with me, Vadi'i confirmed the charges made by Safavyan. The outline of his own new plan was described in his article "Amuzesh-e Motavasete," 7–33.

Table 11. Number of vocational school students compared with total high school students, in selected years between 1941/2 and 1976/7

Year	[A] Total of high school students	[B] Vocational schools students	[B] as a % of [A]
1941/2	28,757	615	2.14
1948/9	37,055	724	1.96
1953/4	103,641	792	0.76
1956/7	145,113	1,545	1.06
1962/3	309,855	9,117	2.94
1966/7	443,751	15,224	3.43
1970/1	1,056,857	23,325	2.20
1972/3*	1,477,774	47,561	3.22
1974/5	1,723,292	69,682	4.04
1976/7	2,442,391	180,412	7.39

Sources: Computed from data in: SBB/MA, *Dowran-e Pahlavi*, 40–41; SSHBA, *Amuzesh-e Fanni*, 12; UNESCO, *Statistical Yearbook, 1977*, 286–87.
*Data from 1972/3 include students in seven grades, as against six in previous years.

and technological training on an academic level. In addition, graduates of elementary and intermediate schools were offered numerous shorter courses to acquire specific skills.[79] The present discussion deals with the two first categories, with an account of the other two reserved for the following chapter.

The quantitative weakness of vocational education is brought out sharply in Table 11. Between 1941/2 and 1953/4, the total number of secondary students grew by 360 percent, that of vocational students by 29 percent. In the mid–1950s, there was a gradual increase, but figures still fell far short of those for other secondary schools, constituting 3.43 percent of total secondary school students in 1966/7 and back to 2.2 percent in 1970/1. Only after the restructuring of the schools did vocational education start to fare better. Beginning in 1975, the cancellation of tuition fees in vocational schools gave it some additional impetus. But with 7.39 percent of secondary students at vocational schools in 1976/7, it still lagged far behind original expectations. (Parsay, it will be remembered, had spoken of 40 percent.) It also could not keep up with vocational training in other countries of the region. In Egypt, by contrast, which had made exceptionally fast advances, 50.58 percent of high school students studied at vocational schools.[80]

79. SSHBA, *Barresi Amuzesh-e Fanni va Herfe'i dar Sath-e Teknisyan*, ed., ʿAli Akbar Shirtavaneʾi (Tehran, 1973), 6–8.
80. George D. M. Hyde, *Education in Modern Egypt: Ideals and Realities* (London: Routledge, 1978), 42.

The disproportion is well illustrated by the following: under the third development plan (1963/4–1968/9), 400,000 students were expected to graduate from regular high schools, and 28,000 from vocational high schools. At the end of the five years, it turned out that as many as 658,000 had graduated from the regular schools and just over 16,000 from vocational schools.[81] These figures are surprising in view of the country's rapid urbanization and industrialization, a trend which usually gives a boost to vocational schools. (The urban population grew from 23.8 percent in 1941 to 44 percent in 1976; manpower engaged in industry from 14 percent in 1956 to 36.5 percent in 1977.)[82]

Especially conspicuous was the failure of agricultural education. At the end of the shah's rule, over half of the population still lived in rural areas, and one-third of the total labor force was engaged in agriculture. The White Revolution aspired to mechanize agriculture as part of the overall agrarian reform. Yet in 1972/3, only 9 percent of all vocational students were training for agriculture (as against 66 percent for industry and 25 percent for the service sector).[83]

The share of girls in vocational schools was also extremely low, though growing slowly in the 1970s. In 1962/3, only 9.9 percent of vocational students were girls (904 students); in 1972/3, 18.6 percent (8,850 students). (For comparison's sake: the share of girls in regular high schools grew over the same period from 31.5 percent to 33.5 percent.)[84]

No less significant than the quantitative failure was the defective qualitative level. Applicants were mostly elementary school graduates with a poor academic record; the level of instruction was low; the schools lacked proper equipment; the curriculum was not properly geared to the needs of the economy; and the graduates had little motivation to go to work in the trades they had trained for. Here again, the main problem was the deep-rooted perception equating education with theoretical instruction. Inasmuch as the introduction of new technologies made any dent in this at all, it generated an interest in university education in technological subjects, not in a career as a

81. For the plan, see SBB, *Barname-ye 'Omrani-ye Sevvom-e Keshvar—1342–1347* (Tehran, 1963), 119–25; for the results, see SBB, *Barname-ye 'Omrani-ye Chaharom-e Keshvar—1347–1352 (Tehran, 1968)*, 234–35. On the imbalance between the requirements and the actual supply of skilled manpower, see SBB/Vezarat-e Kar, *Nata'ej-e Amargiri-ye Niru-ye Ensani—1351* (Tehran, 1972); Rahnama, 2:64–65.

82. SBB, *Barname Chaharom*, 59–74; *Iran Almanac, 1978*, 418.

83. SSHBA, *Amuzesh-e Fanni*, 9–22.

84. SBB/MA, *Degarguniha-ye Ejtema'i va Eqtesadi-ye Zanan dar Iran* (Tehran, 1973), 47–48.

technician. Thus students moved to vocational schools not from preference but from lack of choice. The average entrant was one who had failed to gain a place in other schools, and who had come from a lower social class than the typical student entering regular high school.[85]

The social background of vocational school students is analyzed in a classified survey by the Population and Manpower Division of the Plan and Budget Organization (the PO). The survey covered all the 12,000 students in the twelfth grade who finished school in the summer of 1975.[86] It revealed that 29.6 percent of their fathers were illiterate (*bi-savad*), the fathers of another 49.5 percent had had up to six years of schooling, and only 4.2 percent of the fathers had academic degrees. The fathers of female students were better educated: only 10.6 percent were illiterate, 45.1 percent had up to six years of schooling, and 11.9 percent had academic degrees. (This was not because their fathers preferred vocational training for their daughters in the first place; but having failed to enroll them in regular schools, they preferred vocational schools over no schooling at all.)

No similar survey exists for regular high schools. The only comparison that can be made is with applicants for university admission. (Since most high school graduates took the entrance examinations, the data reflect their background almost as well as a specific high school survey would have done.) Among the candidates in 1973/4, only 15.1 percent had fathers who were illiterate, the fathers of another 60.3 percent had had up to six years of schooling, and 8.0 percent of the fathers had academic degrees.[87]

As for their occupations, the survey of vocational schools reveals

85. These problems and the need to change the public's opinion of vocational education were discussed at a seminar of the Plan and Budget Organization and the OECD on "Planning and Development of Manpower in Iran," in September 1969. See mainly the following papers: Afshan Hassam-Vaziri (from the Ministry of Science and Higher Education), "Industry, Technical Education and Vocational Training in Iran: An Analysis of Related Problems"; Ebrahim Farabakhshyan (from the Ministry of Labor), "Manpower and Related Problems of Vocational Education" from the archives of the Plan and Budget Organization.

86. The survey was conducted by Dr. Farrokh Aminzade, head of the division, and I have its copy. It was initiated to find out about their expectations for further study or employment. The questionnaires were distributed to 12,000 students, but only 9,984 forms were filled out properly and only these were used. See SBB, Daftar-e Jam'iyyat va Niru-ye Ensani, *Gozaresh-e Barresi-ye Khastha-ye Shoghli Honarjuyan va Daneshmandan-e Madares-e Fanni va Herfe'i-ye Keshvar* (Tehran, 1976).

87. Data on the background of the applicants are included in the survey of the SSHBA, *Ahval-e Shakhsi-ye Davtalaban-e Tahsilat-e 'Ali: Emtehanat-e Sarasari, Tir 1352* (Tehran, 1973), 86–90. The survey includes all applicants who took the general competitive examination (see Chapter 11).

that 65 percent of the fathers were farmers or unskilled urban workers, 15 percent held administrative positions, and only 2.5 percent had occupations requiring higher education (although, as has been seen, 4.2 percent had academic degrees). The survey of the university applicants shows that as many as 28 percent of their fathers had administrative positions, 18 percent worked in agriculture or in service industries, 22 percent in commerce, and 32 percent held positions requiring higher education (even though only 8 percent had degrees). According to the director of the survey, it confirmed the popular perception that vocational schools were for the less successful students and for children of the lower classes.[88]

The low income awaiting vocational school graduates was no incentive either. According to a National Iranian Oil Company (NIOC) report from the early 1960s, a general secondary school graduate (fresh out of school) earned almost three times as much as an experienced skilled worker in a modern industrial plant. Under these circumstances, it was not surprising that youth preferred an academic education over vocational training.[89]

Many graduates of vocational schools believed that they might still make up for their original failure to gain entrance to a university after all, or at least find a desk job. The above-mentioned survey of vocational school graduates includes the following astonishing findings: 88 percent claimed to have chosen vocational school out of a sense of personal commitment ('alaqe; literally "attachment"), and 91 percent said they were "satisfied" with their choice; but only 6.7 percent said they wanted to work as technicians. Instead, as many as 75 percent wanted to go on to a university, even though their training had, after all, been meant to turn them away from academic study. And at the university level, only 14 percent wanted to take up technological subjects. Even more revealing were their replies about their preferred occupation: 54.1 percent wanted to be engineers; 14.1 percent preferred desk jobs; 12.7 percent wanted to be teachers (a profession not attractive to graduates of regular high schools).[90] With regard to their detachment from manual

88. This was emphasized in the above-mentioned survey conducted by Aminzade (see above, note 86).

89. William H. Bartsch, commenting on the NIOC "Report on Salaries, Wages, and Benefits of the Principal Employers of Iran in Farvardin 1343," which he quotes in his article "The Industrial Labour Force of Iran: Problems of Recruitment, Training and Productivity," *MEJ*, 25 (Winter 1971), 15–30. Later comments show that the situation had not changed; see: *KI*, 12 May 1969, 6 September 1971; *Ettela'at*, 14 September 1971; *Kayhan*, 7 June 1976.

90. SBB, *Khastha-ye Shoghli Honarjuyan*, 23–34. For criticism of the view that vocational

work, at least reality was not far different from intention: according to data from the Ministry of Education, in the forty years up to the late 1960s only 25 percent of the vocational school graduates had worked in their fields of specialization, and many of them had apparently done so for only a short while.[91]

Given this state of affairs, industrial managers were not keen on hiring the graduates of vocational schools. 'Ali Reza'i, a leading industrialist, claimed at a seminar organized by the OECD and the PO in 1969 that although Iran needed working hands, the educational system produced "advice-giving heads."[92] Industrialists thought it economically unsound to pay the relatively high salaries the graduates expected.[93] Instead most factories preferred to hire cheap unskilled labor from among the recent migrants to the towns and train them on the job.[94] A PO study showed that only 2 percent of the total "skilled" operatives and master craftsmen employed in factories had ever benefited from any formal preemployment vocational training. A study by Tehran University indicated that only 1.3 percent of foremen and 2 percent of technicians were graduates of *honarestans*.[95] A vicious circle was thus set up: poor students went on to vocational schools; their qualifications at graduation were still low; they had little motivation to take up manual work; their income remained low; and their example caused the number of vocational school entrants to remain low.

The shah and his ministers, as well as professional educationalists and economists, were all aware of the problem and gave warnings about its consequences.[96] The PO Manpower Division frequently

---

training was a stepping stone toward administrative employment, see: Jacobs, 170; Bartsch, 24; *KI*, 27 October 1964, 24 January 1965.

91. Bartsch, 23–24; *KI*, 11 April 1970. The low standards of both students and teachers, the theoretical bent still noticeable in vocational training, the lack of suitable equipment and the failure to coordinate between industry and the vocational schools were stressed by many Iranian and foreign experts. See: PO, *The Fourth National Development Plan* (Tehran, 1968), 263; George B. Baldwin, *Planning and Development in Iran* (Baltimore: Johns Hopkins University Press, 1967), 139–64; Jacobs, 153–76; Bartsch, 15–30.

92. *KI*, 18 September 1969. Similarly an article by Houshang Mehr-Ayn, ibid., 29 July 1970; ILO, *Employment*, 69–70; Bartsch, 23.

93. See the above-mentioned survey of graduates, 35–38; and survey by Bartsch, 21–24, 28.

94. Thus, for example, at twenty-one of the twenty-three factories surveyed by Bartsch (Bartsch, 18–21).

95. Ibid., 24; Hessam-Vaziri, 5–6.

96. For examples of the shah's many statements to that effect, see: Pahlavi, *Ta'lifat*, 3:2234 (from a speech to the government in 1959), 4:3270–72 (in an interview in May 1963); idem, *Mission*, 252–54; *KAEA, 1970*, 52–56 (from a speech of 18 July 1970); and quotations in *Ettela'at*, 23 September 1967, 4 August 1968.

pointed to the discrepancy between demand and supply for graduates of vocational and regular high schools. Already in its first manpower survey (conducted in 1958 together with the Ministry of Labor), it stressed "the grave shortage of skilled manpower" and warned that "unless immediate decisive steps are taken . . . the economic plan will soon be faced with grave problems."[97] A PO survey in 1975 (intended to evaluate long-term labor needs) drew similar conclusions, as did the Institute for International Political and Economic Studies in a 1974 study on the future of the Iranian economy.[98] The five-year economic plans, the annual conferences on education, the Royal Institute for Research on Education, and many other institutes and individuals echoed their findings.[99]

Acknowledging that the problem was rooted in social conceptions, the government tried to enforce change through indoctrination. The shah placed himself at the head of a campaign to convince people that the "moral worth (*sharaf*), respect (*ehteram*) and honor (*'ezzat*)" of manual work was not inferior to that of any other occupation.[100] His ministers of education echoed him, as did the annual conferences on education. The 1972 conference, for example, recommended measures to ensure that people possessing "professional qualifications will enjoy high social prestige (*heythiyyat*) and status (*mowqe'iyyat*), will be suitably compensated, morally and materially, and will gain the appreciation due to them for their contribution to the economy and to society."[101] Such verbal tributes had no more than a marginal effect.

The 1971/2 restructuring of the school system did stimulate a modest increase in the number of vocational schools, but did little to change the public's opinion of vocational training. An additional attempt was made in 1975 by canceling tuition at vocational schools. Since this

97. SBB va Vezarat-e Kar, *Barresi Manabe' va Ehtiyajat-e Niru-ye Ensani dar Iran* (Tehran, 1975), pp. i–iii.

98. SBB/Mo'avenat-e Barname Rizi, *Pish Bini-ye Deraz Modat-e Eshteghal* (Tehran, 1975), 1–24; Mo'assese-ye Pezhuheshha-ye Siyasi va Eqtesadi Beynolmellali, *Tajziye va Tahlil az Ayande-ye Eqtesadi-ye Iran* (Tehran, 1974), 3–5.

99. SBB, *Gozaresh-e Ejra'i-ye Barname-ye Haft Sale-ye Dovvom* (Tehran, 1964), 57–59; idem, *Barname Sevvom*, 119–24; idem, *Barname Chaharom*, 234–48; PO, *Iran's Fifth Development Plan; 1973–1978* (Tehran, 1975), 199–201; *KAEA, 1968*, article 6 of the resolutions; *KAEA, 1969*, article 25; *KAEA, 1970*, articles 4, 12, 15–17; *KAEA, 1971*, articles 6, 9–11; *KAEA, 1972*, article 2; *KAEA, 1973*, articles 11–12, 19–26; *KAEA, 1974*, articles 36–39; SSHBA, *Amuzesh Fanni*, i.

100. Pahlavi, *Ta'lifat*, 3:3014–20; idem, *Mission*, 252–54; and his speeches quoted in *Ettela'at*, 6 and 8 August 1968, 30 November 1969, 19 July 1970, 4 September 1976 and in *KI*, 7 August 1968, 12 May 1969, 18 July 1970, 6 September 1971.

101. *KAEA, 1972*, article 15 of the resolutions.

measure was not implemented until 1975/6—very close to the end of the shah's regime—it is difficult to assess. But, as Table 11 shows, the fastest growth did occur between 1974/5 and 1976/7. Yet the change remained quantitative alone. As long as social attitudes remained as they were, laws and regulations were incapable of effecting a real change. Moreover, my conversations with many parents and students revealed that the cancellation of tuition fees was not thought of as conveying an appreciation for vocational education, but rather as a sop thrown out to the underprivileged. Thus, in a way, it reinforced the old beliefs.

There is no better way to conclude this section than to quote from the conclusion of the PO vocational school survey:

> The yearning for degrees, which constitutes one of the main problems of the Iranian society today, has been conspicuous in this survey too. Although the graduates of . . . [vocational] schools did not stand much chance of being accepted at a university, and although many of them do not have the qualifications for academic study, yet 75 percent of them want to continue their studies at a university . . . . If vocational education is doomed to become a copy of the regular high school system, i.e., to supply university candidates, why do we have to invest in vocational education sums that are [proportionally] several times higher than those invested in the regular high schools?[102]

"A Bridge to Nowhere"

In the 1970s, Iran had become a prime example of the truth of Ivan Illich's saying that the very "existence of schools produces the demand for schooling."[103] Demand had risen dramatically, and, as has been shown, with regard to elementary and secondary education supply had—after some time lag—virtually caught up with it. But for the underprivileged, the ultimate escape from poverty was through higher education, and at that point the fairly balanced supply-and-demand situation broke down.

Right down to the end of the shah's regime, the high school certificate continued to be seen as a passport to university admission. The quality of secondary education was such that it did not point its graduates toward any other destination and failed to signal to weak students that

102. SBB, *Khastha-ye Shoghli Honarjuyan*, 47–48. According to the SBB, a year at regular high school cost between 8,000 and 9,000 Riyals per student, in vocational schools between 150,000 and 300,000 Riyals: *KI*, 27 October 1964.

103. Illich, 50–56, 105.

they stood no chance of entering the university. Graduates of both regular and vocational high schools thought of higher education as the only "natural" path for them to proceed along and as the only proper "return" for the efforts they had invested in the *diplom*. But the government had failed to balance demand and supply at the higher level, and indeed for a number of years deliberately blocked university expansion (see Chapter 11). The result was that only a small—and constantly diminishing—percentage of aspirants to a university education were able to enter that promised land.

To understand the full magnitude of this problem and its social and political repercussions, one must realize how great was the desire of high school students to go on to the university. My own experience in Iran just prior to the fall of the shah confirmed that this was the main question on their minds, and indeed on the minds of their entire family. Admission to their preferred school and faculty was the most important issue in their lives. Consequently, high schools were graded according to their success in having their graduates admitted to prestigious universities and popular departments.[104] The disparate resolve of candidates to enter a university was attested to in the above survey of participants in competitive examinations. Of those taking the examinations in the year surveyed, 26 percent had already taken them three or more times before; 61.8 percent said that if they failed they would try again (only 14.4 percent said they would not; 23.8 percent were not sure). Asked "under what conditions" they would be willing to forgo their present plans for a higher education, 68.0 percent answered "under no circumstances" or on condition that they went to study abroad; 26.1 percent were willing to give up higher education provided they be granted a "respected" and "well-paid" position. For the sake of a university education, 77.3 percent were willing to move away from their hometowns (a surprisingly high figure in view of the many candidates from Tehran). No fewer than 71 percent were willing to take up subjects they had not originally listed as their preference.[105]

The numerical results of these trends are set out in Table 12, showing the steep decline in the percentage of high school graduates gaining university admission. Admission figures do not include those who were accepted by colleges rather than universities (for these, see Chap-

---

104. A headmaster of one of the most prestigious high schools in Tehran told me in 1976 that this was the only yardstick by which students and parents evaluated his school.

105. Kotubi, *Amuzesh-e Motavasete*. For a similar conclusion reached by the Royal Institute for Research on Education, see Chapter 11.

Table 12. Number of high school graduates compared with university admissions between 1961/2 and 1978/9

Year	[A] High school graduates	[B] University entrants	[B] as a % of [A]
1961/2	15,924	5,781	36.3
1966/7	38,198	12,210	32.0
1971/2	78,494	23,054	29.4
1975/6	177,850	25,138	14.0
1978/9	235,000	28,500	12.1

Sources: Computed from data in: SSHBA, *Amuzesh-e 'Ali*, 1975/6; Nasafat, 38–39. Estimated data for 1978/9: *Iran Almanac, 1978*, 440–43.

ter 11). In any case, these institutions were not considered prestigious enough.[106]

Under Reza Shah, most high school graduates had been admitted to Tehran University or sent abroad at government expense. The rest moved into prestigious desk jobs, which at that time their high school certificates were still capable of securing for them.[107] In the mid-1950s, 50 percent of the graduates still moved on to Iranian universities. From then on, the decline set in.

Revealing as they are, the percentages in Table 12 do not tell the full story. To do so, one must also look at the absolute figures: the discrepancy between high school graduates and university admission grew from some 10,000 in 1961/2 to over 200,000 in 1978/9. These are net figures, arrived at after deducting the numbers of those who eventually found a place in one of the colleges or went abroad to study (together, these two groups accounted in the late 1970s for fewer than 50,000 students). In each of the three last years of the shah's rule, between 250,000 and 300,000 young people applied for university admission;[108] the highest actual admission figure (that for 1978/9) was a little short of 30,000. Thus, in these final years there were well over 200,000 young people each year who had their hopes dashed by a cruel reality. Since they were not trained for anything else and since—unlike in the past—their high school certificates were no longer sufficient to

106. For the low appeal of such schools, see the survey conducted by Morteza Nasafat, head of the Center for Psychological Research (Mo'assese-ye Tahqiqat-e Ravanshenasi) of Tehran University, on the "Opinions of Iranian Students": *Sanjesh Afkar-e Daneshjuyan-e Keshvar* (Tehran, 1975/6), 38–39.

107. See also Masha'ekhi, "Hadaf-e Matavasete," 1–15.

108. In most years in the 1970s, the number of applications equaled or somewhat exceeded the total of that year's high school graduates. Making up for the small number who did not apply were others who had been turned down before and were now trying again.

secure them attractive administrative employment, their frustration was shattering. Their entire families joined in their grief. Their collective frustration and anger made them turn against the regime, and they became a potential threat to its stability. Supporters of the conflict theory (see Introduction) and some experts examining Iranian education had long warned that in certain circumstances the spread of education might threaten rather than underpin political stability. Now, in a way, they were being proved right. Clearly, many of the young people who turned against the shah in 1978 were partly, and often enough principally, motivated by such sentiments.

Demonstrations and strikes of high school students had already occurred in October 1970, triggered by a decision of the Ministry of Education to raise the standards of the matriculation examinations. The minister claimed that the intention was to improve the quality of secondary education,[109] but the ministry obviously also meant to regulate the number of university entrants and signal to some high school students to lower their expectations. The government soon restored order but found itself compelled to compromise on the examinations. The unrest was all the more significant in that it occurred against the background of a generally quiescent political atmosphere at the time. In the last quarter of 1977, and even more so during 1978, students took an active part in the demonstrations against the shah. Their motives for joining the rank of the opposition were obviously complex, but frustration at finding the road to higher education blocked undoubtedly played a significant part.

The sense of outrage on the part of those rejected by the universities was plain to see in Tehran on the yearly occasion when the results of the competitive examinations were made known. The lists were posted on the walls of the Ministry of Science and Higher Education and then printed in the daily newspapers—itself a sign of the public interest they elicited. There were scenes of frantic joy for a few, and of pain and despair for many. Tens of thousands of families sank into despondency. Their frustration and outrage were all the greater because those rejected were now liable to immediate conscription, instead of enjoying the automatic deferment accorded to students.

Those in charge of educational planning were not unaware of the political reverberations of the situation. The resolutions of the committee on pre-university education at the 1976 Conference on Education

---

109. *Ettela'at*, 27 and 28 October 1970. For the proposed changes and the subsequent demonstrations and strikes, see *KI*, 19 and 28 October 1970; *Ayandegan*, 19 and 21 October 1970.

did not mince words in speaking of them: "The existing curriculum
. . . leaves our young people no choice but to go on to university . . . .
Teaching methods are not geared to our social and economic needs.
They lead to a deterioration in the level of schooling *and to the youngsters'
dissatisfaction, and promote tendencies toward rebelliousness (ʿasyan) . . .
among those failing in the competitive examinations.*"[110] Professor ʿAbbas
Safavyan addressed the conference as follows: "We have placed all the
youngsters . . . behind a huge dam with a very narrow breach through
which only a few can steer their course into the universities." Yet, he
added, the school system continued to impress on youngsters that only
through university education could they "reach the highest peak of
happiness."[111]

Opposition circles were even quicker to realize that the dissatisfaction
of high school graduates could have serious political consequences.
Thus, for example, Jalal Al-e Ahmad wrote in his *Gharbzadegi* (West-
strickenness): "each year about 20,000 high school graduates spew forth
until, lo and behold!, they become potential fuel for all future dissatisfaction, complexes, crises, and perhaps revolutions."[112]

In quantitative terms, elementary and secondary education had indeed gradually turned into a success story, but taken as a whole, Iran's
educational system failed to formulate an appropriate educational philosophy. For rapidly growing numbers, high school education became
(to use Illich's phrase) a "bridge to nowhere." In the mid-1970, educationalists warned the shah of the grave social economic and political
dangers inherent in the prevailing situation, but when attempts to
expand higher education were eventually made, it was a case of too
little, too late. The pent-up frustrations of the would-be students added
their weight to the many other components of the turbulence that
brought down the shah.

110. VʿU, *Nohomin Konferans-e Arzyabi-ye Enqelab-e Amuzeshi, 1976*: from the archives
of the Ministry of Science and Higher Education (emphasis added). A summary of the
resolutions was published in *Kayhan*, 4 and 7 September 1976.

111. See his speech quoted in *Kayhan*, 7 September 1976.

112. Jalal Al-e Ahmad, *Plagued by the West (Gharbzadegi)*, trans. Paul Sprachman (Delmar, N.Y.: Caravan Books, 1982), 89. The figures quoted above relate to the early 1960s.

10

Higher Education

The rapid expansion of higher education in the West—sometimes called the educational revolution—started in the late nineteenth century.[1] In the developing countries its expansion began after World War II but did not gather momentum until the 1960s. Although still lagging behind the West, progress in the Third World as a whole was nevertheless fast: whereas in 1960, only 3.6 percent of those between the ages of eighteen and twenty-three were at seminaries, colleges, or universities, no fewer than 9.0 percent attended in 1975. The figures for Iran, however, were lower than that average.[2] It was to correct that shortfall—both quantitatively and qualitatively—that the shah initiated his own educational revolution and incorporated it as (part of) the twelfth principle of the White Revolution in 1967.

Contrary to the earlier policies of reform (*eslahat*), the intention now was for a change on the scale of a revolution (*enqelab*). The proclamation of the educational revolution in 1967 (the fifth year of the White Revolution) marked a turning point: for a century or so, the emphasis had

1. Martin Trow, "Reflections on the Transition from Mass to Universal Higher Education," *Daedalus*, 99, 2 (Winter 1970), 1–42.
2. If we look at the age group between 20 and 24, we see that in Turkey 6.6 percent were studying in 1975 (compared with 2.9 percent in 1960), in Egypt 13.5 percent (as against 4.9 percent), and in Iran 5.0 percent (1.2 percent). By comparison, for all the countries classed as "developed" by UNESCO, the 1975 average was 29.6 percent (15.1 percent in 1960). For North America alone, the figures were 48.1 percent and 29.7 percent, respectively. UNESCO, *Statistical Yearbook, 1977* (Paris, 1978), 102–4, 128–70.

been on elementary and secondary education; now higher education had top priority.

One factor in the shah's considerations was that, despite his obsessive fear of political opposition activity among students, he had by 1967 come to feel strong enough to disregard that risk. (Had the 1968 wave of campus disturbances in the West occurred earlier, it might well have deterred him;[3] but by the time it erupted he was set on his new course.) Other factors, as noted before, were the manpower needs created by the White Revolution reform schemes, the fast-growing demand for higher education, and the availability of greater funds from oil income.

An outward sign of the shift of priorities was the establishment in October 1967 of the Ministry of Science and Higher Education, soon to acquire greater authority than the Ministry of Education. In the following years, the annual conferences on education, the shah's pronouncements, as well as government policy statements all attested to the same trend. The 1970 conference, for instance, stated explicitly that higher education was to be given highest priority (article 4).[4] In the early 1970s, however, the trend was reversed again. There was a growing recognition that the advance of higher education depended largely on elementary and secondary education, and a more balanced policy was sought. At the end of the period discussed, education at the lower levels was again the focus of attention. This time, the outward sign was the dissolution, in August 1977, of the Ministry of Science and Higher Education and the reassumption of responsibility for education at all levels by the Ministry of Education.

One of the first steps of the Ministry of Science and Higher Education during its ten-year lifetime was to call for an annual conference on educational policies. The first conference, in August 1968, was attended by the shah, the prime minister, the ministers whose work had to do with education (science, education, labor, economy), the head of the Plan and Budget Organization, the chancellors of all the universities, and distinguished professors. It outlined "the philosophy and aims of

3. Apprehension of the possible impact of the student riots in the West on political activity by Iranian students were expressed at the Gochsar conference on education on 2 May 1968 by Rahnama, the first minister of science and higher education (hitherto: the minister of science): MAM, document 4714.

4. At the first conference, two clauses in the resolutions dealt with pre-university education, the rest (forty-one) dealt with higher education. At the second conference, all thirty-three clauses dealt with higher educations as did twenty (out of twenty-two) in 1971 and nineteen (out of twenty-one) in 1972. After that, the references to pre-university education gradually increased.

the educational revolution" in fairly general terms.[5] From 1969 until 1976, further such annual "Conferences for the Evaluation of the Achievements of the Educational Revolution" (*Konferans-e Arzyabi-ye Enqelab-e Amuzeshi*) were held to review the implementation of existing plans and outline further measures for promoting higher education.[6] The personal participation of the shah lent them added weight. His vigorous criticism inspired lively and often highly critical discussions. During peak period's of the shah's power, no other area of Iranian life came under such heavy criticism as education did.

Quantitative Expansion

Actual Growth

As far as the numerical growth of higher education is concerned, the shah's reign can be divided into three subperiods—more or less co-inciding with the three stages of his political strength. From 1941 to 1953, the shah and his governments jointly pursued a policy of ex-panding higher education, with the concurrence of most intellectuals and educationalists. But political instability and economic difficulties prevented the government from taking much practical action. In the second subperiod, from 1953 up to the educational revolution, the shah—defying the view of educationalists and ignoring growing public demands—acted to block the growth of higher education. The role of students and faculty in the crises of the early 1950s and the early 1960s had led the shah to view them as potential dissenters liable to threaten political stability and his own rule. Finally, from 1967 until close to the end of his reign, he reversed his course altogether and (for reasons already noted) actively promoted an unrestrained expansion of aca-demic education. University heads who had previously pleaded for expansion now sought to curb the rapid pace in order to avoid a decline in standards. The ups and down of educational policy can be traced by following the dates for establishing new universities and the number of students at them.

In the first period, all difficulties notwithstanding, there was a certain momentum in founding new universities. A law dated 24 May 1949 provided for the establishment of new universities in four provincial

5. Rahnama, 1:78–80, 124; 2:160.
6. On the aims of the conferences, see *Ettela'at*, 10 May 1969, 18 July 1970, 22 June 1971.

Table 13. Iranian universities in 1976/7

University	Location	Year established	No. of students in 1976/7
Tehran	Tehran	1935	18,183
Azerbadegan	Tabriz	1947	7,628
Ferdowsi	Meshhed	1949	5,647
Pahlavi	Shiraz	1949	5,129
Isfahan	Isfahan	1950	5,863
Gondi Shapur	Ahvaz	1955	3,424
Melli	Tehran	1960	8,185
Aryamehr	Tehran	1966	3,228
Tarbiyyat-e Moʿallem	Tehran	1974	2,957
Sepahyan-e Enqelab	Varamin	1974	4,278
Farah Pahlavi	Tehran	1975	1,430
Baluchestan	Zahedan	1975	206
Bou-ʿAli	Hamadan	1976	18
Razi	Kermanshah	1976	1,445
Gilan	Rasht	1976	757
Farabi	Tehran	1976	38
Kerman	Kerman	1976	277
			68,693

Sources: Computed from MTBRA data.
Note: The names of some of the universities were changed after their establishment. Listed above are their names as of 1976/7.

capitals (listed in second to fifth place in Table 13).[7] They were set up with little planning and with scant regard for the availability of teaching and research staff. Rather, their creation reflected the pressing needs for skilled labor, pressures from the junior staff of Tehran University and from the liberal intellectuals in general, and the shah's own interests in the matter. They were founded around local hospitals (which served as the nucleus of their medical schools) and also included the humanities. In general, the staff comprised local physicians and Tehran University teachers who had received a special bonus to go out to the provinces. The haste that characterized creation of these schools had already been displayed when Tabriz University was set up in January 1947. At that time, the Ministry of Education had sent two Tehran professors, Mostafa Habibi (from the school of medicine) and Khanbaba Bayani (humanities), to inquire into the possibility of founding a university there. Within two months they sketched plans for faculties of medicine and the humanities; these were set up the same year but

7. *MQ,* term 15, 183–84. Tabriz University had been founded before the law was approved.

functioned separately for several years. The new university was to be staffed by faculty sent out from Tehran (and thus absorb the surplus of young academic staff there). In this case, it should be mentioned, the shah's regime only continued what had been started earlier by the short-lived Azerbayjan Republic. It was the Pishavari government that had first established a university at Tabriz, but the Iranian documents during the shah's rule gave no credit to this pioneer initiative.[8] In the next three years, universities were founded along similar lines in Meshhed, Shiraz, and Isfahan. In their first years, they had only faculties of medicine. In Meshhed, a faculty of humanities was added in 1955, in Shiraz in 1954, and in Isfahan in 1957. (Isfahan also got a pharmacological faculty in 1954.) The growth of colleges was proportionately slower: until 1953, only six new colleges were added to the five existing in 1941.[9]

In the following period, by contrast, only three new universities were founded in the space of thirteen years (1951–1974). At first, the slowdown had to do with the need to consolidate the earlier provincial universities; later the reasons were primarily political. The first university to be established in this period, Gondi Shapur, resembled the ones listed above. It started out as a medical school only, and fourth-year students were initially sent to continue their studies at Tehran University.[10] The National University and Aryamehr were different: both were prestigious private schools concentrating on teaching specific skills. The National University focused on social science and economics (its first faculties were those of economy, banking, political science, and architecture; in response to growing demands, faculties of medicine and science were added later). Aryamehr was designed to be a school of technology and remained one.[11] Higher education for high school graduates who had found no room at the universities was to be provided by the colleges, which developed rapidly in this period. Their number grew from twenty-five in 1963 to fifty-seven in 1967. They were to solve two other problems with one stroke: supply more skilled men to meet the needs of the economy and offer vacancies for

8. On the founding of Tabriz University and its first years, see: MAM, documents 441 and 4698; Khanbaba Bayani, "Daneshgah-e Tabriz," AP, 1948/9, 7:21–34. With some resentment Al-e Ahmad (Gharbzadegi, 89) mentioned Pishavari's initiative to establish a university "as a symbol of the independence or autonomy of the province," but, he continued, all traces of this "have been rubbed off the books."

9. MAM, document 441.

10. Ibid., documents 441 and 4769.

11. On their foundations, see MAM, documents 4696 and 4695, respectively.

young academics or additional source of income for the established faculty at the other schools.

In the third period, it was declared policy to expand higher education. Yet unlike in the early 1940s, new schools did not spring up instantly. Since the aim now was to achieve higher academic standards, and since leading professors insisted on it, great attention was devoted to planning, staff recruitment, and the general campus infrastructure. Thus universities planned in the late 1960s actually opened only in the mid-1970s: two in 1974, two in 1975, and five in 1976 (see Table 13). Several other projected universities, among them the Open University (Daneshgah-e Azad), were still at the planning stages when the shah lost power.[12] In the same period, a rapid growth of colleges was seen: from fifty-seven in 1967 to 111 in 1970, 148 in 1973, 195 in 1974, and 231 in 1976. Many were private institutions, which, given the growing demand, were now viewed as profitable investments.

Throughout the period, Tehran University remained the largest school. It thought of itself as the "mother university" (*daneshgah-e madar*), setting the model for all others. It felt obliged to teach any subject taken up in any other schools. Government attention and public regard both focused on it. But in 1963, the Pahlavi University was founded in collaboration with the University of Pennsylvania to replace Shiraz University along entirely different lines. Its curriculum, similar to that of American schools, was based on gaining credits in a semestral system. The academic staff was made up predominantly of graduates of American universities, and instruction was in English.[13] From my visits to the university and interviews with its chancellor (Farhang Mehr), and from numerous statements made by some of the deans in office in 1976/7, it became clear that they regarded it as an elitist school (though not necessarily reserved for children of elite families). It was to remain small and prestigious, valuing quality rather than quantity, and prepare its graduates for advanced specialization. With the shah's encouragement, its staff aspired to turn it into an important regional center for higher education, attracting students and staff from the entire Middle East. This was also the rationale for making English the language of instruction. (More realistically, it was argued that most students would continue their studies in English-speaking countries.)

12. For the idea behind it and the intention for providing "mass higher education" see Daneshgah-e Azad-e Iran, *Daneshgah-e Azad-e Iran: Rah-e Now dar Amuzesh-e 'Ali* (Tehran, 1974).

13. Daneshgah-e Pahlavi, *Majmu'e A'innameha, Asasnameha va Moqarrarat-e Daneshgah-e Pahlavi* (Shiraz, 1971); idem, *Daneshgah-e Pahlavi dar Chahar Sal-e Godhashte: 1963/4–1967/8* (Shiraz, 1967).

Table 14. Number of university and college students in selected
years between 1941/2 and 1976/7

Year	[A] Total of students in higher education	[B] University students	[B] as % of [A]
1941/2	3,367	1,814	53.9
1946/7	5,883	4,311	73.3
1951/2	7,463	7,340	98.3
1953/4	9,845	9,685	98.4
1956/7	11,334	11,276	99.5
1961/2	22,856	21,111	92.4
1966/7	36,882	27,385	74.2
1971/2	97,338	47,176	48.5
1974/5	135,354	58,461	43.2
1975/6	151,905	65,372	43.0
1976/7	154,215	68,693	44.5

Sources: Computed from data of MTBRA and SSHBA.

The many colleges operating alongside the universities were of divergent types: some (eighty-six of the 231 existing in 1976) offered academic degrees, and a few (e.g., Daneshkade 'Ilm va San'at and Daneshkade San'ati Politeknik) had gained considerable prestige and had in fact become small single-faculty universities. Most offered the degree called *fowq-e diplom* ("higher diploma") for specific occupations (like accounting, translation, music, teaching, or social work). Many of them were located in Tehran where the demand was highest: ninety of the total number were in the capital, including fifty-one of the eighty-six offering academic degrees. According to the data of the Royal Institute for Research on Education, thirty-five of the 1973/4 total of 148 colleges were private, and they attracted a quarter of the total college students. Yet, with few exceptions, colleges—whether public or private—lacked the prestige necessary to make them an attractive alternative to the universities.[14] Nevertheless, given the high proportion of candidates rejected by the universities, they were in great demand. They entitled a young man to call himself a "student" (*mohasel* or *daneshju*) and were thus better, though perhaps barely so, than no postsecondary education at all.

Table 14 gives figures for the expansion of higher education and for the ratio of university to college students for the entire period of the shah's reign. During the first period of expansion, between 1941/2 and 1953/4, the university student body grew 5.3 times larger while the

14. This was well brought out, for example, in Nasafat's survey of student views and attitudes (Nasafat, 31–32).

number of secondary students multiplied by 3.4). Consequently there was a sharp drop in the share of college students: from 46.1 percent in 1941/2 to 1.6 percent in 1953/4. In the second period, university expansion was slow: between 1953/4 and 1966/7 the number of students multiplied by 2.8 (that of secondary students by 4.3). The early 1960s were the lowest point: an increase of only 29.7 percent between 1961/2 and 1966/7 (as against 49.2 percent in secondary education). Colleges, on the other hand, now expanded quickly: their share in the total student population went up to 25.8 percent in 1966/7. In the third period, both forms of higher education gathered momentum, but the colleges retained their advantage: between 1966/7 and 1976/7, the number of university students multiplied by 2.5, but that of college students by nine.

At most of the older universities, the student body had long reached maximum capacity. Tehran University, for example, had topped the 15,000 mark already in 1966/7; in the next ten years it grew by less than 3,000. Originally created by fusing several existing colleges, it again had campus buildings spread out in different quarters of the city in the 1970s. Its president, Dr. Hushang Nahavandi, claimed in 1976 that academic as well as administrative restraints made further expansion "impossible." The universities planned in the late 1960s were only beginning to function in the mid-1970s and could not meet the expanding demand. The two schools opened in 1974 were in fact not new, but were older institutions now being remade into universities. Another seven set up in 1975 and 1976 had a total of only 4,171 students between them in 1976/7. The share of college students continued to grow, reaching 57 percent in 1975/6. It declined slightly the following year, but the basic trend was not reversed for the remainder of the shah's reign.

The direct influence of the court on the universities was most conspicuous in the transition from the above-mentioned antiexpansionist to the expansionist subperiod. In the early 1960s, the shah and the court pressured heads of the universities to block the expansion of higher education. Already in the mid-1960s an Iranian who has been influential in the formation and administration of higher education policy indicated in an interview that the decision to restrict university admission "had come from above." The idea was to limit higher education to those "who had the most at stake" in maintaining the present system.[15] A SAVAK general who was close to the shah told me after the revolution that at the time the shah viewed the students as a group

15. Zonis (*Elite*, 36–37), who interviewed this official, did not identify him.

influenced by antimonarchical ideologies and a communist worldview. Until 1967, it was therefore his policy "to restrict higher education."[16]

The opposite was true of the later period: the forced rate of growth after 1967 was, to some extent, opposed by university presidents, deans, and professors, who felt that the government was pressuring them to expand regardless of academic standards.[17] Behnam claimed that when Nahavandi concluded that Tehran University could not expand any more, he had to make use of his personal access to the empress to convince the authorities. The chancellor of Pahlavi University, his deputy, and the deans considered it their main achievement to have successfully resisted government pressure for quantitative expansion. Here, too, their ability to withstand pressure was explained (even by Professor Mehr himself) in terms of the chancellor's personal ties with key government figures. The fact that the regime now allowed public criticism of educational policy made it easier for them to stand up to the government. But not all universities and colleges could or wanted to do so, and overall growth was quite rapid after 1967.

Nonetheless, the ratio of supply to demand made it difficult for students to gain admission to a university. This imbalance, as well as the extra prestige attaching to study abroad, led to an increase in the number of students leaving for universities in the West. Precise numbers, however, are impossible to come by, since most now paid their own way and only a few had their studies financed by the government. The Ministry of Education kept no records of students abroad. Beginning in 1967, the Ministry of Science tried to do so but found it could trace only those who asked to leave the country before doing their military service or who applied for foreign currency allowances. The Department of Students Affairs in the ministry had particulars for 18,035 students in 1971/2, but estimated that the total was 25,000 (compared with about 3,000 in 1956, 14,000 in the late 1950s, and 17,000 in 1968).[18] In 1977, the Royal Institute for Research on Education and the Institute for Research and Planning in Science and Education in the

16. The general served in the SAVAK for thirty years and was close to the shah in the 1970s. The interview with him was held in Tel Aviv in 1980.

17. These sentiments were expressed then, among others, by the following: Nahavandi (chancellor of Tehran University), Behnam (his deputy), Nasafat (head of the Institute for Psychological Research at the same university), Nikgouhar (head of the Institute for Social Research), Vadi'i (deputy minister of education), Mehr (chancellor of Pahlavi University), Shir'alipur (his deputy) and the deans Mo'idi (engineering), Nasr (medicine), and Hadidi (humanities).

18. V'U, Daftar-e Omur-e Daneshjuyan, *Amar-e Daneshjuyan-e Irani Moqim-e Keshvarha-ye Kharej* (Tehran, 1972/3), 73. Data for 1956 are given in *Ettela'at*, 20 June 1968; and for 1971: *Ayandegan*, 11 September 1971.

Ministry of Science put the number at over 40,000—equivalent to more than a quarter of the total students at all local institutions of higher education or to two-thirds of all university students in Iran.[19]

Trying to Plan Ahead

Planning ahead for education and directing its course to go hand in hand with social and economic change and provide the skilled and specialized manpower needed by the nation are difficult tasks at the best of times, but particularly so in developing countries. At the time discussed here, some developing countries, (e.g., India and some states in South America) had a planning machinery, but their educational systems were slow to expand; in others (such as Mexico and Sri Lanka) education was expanding fast, but without the benefit of planning.[20] By and large, in the developing countries, planning for education and for professional training was "the weakest part" in planning for social and economic development.[21] They lacked an appropriate tradition, and for some people—mainly in Muslim countries—planning was even regarded as human interference with God's authority.[22] The dearth of accurate data on past and present developments added further difficulties. Coordination between the different bodies dealing with edu-

19. According to Dr. Safavi (deputy head of the latter institute) and Mr. Razedan (the director of the former), these estimates were accepted by both institutes. Data published by U.S. immigration authorities indicate that at the end of 1977 there were over 12,000 Iranian students in the country (the largest group of students from any foreign country) and that an additional 27,000 were staying in the country (without permits) upon graduation or after quitting school: *NYT*, 14 December 1977.

The fact that increasing numbers of Iranians were studying abroad accelerated the brain drain. Thus, according to official Iranian data from the early 1960s, about half the graduates of Tehran University's medical school left the country and many of them did not return (*Echo of Iran*, 24 May 1965). A decade later Iran became the fifth largest supplier of physicians to the United States; see Hossain Ronaghy et al., "Physician Migration to the United States: One Country's Transfusion Is Another Country's Hemorrhage," *Journal of the American Medical Association*, 227 (1974), 538–42. According to another source, only 7 percent of the Iranians who had graduated abroad between 1950 and 1968 returned to Iran (Hamid Mowlana, "US-Iranian Relations, 1954–1978: A Case of Cultural Domination," unpublished paper presented to the Middle East Studies Association annual conference, Salt Lake City, November 1979, 5).

20. Adams and Bjork, 143, 156; Taiwo, 5.

21. Frederick Harbison, "Human Resources and Development," in UNESCO, *Educational Planning*, 62–63.

22. A Jordanian citizen took the attitude that planning ahead was tantamount to heresy, since only Allah knows the future (idem, "Human Resources Assessments," ibid., 117).

cational and economic planning and between planning and executive organs posed another serious problem.[23]

Compared with other developing countries, Iran made an early start with economic planning (in the late 1940s), as well as manpower planning (in the mid-1950s). But serious efforts to plan the development of education and to adapt it to current needs started only with the formation of the Ministry of Science and Higher Education in 1967. Until then, planning—and to a degree implementation as well—were divided among several bodies: the divisions for planning and vocational training at the Plan and Budget Organization; the Ministry of Eeducation; and the universities. The assessment of manpower needs was in the jurisdiction of the Plan and Budget Organization, and planning for manpower training in that of the Ministry of Education. Coordination between them was haphazard, and some ministries continued to train their own staff.[24] Often enough, therefore, the actual development of education differed considerably from what had been planned. Moreover, social and economic change was so rapid, particularly after the White Revolution had begun, that plans quickly became outdated.[25]

The formation of the Ministry of Science and Higher Education on 18 October 1967 was meant to correct this situation. But the ministry, itself formed without adequate prior planning, failed to perform its major tasks. Its functions were not specified clearly enough.[26] Prime Minister Hoveyda said rather vaguely that it had been formed to deal "more emphatically" with the problems facing higher education, and thus promote the (newly launched) educational revolution. Rahnama, its first minister, was no more specific.[27] Only in mid-December did

23. On difficulties in collecting statistical data on education in developing countries and their impact on educational planning, see Kendall, 7–19. For coordination difficulties: Hutchitner, 85–96; Harbison, "Human Resources Assessment," 191.

24. Harry Melville, *Iran: Science Policy and Organization* (Paris: UNESCO, 1969), 6; Baldwin, 139–41; Rahnama 2:11; *Ayandegan*, 5 August 1968; *Ettela'at*, 5 May, 20 July 1969. Recommendations for changes were made at the annual conferences on education: *KAEA, 1968*, article 15 of the resolutions; *KAEA, 1969*, resolutions 3, 7, and 28; *KAEA, 1970*, article 29.

25. See J. Defay and J. Spacy, eds., *Structures d'Organization du Ministere de la Science et de l'Ensignement Superieur* (Paris: UNESCO, 1969), 4–7.

26. For the tasks of the ministry, called Vezarat-e 'Ulum va Amuzesh-e 'Ali, see: Rahnama, 2:7, 69; and *KAEA, 1968*, resolution 14. Already in 1964 the Ministry of Culture and Arts (Vezarat-e Farhang va Honar) had been formed by removing certain departments from the Ministry of Education.

27. For Hoveyda's statement, see *Ettela'at*, 19 and 23 October 1967; for Rahnama's, ibid., 8 November 1967.

the government approve its terms of reference: the new ministry was to be in charge of planning for the *entire* educational system and have direct operative responsibility for *higher* education.[28] The appropriate law was not passed until on 1 February 1968 (some four months after the ministry had started operating). It included the earlier government directives and also empowered the ministry to decide on the establishment, or suspension, of institutes for higher learning; to supervise them; to coordinate research; and to supervise studies abroad.[29]

The ministry itself viewed planning as its main task. Rahnama said that in its planning work and its policy recommendations, the ministry would be guided by the country's "needs, possibilities and targets" for the next twenty years. His approach was in line with recommendations soon to be made by a UNESCO committee.[30] In his speech at the Gochsar conference in 1967—the first conference of the minister and his senior staff with the heads of the institutes for higher learning—Rahnama stressed the need for formulating a "science policy" (*siyasat-e 'ilmi*) for the long run.[31] The subsequent annual meetings all emphasized the centrality of planning as a precondition for educational reform. The resolutions of the first conference stipulated that new colleges or universities were to be established only according to the future needs of the economy. In his opening address to the 1969 conference, the shah made the same point over again. Later conferences made similar recommendations.[32]

The most important planning body created by the ministry was the Institute for Research and Planning in Science and Education (Mo'assese-ye Tahqiqat va Barname rizi 'Ilmi va Amuzeshi), which started work in July 1969. Its main significance lay in assigning the formulation of educational policies to such a semi-independent body. When conducting my research in Iran, I observed the highly valuable work done in this regard, mainly by its successive directors (Professor Mehran and Professor Naraqi), its deputy director (Safavi), and members of the staff (mainly Moftakhar, Shirazi, Hassam-Vaziri, and Mansur al-Haqq). Most of them had studied in the West and had specialized

28. *Echo of Iran* and *Ettela'at*, 17 December 1967.

29. MAM, document 4703. For a similar definition of its function, see Rahnama, 1:81 and 2:6, 133.

30. Rahnama, 1:56–58, 78–84, 128–38; 2:7, 15. Similarly in *Ayandegan*, 17 December 1967; *Ettela'at*, 23 June 1971. For UNESCO recommendations, see Melville, 4.

31. MAM, document 4714.

32. *KAEA, 1968*, articles 14–16 and 19 of the resolutions; *KAEA, 1969*, articles 6–7, 22, 27–28; *KAEA, 1972*, resolution 3. Similarly, *KAEA, 1971*, articles 7–8, 11; *KAEA, 1973*, article 17; *KAEA, 1974*, articles 37, 53.

in areas relevant to their work at the institute. The Ministry of Science put up the necessary funds yet gave the institute some freedom of action. The main obstacles it encountered were the lack of accurate (mainly, statistical) data and the difficulty in securing the cooperation of the universities and colleges. Its planning work was hampered by its lack of a suitable scientific infrastructure; so it concentrated instead on collecting data. In the mid-1970s, it had the best library in the country on Iranian education. It conducted dozens of statistical studies on the history and current situation of education, particularly higher education. But it was less successful in planning. Although a few forecasts of the development of higher education until the end of the century were drawn up, they were all couched in very general terms. Moreover, several members of the institute told me that social and economic development was so rapid that some of the findings were no longer realistic by the time the relevant research project was concluded, and were therefore shelved. Those that were eventually published—so the heads of the institute themselves attested—did little or nothing to guide government policy.

While the Institute for Research and Planning was to engage in long-term planning, the annual conferences on education were to formulate immediate policies and the Central Council on Education (Shura-ye Markazi-ye Amuzesh) was to devise practical methods of implementation. The foundation of such a council had been recommended in a UNESCO report of January 1969, with a view to bringing together "a team of experts" composed of "the highest officials" to study the problems of education from a wide interdisciplinary point of view. Its formation was discussed at the 1969 conference, and it was set up already by October of the same year. Going beyond the UNESCO recommendations, it was also charged with supervising the implementation of educational policies.[33] Addressing its members, the shah defined it as the "highest authority in the country for the study and analysis of the educational system," whose recommendations were "to guide the government and the other relevant bodies in carrying out their duties." It should use scientific methods and a revolutionary approach.[34]

The council established a number of committees (somewhat confusingly called "councils" as well). The most important were: the Committee for Educational Organization (Shura-ye Nezam-e Amuzesh), the Committee for University Coordination (Shura-ye Hamahangi-ye Daneshgahha), the Committee for the Foundation, Expansion and Dis-

33. Melville, 5; Rahnama 1:82; KI, 29 May 1969.
34. Ettela'at, 27 July 1970.

solution of Institutes of Higher Learning (Shura-ye Tasis va Towse'e va Enhelal Mo'assesat-e Amuzesh-e 'Ali), the Committee for Students' Welfare (Shura-ye Refah-e Daneshjuyan), and the Committee for Rural Education (Shura-ye Amuzesh-e Rusta'i).[35] A 1974 amendment to the law setting up the Ministry of Science envisaged several more committees: the Central Committee for Universities and Institutes of Higher Learning (Shura-ye Markazi-ye Daneshgahha va Mo'assesat-e Amuzesh-e 'Ali), for the coordination of these bodies; the Committee for Scientific Research (Shura-ye Pezhuheshha-ye 'Ilmi); and the Organization of Students' Affairs (Sazeman-e Omur-e Daneshjuyan).[36]

The Ministry of Science also encouraged universities to form their own planning units, as recommended by the first conference on education, and all universities did so at some time in the early 1970s. Yet even at the end of the period reviewed here, there was no comprehensive planning, and the actual development of the universities was certainly not the result of planning.[37] There was a keen awareness of the vital role of planning, and appropriate organs were eventually formed, but as in so many other fields of the White Revolution, the problem was implementation.

The total failure of the committees is best illustrated by the performance of the committee in charge of establishing new institutes for higher learning. From its inception, it abstained from initiatives of its own and limited itself to the rather passive role of pronouncing on plans submitted to it. This, however, was not suited to the realities of the time. According to one of its members, A. Mokhtari, in the conditions prevalent in the early 1970s, any person with drive and initiative could persuade the committee to approve the school he wished to found. He stated that the committee usually failed to assess the appropriateness of the suggested field of study or relate it to the country's needs; nor did it investigate the credentials of the private investor or of the proposed staff. In fact, it approved almost all the plans presented to it.[38] The Royal Institute for Research on Education also criticized the

35. For details on their founding and terms of reference, see *Ettela'at*, 6 October, 29 November 1969.

36. The text of the amendment is included in a letter from the prime minister to the minister of science, no. 41956, of 19 August 1974 (from the archives of the Ministry of Science).

37. This was the view that the vice presidents for planning of Tehran and Pahlavi universities (Behnam and Shir'alipur) expressed before the revolution. On the various committees, see: resolutions of the first conference on education (article 19), the second (article 28), and the third (30 and 31); *Ettela'at*, 24 September 1968; 18 July 1970; 26 June 1971.

38. Mokhtari was the head of the Department for Academic Employment in the

committee for failing to establish criteria for new schools; instead, it simply limited itself to the function of "approval or rejection." The institute found that new schools became a profitable business, that they offered subjects not relevant to the needs of the economy, and that the level of instruction was unsatisfactory. With this in mind, the experts at the institute wrote in 1974/5: "Generally, and with very few exceptions, the spread of private institutes for higher education did not contribute to raising the level of academic training. Most of them were established as an investment, and concentrated on fields requiring low budgets. . . . [They] caused an inappropriate multiplication of students and a decline in academic standards for the sake of profit." They concluded that the private colleges not only were unlikely to help overcome current problems but might well have "crisis-engendering consequences" (*'avaqeb-e bohrani*) unless countermeasures were taken before the end of the fifth economic plan (March 1978). If a crisis had not occurred so far, they stressed, this was only because rapid economic development provided jobs for the graduates.[39] In fact the private colleges produced graduates who expected to work in prestigious occupations and earn high pay, but who had limited qualifications, and specializations ill-suited to the needs of the country. When the economy slowed down in 1977, the graduates found their prospects seriously limited.[40] When the fifth development plan came to an end, Iran was indeed experiencing a crisis much more acute than the experts of the Royal Institute had anticipated. Its effect on the overall sense of ferment is impossible to assess. But for many graduates of private colleges, their dashed plans for a good career were sufficient motivation for resenting the existing order.

Even where there was appropriate planning, the actual development of the educational system did not proceed as planned. For example, according to the fourth development plan (for 1968–1973), drawn up when the Ministry of Science was already in existence, the student body was to grow by 60 percent, rising to 60,000 in 1973. This figure was considered "desirable" (*hadd-e matlub*), not as the minimum. But in actual fact the 1973 figure topped 115,000. Moreover, the plan had prescribed that by 1973 some 55 percent of the students would be in

---

Ministry of Science and a member of the committee.

39. SSHBA, *Amuzesh-e 'Ali*, 10–14.

40. The change in the economic climate became evident during 1977 and was clearly reflected in the policies of the Jamshid Amuzegar government (August 1977–August 1978). For details, see *Middle East Contemporary Survey, 1976–77*, 369–402; *Iran Almanac, 1978*, 209–30.

science, engineering, and technology, but the actual figure was around 48 percent. The plan had provided for an aggregate of 56,420 students to graduate during the five years; the actual figure was 81,952, with a surplus of some 19,000 in the humanities and of 8,000 in science, but a shortfall of 8,000 in engineering, 4,600 in agriculture, and 1,100 in medicine. Referring to these discrepancies, the report of the Royal Institute concluded that the estimates were the result of "baseless assumptions" rather than of research or scientific forecasting.[41]

To be sure, some of the obstacles in the way of proper planning were of an objective nature. The rapidity of social and economic change between 1967 and 1977 might well have made nonsense of even the best planning bodies and procedures. As it is, it is important to note that in the last decade of the shah's reign, for the first time in Iran, the foundations for planning and supervision were being laid down. Yet, all in all, planning had failed, and so had attempts to make realities conform to the plans. In what may be viewed as an admission of failure, the Ministry of Science was dissolved in 1977. The official reason given by Manuchehr Ganji, who was minister of education at the time, was the need to ensure "comprehensive planning" of the educational system—this time by returning responsibility for it to the Ministry of Education.[42] It was the very same argument that had been put forward ten years earlier to set up the Ministry of Science in the first place.

The Quest for Higher Quality

In his book *Mission for My Country* published in 1961, the shah drew up a harsh indictment of Iranian education. He wrote that children were being taught to evade responsibility and were being raised on tales (*dastan*) rather than on science; and that their teachers discounted critical thinking, overemphasized "uncritical memorization," and made their pupils look down on manual work. His criticism of the universities was even more scathing. He accused professors of having scant regard for their students and for their teaching duties, condemned the paucity of scientific research, and spoke of the low general level of the universities.[43] This section will explore the qualitative deficiencies existing at the outset of the educational revolution, the measures taken to correct them, and the degree of success they had.

41. SSHBA, *Amuzesh-e 'Ali*, 12–14.
42. *Kayhan*, 9 August 1977.
43. Pahlavi, *Mission*, 238–56.

Academic Staff

Critics of the educational system pointed to the university teaching staff as the primary source of its faults. As was customary, the shah set the tone; others followed suit. In 1961, shortly before the beginning of the White Revolution, he wrote:

> Some of our professors still regard themselves as little gods whose opinions must not be disputed and whose time must not be wasted upon the students. Such a professor may march into his classroom, deliver his lecture, and march out again. He may believe a student is disrespectful if he asks for supporting evidence for one of the professor's statements or presumes to suggest an alternative interpretation. Without any advance notification the professor may repeatedly fail to come to his class. He may neglect to establish office hours for students consultation, and except for lecture she [sic] may spend virtually no time in the precincts.[44]

At the time of the educational revolution in 1967, the shah went on the offensive again, with the prime minister and the minister of science echoing his words.[45] As usual, the press took its cues from them. Among the points most commonly made in negative press comments at the time were the following: that faculty often owed their appointments to personal connections rather than to their qualifications; that some of their dissertations "were not worth the paper they were written on"; and that they were not really devoted to teaching or research.[46] The following passage from an Iranian magazine in 1968, though touching only on some of the accusations, reflects the tone then current:

> There still are some distinguished professors in various universities who teach exactly the same things they taught when Tehran University was first established. . . . Most university lessons are poor translations of foreign textbooks which are being typed and stencilled, then sold to students year after year at exorbitant prices, by the professors concerned. . . . There are professors who are more inaccessible than a taxi during rush hour. Others will not give good marks unless the students call on their houses

44. Ibid., 258.

45. See, for example, the shah's statement at the opening session of the 1968 conference on educational reform (*Ettela'at*, 8 August 1968); Hoveyda's statement on 27 July 1968 (*Ettela'at*, 27 July 1968); and Rahnama's statement at the Gochsar conference (MAM, document 4714).

46. For some typical pejorative comment, see: *KI*, 5 March, 24 June, 1 July 1967, 2 and 15 June, 1 August 1968, 15 June 1969, 4 March 1970, 15 September 1971; *Ayandegan*, 17 December 1967; *Khandaniha*, 16 March 1968; *Ettela'at*, 19 February, 20 June 1969, 2 March 1970; *Ferdows*, 2 August 1971.

and offer them some presents. . . . There are many professors who have published nothing in their lives.[47]

   The shah may have had reasons other than his sincere disappointment for turning against the professors. He may have wanted to point at a scapegoat for the faults of higher education and to weaken the teaching body, some of whom were less than totally loyal to him. After the student riots in the West, he may have wanted to signal to the students that he was on their side and that action on their part was therefore unnecessary. But his overriding worry was no doubt the constant decline in university standards since the beginning of the White Revolution. The new universities and colleges clamored for staff at a time when rapid economic development opened up new, better paid, and no less prestigious opportunities for young academics. Moreover, to complement their low pay, many professors accepted additional positions, adding to their load and diminishing their contribution to their primary university job—mainly in research.
   As in other developing countries,[48] industry and the administration were the principle competitors for the employment of gifted graduates. The university professor (*ostadh*), who had enjoyed such great prestige in the past, lost much of it in the last decades. Higher income, more power, and quicker advancement were now to be found outside the universities. In the words of Alfred [Shaul] Bakhash: "The financial problem could have been less significant had the position of a professor contained more prestige in society. The prevalent view is that the prestige of professors has considerably declined. Power and prestige are now [1969] in other places—government administration and the industry."[49] Moreover, salaries at universities were declining constantly. Although quite high in comparison with their colleagues in many other developing countries, professorial salaries were low when compared with those of other professionals in Iran, and the gap was widening.[50] In the mid-1970s, an associate professor at a state university earned less than $1,000 (then 70,000 Riyals) a month, less than a first-year engineer in the private sector or veteran government employee. (As a point of reference: $1,000 was the rental for a house in a good—

47. *Ettehad-e Melli*, 3 September 1968, quoted by *Echo of Iran*, 4 September 1968.
48. See, for example, Fahim Qubain, *Education and Science in the Arab World* (Baltimore: Johns Hopkins University Press, 1966), 54–55.
49. *KI*, 12 May 1969.
50. The salary structure of some Iranian universities is analyzed in Cyrus Manzoor, "University Reform in Iran: Problems and Prospects" (Ph.D. diss., Tufts University, 1971), 59–61.

though not in the most prestigious—neighborhood of Tehran.) Under these circumstances, the universities had to make do with less qualified staff, or with professors holding other positions as well.

In the mid-1970s, one could hardly find a professor who did not hold more than one appointment. Most professors at medical schools also had a hospital appointment and often their own private clinic as well; those at engineering schools often held a second position in industry, had their own private business, and/or had a second teaching position at one of the many new colleges; professors at the law schools and in the humanities and other fields had second jobs in the administration, or were in private business, or else taught at a college. This state of affairs was not unique to Iran and had its parallels in many developing countries. But it had become considerably more common in Iran with the advent of the White Revolution and affected both instruction and research.[51] Moreover, while the teaching load on the senior staff was below the norm, that on junior staff was much above average.[52] A UNESCO report stated that the load "is not necessarily due to the duties they have to perform in one department; it is due to the fact that in order to earn reasonable remunerations they have to teach in other departments of the universities or, worse still, have to travel to other institutions remote from the[ir] university and give similar lectures there." The report warned that this was bound to lead to a lowering of standards.[53]

The annual conferences on education, in which professors were in the majority (as representatives of the universities or of the government), adopted a series of recommendations that—had they been applied—would have offered at least a partial solution. They counseled to lessen the teaching load of professors; to raise their salaries and take measures for their welfare (*refah*); and to set down clear-cut criteria for their promotion. Already the first conference demanded that professors

51. According to the study by Zonis on the political elite of Iran (p. 189), elite members held an average of 1.8 jobs each. Only 20.3 percent held only a single paid position. Although there are no similar surveys for later years, my impression was that the tendency to hold additional positions had increased. In Lebanon, by comparison, members of the political elite held an average of 1.6 positions in the late 1960s; see I. Harik, *Man Yahkum Lubnan* (Beirut: Dar al-Nahar, 1972), 33. For similar problems in other Arab countries, see Waadenburg, 119–20.

52. This point was emphasized in the report to the shah by the head of the Royal Institute for Research on Education (Baheri report, 1975, 3). It was based on a study conducted by the institute which found a considerable discrepancy in the teaching load of senior and junior staff: SSHBA, *Moshakhkhasat-e Amari Barnameha-ye Amuzeshi dar Daneshgahha va Mo'assesat-e Amuzesh-e 'Ali-ye Iran* (Tehran, 1975), 10–11.

53. Melville, 8. See a similar warning by Rahnama, 2:25.

should only hold full-time (*tamam-vaqt*) jobs, in other words, no partial employment and (even more significant) not more than one paid position either (articles 21 and 22 of the resolutions). The shah and the ministers of education backed this policy,[54] and the universities issued appropriate regulations.[55] But it soon became evident that the universities were not able to carry out what they themselves had decided. In practice, the meaning of "full-time" became lopsided: part-time employment was indeed banned, but holding more than one full job was not. The next conference (1969), aware of this distortion, declared that "the meaning of full-time occupation has not yet been perceived accurately . . . a full-time professor is one who does not have any other paid position . . . and devotes all his time to the service of the university" (article 17 of the resolutions). But that clarification did not suffice either to produce actual change.

Eventually, the government and the heads of institutes of higher learning realized their inability to overcome the difficulties that stood in their way. Many colleges would have collapsed without the services of teachers holding positions elsewhere. Limiting professors to a single job would have required a revision of the salary scale. Moreover, a professor forced to choose between his academic position and his other occupations might well have decided to abandon teaching. A team chosen by the Royal Institute for Research on Education in 1975 to look into the matter reached gloomy conclusions. Their judgment was that under the prevalent conditions the "full-time" principle could not be applied. It might be feasible at the conclusion of a long process of raising the status and level of the faculty, but certainly not at its outset.[56] A survey by another team of the institute which investigated the views of the faculty found them opposed to such regulations as long as there was no basic pay increase.[57] The upshot was that in 1975 the head of the institute, Mohammad Baheri, reported to the shah that if the full-time rule were applied, the best professors would abandon their academic jobs.[58]

54. See the statement by the shah in *Ettela'at*, 20 July 1969; and the view of the minister of science (Rahnama, 1:147).

55. The first to do so was Tehran University. According to new regulations of December 1969, the university was not to approve appointments for more than one full-time job for new staff (*Ettela'at*, 29 December 1969). But it did not even try to impose similar restrictions on those already on its payroll.

56. SSHBA, *Atharat-e Moqarrarat-e Khedmat-e Tamam-Vaqt dar Daneshgahha va Mo'assesat-e Amuzesh-e 'Ali* (Tehran, 1974/5), 119–23.

57. Idem, *Ara'-ye A'za'-ye Hey'at-e 'Ilmi dar bare-ye Ejra'-ye Moqarrarat-e Khedmat-e Tamam-Vaqt dar Daneshgahha* (Tehran, 1974/5).

58. Baheri report to the shah, 1975, 6.

Pahlavi University was the only university or college to implement the rule, but was able to do so only because it offered substantially higher salaries.[59] In return, it required the full-time presence of professors on campus (eight hours, five days a week). The rule was applied more or less effectively: while in Tehran I often had a hard time locating professors and frequently interviewed them at government offices or private firms; at Pahlavi University, they were present on campus and much more easily available. The deans of all faculties (particularly the deans of medicine and engineering) stressed that they were constantly being approached by professors asking for permission to accept additional positions, but no exceptions were made (even though this led to a number of resignations). At Pahlavi, and only there, full-time employment meant devoting one's entire workday to the university.

Salary reform was of course related to the overall issue of university funding. All the education conferences passed resolutions asking for salary scales to be reexamined. Each looked into the matter of "faculty welfare," to include help in housing (one of the most pressing problems in Iran at the time). But there was little change in overall university budgets, and the expectations raised by the conferences remained unfulfilled and turned into resentment. In the absence of salary reform, the universities were unable to attract the best staff, let alone confine them to their academic duties. This in turn became an additional reason for the decline in instruction and research.

Research

New universities in developing countries, those of the Muslim world included, have generally concentrated on teaching rather than research. Inasmuch as they engaged in research, the accent was on cultural and social science studies rather than natural science or technology.[60]

Neither the Islamic heritage nor the training of many of its faculty (usually in the West) can be held accountable for this lag. True, the traditions of Islam imposed significant limitations on the areas and nature of research and investigation, but original writing (and its publication) were important cornerstones of the traditional education. The reasons for falling behind in research, rather than having to do with

59. Manzoor, 59–60. In line with American university practice, Pahlavi salaries were set by means of individual agreements; in the mid-1970s, many professors there obtained a considerable raise.

60. Waadenburg, 121. See also the views of Jamshid Taqizade, a Tehran University professor, in *Rastakhiz*, 10 January 1977.

the heritage of the past or the models emulated by the new universities, must be sought in the social, economic, and political circumstances in which the new academic centers had sprung up.

Beginning with Dar al-Fonun, there emerged at the new Iranian higher schools a twofold heritage that became, as it were, a substitute for academic research: the "tradition" of producing translations of foreign textbooks or other standard texts, and the "tradition" of publishing abstracts. Both stemmed from the initial desire to teach sciences in Persian and from the necessity to hire foreign professors to do so. Going back for over a century, these became deeply rooted. "Research" often meant no more than translating or adapting foreign professional literature. At least initially, the new universities did not value research (properly so called), and many senior professors had no significant original publications to their credit.[61] The shah himself juxtaposed what he expected and what he found at the universities:

> A great university professor is essentially research-minded. He possesses an attitude of deep humility towards the wonders of nature. . . . He is a modest man of almost childlike curiosity and thirst for knowledge. Constantly he nourishes his teaching with fresh research. To him, the subject-matter that he is teaching is never a dead body of knowledge, to be repeated parrot-fashion year after year; instead it is something living and constantly growing through his own research and that of others, including his students, whose contributions he gladly acknowledges.
>
> But upon the slightest provocation certain of our professors will tell you what distinguished men they are and how many distinguished positions they hold, their intellectual arrogance betrays their lack of the scientific spirit. Some of them conduct no real research of their own but copy their lectures from foreign works, with or without credit being given to the original authors; or they originate some writing which they support with no scientific evidence; or they deliver the same lectures year after year without ever bothering to bring them up to date. If a university professor knows nothing of scientific method, how can he teach it to his students?[62]

Many prominent professors, in particular the heads of research institutes, often made similar comments in the late 1970s. This group included Nasafat (head of the Institute for Psychology), Nikgouhar (director of the Institute for Social Research), professors Sadiqi and Behnam (all four from Tehran University); Safavi and Moftakhar (from the Institute for Research and Planning in Science and Education);

61. SSHBA, *Amuzesh-e 'Ali,* 47–52; Jacobs, 158–59; Manzoor, 103–31.
62. Pahlavi, *Mission,* 258–59.

Razedan (from the Royal Institute for Research on Education); Mehr, Shir°alipur, and Mo'idi (from Pahlavi University); and Rasekh (from the Plan and Budget Organization).

It would of course be rash to generalize about the research produced at Iranian universities, and it is clearly outside the scope of this book to evaluate the work of individual researchers. But the general impression, strongly reinforced by the sources mentioned above, is that neither the universities as a body nor many of the faculty individually put great value on or devoted much time to research. Perusal of lists of publications by professors at the faculty of social sciences of Tehran University (prepared by themselves for a book on the faculty) shows that most of the items were booklets consisting of lecture abstracts, or translations of foreign books and articles. Only a few could be described as original research. Many staff members had not published anything in international scholarly journals. Studies of the Royal Institute and the Institute for Research and Planning supported the same conclusion.[63]

This state of affairs had developed for a variety of reasons. To begin with, original research was not made a prerequisite for promotion. This, and a general lack of awareness of the vitality of research, made it appear a thankless effort with nothing to show in return.[64] Second, the heavy teaching load of the academic staff left professors "no time to think about original work nor to supervise students" (as the 1969 UNESCO report put it); Rahnama, the first minister of science, took the same view.[65] Third, as in other developing countries, links between the universities and industry were feeble, and it was unusual for industrial firms to place research projects with universities or finance research there.[66] (It is a moot point whether this held back research[67] or whether, on the contrary, the backwardness of research caused the lack of industrial support.) Fourth, until the last years of the shah's reign, academic education was mainly restricted to the undergraduate level. Fifth, as the UNESCO report stated, the method of instruction produced a "non-inquiring attitude" on the part of the students: "They are taught, they absorb and they reproduce information when required.

63. SSHBA, *Amuzesh-e °Ali*, 47–52.

64. See the views of Professor Fazlollah Reza (chancellor of Tehran University in the late 1960s), in *KI*, 1 February 1969; of the first minister of science, in Rahnama 2:25; and of Dr. Mostowfi (professor at Tehran University), in *Khandaniha*, 19 December 1970.

65. Melville, 8; Manzoor, 64–76; Rahnama, 2:25; *Ettela°at*, 30 July, 29 September 1968.

66. Qubain, 510; similarly the findings of the OECD study cited in *KI*, 14 January 1969.

67. For this view, see Melville, 8; Manzoor, 124–26; SSHBA, *Amuzesh-e °Ali*, 46.

The authority of the teachers is regarded as absolute and thus ideas do not gradually change. This is the very antithesis of the approach to research and to the application of new knowledge." Moreover, since the faculty themselves lacked research experience, they could hardly have been expected to promote in their students the qualities of good researchers.[68] The sixth reason had to do with inadequate scientific equipment. It was often obsolete and sometimes improperly used and badly maintained. Some heads of research institutes complained that decisions about its procurement—over which in many cases they had no control—were made according to how much profit was in it for the administrative personnel.[69] The UNESCO experts observed that "virtually no equipment of an advanced kind is available for research, the budget of the universities being wholly expended on staff salaries and the maintenance of buildings."[70] Finally, the small share of research in the total higher education budget must be mentioned, as well as the fact that allocations for research were often diverted to other purposes.[71] Ironically, the faculty did not always find a use for even the small amounts available.[72] But when, toward the end of the shah's reign, research institutes no longer suffered from budget restrictions (as stated, for example, by Nikgouhar), research did not develop. At that point, the low budgets were the result of the weakness of research, not its reason.

A vicious circle was thus set up: there was no public recognition of the importance of research or appreciation for those engaged in it; neither was the government aware of its vitality; the universities did not promote it or reward those conducting it; consequently, the academic staff often neglected research efforts, and the students were not trained for research.

Only when the educational revolution was launched in 1967 was greater attention given to research—for the first time since modern universities had come into existence. Hoveyda, the prime minister,[73]

---

68. Melville, 8.

69. For criticism in this regard, see the resolutions of the committee for research in the 1976 Conference on Education cited in *Kayhan*, 2 September 1976. Similar accusations are contained in interviews by Jamshid Taqizade and Nikgouhar in *Rastakhiz*, 10 January and 1 March 1977, respectively.

70. Melville, 9.

71. In the late 1960s, only 2 percent of the total budget of the universities was for research. This, according to most sources, did not change in the 1970s (*Ettela'at*, 27 August 1968). For the misuse of research budgets, see Manzoor, 115–20.

72. See the words of the minister of science, Rahnama, 2:111–12.

73. *Ettela'at*, 28 July 1968.

and Rahnama, the minister of science,[74] urged the university to expand research activities. The educational conferences stressed the same theme. The 1968 conference called for increased research budgets and demanded that research be made a prerequisite for employment and promotion of faculty (articles 10–13, 21, 24 of the resolutions). The 1972 conference added an appeal for coordinating academic research with the needs of the economy (article 5). The 1975 conference expressed its displeasure at the backwardness of research and again recommended bigger allocations as well as incentives to those engaged in it (articles 27–32).[75] The establishment, in 1969, of a council for scientific research by the Ministry of Science has already been noted. The universities, for their part, established "research councils" (*shuraha-ye pezhuheshi*) in the early 1970s as well as a number of research institutes.

But neither verbal encouragement nor the practical steps listed above engendered significant change. None of the major obstacles were effectively removed. Many professors told me that research was still not regarded as a yardstick for advancement; that the teaching load had not been significantly eased; that teaching methods had not changed; and that research and the researchers remained largely dependent on the administrators.[76] With the blessing of the shah (and perhaps in a bid to please him), the growing research budgets were usually allocated to overambitious projects, such as nuclear energy and cancer, running counter to the recommendations of the conferences on education for greater relevance to the needs of Iran and the Iranians. Criticism in this regard was brought before the shah in the 1975 report of Deputy Court Minister Baheri.[77] But still nothing much changed. In many press interviews, Nikgouhar blamed the university heads for a "total lack of understanding" of the significance and essence of academic research. In 1977, he told a journalist that research was still not thought of as an honorable occupation (*shoghl*) and that the educational system failed to encourage it. He added: "If we are in fact determined to become technologically independent, we must begin as a first step by founding centers for advanced research. . . . We have the budget and the manpower . . . what we lack is a . . . policy. . . . Unfortunately, research . . .

74. In his statement at the Gochsar conference (MAM, document 4714; Rahnama, 1:98–117).

75. Similarly at the 1969 conference (article 23), the 1970 conference (articles 20–22), the conference of 1973 (articles 38–39), and that of 1974 (article 47).

76. According to one expert, the administrative staff continued to make all decisions, until the end of the period discussed, on the purchase of equipment. (In his words: "According to the agents with whom they are connected.")

77. Baheri report, 1975, 6.

is not being coordinated with the needs of the country. . . . Research in itself is still not regarded as an occupation [in its own right]. . . . Those engaged in research do not enjoy distinguished social standing."[78]

Dr. Jamshid Taqizade, who received a special award from the Tehran University research council in 1976, told an interviewer that at the universities "as well as within social circles" appreciation for research was still lacking. As proof, he mentioned that his colleagues made no great efforts to publish in scientific journals or to participate in international conferences.[79]

In short, while the launching of the educational revolution did signal the beginning of a change, the basic problems obstructing academic research remained much as before.

Teaching

Despite the almost exclusive accent on instruction (to the near-exclusion of research), teaching, too, remained beset by weaknesses. The main reasons were: the deficient standards of the teaching staff; the low level of freshmen arriving from secondary school; and the heritage of traditional methods of instruction and study. Moreover, the expansion of higher education since the 1960s had been too rapid to allow for gradual improvement in quality. In this respect, too, the educational revolution signaled that by the late 1960s the government was ready to take the initiative for reform.

Here, too, it would be misleading to generalize. Yet prolonged observation of campus life at a number of Iranian universities in the 1970s convinced me of the persistence of a series of basic faults. The heavy load on professors and the lack of original research left their imprint on the method and level of instruction. Many professors reached the campus in time (or barely in time) to go straight to their class and left the campus immediately afterward. Many classes were canceled, often without prior notice.[80] Many students complained that professors did

78. *Rastakhiz*, 1 March 1977. The Committee for Scientific Research voiced similar criticism in its report to the 1976 Conference on Education, adding that there were instances of expensive equipment being stored without any use being made of it (report cited by *Kayhan*, 2 September 1976).

79. *Rastakhiz*, 10 January 1977.

80. A similar description was given in a survey conducted by the Royal Institute for Research on Education in 1974/5 which examined this very question: SSHBA, *Tashkil Jalasat-e Dars dar Daneshgahha va Mo'assesat-e Amuzesh-e 'Ali: Sal-e Tahsili 1353/4* (Tehran, 1974/5), 85–92, 147–63.

not prepare properly for class and had little time to guide their students or help them in their research. Many others complained that professors taught outdated material or gave precisely the same lectures "for dozens of years."[81] With regard to some professors, such accusations were certainly baseless; for many others, they were not.

In almost all classes I attended, the professor lectured in front of the class, with the students carefully taking notes they would then memorize. Argument and discussion were rare. Most professors left no time for questions, and some did not allow any or answered with annoyance. A foreign observer could not fail to be impressed by the distance separating faculty from students, recalling the shah's reference to them as "little gods." To be sure, there were exceptions, but, for all the dangers of undue generalization, the characterization given here seems to describe the rule.

Many professors accused the students of an "unserious approach to their studies,"[82] but I found most of them to be extremely studious. Because of the introduction of a single competitive entrance examination at all universities (see next section), they represented the pick of the high school graduates and were highly motivated to add to their initial success. They were ready to do their utmost to earn their degrees but did so in the only way they knew: first and foremost by memorizing.

The result of these attitudes—on the part of professors and students alike—was a teaching method based mostly on transferring information (often highly theoretical and outdated) by means of lectures and memorization. While there was no disputing these facts, various explanations were offered for them. Faculty members claimed that students chose to memorize lectures because they were unable or unwilling to consult the scientific literature, mostly in foreign languages. Students, on the other hand, claimed that they had no choice because their examination papers were graded according to their familiarity with their professors' presentations. Memorization, they claimed, was the only way to get high grades. It was a common sight at exam time to see students (including science students) pace the parks, the yards, and corridors, memorizing lecture notes.

Differences of opinion also existed as to the reasons for the absence of discussion and analysis. Many students claimed that professors did not encourage questions simply because they were unqualified, or un-

81. Such charges appeared in *Khandaniha*, 16 March 1968; *Ettela'at*, 4 September 1968; *KI*, 1 August 1968, 15 June 1969. See also the shah's statement quoted at the beginning of this section.

82. For such claims, see *KI*, 5 June 1969; *Ayandegan*, 19 November 1970.

prepared, to answer them. The shah and the minister of science claimed that the faculty viewed questions as tantamount to a challenge of their knowledge and authority.[83] Professors with whom I discussed these charges dismissed them as ridiculous. Their explanation was that the students failed to ask intelligent questions because they did no reading on their own. Others said that this was the heritage of the past, when the authority of the professor was absolute. Some observers spoke of an "unholly alliance" between students and professors—both equally concerned only with "getting through the year."[84]

Around the time of the educational revolution, the universities became the butt of a great deal of public criticism—more so than perhaps any other sector of the contemporary scene. *Echo of Iran* wrote that university education was nothing more than an extension of the secondary schools and suffered from all the defects of the latter.[85] Majlis member Saʿid Vaziri said the Iranian universities trained "adult simpletons, with brains of children."[86] The annual conferences on education focused on the same problems and called for their eradication. But the force of deeply rooted traditions and the objective circumstances of rapid growth proved stronger. Both faculty and students seemed equally interested in maintaining the status quo.

Admission Policies

As already noted, many problems in higher education originated at the lower levels. University entrants arrived with insufficient knowledge and inappropriate study habits. The Ministry of Science, acknowledging that this could not be quickly remedied, endeavored to solve part of the immediate problem by a more methodical admission policy. This was all the more pressing because of the growing discrepancy between the number of students leaving secondary school and the number of university vacancies. Until 1968/9, each school set its own competitive entrance examinations. Candidates therefore often applied at more than one place and had to travel all over the country to take the examinations. Even for the same subject, requirements often differed from one school to the next.[87] More important, many candidates

83. Rahnama, 1:92; for the shah's view, see *KI*, 7 August 1968.
84. *Ettelaʿat*, 2 March 1970; *Ayandegan*, 10 March 1970; *Ferdows*, 2 August 1971.
85. *Echo of Iran*, 10 October 1965.
86. *Ayandegan*, 3 February 1968.
87. This was criticized by Rahnama at the Gochsar conference (MAM, document 4714). For similar criticism, see *Ettelaʿat*, 2 September 1967, 20 May, 13 September 1969; *Paygham-e Emruz*, 14 October 1967.

doubted that admission honestly depended on their tests; family ties, they claimed, counted for more.[89] Already the first conference on education demanded in its resolutions (article 37) to "simplify" admission procedures and "render [them] more efficient" and to establish "logical criteria" capable of securing "a just selection."

Early in 1969 the Committee for University Coordination formed the Center for Examination Studies (Markaz-e Azemun Shenasi), which co-opted representatives of the universities and the Ministries of Education and Science. It was authorized to work out a new selection method, and on 18 May 1969, it presented to the Majlis a draft law for the "rationalization of . . . university entrance examination." The law was passed, and beginning with the academic year 1969/70, examinations were administered under it.[89] A single unified entrance examination was introduced at all state universities (as well as at some of the colleges offering academic degrees). A candidate could register for several departments in one or more universities and take the examination in a single town of his choice.[90] In other respects, each university could go on setting its individual requirements (e.g., with regard to the maximum age of applicants or the refusal of candidates who had named it as second or third choice). The examination was designed to check both the candidate's knowledge and his aptitude for the specific field he had chosen. If he passed, he was admitted to the department of his first choice. The system greatly simplified procedures for both the students and the universities; enabled the latter to pool their efforts for establishing scientific selection criteria; and strengthened public confidence in the fairness of the examination. Given the general tendency to distrust the administration, it was unlikely for any system to gain complete public confidence. Even Baheri admitted that some "rotten and corrupt (*fased*) practices" still persisted.[91] But the new system marked an important step forward, away from the nepotism and favoritism of earlier times. This was also the public perception.[92] It is thus possible to conclude that taken as a whole, the new system improved the chances of the best candidates to secure admission.

However, it also brought into being a set of new problems. Concentrating almost exclusively on material from the high school syllabus, the new examination largely duplicated the tests the candidates had

---

88. For such charges, see *KI*, 20 May 1969; *Ettela'at*, 9 February 1970.

89. For the text of the law, see *KI*, 20 May 1969; *Ettela'at*, 9 February 1970.

90. In 1969/70, each applicant could register for five departments; later for ten.

91. Baheri report to the shah, 1975, 12.

92. Years later, when making a case for its cancellation, *Kayhan* (19 August 1977), mentioned this as its *only* virtue.

taken only a little while earlier upon completion of high school. They therefore came to resent the examination as unnecessary. This was at least partially confirmed by a study of the Royal Institute for Research on Education showing a clear correlation between the grades students got on the two sets of examinations.[93] Another problem was that the universities did not set minimum standards and accepted the students who had the highest scores. This led to the acceptance of many weak students, mainly by the less popular departments and at schools for which there was not much competition.[94] Moreover, some administrative difficulties persisted. Popular private schools such as the Pahlavi, Aryamehr, and Melli universities, did not participate in the general competition and made their own selection. Minor colleges, on the other hand, were likely to be saddled with students who had failed to be admitted to the schools that were high on their priority list. But some students gave up and decided not to accept offers of admission from schools at the bottom of their list (perhaps their ninth or tenth choice). To illustrate: at the school of medicine of Tehran University 91.6 percent of those who passed the examinations in 1972/3 did eventually enroll; at the colleges, 53.4 percent of those accepted did not.[95]

In the early and middle 1970s, there was mounting criticism of the new system by educationalists, rejected candidates, and the media, and there were calls to abrogate it altogether.[96] The conferences on education, mindful of the need for an improved method, took up the issue. In 1973 (articles 29 and 31 of the resolutions), and again in 1974 (article 30) and 1975 (articles 14 and 23), they demanded the cancellation of that part of the examination testing the candidate's familiarity with the high school syllabus (i.e., the main portion) and instead put the emphasis on testing the student's aptitude for his chosen field. Accordingly, beginning in 1976/7, the system was revised so as to make greater use of candidates' score on the earlier examination without testing them twice over.

Two other shortcomings, however, remained. First, the revised system limited competition between universities. While it was true that schools in high demand could pick their candidates, they could not set

93. SSHBA, *E'tebar-e Emtehan-e Entekhab-e Daneshju*, vol. 1: *Tahlil Nomarat-e Tahsilat-e Dabirestani va Emtehanat-e Vorudi va Rabete-ye An*, ed., Morteza Nasafat (Tehran, 1972), 141–46.

94. For such arguments by scholars of the Royal Institute, see idem, *Barresi Raveshha-ye Emtehanat-e Entekhab-e Daneshju dar Mo'assesat-e Amuzesh-e 'Ali, Sal-e Tahsili 1351/2*, eds., Morteza Masafat and Parviz Razedan (Tehran, 1973), 68.

95. Ibid., 68–69.

96. See, for example, an article in *Kayhan* of 19 August 1977, quoting diverse views.

a higher standard for admission. Second, the universities' loss of the right to set the examinations or even select their students was criticized as one more step limiting the freedom of the universities.[97]

To sum up: if one can speak of an educational "revolution" in Iran, it is in the quantitative sense. In absolute numbers, expansion was rapid. But even so, it could not keep abreast of demand.

There was a keener awareness than before of the need for qualitative improvement. Higher education now had priority over the lower levels of schooling, and many plans were prepared to advance it. Political stability, the unquestioned authority of the shah, and his personal interest in the universities all helped in their development. But the fact that this happened under the pressure of fast-growing demand for higher education and at a time of rapid social and economic change worked against them. One way or another, a final judgment cannot be made: the space of barely a decade at the disposal of the educationalists was too short a time to plan, persuade, and implement. Some ten years after the educational revolution was launched, the upsurge of opposition forces paralyzed the government. And the new regime was to take an entirely different course (see Epilogue).

97. Such was the claim, among others, of the organ of the Mardom [opposition] party (*Seda-ye Mardom*, 15 July 1971).

11

Social Origins of the Student Population

Is education a ticket to upward social mobility, or is it, on the contrary, merely an instrument by which the political and social elites perpetuate social gaps and preserve their own superiority? The controversy over this question has become a central issue in the sociology of education, marking off supporters of the functional theory of education from proponents of the conflict theory. Yet even those who held that a university education "was one of the most important avenues"[1] for social advance conceded that elementary and secondary education, home background, and the traditions of a student's social class had something to do with motivation and achievement. Conversely, their opponents did not altogether deny the power of education to impart mobility along with knowledge. Empirical studies have not provided results that can be universally applied. Developed and developing countries each have their own characteristics. Among the latter, again, there seem to be wide variations.[2]

In the Muslim Middle East education should, on the face of it, have had a better chance of promoting mobility than elsewhere in the Third World. The importance traditionally attached to 'ilm in Muslim society made it an important asset in determining status. In modern (as in former) times, class membership was not defined by birth as much as

1. Shapira and Etzioni-Halevi, 14–21; similarly Eisenstadt, "Stratification," 145.
2. For examples, see Adam Crule, *The Role of Education in Developing Societies* (Accra: Ghana University Press, 1961), 7–8; Coleman, *Education and Political Development*, 30–32; Philip J. Foster, "Ethnicity and the Schools of Ghana," *Comparative Educational Review*, 6 (October 1962), 128.

by the position a person came to hold.[3] Studies of Middle Eastern elites beginning with the 1960s emphasized their high level of education (see Chapter 12). At the same time, a significant change in the social philosophy of the Middle Eastern regimes led to a view of education as the right of the many rather than the privilege of the few.[4] But it remained an open question to what degree a student of humble origin could turn that right into a reality.

In Iran, specifically, both the pre-Islamic and the Muslim-Shi'i traditions stressed that education conferred, or was capable of conferring, social status. But in reality, from the old dynasties and well into modern times, a rigid social structure limited mobility.[5] In the modern era, especially under Mohammad Reza Shah, a growing popular demand sprang up for higher education on the part of people wishing to achieve, in the words of Marvin Zonis, "satisfaction, status, power, and mobility"; but elite groups strove to frustrate them so as to preserve the educational gap and through it their own status.[6] The slow pace of expanding higher education made it impossible to meet popular demand. Referring to the period up to the educational revolution, Zonis concluded that higher education had become yet "another distinction that the elite would possess," making the existing gap "nearly unbridgeable. For with the tendency to restrict higher education to scions of elite families and the establishment of higher, or at least modern, education as a chief requirement for service in the upper reaches . . . access to elite status through official channels was closed. Modern education became a distinguishing characteristic of the elite, but an education that it was all but impossible for the children of the masses to acquire."[7] Yet he, too, recognized elsewhere that "only a university education can make access to the higher reaches of society feasible."[8]

Empirical research, or what there is of it for the period under consideration, does by and large support the view that in Iran education perpetuated, and possibly widened, social gaps. Yet for a small but ever growing number of young people, education became an important

3. Manfred Halpern, *The Politics of Social Change in the Middle East and North Africa* (Princeton: Princeton University Press, 1963), 57–59.

4. Qubain, 57–59, 502–3.

5. Rosenthal, 322–24; Bill, *Intelligentsia*, 41–54.

6. Marvin Zonis, "Higher Education and Social Change: Problems and Prospects," in Ehsan Yar-Shater, ed., *Iran Faces the Seventies* (New York: Praeger, 1971), 217–18.

7. Zonis, *Elite*, 167.

8. Idem, *Higher Education*, 237.

(in fact the most important) single avenue for mobility. For all, it was the "prerequisite of social mobility."[9]

The Rising Prestige of Higher Education

In the period under review, the prestige attached to higher education and the standing it gave to academics continued to rise. The consequent demand for higher education peaked in the years of the White Revolution. Both those wishing to perpetuate their status and those eager to improve it were at one in acknowledging the importance of education. An outward expression of this trend was the appreciation and admiration—not to say adulation—of academics in Iranian society. As in other developing countries, special prestige was accorded to holders of the degrees of *doktor* or *mohandes* (engineer). The form of address *aqa-ye doktor* or *aqa-ye mohandes* (parallel to the German *Herr Doktor, Herr Ingenieur*) was a mark of honor and standing. Both in their professional and in their social circle, and often enough also within their immediate family, they were spoken to, or spoken of, by their academic titles. The wife of a doctor was, and still is, often referred to as *khanom-e doktor* regardless of her own education (again similar to the German *Frau Doktor* common in the past and still heard today).

Their degrees, it seems, lent added weight to their general views, even on subjects remote from their areas of expertise. Special respect was reserved for graduates of universities abroad, regardless of the level of the institution they had attended or their own achievements there. On their doorplates and prescription forms, physicians were careful to note that they had studied abroad, or to name the country or university they had been to, for example: *tahsilkarde-ye daneshgah-e Amrika* (graduate of an American university) or *motakhasses-e daneshgah-e Englisi* (specialized at an English university). Engineers, lawyers, and, to a lesser degree, other graduates adopted the same practice.

Elite families made every possible effort to ensure the status of their children by providing them with a higher education and, as more opportunities opened up for doing so, with advanced degrees from especially prestigious schools, preferably in fields considered most desirable, socially speaking. While conducting research in Iran, I encountered many examples of this practice. Parents made use of their own standing and of family connections to guarantee academic

9. Hyden, 1:199.

achievement for their children. To cite an example: one of the rich families (closely associated with the shah) "designated" their son (then in his early twenties) as a future foreign minister. His father told me that the young man *must* therefore have a doctorate from a *leading* American school. When the latter had some difficulties at his chosen university (in fact, one of the most prestigious institutions in the Unites States), the family did not hesitate to turn to the ambassador of a foreign country who was based in Tehran; they asked the ambassador to have his foreign minister intervene with the son's professor (a noted orientalist), since they knew that the minister was personally acquainted with the American secretary of state and, so they believed, with the professor. Another father whose son had similar problems told him to offer a "nice present" to his professor or even propose a donation to the university.[10] How many students paved their way in this manner cannot even be guessed at. In the present context, the only purpose is to illustrate the importance such families attached to securing for their children the best possible education at the most prestigious schools. In many other cases, families took on additional jobs, or raised loans, to help their children through college or university. Failure to gain admission, or pass the examination, sometimes led to suicide.[11] This was not an entirely new phenomenon in Iran, but the trend became more marked in the 1960s and 1970s.

Lower down the social scale, people thought of higher education as the chief means to achieve status and power. Because they lacked other assets, education was the only thing they could give their children to make it possible for them to forge ahead. Those who had an education could penetrate social barriers and perhaps marry into circles higher than their own. Several such couples (usually with a husband of lower class origin but with a better education than his wife) told me that had it not been for the husband's education, the wife's family would not have consented to the match; neither—often enough—would the woman herself. Women looking for matrimonial partners through newspaper advertising (a rather rare thing in Iran) often specified higher education as a condition.[12] In 1967, students at the Tehran polytechnic whose studies led to the *fowq-e diplom* (high diploma) asked the minister of science to approve academic degrees for them. One of

10. I know the names of all those involved in both cases, but I am not at liberty to make use of them. The first student had to quit his studies at the university.
11. For some examples, see *Tehran Journal*, 8 August 1963; *Ettehad-e Melli*, 5 July 1975.
12. See, for example, a matrimonial notice in *Zan-e Ruz*, 3 May 1975, p. 61.

the reasons they stated was that "distinguished families" did not "recognize" their degrees as academic and therefore refused to allow their daughters to marry them. The minister investigated their claim and said he had found it accurate.[13] A leading sociologist who occupied a prominent post at the Ministry of Plan and Budget in the mid-1970s told me that this was the prevalent perception in Iran. Higher education, he said, was a principal "weapon" for "penetrating the social bastion." He added that such perceptions had "devastating" practical results: since people did not "recognize" the degrees granted by the technological colleges, many talented students refused to attend them. With this in mind, he recommended to the government that it authorized these colleges to grant academic degrees rather than the *fowq-e diplom*. (His suggestion was rejected).

All in all, the period under review was one of a growing recognition—throughout all strata of the population—of the importance of higher education and hence of greater demand for it.

Government Policy

The Shah's Approach

In his public statements throughout his reign, the shah spoke for the right of *all* Iranian children to higher education. Soon after his accession, for example, he stated that room should be found at the university for everyone wishing to study and possessing the aptitude for it, and that financial consideration must not be allowed to stand in his way. In the late 1940s, he even stated that it was "the duty" of the government to give a higher education to lower-class students and to grant them financial assistance for that purpose. He reverted to the theme in still more resolute terms at the time of the White Revolution.[14] Yet for the most part, he did no more than pay lip service to this idea. In contrast to his active role in the development of pre-university education, the shah's policy vis-à-vis higher education was to let those who had a vested interest in the prevalent social order monopolize university admission for their young people. This changed only in the late 1960s when the government began helping lower-strata students up the educational ladder. As in so many other fields, the change was

13. *KI*, 19 December 1967, 2 June 1968.
14. For the shah's speeches, see Pahlavi, *Ta'lifat*, 1:1120 (1943 speeches), 2:1370–71 (1952 speeches), and 2:1407–9 (1953 speeches). For his words on the eve of the White Revolution, see Pahlavi, *Mission*, 238–56.

swift and sudden, but came too late to effect a real change in the time left before the fall of the shah.

The shah's initial resistance to a broader social approach to higher education was attested to both by educationalists supporting his line (Sadiq, for example) and by experts (like Sadiqi, Siyasi, and Vadi'i) who, although holding prominent position in the educational system, did not identify with his policy. Many others (like Rasekh, Mehr, Mehran, and Naraqi) held that the present state of affairs was an unavoidable stage of social development rather than of intentional policy. A SAVAK general told me (after the Islamic Revolution) that the shah had sincerely wished to encourage lower-class students, but that the SAVAK had advised against it, pointing to the potential dangers to his rule. He added that after the crackdown against the opposition in the early 1960s, the shah wanted to reopen the universities to such students, but the SAVAK pointed to recent campus disturbances and to the role of the intellectuals in the opposition and was once more successful in postponing any change.

For this period, then, Zonis is right in saying that higher education served to widen social gaps and to make them "nearly unbridgeable."[15] But by the time his book, researched in Iran in the mid-1960s, came out in 1971, such a conclusion was no longer correct. With the declaration of the educational revolution, the shah changed direction. By that time, he had come to feel confident enough not to fear opposition from the intelligentsia anymore. In addition, a close aide, the SAVAK man in charge of internal intelligence, had assured him that the SAVAK possessed adequate tools to meet a challenge (if there was one) from the students and the intelligentsia.[16] Moreover, as the SAVAK general said, the shah himself had told him on many occasions that he no longer viewed the students (the leftists excluded) as a threat; rather, he now thought of a socially broader higher education—for which they were so eager—as an additional guarantee of their families' support for his regime. Sadiq, for his part, said the shah had told him that the danger from high school graduates denied university admission was disproportionately higher than the "hypothetical danger" of opposition by students and graduates. Moreover, the fact that higher education remained under strict supervision (see Chapter 13) and that the authorities were largely in control of employment for the graduates, led the shah to believe that he could recruit them as supporters of the regime.

15. Zonis, *Elite*, 37–38, 167.
16. Based on an interview with the SAVAK general quoted above.

Student Welfare

The principle of supporting needy students was set forth already at the Gochsar conference when Rahnama proclaimed it to be an integral part of the educational revolution. He rejected the total abolition of tuition fees as "unjust to the weak," who would then eventually have to "finance the studies of the rich" as well, but advocated monetary grants to those in need.[17] Subsequent conferences supported similar policies and outlined additional guidelines and programs to support them.[18] To coordinate student affairs in general, but especially to deal with the matter of financial assistance, the Department for Students' Affairs (Daftar-e Omur-e Daneshjuyan) was established in the Ministry of Science in 1969. Similar offices were then set up at all the universities. In 1973, a foundation for student welfare (Sandoq-e Refah-e Daneshjuyan) was formed at the ministry to provide financial and other support for students.[19]

Already in the academic year 1968/9 the Ministry of Science made it possible for needy students to receive an allowance as well as a variety of loans and grants.[20] Beginning in 1969/70 students could postpone payment of tuition fees until after graduation.[21] According to a survey conducted by Nasafat in 1971/2, 29.3 percent of the students on the campuses investigated were exempt from paying any tuition and another 19.3 percent enjoyed partial exemption.[22] With the inception of the educational revolution, dormitories and cafeterias were set up at all universities, offering accommodation and meals at reduced prices. (The price of a full meal at Tehran University for example, was 20 Riyals—the equivalent of two soft drinks or one sandwich at a popular downtown restaurant.) According to a survey by the Royal Institute for Research on Education, about a quarter of the university students (excluding colleges) lived in dormitories in 1974/5. According to Nasafat (who included colleges), 51.3 percent did. Nasafat also found that 92.3

17. MAM, document 4717; Rahnama, 2:16–17.

18. See, for example, articles 39–41 in the 1968 conference resolutions, articles 30 and 31 in the 1969 resolutions, articles 20 and 25 in 1970, articles 19–22 in 1972, 8 and 9 in 1973, article 32 in 1974, and 24–26 in 1976.

19. An appropriate law, and regulations for its application, were approved subsequently, but did not set explicit priorities for the underprivileged. See letters from the prime minister to the minister of science no. 12370 (20 August 1973) and no. 722 (10 April 1974). The letters from the archives of the Ministry of Education were given to me by the staff.

20. *KI*, 29 September 1968.

21. *Ettela'at*, 7 September 1969; *KI*, 9 October 1969.

22. Nasafat, 182.

percent had access to cafeterias, 64.4 percent were able to benefit from free medical care, 58.9 percent were entitled to loans to finance their tuition, and 40.9 percent were eligible for grants. By the nature of things, students from underprivileged families made greater use of these facilities than others, and this is borne out by Nasafat's study showing considerable differentials in a breakdown according to social origin.[23]

At Pahlavi University, 3,800 dormitory places were available in 1975/6 when the student population numbered 4,719. Other students, including local residents, benefited from a monthly accommodation grant of 2,500 Riyals each. Monthly grants of 3,000 Riyals were given to 16 percent of the student population, and twice that number received loans in the same amount. The cafeteria served daily meals to an average of 71 percent of the students. (For three meals a day, students paid 45 Riyals—one quarter of the price of the food used). Textbooks were sold at a campus bookshop at a considerable discount. Transportation between the dormitories and the downtown campus was free. After the 1974 rise in oil prices, services improved considerably, as they did on other campuses throughout the country.[24]

Another important step to encourage underprivileged students was the introduction of evening classes. The idea was first raised by the shah in September 1967, and a few months later the first evening courses were offered at Tehran University. Other campuses followed suit.[25] Even more important in this context was the initiative to set up universities in the provinces, particularly in smaller provincial towns and in the less developed provinces. (For a list of the universities, their location, and their inauguration dates, see Table 13.) Contrary to the declared intention, no quota was set for provincial residents, but the very location of the new campuses made it easier for them to enroll.

Some critics considered support for all students, regardless of financial need, as socially unjust. In the conclusion to his survey, for instance, Nasafat stated that although students from the lower strata benefited more than others from the financial support, many "who are in no need at all of such allowances still enjoyed them."[26] A professor of Pahlavi University called it "ridiculous" that the university offered

23. Ibid., 169–83; SSHBA, *Omur-e Daneshju'i, 1974/5*, ed., 'Ali Asghar Shirtavane'i (Tehran, 1975).

24. Information given to me by a prominent official at the Pahlavi University bureau for student affairs.

25. *Ettela'at*, 24 September and 9 December 1967; for similar initiatives in other schools, see *Ettela'at*, 4 August 1970, 4 September 1971.

26. Nasafat, 176.

equal support to students who depended on it and to those "whose parents could buy the entire university." The royal Institute for Research on Education also criticized the lack of "logical criteria" and stated that allowances paid out regardless of need or achievement caused "spiritual corruption" (*fesad-e ruhi*): they encouraged students to consider monetary aid as their "natural right" with no obligation on their part to improve their own standards.[27] In fact, by the mid-1970s, students were in the habit of pointing to the growing oil income and claiming that it was the duty of the government to support them during their university years.

To sum up: important improvements were made in the early 1970s and obviously, taking them as a whole, they benefited the poor more than the rich. But the whole trend did not really come to fruition before the shah's regime was swept away. One thing stands out, nevertheless: no effort by the government was capable of catching up with the rising expectations.

The 1974 Free Higher Education Law

The most significant step taken to meet these expectations was the 1974 law offering free academic study as of 1974/5. This time the shah himself had presented the proposal to the 1973 educational conference, and the law of 21 July 1974 made it official. Under articles 7 and 8 of the new law, all students were eligible for government support to cover their tuition fees, in exchange for agreeing to work in a job assigned by the Ministry of Science upon graduation; two years of work had to be performed for each year of study. The ministry was entitled to direct them to the public or private sector at any location in Iran provided that the employment offered was related to their field of study. The law made it very clear that the government was *entitled* but not *obliged* to employ them. Vocational training at institutes offering the *fowq-e diplom* was made free unconditionally.

According to regulations issued by the Ministry of Science in September 1974, students exempted under the new law would also receive a monthly allowance in an amount to be approved by the Sandoq-e Refah-e Daneshjuyan; and military service as well as the period of internship (for doctors) or clerkship (for lawyers) would be deducted from the overall number of years of obligatory employment. Those

27. SSHBA, *Omur-e Daneshju'i, 1974/5*, 125; idem, *Tahavvol-e Amuzesh-e ʿAli-ye Iran, 1974/5* (Tehran, 1975/6); idem, *Tasvir-e Amuzesh-e ʿAli-ye Iran, 1974/5* (Tehran, 1974/5), 110–20. Similar language was used by Dr. Baheri, head of the institute, in his 1975 report to the shah, pp. 7–8.

continuing at graduate schools would have such employment deferred until after the completion of their studies. Students failing to honor their employment commitment would have to pay "full tuition" retroactively. At the same time the Ministry of Science issued a new tuition scale based on the actual cost of studies in each faculty. The new fees were between three times (in the humanities and social sciences) to ten times (in medicine) higher than before.[28]

The shah and the government saw several advantages in the law: it was the fulfillment of an old promise by the shah; it was believed to strengthen the loyalties of lower-class families since they could now send their children to prestigious universities at which tuition had traditionally been high (such as Pahlavi, Melli, and Aryamehr); the government would have graduates available for employment in areas (mainly in the provinces) and in professions (such as teaching) where the need was most pressing; politically, graduates would be more dependent on government goodwill, and under closer government supervision than before. (For similar arrangements for high school students, see Chapter 9.) Making vocational schools altogether free was expected to encourage young people to opt for technical training.

Despite the government's hopes and wishes, and even though enforcement of the employment obligation was questionable from the start, the new regulations immediately caused resentment among high school and university students and their families. Rather than contributing to stability, as the shah and his government had anticipated, the law ended up doing the opposite.

The reasons for resentment, by rich and poor alike, were manifold. Regardless of their social background, students (particularly girls) resented being tied down with future employment for such a long period. (A student who had benefited from the law during four years at high school and four years at the university would be tied down for twelve years. Medical students and those taking advanced degrees had to sign on for even longer periods.) Another cause of resentment was a change in preference with regard to government employment. Traditionally, this had been the preferred option of academics. But in the past decade, better opportunities and greater prestige had come to be found in the private sector. Without this change, such a commitment would not really have been necessary. But the government had ignored the impact of changing preferences and had failed to assess accurately the degree of resentment the new law was bound to evoke. Yet indications of the

28. Letter of the minister of science to university chancellors (no. 11/2/3780) from 19 September 1974.

trend away from government employment had already been seen in a survey conducted by the Institute for Psychological Research in 1971/ 2. Asked what "type of occupation" they preferred, only 23.8 percent of the 6,387 students questioned answered "employment in government institutions." More than that: among students listed as coming from families of "high" social status, only 16 percent opted for government employment, as against 24.7 percent from "medium"- and 25.9 percent from "low"-status families. Among students of medicine, engineering, arts, and mathematics, the inclination toward public employment was below average; among students of political science and law and natural sciences, above average.[29] The trend away from public employment continued after the survey was made and was reinforced by the 1974 oil boom. More and more, the students and the government were at odds on this point.

In particular, students feared assignment to the provinces. Nasafat's survey found out that 63.9 percent of the 4,373 students who answered the relevant question preferred jobs in Tehran. This applied in almost equal measure to students who had themselves gone to secondary school and to university in the provinces: more than half of the students in Rasht, Qazvin, Bandar Pahlavi, Lahijan, and Babolsar indicated they preferred to work in Tehran, as did over half of the students who had completed their secondary education in Ilam, Hamadan, Semnan, or Hormuzadegan.[30]

What further incensed students was their feeling that—given the new oil income—they had a right to free education without strings attached. This was pointed out by Deputy Court Minister Baheri in his 1975 report to the shah. Ironically, students of lower social background, whom the government believed the law was helping most, were particularly angry. The rise in tuition fees made it impossible for them to enroll as paying students and thus avoid the public-service obligation. Moreover, they believed that well-to-do families would find ways to escape provincial or low-prestige assignments while they themselves, lacking connections or "pull" (*parti*), would get the worst jobs. In this way, they believed, the new regulations would deprive them of some of the benefits for the sake of which they had worked so hard to gain admission.

The fact that the law was passed only two months before the start of the academic year to which it applied, and that the regulations were issued only four days before classes began, caused confusion and hence

29. Nasafat, 225–30.
30. Ibid., 236–76.

additional resentment. A survey by the Royal Institute for Research on Education of the implementation of the law in its first year found that instructions from the Ministry of Science to colleges and universities were far from uniform, and in some cases, downright contradictory. Red tape compounded the problem.[31] Students felt that they had been asked to sign forms without having been given time to study the new regulations or find funds for admission as fee-paying students, and resented the resulting tensions.

The Iranian political environment such as it was at the time did not, of course, make open criticism possible. But those who were in Iran then and were in touch with the campuses were well aware of the students' sense of outrage; I know I certainly was. So, in its own way, was the government. In fact, whether from a desire to ease tensions or in a move intended to make the required educational contracts more attractive to future students, the government did not at first make use of its right to assign jobs to the graduates. Classified reports of the Royal Institute for Research on Education and the Organization for Students' Affairs in the Ministry of Science listed all students who signed obligations on graduation between January 1975 and January 1976. Out of a total of 12,594 graduates, the ministry assigned jobs to 7,408, (to 5,052 in government agencies and to 2,356 in the private sector). The remaining 5,186 continued their studies or were called up for army service. Yet only 432 (or 5.8 percent) reported to the ministry as required. No attempt at enforcement was made with respect to the others. Graduates in medicine, pharmacology, and engineering were particularly reluctant to report, graduates in the humanities and social science slightly less so.

A few months later, in May 1976 (according to data given to me by a senior official in the bureau for the academic professions in the Ministry of Labor) the percentage of those reporting for employment was only 4.8 percent. A further breakdown showed that of those assigned to teaching positions (approximately one half of all assignments), only 2.3 percent had reported. Only 20 percent of the seventy-nine graduates referred to the Ministry of Agriculture did report (mainly for administrative positions). Of the 134 graduates of medicine, pharmacology, psychology, and the natural sciences assigned to the Ministry of Health, not a single one turned up. Even at the more prestigious workplaces (such as the Central Bank, the National Gas Company, the Ministry of Justice, and the Central Bureau for Statistics)

---

31. SSHBA, *Ejra'-ye Firman-e Amuzesh-e Raygan dar Daneshgahha va Mo'assesat-e Amuzesh-e 'Ali, 1974/5*, eds., Hushang Ranku and Parviz Razedan (Tehran, 1974/5), 8–9.

as well as at the Ministries of Finance and Welfare, not one assignee reported for duty.

The situation was not much better in the private sector. A list of the 2,356 graduates referred to it was made available to me by the Royal Institute for Research on Education. Surprisingly, many physicians, engineers, and teachers—for whom there was such pressing need in public employment—were assigned to the private sector. From my own observation of those who did report to the appropriate office, I got the impression that they had particularly high expectations with regard to both the occupations they were seeking as well as the pay they anticipated.

In his 1975 report to the shah, Baheri pointed to other shortcomings of the new system: for one thing, more graduates signed contracts in the fields of specialization less urgently required; for another, students came to increasingly believe that the government owed them suitable employment after graduation. Since many of them had specialized in fields totally irrelevant to the government's manpower needs, Baheri concluded that the new law was more likely to cause resentment than to correct what was wrong in the present situation.

The government could easily have enforced the law (e.g., by withholding diplomas from those failing to report for employment). Why did it fail to do so? According to some officials like Dehqan (head of students' bureau in the Ministry of Science) or Tayyeb and Razedan (both from the Royal Institute), the government did not deem it wise to impose undesired employment on graduates; others (like Mokhtari) thought that the government, being aware of the graduates' resentment, wished to avoid a direct confrontation with them. Many students, however, believed that the initial leniency was only meant to lull them into a false sense of optimism and encourage students to sign the required contracts lightly, while in fact the government was preparing to take action to enforce the law.

It is clear, then, that the government succeeded in eliciting a great deal of resentment but failed to reap any benefit from the law. Had it not rushed to pass the law (presumably to make a show of doing the shah's bidding), it might have found other ways to promote its ends, for instance, by offering incentives for the kind of job it most wanted filled. As it was, the law probably reinforced opposition trends. My own observations convinced me that many students viewed the law as a threat to their career prospects and their personal advancement. The failure to enforce it did not calm tensions either. If anything, it added to the general resentment the particular pique of those who had either paid their fees or taken up the jobs they had been referred to and now felt duped because so many others had done neither. Open opposition to the law was not voiced until 1978, and—among other steps to appease the opposition—the government (in June of that year) waived the requirement to work as assigned: at long last, when it was obviously too late to do any good, higher education was made unconditionally free.

Tuition Payment After 1974

After the 1974 law went into effect, and until it was superseded by the government's new policy in 1978, individual students had to make up their minds whether to claim free tuition and undertake the concomitant obligations, or else pay the (now considerably higher) fees. Those easily capable of affording the fees could weigh their decision according to both economic or noneconomic considerations. Others could still conclude that loans or greater financial efforts on the part of their families were preferable to long years of assigned employment. Others again probably had no choice but to sign on.

The actual methods of financing tuition were investigated by the Royal Institute in 1974/5.[32] Its survey covered all institutes of higher education (ten universities and 151 colleges) and made use of data supplied by the student bureaus on the various campuses. It related to 128,788 out of the total student population of 135,350. Table 15 shows the mode of covering tuition fees according to the different types of schools: universities, independent colleges (granting academic degrees), private colleges, colleges operated by the Ministry of Education (mainly teachers seminars), and colleges under other ministries. Five categories were used: exemptions in return for obligations according to the 1974 law; exemptions carrying no obligation (mainly at colleges in technological fields), exemptions carrying a specific obligation (in training for specific government jobs); personal exemptions (given to outstanding high school students and to children of the universities' academic staff); and those paying full tuition. It turned out that 47.7 percent of all students signed obligations, and only 21.1 percent paid full tuition. A breakdown by types of schools shows that the higher the prestige of a school, the more students paid tuition. This comes out clearly in the first three groups of schools where students had no options except full payment or signing contracts for assigned employment. At the universities, 31.2 percent of the students paid tuition, and 50.3 percent were exempted in exchange for assigned employment;

---

32. SSHBA, *Amuzesh-e Raygan*, 38.

Table 15. Tuition payment or exemption in 1974/5 according to types of institutions (in percentages)

Type of institute	Total no. of students	Exemption in return for job obligation	Uncon- ditional exemption	Exemption in return for spe- cific ob- ligation	Personal exemp- tion	Full tuition pay- ment	Other
Universities	53,420	50.3	0.1	10.2	7.3	31.2	0.9
Independent public colleges	7,286	62.2	—	2.3	3.4	26.9	5.2
Private colleges	38,390	75.4	3.1	1.0	0.1	20.4	—
Colleges affiliated with Ministry of Education	23,458	—	50.9	49.1	—	—	—
Colleges affiliated with other ministries	6,234	18.2	3.5	64.9	0.1	11.2	1.9
Total	128,788	47.7	10.4	16.7	3.3	21.1	0.8

Sources: Computed from data in SSHBA, *Amuzesh-e Raygan,* 1–18, 44–48.

at the independent colleges, the figures were 26.9 percent and 62.2 percent; and at the private colleges, 20.4 percent and 75.4 percent, respectively. On the scale of prestige, the universities placed first, the independent colleges next, and the private colleges third. A comparison of number of students having personal exemptions (for academic excellence or as children of academic staff) bears this out: they numbered 7.3 percent at the universities and 3.4 percent, and 0.1 percent in each of the two other types of school, respectively.

A more detailed breakdown for the ten universities again points to the correlation between the prestige of a school and the student's willingness and ability to pay tuition. This was most conspicuous at the Tehran and Pahlavi universities (where there was also a marked concentration of students with personal exceptions). At Tehran University, 43.1 percent of the students paid tuition, and 42.9 percent signed obligations; at Pahlavi 41.9 percent paid and 38.8 percent signed on. But the average for all ten universities was 31.2 percent and 50.3 percent, respectively.[33]

33. Ibid., 56–61.

Table 16. Tuition payment or exemption of students of medicine, the humanities, and social science in 1974/5 (in percentages)

Faculty	Total no. of students	Exemption in return for job ob- ligation	Uncon- ditional exemption	Exemption in return for spe- cific ob- ligation	Personal exemp- tion	Full tuition pay- ment	Other
Humanities & social science	17,333	66.5	—	1.5	3.2	28.6	0.2
Medicine	6,977	22.2	0.7	1.7	25.1	50.0	0.3
Total	128,788	47.7	10.4	16.7	3.3	21.1	0.8

Sources: Computed from data in SSHBA, *Amuzesh-e Raygan,* 30–38.

Similar differences existed between students at different faculties. Table 16 compares the faculties of medicine with the faculties of humanities and social science. As has been noted, these two stand at either end of the prestige scale. The findings are consistent with this: among medical students, only 22.2 percent undertook obligations under the 1974 law, in the humanities and social science as many as 66.5 percent did so.[34] Similarly, there were 25.1 percent students in medicine and only 3.2 percent in humanities who had personal exemptions.

A breakdown according to degrees shows that those taking advanced degrees tended to finance their own tuition and avoid occupational commitments: out of 82,294 first-degree students at the universities, 22.8 percent paid tuition and 63.9 percent signed obligations; of the 2,394 second-degree students, 38.9 percent paid tuition and 50.0 percent signed commitments; of 3,016 students studying straight for the second degree (mostly in engineering), 70.8 percent paid tuition and only 23.5 percent signed commitments; and of the 7,849 studying directly for a Ph.D. or M.D. (mostly in medical and veterinary schools and in pharmacology), 51.6 percent paid their tuition and only 24.4 percent committed themselves to assigned employment. This was so despite the higher tuition fees involved.[35]

Other findings of the survey show that more women than men paid

34. The long duration of medical training may also have deterred some students from adding another long-term obligation. But conversely the underprivileged may now have found it almost impossible to pay their own tuition.

It would have been instructive to compare the findings with those for engineering students. But many of the latter were at technical colleges (and hence exempted in any case), and the comparative figures would therefore not have been representative.

35. SSHBA, *Amuzesh-e Raygan,* 18–21.

tuition. This was presumably due to their special reluctance to make commitments for their future employment, but also indicates higher social standing. Of the 128,788 students in the survey, 37,479 (29.1 percent) were women. Of these, 25.3 percent paid tuition (as compared with 19.3 percent of the men) and 39.2 percent signed obligations (as against 51.3 percent of the men).[36]

The overall picture, then, is that the schools—and within them, the faculties—accorded greater social prestige attracted a greater share of students willing and able to pay for their tuition. But the steep rise in fees caused well-off students to join the less well-off in resenting the 1974 law.

The Student Population

An examination of the social background of the student population is no easy task. For the early years of Mohammad Reza Shah's regime, the data are insufficient. A check of the available sources reveals that until the White Revolution no such information was gathered by the universities or by other agencies. The personal files of the students yield but little. For the later years, more data are available, but their accuracy is somewhat doubtful.[37] The following summary relates mainly to the end of the period and is based on official and semiofficial sources; for the earlier years, it will be necessary to make do with some general observations by people then involved in higher education.

Sadiqi, the noted sociologist who taught at Tehran University from its first years, claimed that between the 1940s and the 1970s the social background of the students changed considerably: in the earlier period, the students were almost exclusively from the higher strata of society; gradually (mainly after the White Revolution) more and more students from humble origin were to be found on campus. In the absence of relevant statistics, he argued mainly from the appearance of the students, their accent, style of conversation, and manners. Sadiqi told me in the summer of 1977 that this was "one of the most outstanding achievements" of the shah and of the educational system under him—an assessment all the more noteworthy for coming from a man with a consistent record of opposing the shah. Siyasi (also one of the shah's

---

36. Ibid., 16.
37. Many informants suggested that more precise information might be found in the SAVAK files; but the author had no access to them.

opponents) and Sadiq (who supported him all along) both formed the same impression.

Judging by Sadiqi's yardstick, one can discern a social differential between various universities and various faculties in the 1970s. At Tehran University, for instance, in the faculties of the humanities, social science, and education, many students wore modest clothes and many female students used the veil (*chador*) or scarf. Their accent attested to their being first-generation migrants from the provinces. Many of them used buses to come to school. The same could not be said of the faculties of medicine, pharmacology, and the arts. There, students usually arrived by cab (a fairly inexpensive means of transportation in Tehran) or in private cars, sometimes chauffeur-driven. Many students, especially women, wore modern and expensive clothes. Their speech, manners, and conduct as well as the topics of their conversation clearly suggested that they belonged to the upper classes. This is not to suggest, however, that only rich students enrolled in these faculties. Professor Iraj Lalezari (dean of the School of Pharmacology) maintained at that time that there were a number of students of lower-class origin in his and other prestigious faculties, particularly during the last decade of the shah's reign. But all in all, there was clearly a difference between the two types of schools. Interestingly, in the Faculty of Engineering the composition of the student population was somewhat more balanced. Similar differences could be observed between one campus and another: Aryamehr and Melli being the preserve of mostly upper-class students; Meshhed and Isfahan of lower-class entrants. Pahlavi University was exceptional: it was less glamorous, but this stemmed from the unique open atmosphere there rather than from the social affiliation of its student. Even the professors (mostly graduates of American universities) often dressed and behaved differently from the staff elsewhere. The colleges, with few exceptions, resembled the less prestigious faculties at Tehran University.

Places of Birth and Study

The first comprehensive survey of all institutes of higher education was conducted by the Institute for Research and Planning in Science and Education for the 1969/70 academic year. It showed that 72 percent of all students (i.e., college *and* university students) and 61.3 percent of the university students were enrolled in Tehran province (where 20 percent of the total population were living).[38] A later survey, for 1976/

38. MTBRA, *Amar Amuzesh-e 'Ali-ye Iran, 1969/70* (Tehran, 1970), 4–7.

Table 17. Students in 1971/2 according to province of birth and of matriculation (in percentages)

Province*	Population	Students born in the province	Students who completed high school in the province
Central (Tehran)	20.6	34.1	48.7
Khorasan	9.7	7.3	6.6
Azerbayjan Sharqi	9.5	8.1	6.4
Mazanderan	7.1	6.2	4.1
Khuzestan	6.5	5.2	4.8
Fars	6.0	6.1	5.9
Isfahan	5.8	7.0	6.3
Others	34.8	26.0	17.2
Total	100.0% (35,251,000)	100.0% (6,387)	100.0% (6,387)

Sources: Column 2 and 3 computed from Nasafat's survey, pp. 68–85; column 1 based on the 1976 census.
*Provinces containing less than 5 percent of the total population are not listed.

7, showed that the concentration in Tehran had been reduced: to 48.7 percent of *all* students and 53.4 percent of university students alone.[39] The surveys show that during the years of the educational revolution higher education expanded more quickly in the provinces than in Tehran. Most university students studied in the six largest cities of Iran (see Table 13). According to Nasafat's survey for 1971/2, 90.6 percent of the participants in the survey (including college students) studied in the capital cities of the provinces (including Tehran), 6.2 percent studied in other large cities, 1.2 percent in the capital cities of the districts, and only 2 percent in smaller towns.[40]

The survey by Nasafat also included data on the students' provinces of birth and the places where they had completed their secondary education (often indicating residence). Table 17 is based on its findings and compares them with the share of each province in the total population. While Tehran had one-fifth of the population, half of the students completed their matriculation examinations there and had presumably grown up there as well. All other provinces and districts (except for Isfahan) had a higher share of the total population than of high school graduates. A division of all the provinces into three groups—Tehran, the other six large provinces (listed in the table), and the rest of the country—shows the following: at the campuses in Tehran, the share of Tehran-born students was 1.7 times the share of

39. Idem, *Amar Amuzesh-e 'Ali-ye Iran, 1976/7* (Tehran, 1977), 1:1–8.
40. Data relate to 6,230 of the 6,387 students surveyed (Nasafat, 70).

Table 18. Place of birth and matriculation of students in 1971/2 by types of settlements (in percentages)

Types of settlement	Place of birth	Place of matriculation
Provincial capitals	51.1	72.4
Other major cities	30.2	22.5
District capitals	4.9	3.3
Towns	6.3	1.0
Villages	6.8	0.3
Abroad	0.7	0.5
Total	100.0% (6,240)	100.0% (6,294)

Sources: Computed from data in Nasafat's survey, pp. 60–70.

Tehran in the overall population, and the share of high school graduates was 2.4 times as high; in the large provinces, there was no marked disparity between the size of the population (44.6 percent), the percentage of students born there (39.9 percent), and those who had passed their matriculation examinations there (34.1 percent); but the remaining provinces had 34.8 percent of the population, whereas only 26 percent of the students were born there, and—what is more revealing—only 17.2 percent had completed their secondary education locally.

The survey of the Institute for Research and Planning in Science and Education (of the Ministry of Science) that gave a breakdown of the total student population of 1969/70 by province of residence supports similar results. It showed that Tehran province had 470 students per 100,000 inhabitants. In the other more developed provinces the ratio was only slightly lower: 387 in Isfahan and 252 in Fars. But in the underprivileged provinces it was significantly lower: 118 students in Kurdistan, 85 in Sistan and Baluchestan, and 70, 41, and 16 per 100,000 inhabitants in each of the districts of Hormuzadegan, Ilam, and Kahgiluye and Boyed Ahmadi, respectively.[41]

A breakdown by the size of the place of birth or secondary schooling of the students pointed up the advantage of being city-born. Table 18 indicates that over 50 percent of the students were born in the capital cities of 14 provinces and over 70 percent had gone to secondary school there. Yet these 14 cities together accounted only for 20 percent of the overall population (according to the 1976 census). Grouping the above cities with other larger cities, we see that 86.2 percent of the students

41. MTBRA, *Tasviri az Tarkib-e Daneshjuyan . . . Sal-e Tahsili 1969/70* (Tehran, 1971), 2–6.

were born, and 98.2 percent finished secondary school, in major cities, whereas the aggregate share of these cities in the population was only 32 percent. Only 13.1 percent of the students were born in the smaller towns or in villages (which housed well over two-thirds of the population), and only 1.3 percent of them completed their secondary education there.

The contrast is even more marked if applicants rather than students are compared. Such a comparison was made in a survey of the competitive examination for 1972 and 1973 conducted by the Royal Institute. Some of the data relevant to our theme were blurred (perhaps intentionally) by the editors by combining highly developed and underprivileged regions under a single rubric (e.g.: data for Fars were grouped with those of Kahgiluye and Boyed Ahmadi, Isfahan with Chaharmahal and Bakhtyari, and Khuzestan with Lorestan). Furthermore, the survey did not relate to the private prestige universities (Aryamehr, Melli, and Pahlavi) or to any of the colleges (which did not participate in the general competitive examinations). Yet it is clear that the failure rate of applicants from small towns and villages was considerably higher than that of the city-born. To illustrate: people born in Tehran represented just over 29 percent of the applicants in both years; students completing their matriculation examinations there accounted for 33.5 percent (1972/3) and 38.5 percent (1973/4)—while according to Nasafat's survey, there were 51.1 percent Tehran-born *students* in 1971/2, and 72.4 percent completed their matriculation there. At the other end of the scale, *applicants* residing in small towns and villages formed 8.8 percent of the total in 1973/4, but only 1.3 percent of the *student* population surveyed by Nasafat had finished secondary school there.[42]

From the above findings, two important conclusions are clear: first, residents of major cities (particularly of Tehran) and of the more developed provinces had a disproportionate advantage in gaining college or university admission; second, the expansion of elementary and secondary education led to an increase in the number of applicants for higher education from among residents of small towns and (to some extent) larger villages, but their failure rate in the university entrance examinations was disproportionately high. Yet the evaluation of these data is not unequivocal. At the end of the shah's reign, there had, after all, sprung up centers of higher education in the provinces (rather than in Tehran alone, as had been the case at his accession). Furthermore,

---

42. SSHBA, *Ahval-e Shakhsi-ye Davtalaban-e Tahsilat-e ʿAli: Barresi Moshakhkhasat-e Fardi va Khanevadegi, 1973/4* (Tehran, 1974/5), 27; idem, *Ahval-e Shakhsi-ye Davtalaban-e Tahsilat-e ʿAli: Barresi Moshakhkhasat-e Fardi va Khanevadegi, 1972/3* (Tehran, 1974), 30–35.

gradual though the process was, more young people of lower social background were working their way into the colleges and universities at a fairly steady rate. The expansion of secondary education in the provinces during the last two decades or so of the regime and the establishment, from the late 1960s on, of provincial colleges and universities were beginning to leave their mark—however haltingly—on the eve of the shah's overthrow.

Social Background

Education, occupational status, and income, as well as patterns of consumerism, life-style, and social and cultural trends are commonly accepted indicators of a person's place on the social ladder. But for the Iranian student population, information on these points was difficult to obtain. Even for the later years for which some data exist, important information (i.e., for income) is unavailable.[43] Best documented among items likely to shed light on the social status of the students are data on their education. They suggest a clear correlation between the parents' educational level and their children's prospects of acquiring a higher education. Table 19 compares the educational levels of parents of the students in Nasafat's survey with those of parents of applicants for 1972/3 (according to the survey of the Royal Institute). The above-average education of the parents in both surveys stands out at first glance. In 1976, only 1.8 percent of the men and 0.5 percent of the women above the age of twenty in the population at large had had a higher education. By contrast, 13.4 percent of the fathers and 1.5 percent of the mothers of the 1971/2 students (in both universities and colleges) had had a higher education. (The actual gap is even wider: the parents were then in their forties or older, and the percentage of graduates in their age group was lower than the overall 1976 figure.) Similarly, of the total population above the age of fifteen, only 20.5 percent of the men and 8.2 percent of the women had had between seven and twelve years of schooling. But 22.7 percent of the fathers and 16.8 percent of the mothers of students had had that much schooling. (Again, the parents' age group must be taken into account.)[44] But this very marked correlation should not be allowed to obscure the fact that the large majority of parents (63.9 percent of the fathers and 81.7

43. In surveys at Tehran University, students were asked to specify their parents' income, but their responses were so obviously understated that those conducting the surveys preferred to ignore them.
44. SBB/MA, *Dowran-e Pahlavi*, 18–44.

Table 19. Education of parents of 1971/2 students and 1972/3 candidates (in percentages)

Education	Fathers		Mothers	
	of students	of candidates	of students	of candidates
Doctorate	2.4	1.4	0.1	0.1
M.A. or M.Sc.	1.8	0.6	0.1	0.1
B.A. or B.Sc.	6.7	6.6	0.9	0.7
Fowq-e Diplom	2.5	0.6	0.4	0.3
All levels of higher education	13.4	9.2	1.5	1.2
High school	11.0	12.1	6.7	7.5
Intermediate school	11.7	13.9	10.1	10.2
All levels of secondary education	22.7	26.0	16.8	17.7
Complete elementary education	21.3	26.2	25.6	23.3
"Little education"(*kam-savad*)	28.1	17.2	22.1	18.2
Illiterate (*bi-savad*)	14.5	21.4	34.0	39.6
Total of elementary or lower education	63.9	64.8	81.7	81.1
	100.0%(6,030)	100.0%(44,813)	100.0%(5,777)	100.0%(42,603)

Sources: Data on students computed from Nasafat's survey, pp. 80–87; data on candidates computed from SSHBA, *Ahval-e Shakhsi-ye Davtalaban 1972/3,* 92–98.

percent of the mothers) had no more than six years of schooling and 42.6 percent and 56.1 percent, respectively, were illiterate (*bi-savad*) or had "little education" (*kam-savad*).

A comparison of the educational level of parents of students and of parents of applicants is also instructive: as opposed to 13.4 percent of the fathers of students, only 9.2 percent of the fathers of the applicants had had a higher education; the rates for the mothers were 1.5 percent and 1.2 percent, respectively. In other words: the rate of failure in the examinations was higher for the children of less-educated parents.

Even more enlightening are the differences in level of parental ed-

Table 20. Education of fathers of students at Tehran University by faculties in 1973/4 (in percentages)

| Faculty | Sex | Father's education | | | |
		Higher	7–12 years	1–6 years	None
Medicine	F	33.7	34.1	28.4	4.2
(N = 920)	M	19.9	21.7	42.5	15.9
	All	23.4	25.0	38.8	12.8
Engineering*	M	18.3	23.7	39.2	18.8
(N = 994)					
Law and	F	33.1	32.6	30.6	3.7
political	M	7.3	13.6	47.3	31.8
science					
(N = 817)	All	14.9	19.2	42.4	23.5
Humanities	F	17.4	38.9	38.1	5.6
and	M	7.0	8.9	48.7	35.4
social					
sciences					
(N = 1,785)	All	13.0	26.4	42.6	18.0
Arts	F	54.7	34.6	9.6	1.1
(N = 475)	M	23.1	27.0	36.5	13.4
	All	33.1	29.4	28.0	9.5

Sources: Computed from Daneshgah-e Tehran, *Barresi Nemune'i Moshakhkhasat-e Fardi va-Khanevadegi Daneshjuyan-e Daneshgah-e Tehran* (Tehran, 1974).
* There were no female students at this faculty in 1973/4.

ucation for students in different faculties. Table 20 examines such differences among parents of Tehran University students in 1973/4. The information was supplied by the students at the schools of medicine, engineering, and law and political science when registering for the second term. The questionnaires properly answered numbered 994 in the school of engineering (66.4 percent of the total of students there), 920 in medicine (50.1 percent), and 817 in law and political science (53.3 percent). They included data on the place of birth, the source for financing university education, and the occupation and education of the fathers. Later the editors decided to add similar data, presumably from students' files, for the faculties of humanities, social science, and arts. The survey showed that the higher the education of parents, the better able they were to secure a higher education for their children. Most remarkable was that fathers of female students had a higher level of education (and, presumably, of income) than fathers of male students. Thus, 54.7 percent of the fathers of women in the School of Arts had had a higher education, as against 23.1 percent of the fathers of men studying there; 33.7 percent of fathers of women in the School of

Medicine, compared with 19.9 percent of fathers of men; 33.1 percent and 7.3 percent, respectively, in the School of Law and Political Science, and 17.4 percent and 7.0 percent, respectively, in the humanities and social sciences. The highest level of parental education was found with respect to the School of Arts: 33.1 percent of the fathers of students there (male and female taken together) were graduates and only 9.5 percent were illiterate. This may appear strange at first glance but can be accounted for by the fact that this faculty in particular contained many students for whom career prospects were not the primary motivation and who came from a home background in which the arts were held in high regard. In other faculties parental education varied according to the social prestige of the field of study, as was noted above. A comparison of the data for the faculties of Tehran University (Table 20) with those of the countrywide student population (Table 19) shows that the educational level of parents of students at Tehran University was far above the national average.

Reliable data on the economic situation of the students' families proved difficult to obtain. Survey questions on parental income were answered in a manner so patently insincere that some editors preferred not to include the replies in their findings. Dr. Parviz Kardavani, head of the Bureau for Educational Research (*Daftar-e Motale'at-e Amuzeshi*) at Tehran University, claimed that according to a 1975 survey by his staff, some 75 percent of the students marked their fathers' income as below 20,000 Riyals a month (the salary of an unskilled employee). Since this seemed "ridiculous" (*maskhare*), he decided not to include answers to that question in the published version. Those surveys that did include income took care to note that they viewed their findings as "unrealistic."[45] (An example is Nasafat's survey: of the 5,964 students questioned, 44 percent said their fathers earned less than 10,000 Riyals a month, and only 5.2 percent gave a figure of over 50,000 Riyals.) Although all questionnaires were anonymous, and even though they stated expressly that they would be used for scientific purposes only, students evidently viewed them with complete mistrust and thought it prudent to make their parents' income appear lower than it was.

Information on parental employment turned out to be more useful (and allowed an indirect, if not very precise, assessment of income, too). The survey by the Institute for Research and Planning in Science and Education for 1969/70 gathered data on the occupation of 49,778 fathers who were still working at the time of the survey: 47.3 percent

---

45. Nasafat, 99. For similar reservations, see SSHBA, *Ahval-e Shakhsi-ye Davtalaban 1973/4*, 98; SBB, *Khastha-ye Shoghli*, 35.

of them were government employees, 37.8 percent were listed as small businessmen, 8.1 percent were farmers, 4.1 percent owners of large businesses, and 2.7 percent were classed as unskilled workers.[46] It is possible that among the "farmers" were some rich owners of mechanized farms, or that some "small" businessmen were in fact quite rich. However, the large number of government employees stands out. Although the figure for unskilled workers was low, it still indicates that children of lower-class families had already begun to make their way to the campuses. Nasafat reports on the occupation of 5,456 fathers of the 6,387 students he surveyed. He found that 39.4 percent were employed in the administration, in education, or in other white-collar jobs; 12.1 percent worked in technical jobs, 11.7 percent in agriculture, 23.6 percent in commerce, 6.0 percent in service industries, and 7.4 percent in the armed forces.[47] Similar results were listed in the survey of the Royal Institute for Research on Education of candidates for higher education in 1973/4. But a comparison between the two surveys reveals that comparatively more *candidates* had fathers working in technical jobs and in education, whereas the *students* had more fathers in the administration and commerce.[48] This again confirms that the drop-out rate on the threshold of higher education was higher among children of relatively weaker strata.

Even more instructive for the present discussion is Nasafat's breakdown of the occupational status of the fathers. His survey divided all occupations into nine levels: three defined as "low level" (*sath-e pa'in*), three "medium level" (*sath-e motavaset*), and three as "high level" (*sath-e bala*). The division was based on the education, skills, and experience required for each of them, the average income, and the degree of social prestige. The survey found that 48.4 percent of students' parents were at a "low level," 43.6 percent at a "medium level," and only 8.0 percent at a "high level." The lowest jobs (not further specified) of the three grouped as "low level" accounted for 9.3 percent of the fathers[49]—yet another indication of the beginnings of upward mobility at the lowest end of the social scale.

As noted before, well-to-do families managed to secure for their children places in above-average secondary schools—often in private schools (see Chapter Nine)—giving them a built-in advantage in their quest for admission to prestige universities or "desirable" faculties.

46. MTBRA, *Tarkib Daneshjuyan*, 19–21.
47. Nasafat, 91.
48. SSHBA, *Ahval Shakhsi-ye Davtalaban 1973/4*, 88.
49. Nasafat, 91–95.

Two surveys of the Royal Institute for Research on Education compared the grades students earned in high school and their achievements in the university entrance examinations of 1970/1 and 1972/3. They found that graduates of private high schools had an advantage over graduates of government schools; that students who had specialized in mathematics had an advantage over students of natural science; and that the latter had an advantage over those taking the humanities at high schools.[50] (This was reinforced by a survey of the Royal Institute in 1970/1 which found that 40.6 percent of the graduates of private high schools had taken the mathematics specialization, but only 26.0 percent of the graduates of government schools had done so. For the humanities, the figures were 6.5 percent and 13.4 percent, respectively.)[51] The two above-named surveys also found that, other factors being equal, a student's chances of gaining admission showed a clear correlation with the size of his home town (or village).

The trends set out here were further corroborated by the results of the inquiry into the methods of financing tuition (see previous section). The high percentage of fee-paying students, as well as their above-average representation at prestige schools and in prestige fields of study, once more attested to the disproportionate share of the well-off in higher education. It relegated a disproportionate percentage of lower-class students to less "desirable" schools or faculties, alienated them from their more advantaged colleagues, and made them resent the latter's greater freedom of choice. But this survey, too, leaves no doubt that, by the middle and late 1970s, more sons of the underprivileged were moving onto the campuses.

Conclusion

The dearth of data on the social background of students, mainly for the era before the White Revolution, adds to the perplexity of assessing

50. SSHBA, *Entekhab Daneshju 1970/1*, 81; idem, *Entekhab Daneshju 1972/3*, 95. Such findings were confirmed by two other studies of the same institute which examined the social background of candidates taking the general entrance examination in 1972/3 and 1973/4; in a survey of the Institute for Research and Planning in Science and Education in the Ministry of Science which examined the student population in 1969/70; in the survey by Nasafat; as well as in a survey by Tehran University of its candidates for 1973/4. See SSHBA, *Ahval-e Shakhsi-ye Davtalaban 1972/3*, 42; idem, *Ahval-e Shakhsi-ye Davtalaban-e 1973/4*, 36; Daneshgah-e Tehran, *Gozaresh Marbut be Davtalaban va Padhirofteshodegan Daneshgah-e Tehran 1973/4* (Tehran, 1973), 5.

51. SSHBA, *Entekhab Daneshju 1970/1*, 51–75.

the advent of young people from the lower classes at the universities and colleges. What is worse: it is impossible to make a meaningful comparison between the late years of the shah's reign, for which there is a considerable body of documentation, and the early years, for which there is virtually none. But even the evaluation of the findings for the later period is difficult; much depends on whether one chooses to look at a half-empty or half-full glass. There can be no doubt that more students from lower-class families entered the course of higher education, just as there can be no doubt that, numerically speaking, the process remained quite limited. Those who made their way forward often had to make do with less prestigious schools and fields of specialization, and most did not go on after the first degree. The original policy of the shah (as well as the interest of the elites) to limit higher education left its mark on the campuses for quite some time, even after its eventual reversal.

Once the educational revolution was launched and the shah reviewed his policy, the expansion of higher education quickened. But the single decade that intervened until the fall of the shah was not enough time for the new policy to gather momentum and produce results. There was indeed progress, but if "equal opportunities" was the goal, it was still far in the future.

12

Education—
The Badge of the New Elites

Empirical research on elite groups in the Middle East began in the mid-1960s with a study on Turkey followed by a series of other case studies.[1] In most cases, the subjects were people holding prominent positions whom the scholars believed to possess power or to have access to the powerful. The study on Turkey, for instance, related to members of parliament and to cabinet ministers; other studies to the leaders of the Algierian revolution; the ruling party of Egypt; cabinet ministers and members of the revolutionary council in Iraq. Zonis, by contrast, in his work on the Iranian elites, sought "to identify the powerful by locating those with reputation for exercising such power."[2] All scholars

1. Empirical studies were stimulated by modern theories of elite formation, such as Vilfredo Pareto, *The Mind and Society* (New York: Harcourt and Brace, 1935); Gaetano Mosca, *The Ruling Class* (New York: McGraw-Hill, 1939); Robert Michels, *Political Parties* (New York: Free Press, 1915); Harold Laswell, *Politics: Who Gets What, When, How* (Hightstown: McGraw-Hill, 1939).

For case studies, see Frederick Frey, *The Turkish Political Elite* (Cambridge: MIT Press, 1965); William Quandt, *Revolution and Political Leadership: Algeria, 1954–1958* (Cambridge: MIT Press, 1969); Leslie Roos, Jr., and Nuralou Roos, *Managers of Modernization* (Cambridge: Harvard University Press, 1971); Hrair Dekmejian, *Patterns of Political Leadership: Egypt, Israel, Lebanon* (New York: SUNY Press, 1975); George Lenczowski, ed., *Political Elites in the Middle East* (Washington: American Enterprise, 1975); William Zartman, ed., *Elites in the Middle East* (New York: Praeger, 1980); Frank Tachau, ed., *Political Elites and Political Development in the Middle East* (Boston: Schenkman, 1975); Leonard Binder, *In a Moment of Enthusiasm: Political Power and the Second Stratum in Egypt* (Chicago: University of Chicago Press, 1978). For the studies by Zonis and Bill, see in pp. 155 and 278, respectively.

2. Phebe Marr, "The Political Elite in Egypt," in Lenczowski, *Political Elites,* 109–49; For Zonis's approach, see his book *Elite,* 5–8.

agreed that modern development had worked a profound change in the political structure of Middle Eastern countries and had upset the traditional sources of power: whereas in the past, land ownership, Bazar or guild membership, and personal connections at court were the main prerequisites for elite status, they had now been largely replaced by education, professional skills, and local positions of influence. This implied that in more and more societies achievement had come to matter more than descent.

All authors stressed the importance of higher education for membership in the new elites. "In socioeconomic terms," William Zartman suggested, "the new elites are clearly 'modern' rather than 'traditional,' in the sense of being more educated, more dependent on salaried income, and more secular than their predecessors." It was, he added, "education [which] has created the sudden changes and opportunities in social promotion, permitting new roles, creating new classes, providing the basis for new struggles for succession and polity direction."[3] Zonis stressed that although wealth was still important, "formal education has become not only the hallmark of the younger aspirants to the political elite, but a sine qua non."[4] What they failed to say explicitly, however, was that to a considerable extent the new elites were largely the descendants of the old ruling classes who had only reinforced their status by an additional asset: the acquisition of a modern higher education.

The present chapter attempts, as well as can be done, to explore the educational characteristics of the Iranian political, social, and administrative elites, drawing on previous studies as well as new material.[5]

A most salient feature of Middle Eastern elites, confirmed by all empirical studies, is their high level of education, thrown into relief by the high rate of illiteracy in the population at large. One means of tracing this in Iran is by analyzing the reference book *Who's Who in Iran*.[6] It lists members of the royal family, cabinet ministers, most members of Parliament, prominent figures in the administration, business-

---

3. Zartman, 3.

4. Zonis, *Elite*, 31–32.

5. An examination of the economic elite would have been interesting as well and might have come up with very different results. But this group is not easily defined, nor would it have been easy to obtain personal data on its members.

6. Published by *The Echo of Iran* and edited by Jahangir Behruz.

The use of such references as an analytical source has become a well-established practice in the Middle East and elsewhere. See, for instance, Stanley Lieberson and Donna Carter, "Making It in America: Differences Between Eminent Blacks and White Ethnic Groups," *American Sociological Review*, 44 (June 1974), 347–66; Michael Fischer, "Persian Women," 191.

Table 21. Education of people listed in the 1976 *Who's Who in Iran*

Sex	Total no.	% of university graduates	% of Ph.D.s and M.D.s	% of graduates of foreign universities
M	4,170	75.2	31.6	46.0
F	308	52.6	18.8	40.3
Total	4,478	73.6	30.7	45.6

Sources: Computed from Echo of Iran, *Who's Who in Iran: 1976* (Tehran, 1976).

men, intellectuals, scholars, artists, and so forth. The staff of this publication select the names to be listed and send out questionnaires which include a space for education. One of the survey's editors told me that the response was almost total. For those failing to reply, the staff compiled data from other sources. The advantage of such a publication for our purposes is its wide range; its disadvantage is that the information is based on the selected person's own (not disinterested) reply, and that the selection may be tinged by subjective judgment.

Only three volumes of the *Who's Who* were published until the revolution: in 1972, 1974, and 1976. I decided to use the last as the basis for my analysis because it is a fairly valid reflection of the group of ranking Iranians toward the end of the shah's reign. To extract information on the academic background of those listed in the volume, I combed all 4,478 entries. I used the term "graduates" rather broadly, to include holders of the *fowq-e diplom* and graduates of the war academy. Furthermore, I considered a graduate of a foreign university to be anyone having a degree from a western university (regardless of whether he or she had earned other degrees in Iran) as well as anyone who specialized in postdoctoral programs abroad. Only a dozen or so entries did not specify educational levels; I assumed that individuals listed in this way had no academic degrees.

The findings are collated in Table 21. It shows that 73.6 percent of the persons listed were university-educated, nearly one-third had doctoral degrees, and almost half had studied in the West. Only 7.4 percent were women, of whom "only" 52.6 percent were university graduates (as compared with 75.2 percent of the men). Among the women, 18.8 percent had Ph.D.s or M.D.s (as compared with 31.6 percent of the men). All these figures should be compared with the overall illiteracy rates of the population. Furthermore, in the same year, the percentage of graduates in the total population over the age of twenty was 1.8

percent for men and 0.5 percent for women.[7] Education, then, was a major dividing line between the elites and the population at large.

Although we have no source material enabling us to compare these figures with data for earlier years, we do have one documentary source capable of shedding some light on the matter. It is a report prepared in 1939 at the British Embassy in Tehran including biographies of 220 people whom the embassy considered most outstanding (other than members of the royal family). Unlike the *Who's Who*, it does not include artists, scientists, and the like, but concentrates on political and economic figures. The educational background of 200 people was given. Applying the same yardstick as before, it turned out that forty-seven (i.e., 23.5 percent) had academic degrees and ten (5.0 percent) had doctorates. All degrees were from western universities (Tehran University had only been opened four years earlier). Another twenty-five had completed their secondary education in the West. Against the background of the Iranian educational system such as it was at the time, the picture that emerges is of a highly educated elite even then.[8] The process making higher education a badge of the elites had started; a generation later, it was to become an essential requirement of elite membership.

Zonis's study adds important data on the group he defined as the political elite in the mid-1960s. He surveyed 300 people who had "boasted the greatest reputation for political power."[9] For 231 of them, he found educational data: 41.1 percent had B.A.s and another 50.7 percent had M.A.s and/or Ph.D.s; 43.7 percent of the graduates had one or more degrees from a western university; only 8.2 percent had no more than a secondary education; none had less. Zonis compared this data with statistics on the members of the twenty-first Majlis elected in 1963 and with those on the adult male population of Iran as a whole and of Tehran (he excluded women to provide a better basis of comparison, since the entire elite group and the great majority of Majlis members were men). The population figures were taken from the 1956 census (i.e., almost decade earlier), and there had been a slight improvement of the population's education in the interval. Also, the unavailability of a breakdown by age makes the statistics somewhat slanted. On the strength of existing sources, Zonis found that 91.8 percent of the political elite possessed academic degrees, as opposed

7. For a similar description of Turkey, see Daniel Lerner, *The Passing of Traditional Society: Modernizing the Middle East* (Glencoe: Free Press, 1958), 130, 442–43, 445; and Frey, 30.

8. P.R.O., F.O. 371/24582, W. Bullard to Viscount Halifax, 24 February 1940.

9. Zonis, *Elite*, 8.

to only 2.1 percent of the residents of Tehran and 0.5 percent of the population countrywide. None of the elite group had less than a secondary education, but 67.6 percent of the people of Tehran and 83.3 percent of all Iranians had no formal education at all.[10] His figures confirm that the educational level of the elites at the outset of the White Revolution was high and attest once again to the great educational gap between the few and the many.

In two more specific studies, Zahra Shaji'i, from the Institute for Social Research of Tehran University, examined the composition of the Majlis and the cabinet since the 1906 constitution. The study on the Majlis, published in 1965, collated the place of birth and residence, parental occupation and educational level of the members of the first twenty-one Parliaments (1906–1963). All in all, out of 2,777 members who actually exercised their membership in the Parliaments,[11] she gathered data on 2,594 (93.4 percent). I used these data in preparing Table 22. Also in the table are data from the 1976 *Who's Who* for 152 out of the 268 members of the twenty-fourth (1975) Majlis—the last under the monarchy. In line with the three parts of this book, the table is divided into the Qajar era (terms 1–5, 1906–1924), the era of Reza Shah (terms 6–12, 1926–1939), and that of Mohammad Reza Shah (terms 13–24, 1941–1975). Traditional and modern education are shown separately. The table shows that the share of deputies with a traditional education declined gradually until by the time of White Revolution none were left (or, perhaps more correctly, none were recorded). After an initial period of growing representation, the number of traditionally educated deputies began going down from the fourth Majlis on. After a short resurgence in the sixth Majlis, the decline continued uninterrupted.

Conversely, the proportion of deputies with a modern education, in particular university graduates, remarkably high for that time in the first and second Majlis, declined in the third, then held steady until the advent of Mohammad Reza, and subsequently grew consistently and quite quickly. University graduates reached 47 percent in the nineteenth Majlis (elected in 1956) and 48 percent in the twentieth (elected in 1960). In the twenty-fourth Majlis, 80 percent of the members were graduates of new institutes for higher learning and 31 percent of all members had doctoral degrees.

A salient point is that in spite of Reza Shah's anticlerical policy, the share of deputies with a traditional education did not decline signifi-

10. Ibid., 167–74.

11. In the early years, some elected deputies never reached Tehran; they are not included in the survey.

Table 22. Education of Majlis members (in percentages)

Majlis	Total no. of deputies	No. of Members for whom data were available	Traditional Education				New Education			
			Ejtehad	Modarres	Moqaddamat and Sath	Total	Doctoral	B.A. or M.A.	Elementary or secondary	Total
The later Qajar period										
1st	153	106	5	20	21	46	4	15	35	54
2nd	111	103	5	28	17	50	8	17	25	50
3rd	104	97	13	21	35	69	4	13	14	31
4th	105	98	6	19	32	57	2	10	31	43
5th	139	135	4	26	24	54	4	12	30	46
The reign of Reza Shah										
6th	126	120	7	24	31	62	3	9	26	38
7th	132	128	5	19	34	58	3	9	30	42
8th	125	119	3	16	25	44	6	9	41	56
9th	130	129	1	18	26	45	6	10	39	55
10th	135	128	1	21	26	48	8	5	39	52
11th	135	131	1	16	30	47	8	5	40	53
12th	134	132	1	16	32	49	7	6	38	51

The reign of
Mohammad
Reza
Shah

13th	134	132	1	16	24	41	8	6	45	59
14th	134	128	—	15	24	39	9	17	35	61
15th	135	131	—	14	16	30	11	20	39	70
16th	131	126	1	12	20	32	13	15	40	68
17th	79	77	—	14	25	40	14	24	22	60
18th	134	125	—	14	14	28	11	22	39	72
19th	133	128	—	8	9	17	20	27	36	83
20th	176	142	—	5	6	11	20	28	41	89
21st	242	179	—	—	—	—	27	42	31	100
24th	268	152	—	—	—	—	31	49	20	100

Sources: Data for members of the first through the twenty-first Majlis computed from Shajiʿi's study: Majlis, 205–26, 282–83; data for the twenty-fourth Majlis computed from *Who's Who in Iran, 1976.*

cantly in his time, falling by only 5 percent—from 54 percent under the late Qajars to 49 percent at the end of Reza Shah's rule. The main reason was the weakness of modern higher education in the early years of the century. But is also clear that the government did not discourage candidates with a traditional education, provided that they had proved their loyalty to the regime. Only under Mohammad Reza did the expansion of the new education and the shah's changed approach put an end to the membership of traditionally educated deputies.[12]

It is important to note, however, that there is no clear correlation between the education of the representatives and the authority of the Majlis vis-à-vis the court or cabinet. During the White Revolution, for example, when there was a rapid increase in the number of university graduates in the House, the Majlis allowed itself to be used as a rubber stamp by the shah. It should be added as well that the higher number of graduates did not result from popular preference expressed in free elections but reflected in large measure the personal predilections of the shah. Not only education, but also the political process that propelled them into Parliament, set them off from the mass of the population and isolated and alienated them.

Even more impressive was the educational background of the cabinet ministers, by far a more selective and distinguished group. Table 23, based on another survey by Shaji'i, examines this for the years 1906–1971. All in all, she found information on 526 of the total of 611 ministers (86 percent). Her findings are collated here along the same lines as for the Majlis. Traditionally educated ministers disappeared faster than did deputies. By the last years of the monarchy, all ministers had a modern education and most had academic degrees.

To illustrate the point more fully, let us look at the educational background of the ministers in the last cabinet of Amir ʿAbbas Hoveyda—the last cabinet, that is, before the final eruption of the opposition. (It remained in office until August 1977.) Data are taken from the 1976 *Who's Who*. Of the twenty-seven ministers, only one (ironically the minister of culture), the shah's brother-in-law Mehrdad Pahlbud, did not have an academic degree. All the others were university graduates (one of them, war minister Reza ʿAzimi, was a graduate of the war academy); thirteen had Ph.D.s or M.D.s, and twenty-one (77.8 percent) had studied at western universities. Clearly, by the mid-1970s academic degrees had become a sine qua non for top-ranking membership in

---

12. For a comparison with Turkey where the same trends were even more pronounced, see Frey, 43–46.

Table 23. Education of ministers (1906–1971) (in percentages)

	Late Qajar Period	Reza Shah	Mohammad Reza Shah
All ministers	220	62	329
Ministers for whom data were available	177 = 100%	56 = 100%	293 = 100%
Ejtehad	2	2	2
Modarres	10	7	—
Moqaddamat and *Sath*	24	12	3
Total: Traditional Education	36%	21%	5%
Ph.D. or M.D.	14	16	44
B.A. or M.A.	43	52	44
Secondary or elementary	7	11	7
Total: new education	64%	79%	95%

Sources: Computed from Zahra Sahji'i, *Vezarat va Vaziran dar Iran* (Tehran: MTE, 1976).

elite groups, but a mere B.A. was no longer enough for that purpose.[13] (For a similarly high number of university graduates, including graduates of western university, among the political elite under the Islamic regime, see the Epilogue.)

Insofar as education was concerned, the ministers were surpassed by their deputies (*mo'avenin*), who were administrators and technocrats rather than politicians. Early in 1977, there were 145 deputy ministers, and information on 108 of them was made available to me. It came from questionnaires in their files in the Ministry of Information, which they had filled in themselves.[14] All of the 108 were graduates (three of them of the war academy), and 38 percent of them had Ph.D.s or M.D.s. No fewer than 56 percent had taken one or more degrees abroad. Given the shah's predilection to promote young people, pro-

13. Comparative data, showing similar results, can be found for Turkey in Frey, 278–79; for Iraq in Marr, 113; and for Lebanon in Dekmejian, 62–80.

14. I am grateful to the documentation center (markaz asnad) in the Ministry of Information for giving me access to these questionnaires.

vided they were loyal and well-educated, most of the rest (for whom no data were available) were probably university-educated, too.

Senior civil officials were similarly well-educated. A 1970 survey of the Civil Service Commission (Sazeman-e Omur-e Edari va Estekhdami-ye Keshvar) lists the education of the 401 most senior officials, that is, the director-generals of ministries, official agencies, and state enterprises. It shows that only 2 percent of them had less than a full secondary education and another 7 percent had gone to high school but had received no higher training. All the rest (91 percent) had a higher education: 1.2 percent had the *fowq-e diplom*; 51.4 percent had a B.A., 17.9 percent an M.A.; and 20.5 percent a M.D. or Ph.D.[15]

In the same organization, I was able to examine the education of senior civil servants toward the end of the rule of the shah.[16] Early in 1977 there were 365,738 state employees in twelve administrative ranks. For most civil servants, the organization had information on the level, place, and field of education, the appointment, job location according to provinces, age, seniority, and so forth. I elected to concentrate on the officials holding the highest or second-highest of the twelve ranks of the Iranian civil service: an elite group of 592. There were data on 518, among whom thirty-five (6.8 percent) had completed their secondary education but had no academic training; one had the *fowq-e diplom*, 256 (49.6 percent) had a B.A., 110 (21.2 percent) an M.A., and 116 (22.4 percent) a M.D. or Ph.D. In fact, according to civil service regulations of 1973, officials with no academic degrees could no longer be promoted to the highest two grades. (Those in the survey had been appointed before 1973.) Comparison with ministers and Majlis members showed that fewer top government official had studied abroad: "only" 17.2 percent of those for whom data were available in the two highest civil servant ranks had degrees from foreign universities. However, this is an average figure for all levels of higher schooling. A breakdown shows that, significantly, only 7.8 percent of the B.A.s had been taken abroad, while somewhat more (13.6 percent) of the M.A.s and as many as 41.4 percent of the M.D.s or Ph.D.s came from foreign universities.

Educational qualifications for promotion were laid down formally in regulations issued in 1973. They determined that candidates with fewer than twelve years of schooling might enter the civil service at the third

15. Based on a publication by Sazeman-e Omur-e Edari va Estekhdami-ye Keshvar as cited in James Bill, "The Patterns of Elite Politics in Iran," in Lenczowski, *Political Elites*, 27.

16. I am indebted to the officials of the Sazeman-e Omur-e Edari and especially to the staff of its computer services for their support and valuable help in computing the data for me.

grade and be promoted (over fourteen years) up to, but not beyond, the fifth; that those with a complete secondary education might start service in the fourth grade and rise (over twenty years) to the seventh; that holders of the *fowq-e diplom* were to begin in the fifth grade and could (after twenty-two years) reach the ninth; that graduates with a B.A. would start in the seventh grade and could (after eighteen years) be appointed to the twelfth (i.e., the highest) grade. Holders of an M.A. also started in the seventh grade but could reach the top grade after only fourteen years; M.D.- or Ph.D.-holders started in the eighth grade but also needed fourteen years to move to the top.[17] The starting grade of university-educated civil service, it should be noted, was also the highest to which the less-educated candidates could aspire.

With promotion came better pay. For officials with five years' seniority in the service, average monthly incomes (in Riyals) in the mid-1970s were as follows: less than six years of education, 8,629; high school certificate, 11,787; B.A., 18,928; M.A., 27,406; M.D. or Ph.D., 40,107. Once again we find that a "mere" B.A. was no longer enough to secure rapid advancement and to reach the upper end of the pay scales.[18]

Taken as a whole, then, the Iranian elite at the close of the period discussed was highly educated. Can one spot significant differences between the various groups? As a rough generalization, it may be suggested that the higher the prestige and power of a specific group the better its education was. In an attempt to pinpoint the differentials, Table 24 compares the percentages of all graduates as well as of M.D.- or Ph.D.-holders in the five groups discussed such as they were shortly before the end of the monarchy. All ministers but one had a higher education, as did all the deputy ministers for whom we have data. Among the members of the last Majlis "only" 80 percent had university degrees, and among those listed in the *Who's Who*, 74 percent. Of the top administrators and technocrats, who had more power (but not necessarily more prestige) than the Majlis members, 93 percent had degrees. It can be seen that during this period there were no significant variations among the elite groups—all were highly educated. But we can note that this was the result of a gradual process of leveling out earlier differentials. For the mid-1960s, for instance, Zonis found that 91.8 percent of the political elite, but only 69.3 percent of the members

---

17. Sazeman-e Omur-e Edari va Estekhdami-ye Keshvar, *Tarh-e Tabaqe-Bandi va Arzeshyabi-ye Mashaghel* (Tehran, 1973/4), 59. These points were stressed by a high-ranking man at the office of job classification (edare-ye tabaqe-bandi mashaghel) in the Sazeman-e Omur-e Edari va Estekhdami-ye Keshvar, in an interview with me.

18. Sazeman-e Omur-e Edari va Estekhdami-ye Keshvar, *Nata'ej Ejra'-ye Tarh-e Shen-asa'i-ye Vizhegiha-ye Mostakhdemin-e Dowlat dar koll-e Keshvar* (Tehran, 1975/6), 7.

Table 24. Percentage of university graduates among different elite groups at the end of Mohammad Reza Shah's reign

Elite group	Total no. in group	No. for whom data were available	% of graduates	% of Ph.D.s and M.D.s
Members of Hoveyda's last government (in 1977)	27	27	96	48
Deputy ministers in 1977	145	108	100	38
Top-level administrators	592	518	93	22
Deputies in the twenty-fourth Majlis	268	152	80	31
Individuals named in Who's Who (1976)	4,478	4,478	74	31

Sources: Computed from data given in this chapter.

of the twenty-first Majlis, had a higher education. Moreover, if we consider doctoral degrees only, we note that certain differences persisted in the 1970s: 48 percent of the ministers (the most select group) had doctoral degrees; so did 38 percent of the deputy minister; 31 percent of Majlis members and also of those listed in the *Who's Who*; and 22 percent of the senior civil servants.

The array of figures given in this (and the preceding) chapter bear out that, to a marked degree, education had become the "hallmark" of elite membership and that educational qualifications were well on the way toward replacing lineage as the key to positions of power. To what degree, then, could people of lower-class origin move into positions of power by virtue of educational achievements? Empirical studies on Middle Eastern elites leave little room for optimism: upward mobility through education was not entirely absent, but remained limited. Zonis's pessimistic conclusion—correct at the time—reflected the shah's earlier policy of limiting higher education.[19] Once that policy was reversed, university development gathered momentum and lower-class applicants found their prospects improving. They were justified in assuming that, in the longer run, a good education would enable

19. Zonis, *Elite,* 167.

them to better their status. But while more of them were arriving at the campuses, students of elite descent were already busy securing advanced degrees for themselves, making a Ph.D. rather than a B.A. the key to real prestige and power. By stressing advanced degrees, preferably taken at prestige universities, they managed to stay a jump ahead of the growing crowd of university entrants. In other words: even when more students from a lower-class background arrived on campus, higher education still remained more of an instrument for legitimizing the power of the elites than an avenue for upward mobility.

It should be stressed that the type of education that came to be the badge of the influential and the powerful was, at the time we are speaking of, modern and western. As such, it not only marked off the elites from the masses but also barred segments of the traditional elites, particularly those that formed part of, or were associated with, the religious establishment. To a degree at least, the shah had succeeded in promoting an alternative to the traditional elites. But for all their modern higher education, the political, administrative, and military elite groups became isolated and alienated from the live body of the Iranian people. They lacked a power base of their own because that was the way the shah wanted it. Being dependent only on him, they had no popular support and no hold over the public (or any significant sector of it). This was the reason they could not come to his aid in his hour of need. It then turned out that the ulama had remained more powerful and influential than the modern elites, in their modern educational shell, knew or wanted to know. In their inmost hearts the vast majority of the people had withstood the accelerated secularization process and had remained loyal to the religious values and their professional representatives. What is more, large segments of those with a new education resented the shah's rule for a variety of other reasons and joined the ranks of the opposition. Divorced as they were from the deeper realities of the country, the new elites could not stop the clerics from regaining their old mastery over the people at large (and for some time at least over a considerable part of the intelligentsia to boot).

13

The Struggle for
Academic Freedom

As in Europe during earlier centuries, established religion and government authority combined to deny academic freedom to the young institutes of higher learning in Muslim lands during the nineteenth and twentieth centuries.[1] And as in Europe under modern totalitarian regimes, it was the government's hand that eventually proved heavier than that of the religious establishment (except, of course, for Khomeyni's Iran where the two became identical). But then, academic freedom is part and parcel of the wider sphere of freedom of thought and expression, of opinion, speech, and publication. Where these are absent, one would not expect academic freedom (*Lernfreit* and *Lehrfreiheit*, to use the classical terms of the West) to exist either.

The advantage of *ejtehad* (independent investigation) which Shi'i ulama have over their Sunni colleagues might, on the face of it, appear to be conducive to the emergence of academic freedom in Shi'i communities. But *ejtehad* is the prerogative of a very small number of individuals, and relates to the interpretation of religious law. In Iran, as we have seen, *ejtehad* or no *ejtehad*, clerics opposed each successive stage in the introduction of modern education in the name of Islam.

As for government control, this presupposes the existence of a strong central government capable of exercising such control. In the case of

1. For a definition of "academic freedom," and discussion of its vicissitudes, see: "Academic Freedom," *Encyclopaedia of Social Sciences*, 1:384–87; Brubacher, 625–38; Joseph Ben-David and Randall Collins, "A Comparative Study of Academic Freedom and Student Politics," *Comparative Education Review*, 10 (February 1966), 220–48.

Iran, this meant that whenever the shah was strong, the universities were weak; when the shah was weak (as happened in 1941–1946, 1951–1953, and again in 1977–1979), they gained a greater measure of freedom. It was at such periods of faltering authority at the center that, paradoxically, demands for greater academic freedom were made and the government was criticized for circumscribing university autonomy too narrowly. When freedom of expression was suppressed as a matter of general policy, nobody expected, let alone appealed for, academic freedom.

Tehran University under Reza Shah (1935–1941)

Under the authoritarian rule of Reza Shah, Tehran University was fully controlled by the government. Controls were, however, applied selectively. The legitimacy of the regime, its ideology and tenets must not be questioned. Research likely to controvert them was banned without hesitation, but when it was a matter of defying religious objections, the shah upheld academic opinion against its detractors. Thus he helped smuggle skeletons into the medical school, in order to advance teaching and research.

By and large, the university (there was, as will be recalled, only one) was administered as though it was a department of the Ministry of Education. In administrative terms, there was not much difference between the university and secondary, or for that matter, elementary, schools. Professors were hired and dismissed by the ministry. Faculty members then teaching at the university whom I later interviewed (like Sadiq, Siyasi, Sadiqi, and Mahdavi) all stressed that their having to go to the ministry to collect their salary personally was the most blatant reminder of their dependence on the government. All said it made them feel as though they were lowly ministry clerks. Some of their colleagues, they maintained, were dismissed simply because they were not acceptable to the ministry's political or administrative staff.

In these initial years, appointments or promotions were often made on the strength of personal connections rather than solely on the basis of academic excellence.[2] The "regulations for professorial appointments," approved by the Supreme Council of Education on 24 Decem-

2. See, in this regard, a speech by Siyasi at the Sorbonne (10 May 1948), as quoted in his book *Do Mah dar Paris* (Tehran: Daneshgah-e Tehran, 1950), 69–70; also an interview with him in the *Majale Daneshkade-ye Adabiyyat*, 13. See similarly Sadiq's words in his *Yadegar*, 2:345.

ber 1934 and valid throughout the reign of Reza Shah, gave the Ministry of Education total control over this area. Vacancies were to be announced by the ministry, which specified the qualifications needed and made the selection.[3] Similarly, the "regulations for student admission," approved on 27 December 1934, stated that "registration of candidates and their selection . . . the method of the examination and other related issues, will be made according to regulations . . . approved by the Ministry of Education."[4] The kind of (formal and informal) understanding existing in the West between the academics ("who have complete autonomy in running their own affairs") and the government ("which has effective means of letting its views be known and seriously considered without openly interfering with the universities"), with civil servants forming "an effective buffer between politics and universities,"[5] was entirely lacking in Iran. Instead, there was complete subordination. Whereas in the West civil servants had an educational background similar to that of the academics, in Iran the gap between the two groups was wide at that time. Civil servants and academic staff regarded each other with animosity and mistrust.[6]

The Council of the University (Shura-ye Daneshgah) was supposed to be the supreme authority laying down academic policy. But throughout the reign of Reza Shah it was never convened for an ordinary session with an agenda announced ahead of time. Throughout this period the minister of education was, ex officio, also chancellor of the Tehran University. As such, he summoned the deans of the faculties and some other professors to discuss university affairs. Siyasi maintains that in these sessions, whether they were counted as council meetings or not, there was no serious discussion and no decisions were made. Usually, the minister lectured the others on his views and policies, and these were taken to be the decisions of the meeting.[7]

Under the 1934 law establishing the university, a separate chancellor should have been selected, and the tenure of the minister was formally defined as "temporary."[8] But in fact all the ministers until February 1943 were unwilling to give up the prestigious post of chancellor and

---

3. *AP*, 1934/5, 636.

4. Ibid., 313.

5. Ben-David and Collins, 229; Lord Chorley, "Academic Freedom in the United Kingdom," *Law and Contemporary Problems*, 28 (Summer 1963), 647–71.

6. See an interview with Siyasi in the *Majale Daneshkade-ye Adabiyyat*, 13. (For the hostility of civil servants toward the new academics, see Chapter 7.)

7. See Siyasi's interview in ibid., 12–14.

8. See the prime minister's speech of 15 March 1935, as quoted in *AP*, 1935/6, 39–40.

held both offices.[9] In his memoirs Hekmat (the first to hold both positions) said that when first appointed he wished to make one of the professors chancellor. He handed the prime minister, ʿAli Forughi, a list of three, asking him to get the shah's approval for one of them. A few days later, Forughi returned the letter with a note from the shah reading: "Hekmat has founded the university and he will be its chancellor."[10]

In retrospect, there were conflicting views on whether his double tenure helped safeguard the university's autonomy. Sadiq, whose animosity toward Hekmat could be discerned even forty years later, accused him of being "greedy for honors" (*jah talab*) and blamed him for refusing to give up the chancellorship. Sadiq added that Hekmat used his authority to serve the interests of the government rather than of the university. Siyasi, who was more sympathetic to Hekmat, claimed that the academic staff saw an advantage in the latter's twofold position, believing that his status enabled him to advance the university's interests. He and his associates thought that when a minister like Hekmat, sympathetic to the cause of modern learning, doubled as chancellor, this was an asset in advancing the university's freedom.[11]

Whichever view one took, an additional disadvantage was obvious: this practice exposed the university to a great deal of disquiet whenever there was high turnover of ministers. True, this was not felt so much under Reza's rather stable rule (between 1935 and 1941, there was only one change of minister/chancellor). But if we look ahead to the early stage of Mohammad Reza's rule, we find that there were four ministers/chancellors in the first seventeen months of his reign. Each change occurred amid rumors about policy revisions and new academic appointments, generating considerable insecurity among the faculty. And in fact the appointment of a new minister was often followed by a series of academic appointments and dismissals. Rather than competition for academic excellence, the university staff had to compete for the sympathy of successive ministers/chancellors.

During this period, no one openly criticized the university's lack of autonomy. Yet from the many publications immediately following the

---

9. Under Reza Shah these were Hekmat (from the establishment of the school until 13 August 1938) and Esmaʿil Marʾat (from then up to the abdication of the shah). Under Mohammad Reza Shah, until the law for the university's independence was passed, the following served as ministers as well as chancellors: Sadiq, Mohammad Tadayyon, Mostafa ʿAdl, and Siyasi.

10. Hekmat, *Khatere*, 361–62.

11. Based on my interviews with Sadiq and Siyasi. See also the latter's interview with *Majale Daneshkade-ye Adabiyyat*, 9–11.

shah's abdication, one can safely conclude that there was growing resentment among academics and that the lack of freedom on the campus and in society at large was keenly felt by them. It is also known that some academics—especially Siyasi, Mas'ud Kayhan, Sa'id Malek, and Sa'id Nafisi—discussed such problems among themselves and outlined programs to secure greater freedom for the university.[12] But, Reza's rule being what it was, they not only failed to advance their aims, but even stopped short of explicit criticism. This changed dramatically with the abdication of the shah.

An Interlude of Independence (1941–1954)

The abdication of Reza Shah removed all restraints. Academic staff and the media began to speak out strongly against the lack of independence (*esteqlal*) for the university. Demands, sometimes couched in terms of an ultimatum, were made to ensure its autonomy. Typical was an editorial in *Kayhan* (2 December 1942):

> From its first day, some reactionary and self-seeking elements have been interfering in the university's affairs, committing acts of sabotage and destruction against the academic staff, and preventing the university's growth. . . . Such groups disregarded the law for the establishment of the university, [and] passed illogical and inefficient decisions . . . contrary to the spirit of law.
>
> A university without comprehensive and complete independence is useless. A university whose foundations are shaken daily by ministers who come and go . . . cannot fulfill its duties. . . . A university whose chancellor is being changed with every change of government, each lasting three months, cannot implement a proper and efficient plan and work according to scientific standards. In all countries where universities exist, there exists academic freedom and interference in the university's affairs on the part of unauthorized people is [considered] a crime.

Yet actual steps to safeguard the university's autonomy and place it on a firm legal foundation were delayed until the appointment of Siyasi as minister of education and chancellor (24 June 1942). Siyasi had earlier declined similar offers by Prime Ministers Forughi and 'Ali Sohayli (saying that he refused to serve under foreign occupation). In accepting the offer of Ahmad Qavam, Siyasi said he had a twofold aim: making the university independent and implementing the compulsory education law. As soon as he was in office, he started appointing prominent

12. For such a grouping of professors, see the interview with Siyasi in ibid., 1–12.

professors, such as Hashtrudi, ʿAli Kani Jenab, and Mehdi Jalali, to key positions in the university.[13] He proceeded to set up a separate, independent administration to deal with the university's financial and administrative affairs and appointed Dr. Mahmud Mehran to head it.[14] Siyasi's double role of minister and chancellor undoubtedly helped smooth the transfer of authority.

At the same time, Siyasi set up faculty councils in the university. By the end of 1942, all of them had met and had elected their own deans (hitherto appointed by the minister/chancellor) as well as one additional faculty member, who, together with the dean, would represent the faculty on the university council. The council of the faculty of humanities elected Siyasi as its dean.[15]

When the university council met for the first time on 13 December 1942, it approved the procedure for electing the chancellor. Meeting again on 2 January 1943, it elected Siyasi by secret ballot. Even though the council chose Siyasi in his capacity as dean of humanities rather than by virtue of his ministerial office, Siyasi saw a flaw in the fact that his long struggle for new election procedures should in the end lead back to the old double tenure. Accordingly, he asked the council to reconsider. The secret ballot was repeated—with the same result.[16] It reflected the councillors' high personal regard for Siyasi and their acknowledgment of his concern for academic freedom, but also attested to their expectation that he would be able to use his influence in the cabinet. This time, Siyasi accepted, and his election was confirmed by royal decree.[17]

Only then was the matter raised in the Majlis, the first time that it was taken up there. Deputy Ehsan Naraqi argued that it was "intolerable" for the holder of a cabinet office to fill a chancellor position as well. Siyasi answered that he had been elected by a secret, democratic vote on the strength of his academic standing and not because he was a minister.[18]

As it turned out, Siyasi was the last minister of education to double

---

13. For their purpose in advancing the school's independence, see ibid.

14. *AP*, 1942/3, 8–11:xii. See also interview by Siyasi in ibid., 14–15.

15. Meeting between June and December 1942, the other councils elected the following deans: sciences, Sahabi; theology, Mohammad Kazem ʿAssam; law and political science, Qasemzade; engineering, Gholam Hoseyn Rahnama; medicine, Amir Aʿlam. *AP*, 1942/3, 5–6:xxix, 8–11:xi.

16. Nine members voted for Siyasi, two against, one was absent (ibid., vii).

17. For his considerations in accepting the nomination, see Siyasi's interview in *Majale Daneshkade-ye Adabiyyat*.

18. For both speeches, see in *MM*, term 13, 2019–20.

as chancellor. He lost office in June 1943, but remained chancellor until 1954. On 4 February 1943, an official ceremony was held to mark the university's anniversary and to declare "the independence of the university" (*esteqlal-e daneshgah*). The shah, the empress, cabinet members, Majlis deputies, and prominent professors participated—a distinguished forum calculated to underscore the importance of the occasion. In his speech, Siyasi asserted that Mohammad Reza Shah's declaration of university independence was no less important than his father's decision to set up the school. Trying not to sound too critical of Reza Shah while soliciting the support of the young monarch, he said that although the law of 1934 had upheld the independence of the university, it "could not" become independent in its initial years. As a "newborn child," it needed support and nourishment, and independence from the ministry would only have harmed it. But now it had become mature.

> Beginning a year and a half ago [i.e., with the abdication of Reza Shah] it was clearly felt that this huge body had developed sufficiently and . . . deserved the independence prescribed for it by the law. The first to become aware of this fact was [Mohammad Reza Shah]. . . .
>
> There may be some who may still fail to perceive the need and value of university independence. It will be useful to remind them that institutes of higher learning have needs in a variety of fields such as professors, teaching and research aids, laboratories, etc., on which decisions must be made. . . . The only authority to define these needs are the academic authorities and not government officials and government ministries. . . . Moreover, the university is not only an institute to spread existing knowledge, but it is a place for conducting new research, new discoveries and expanding the knowledge of sciences and technology. It can fulfill such functions only if it is free from any nonacademic influence; most significantly, any influence of political and religious views should be prevented. . . . [They] are like rocks which divert the flow of the river from its natural course. . . . The independence of the university depends on the structure . . . the admission policy, the curriculum, and the disciplinary regulations being defined by itself . . . and on scientific research being carried out freely. When this is achieved, no one will be able to impose on the university teachers, deans, or a chancellor, who lack scientific-technological qualifications . . . [or] to impose political views on the university.

The shah in turn promised his support: "Personally, I attach much importance to the university and treat it with great attention and respect. The university is the cradle of education and science . . . the most important center of culture and uplift . . . the source of happiness and the strength of the nation. . . . An important organ of such great value must be absolutely independent and free."[19]

In fact, during the following decade or so, the university was relatively free from nonacademic influence. Reviewing his chancellorship (1942–1954), Siyasi was able to tell me that this was a "period of freedom par excellence." Government attempts to interfere in internal university affairs, he said, met a united front of academics who vigorously refused to submit to any dictate by the regime. But toward the end of his tenure he saw serious threats to university independence. In fact, his own resignation was the result of the political changes already discernible following the crackdown against Mosaddeq and his followers. According to Siyasi, the shah was now determined to tighten his grip on the universities. At the last session of the Council of the University in which he participated as chancellor, in April 1954, he ostensibly appealed to his colleagues while actually addressing the government. His "testament," he said, was a brief note:

> "Keep the university away from politics." It is clear to me beyond any doubt that this body can be independent, and is capable of standing erect in the face of the various events and developments, only if it keeps always from politics and dedicates all its efforts to research. . . . Only in this way will all political trends, all governments, and all the officials honor this institute. . . . Noninterference has been the motto of the Council of the University until now, and for me personally, it is a source of honor, pride, and happiness that I was able to ward off such dangers and keep the road open for the advancement and progress for this important scientific institute.[20]

Autonomy on the Wane (1954–1963)

The lesson the shah drew from the period of upheaval in the early 1950s—when students and faculty took an active role in opposing him—was to tighten control over the institutes of higher learning. The stronger he grew politically, the more he was able to circumscribe university independence. One means was to prevent the establishment of new universities and thus block the quantitative expansion of the student body. Political considerations again became important in hiring new faculty. Those suspected of leftist tendencies were categorically

19. The speeches are cited in *AP*, 1942/3, 8–11:xvii–xix as well as in the dailies *Iran*, 4 February 1943 and *Behnam*, 6 February 1943.
20. *Majale Daneshkade-ye Adabiyyat*, 3 (March 1955), 2:96–97.

excluded. Opponents from the liberal movements of the center were luckier: since they were prowestern, the shah believed they were not likely to challenge his rule again, so he permitted their employment. Still, his agents worked to prevent them from using their positions to spread views detrimental to him or his policies. Siyasi, for example, though a close associate of Mosaddeq, continued as dean of humanities throughout the 1950s, and many other National Front activists remained in their university posts. But as the shah's power increased, so did the activities of security agents on the campuses.

All this did not prevent students and faculty from joining the new opposition movements of the early 1960s—in fact, it may have driven them to do so. But unlike in the crisis of the 1950s, the regime was now determined to nip the opposition in the bud. Putting soldiers and police on the Tehran university campus on 22 January 1962 attested not only to the campus having turned into a new center of dissent but also to the government's determination to crush all signs of opposition. The event caused the chancellor, Dr. Ahmad Farhad, to resign. In his letter of resignation to the prime minister, Dr. ʿAli Amini, he described the behavior of the security forces as follows:

> Soldiers and paratroopers ... attacked boys and girls indiscriminately. ... Many of the students were beaten to the point of death.
>
> I have never seen or heard so much cruelty, sadism, atrocity, and vandalism as on the part of the government forces. Some of the girls were criminally attacked in the classrooms by the soldiers.
>
> When we inspected the University building, we were faced with a situation as if an army of barbarians had invaded an enemy territory. Books were torn, shelves were broken, typewriters smashed, laboratory equipment stolen or destroyed; desks, chairs, doors, windows and walls were vandalized by the troops fighting unarmed students without interference from their officers.[21]

Years of Strict Control (1963–1977)

The subordination of the campuses gathered momentum beginning with the White Revolution and reached its peak with the proclamation of the educational revolution.

Paradoxically, the educational revolution expounded two contradictory policy lines: the importance of independence for the institutes for higher education as well as the vital need for government supervision

21. The letter is quoted in Zonis, *Elite*, 72–73.

(*nezarat*) and control (*moraqebat*). A good illustration of this is the speech made by the first minister of science, Rahnama, at the Gochsar conference of May 1968. He went into great detail to emphasize the importance of complete autonomy for the universities as a sine qua non for their advancement and the advancement of science, and denied charges that his ministry was striving for "supremacy" (*siyadat*) over the universities. In the same breath he asserted that "under the prevailing circumstances" it was essential for the ministry to exercise a measure of "supervision" and "direction" over them.[22]

The same contradiction runs like a red thread through the resolutions of the annual conferences on education from 1968. To illustrate: the 1968 conference resolutions, having affirmed the principle of autonomy, went on to stress that in the interest of an efficient implementation of the educational revolution the government needed "to exercise its legal duties to supervise the institutes of higher education and research" (article 8). The Ministry of Science was to supervise "teaching and research" and not limit itself to controlling "administrative and financial" matters (article 23). The 1970 conference even suggested that the government should supervise "the competence (*selahiyyat*) and the teaching qualifications (*qodrat-e tadris*) of the academic staff" (article 22).

True, some government supervision was inevitable. Even the 1969 UNESCO report to the government of Iran conceded that much.[23] It recognized that whenever a developing country strives for a rapid expansion of education but there are insufficient funds in the private sector to accomplish this goal, the government is entitled to intervene in order to bring the development of the universities into line with the needs of the state. Such rather vague arguments were then made to serve as a cloak for the total subordination of the institutes of higher learning.

Once supervision came to look legitimate, the necessary institutional framework quickly came into being. Early in 1968 a "supervision department" (*daftar-e nezarat*) was formed in the Ministry of Science under Dr. Khatib Shahidi. It soon appointed inspectors (*bazres*) for all institutes of higher education.[24] Early in 1969, the shah appointed a "Supreme Supervision Committee" (Komite-ye ʿAli-ye Nezarat), in which the prime minister, the court minister, and the minister of science participated, and which was to report directly to him. The committee organized "teams of inspectors" (*hey'atha-ye bazresi*) in the universi-

---

22. The text of his speech is cited in document 4717 in MAM.
23. Melville, 5–7.
24. For their duties and functions, see MAM, document 4717.

ties.[25] Later, in 1975, the Rastakhiz party formed its own "follow-up committee" (komite-ye peygiri) to look into the progress of the educational revolution.[26] The Royal Institute for Research on Education (in the Court Ministry) and the Institute for Research and Planning (in the Ministry of Science) both served similar purposes. Designed to assert the progress of the educational revolution, they in fact closely observed the functioning of the institutes for higher learning and their staff, usurped much of the latter's authority, and cut down on their freedom.

The concentration of power in the newly formed Ministry of Science also infringed on the autonomy of the universities. For example, the authority for setting up, expanding, or closing down institutes for higher education, and for setting admission policy, was now largely concentrated there. Chancellors were again nominated by the shah, and some of the nominees were not members of the academic staff. The boards of trustees—established after 1967 to strengthen the universities' independence—were now often headed by members of the royal family, government figures, or people close to them.

Even more harmful than the formal measures was the informal interference on the part of the security services. Students and staff felt that they were being closely and constantly observed, and that any expression of views not in line with official policy would be held against them. Strict checks by security officers at the gates of Tehran University were the first outward sign. Considering the campus a sensitive political site, security men admitted only authorized people (staff or students) or people carrying special permits. All were checked to prevent arms or propaganda material being smuggled into the campus. As in all other public places, pictures of the shah were placed in every classroom, library, cafeteria, and so forth, and statutes of the shah appeared in all the open spaces. Often, when demonstrations were expected, classes were suspended ahead of time to empty the campus of students. On "sensitive" dates (such as the anniversary of the 1962 student riots on 22 January) when students were especially prone to demonstrate, trucks with soldiers and policemen were stationed next to or on the campus. The few disturbances I witnessed (at Tehran University as well as at the 'Ilm va San'at college), and others of which I was told

25. *Ettela'at*, 25 March 1969; *KI*, 10 May 1969; Alfred Bakhash termed the teams "watchdogs" whom the shah appointed to supervise the universities: see his article "Towards Tighter Control," in *KI*, 4 June 1969. Many others, however, viewed the teams, acting under the shah's personal supervision, as an important means to advance the educational revolution. See, for example, *KI*, 10 and 11 June 1969.

26. It was formed upon the recommendation of the 1975 Conference on Education, article 43.

followed a set pattern: a sudden eruption by a small but apparently well-organized group, creating a disturbance in classrooms, libraries, laboratories, and cafeterias and causing some damage to property. The ringleaders usually disappeared before the police arrived, or could identify them, even though police units were stationed on campus or close by. Order was quickly restored. Often enough, those arrested were not seen on campus any more. The media were not allowed to report campus unrest.

The SAVAK was busy checking on professors and students. Even today it is still difficult to say how systematic and comprehensive their supervision was. Clearly, the image of the SAVAK was more threatening than the reality. While I was searching for data on the social background of the students, many friends referred me—whether ironically or not—to the SAVAK files. Only there, they claimed, would I find all the relevant information on students and faculty. Since they felt this way, it is no wonder they were afraid to speak their minds. Veteran professors who had special reasons to believe that they were being watched (for instance, Siyasi) would not meet with me unless I produced a letter from the Ministry of Science recommending that they do so. Others (like Sadiqi) insisted on a colleague of theirs being present at our meetings.[27] Still others refused to talk about sensitive issues in their offices and would only do so during walks on the campus or, preferably, outside the university. They had no doubt that even some of their students were SAVAK agents who reported to their superior on whatever they considered suspect. Vadi'i told me in 1973 that he was asked to "explain" some of the views on agrarian reform that he had expressed during a course on agricultural cooperatives. According to a SAVAK general (interviewed after the revolution), there was a special SAVAK bureau to deal with the universities. Some of the informants were paid agents, but most were students who cooperated with SAVAK in return for financial support for their studies. Others cooperated for what he termed "ideological reasons." There were several informants in each department so that their information could be double-checked. He believed the SAVAK was thus fully informed of all major campus developments.

Refraining from dissent was not considered sufficient. Students and faculty were expected to display their active support for the regime,

27. The meetings with them were held in the spring and summer of 1977. Later that year, I better understood their insistence, for it became evident that they were leaders active in organizing opposition to the regime. In 1982, when I met Siyasi in London, he confirmed that at the time of our 1977 meetings they were already very active in opposition affairs.

among other things by participating in the demonstrations marking the anniversaries of the White Revolution and by appearing at the celebrations of the shah's birthday.

Books unflattering to the shah, let alone openly critical of him, were not to be found in the libraries or bookstores. The books of Khomeyni, for example, were not available;[28] even Zonis's book on the political elite of Iran was missing from the shelves of Tehran University.[29] Many books published during the years of the shah's low fortunes (mainly in the early 1950 and the early 1960s) were later removed from the libraries. The logic behind the blacklisting of books was not always clear. For example, Adamiyyat's book on liberal thought in nineteenth-century Iran was not available in the Tehran University library, presumably because it was held to glorify the struggle for liberalism.[30] Given this climate of censorship, the number of new titles published in Iran was small even though literacy was increasing.[31]

There was only one field to which no restrictions applied: that of religious books. Many such books appeared in the 1970s and found a ready market. Outsiders were struck by the fact that the major bookstores near the university displayed so few books on political or social science and so many new books on Islam. This of course reflected a situation in which "unobjectionable" social and political literature was hard to come by, while religious books were not subject to censorship, but may also have foreshadowed the impending Islamic revival.

Students and faculty had no free access to xerox machines. At Tehran University's central library, for example, their use had to be approved by an authorized official, and the actual copying was done by the library staff. A prominent official of the library explained to me then that this was to prevent students from smuggling propaganda material into the campus and duplicating and distributing it there. Free access by students, he maintained—echoing a typical government propaganda line—would enable "communists" to spread their propaganda.

Professors were expected to portray the regime and its achievements

28. Professor Michael Fischer (from Rice University), who spent a long time in Qom in the mid-1970s, told me that Khomeyni's books were kept there "discreetly" in some libraries and were lent only to "reliable" people. In closed circles, of course, books expressing dissent were passed around.

29. The book was initially bought by university libraries but later removed. In the catalogs (at least at Tehran and Pahlavi universities) it was still listed, but no copy could be found.

30. The book was kept at the National Library but could only be obtained by special permission from the director. Xeroxing from it was not allowed.

31. Robert Graham, *Iran: The Illusion of Power* (New York: St. Martin's Press, 1979), 200–201.

in a positive light in their lectures and papers, as well as in their extracurricular activities. Again, no definite assessment can as yet be made of the methods and dimensions of such practices. One example of "blatant government interference with academic affairs" occurred at a symposium by the Aspen Institute at Persepolis in 1975. According to J. Green, "in addition to obvious SAVAK attendance . . . agents put pressure on Iranian contributors of the volume which grew out of the conference. The book . . . in many places reflects the views of the regime rather than objective scholarship."[32] The government's habit of inviting foreign scholars—especially during the 1971 celebrations—was another method of persuading Iranologists of the success of the white revolution. (There was a special bureau in the Ministry of Information to deal with such guests.) Interviews by foreign scholars regarding Iran, as well as articles on current issues, were systematically scrutinized by the authorities in Tehran.

The government objected to the setting up of student unions. Despite declarations about the importance of student organizations and student participation in decision making on issues concerning them, the minister of science made it clear that the "time was not yet ripe" for this. The maximum the authorities were willing to allow was to let students choose one of five outstanding students in each department to represent them in negotiations with that department. The official argument was that academically distinguished students would represent their colleagues best.[33] Actually, the rule was intended to prevent activists from being chosen. To move beyond that toward student unions, properly so called, was regarded as politically risky. The only student group allowed by the authorities was The Organization of Jewish Students (Sazeman-e Daneshjuyan-e Yahud). Jewish students were generally considered to be loyal to the regime.[34]

Despite all this, the shah did not prevent past opponents of the regime from joining the academic staff. Men who had been among the leaders of the opposition movements of the 1950s and 1960s (Sa-

---

32. The book (*Iran: Past, Present and Future*) was edited by Jane W. Jacqs and published in New York by the Aspen Institute for Humanities in 1976. See Jerrold D. Green, "Pseudo-Participation and Countermobilization: Roots of the Iranian Revolution," *Iranian Studies*, 13 (1980), 49–50. Similarly, Green's book, *Revolution in Iran: The Politics of Countermobilization* (New York: Praeger, 1982), 74.

33. MAM, document 4717; SSHBA, *Tarikh Amuzesh-e 'Ali*, 21–22.

34. In this organization I met students opposed to the shah (some of them with leftist views), but they took care not to use the organization for spreading their ideas. Most of the students were indeed loyal to the regime (as were most Iranian Jews in general) and took pains to make this clear in their formal activities.

diqi, Siyasi, Karim Sanjabi—among many others) kept their university positions. Some known for their antishah sentiments during their years of study in the West were given new teaching posts. Originally, this was one of the shah's methods of recruitment and cooptation.[35] Later, he simply trusted his power and the newfound stability of his regime. In any case, he did not envisage any danger from liberal intellectuals with prowestern tendencies. The SAVAK general I interviewed said that the shah had unqualified faith in the West and did not believe that any prowestern professional group would endanger his regime. Similarly, he did not expect any danger from the ulama. So whereas any sign of leftist opposition (whether in the universities or elsewhere) was brutally suppressed, the shah was much more lenient with opponents from among liberal intellectuals or from the ranks of the ulama.

Loss of Control at the End of the Regime (1977–1979)

With the emergence of the revolutionary movement, the shah was again forced to concede some degree of liberalization. Soon enough, this deteriorated into a total loss of control.

During the 1977/8 academic year, student demonstrations became more frequent and their participants more numerous; political, social, economic, and Islamic themes came to the fore; and violent incidents multiplied and escalated in intensity. The first riots of the academic year occurred at Tehran University on 9 October. Masked students demanded among other things that male and female students be kept apart on campus. They burned student buses, caused some other damage, and distributed pamphlets calling on female students not to frequent the "boys' cafeteria" or ride the "boys' buses." Campus agitation came to a peak on the eve of the shah's visit to the United States the following month. Students demonstrated and held antishah "political picnics." Violence ensued; buildings and property were damaged. Most institutes of higher learning were closed temporarily until order was restored. In some cases, courses were canceled altogether for the duration of the current term, and students who had registered for them lost credit points. The demonstrations were exceptional not only for their duration and the degree of violence involved, but also because of the emphasis on religious-motivated demands. The security

35. For such practices of the shah, see Zonis, *Elite*, 23–25, 323–33.

forces exercised unusual restraint, and, unlike in the past, the media were permitted to cover student activities and demands.[36] By mid-November, student unrest had spread to virtually all the country's universities and colleges.

Earlier in 1977, academics had already taken to addressing open letters to the prime minister or other senior officeholders to protest against infringements of the constitution, violations of human rights, unjustified limitations of political freedom, and disregard for the independence of the university as well as the courts. Toward the end of 1977, this practice became even more common. Demands for much greater autonomy became central to the letter-writing campaign.

The government's response came in September 1978 (i.e., shortly before the opening of the next academic year) when the Law for the Independence of the University (*Qanun Esteqlal-e Daneshgah*) was presented to the Majlis. The law prohibited governmental interference in academic and administrative affairs of the universities (article 8 and elsewhere); made the selection of the chancellor the prerogative of the boards of trustees (article 12); and declared the university councils responsible for academic affairs.[37] The law was, in fact, a belated acknowledgment by the shah of the demands put forward by professors in the early 1940s. Now it was the shah who sought to appease opposition by proposing the law himself. Sadiq, then chairman of the Senate committee on education, tried to speed it through both houses of Parliament. But now the professors objected, arguing that the proposed law offered no sufficient guarantee for their independence. They opposed the concentration of power in the hands of the boards of trustees, whose composition was still influenced by the government (article 4). Shapur Bakhtyar, one of the leaders of the National Front, was speaking for many of the faculty when he said: "The independence of the university is meaningless unless the faculty has complete financial, academic and administrative freedoms." Many professors demanded to revive, in all the universities, the situation that had existed at Tehran University during Siyasi's chancellorship.[38]

The public debate concerning the draft law echoed the arguments employed earlier, in the first years of Mohammad Reza's reign. So did some of its language. But by now the wording of the law was no longer all that important. What mattered was the actual power wielded by the central government, and that power was rapidly declining. Just as

36. *Ettela'at*, 13,16,17 October; *KI*, 13,16 October 1977.
37. For its full text, see *Ettela'at*, 22 September 1978.
38. See, for example, *Kayhan*, 3 October 1978.

earlier on, a liberally worded law would not have helped the universities against the powerful center, so now, in 1978, the universities had gained almost unlimited freedom because the center was faltering. Whether the law was passed or not could make little difference.

Conclusion

Except for brief interludes, the Iranian universities were under strict government control. Fear, frustration, and lack of security prevented the development of creative intellectual activity at the institutes of higher learning and significantly restricted their contribution to a possible Iranian cultural revival in a modern mold. It is, of course, difficult to assess accurately how much damage was done to higher education (and the state at large) by denying employment to people with appropriate academic but insufficient political credentials. Similarly, the extent of damage caused by professionals refusing to return home after the completion of their studies abroad because of their resentment of the shah's policies. Even those eventually appointed to teaching posts had to watch their step, particularly if they taught social sciences, law, or the humanities. Faculty members distrusted one another, suspecting their colleagues of being "collaborators." The trust and cooperation essential for the advancement of science never had a chance to develop. In some ways, this affected extracurricular activities most of all. There were no public debates on campus on problems facing the nation except on the initiative of the government and in circumstances enabling it to dictate the views expressed. Student activities were similarly throttled.

Like Reza Shah, his son viewed the academic staff as professionals useful only in their narrow field of expertise but allowed to speak in justification of official policies. The universities were expected to be— and at most times were—centers of conformism. Such attitudes were bound to be counterproductive. For some, the stifling of the campuses became yet another incentive to join the revolutionary camp. In the last analysis, the most devastating effect of strangling academic freedom was that it prevented the emergence of a nucleus of liberal-minded intellectuals strong enough to secure for the centrist movements a greater share in Khomeyni's revolutionary regime.

One final point stands out: the small number of intellectuals in the late nineteenth century (living in a mostly illiterate society) seem to have had a greater influence on developments during the Constitutional Revolution than their much more numerous fellow intellectuals (operating in a much more "educated" society) had on the course of events during the Islamic Revolution and since. The lack of genuine academic freedom must be thought of as one reason for this. The matter certainly deserves further study.

Conclusion

In Iran, as in other developing countries, education was much appreciated, and educated people enjoyed considerable esteem in society. True, educationalists, statesmen, and others in the various strata of Iranian society had different, sometimes divergent ideas about the aims and the nature of education. There were differences of opinion concerning the ideals that the educational system should impart to students, as well as over educational priorities (should quality be emphasized over quantity or vice versa?). Some of the differences stemmed from distinctive philosophies and worldviews, others from sectarian interest, and still others probably from genuine and objective perceptions of the kind of education the country needed at a given juncture. But the common denominator for virtually everybody was the belief in education as a powerful, not to say omnipotent, vehicle for the advancement of man and society. For many, to use James Coleman's words, education had indeed become "an article of faith." The profundity of appreciation was matched by the intensity of the expectations from it. Were they met? The answer depends on which half of the glass one chooses to look at. This book has pointed to significant achievements, but also to many shortcomings.

At its conclusion, it is therefore appropriate to ask two questions: how much has education itself changed in modern Iran? and how much has education changed Iran? Before answering, we should keep three points in mind. First, the Islamic Revolution may warp our judgment because it reversed a major trend. Later assessments may make it apparent that the contributions of the new education were more com-

300

prehensive and more durable than they appear today, only a decade or so after the fall of the monarchy. Second, although the model for imitation was the West, the outcome should be examined primarily against the background of Iranian history. Third, although the first attempts to adopt at least elements of western education go back to the early nineteenth century, mass elementary education and the rapid growth of higher education belong to the last generation, or even to the era of the White Revolution exclusively. With these points in mind, we can identify some important contributions.

The most basic answer to the first question is that the religious establishment lost its age-old monopoly over education at all levels and had to watch it being sequestered by the (shahs') government. Once the government had control, it changed the structure and contents of the schooling system. The "new" (western) structure totally replaced traditional schooling at the elementary and secondary level and over-shadowed (but did not quite dislodge) the *madrese* in higher education. As for the contents, new subjects, not previously included in the traditional religious curriculum—in fact banned on religious grounds—became the stock-in-trade of the new education.

The Islamic Revolution introduced significant changes both in style and content (see the Epilogue). Yet even the Islamic regime could not quite uproot the new education, much as it had initially been rejected by the ulama. The triumph of the new education lies in the fact that the revolutionary leaders neither tried nor even expressed the wish to wholly reverse the process. Rather, they strove to use it (albeit with some significant revisions) to advance their own goals. Although the clerics now exercised much control over the educational system, it remained a government agency, headed by a minister who (at least until 1991) was not himself a cleric. All levels of education (with the exception of the *madreses*, of course) remained much closer to the—western inspired—schools of the shahs' days than to the old traditional schooling system. Inconsistently perhaps, modern sciences also continued to be taught.

No less significant was the rapid quantitative expansion. Although the first contacts with western higher education go back almost two hundred years and modern elementary and secondary schools have existed for a century, the initial steps were extremely hesitant and slow. Rapid expansion did not occur until the last generation. Quantitatively, that was the era of the educational revolution in Iran. For all its flaws and shortcomings, the nascent Islamic regime found an educational infrastructure covering virtually all parts of the country. If the Islamic regime could—and did—introduce changes in content and style, it was able to do so because it had inherited a working institution. This important institution was readily available for its use.

Yet, rapid expansion under circumstances of social and economic changes has made the advancement of education notoriously difficult in many countries; and Iran was no exception. Under the prevailing circumstances it was extremely difficult to improve the quality of education, or to plan and coordinate the development of the educational system in line with the ever changing social and economic realities and plans. In fact the new schools had serious flaws. At the elementary and secondary levels they were: low teaching standards; textbooks that were outmoded or in short supply; mostly nonexistent teaching aids; many unsuitable school buildings. In addition, attempts to unify the curriculum failed to do away with the differences in the quality of schooling between cities and villages, between rich and poor neighborhoods in the cities, and so on. This meant that the graduates of many (mainly rural) elementary schools were not qualified to move on to high schools; and many graduates of high schools were turned down by colleges and universities. Similarly, some of the defects of traditional schooling, such as rote learning, were carried over into the new schools. Owing to the predominantly theoretical nature of schooling, dropouts remained unprepared for work in the productive sector. Technical and vocational education lagged far behind. All this indicates inherent deficiencies in the pre-university system which greatly diminished the potential benefit of its rapid expansion.

A similar list can be drawn up for postsecondary education: overdependence on the government exposed the universities to the reverberations of the frequent political changes; the lack of academic freedom prevented them from becoming centers of creative intellectual activity; higher education was not coordinated with the needs of the country; and research was almost totally neglected. The consequent need for foreign experts and technicians at all levels reinforced the Shiʿa's native xenophobia which dovetailed with the "anti-imperialist" sentiment of the less religious trends.

There were other areas in which the new education had failed to meet expectations more than partially. It evidently failed to impart modern orientations, values, and attitudes to its graduates. Intellectual curiosity and openness to change remained attributes of the few.[1] But

1. For the models of "modern man" and an "open" mind as formulated by Inkles and Rokaij, see Chapter 10. For Lerner's typology of the "mobile person," see Lerner, 47–52. A study of Syria, using Lerner's Empathy Index, has shown that "while high education, elite occupation, urban residence, and particular religious affiliation do not definitely lead to the ability and willingness to identify with a larger unfamiliar sphere

then it also failed to provide graduates with the cognitive skills and the expertise needed by the rapidly developing economy, and by society as a whole. The list could easily be lengthened.

Despite these shortcomings, education has undoubtedly been one of the most important—if not the most important—social instrument shaping modern Iran. The many graduates of schools at all levels, and the millions of pupils at schools at the close of the last shah's rule, have shaped the new face of the country. Graduates of local and foreign universities held the highest positions in politics, the administration, and the economy and played a significant role in cultural life. It is indeed hard to think of another social institution that contributed more to the making of modern Iran.

Some of the basic trends fostered by the new education proved powerful enough to last even when the basic tenets of the Islamic regime would have suggested that they be reversed. Most important in this regard was its contribution in fostering national identification—at least among the Persian-speaking population—which was one of its major aims in the Pahlavi era. Its ability to be used in this way stemmed from the introduction of a uniform nationwide educational system administrated by the government. With this aim in view, great emphasis was placed (mainly in elementary schools) on the teaching of the Persian language and its literature and of pre-Islamic Persian history. Love of the homeland became a pivotal motif. In due course, the concept of the nation-state won out. Indeed, when the clerics came to power they found that they had gradually to adjust their world vision to the realities thus created.[2] Moreover, the schooling system had significantly narrowed (though not eliminated) the gap between the center and the periphery—another contribution to the emergence of a national identity as well as to the modernization of the country.

Westernization was one of the main aims of the regime at least under the Pahlavis (and of many Iranian intellectuals in much earlier times).

---

of human activity, the converse factors (low education, low occupational stratum, etc.) do lead rather definitely to the inability and unwillingness to identify with larger and unfamiliar sphere of human activity, as measured by the Empathy Index" (Lerner, 434–37). Szyliowicz was of the opinion that Iranian education would continue "reinforcing those values, attitudes and social characteristics that maintain social, cultural and political patterns": (*Modernization*, 448–53).

2. For the ideological changes in the Islamic Republic's worldview in its first decade in power, see my book *Iran: A Decade of War and Revolution* (New York: Holmes and Meier, 1990), mainly 386–93. For the Islamic regime's initial ideology and subsequent policy regarding the national question, see my article "Khomeini's Vision: Nationalism or World Order?" in David Menashri, ed., *The Iranian Revolution and the Muslim World* (Boulder: Westview, 1990), 40–57.

There can be no doubt that education contributed the most to its at least partial success. Whereas national sentiment was promoted mainly at the lower educational levels, westernization was advanced primarily by higher education, most notably by young graduates of foreign universities. Arguably, westernization was too rapid—leading to what Jalal Al-e Ahmad called *gharbzadegi* (West-strickenness). Although higher education was a matter for a narrow class and its effect on society at large was not as widespread as that of primary and secondary schooling, it served as a major channel of westernization. In this regard, the attempt by the Islamic regime to reverse the process has been more conspicuous. But even here, although the cultural influence of the West was criticized, the need to acquire some "products" of western civilization (notably technology) continued to be upheld.

Education also had a major impact on improving the status of women. True, the education of girls continued to lag behind that of boys. But women graduates came to hold (sometimes prominent) positions in many fields which until very recently had been closed to them (such as medicine, the civil service, and even politics). Here, too, the Islamic regime—despite its totally contrary attitudes—could not, and did not wish, to altogether reverse the process.

No less important, university graduates (who had been in the forefront of earlier struggles: in the Constitutional Revolution, during World War II, in the movements of the 1950s and 1960s) were vital in the coalition that brought Khomeyni to power. The concept of freedom and the principles of constitutional rule were the input of highly educated persons whose activities go back to the late nineteenth century. The political parties existing at the time of Khomeyni's advent, whether the National Front and the Freedom Movement or the other movements of the center, or the Tudeh and Mojahedin-e Khalq, were predominantly led by academics. As authors, journalists, and publishers, the educated class made similarly outstanding contributions; they were also leaders in the process of industrialization. Khomeyni's inability to do without properly trained professionals attests to the irreversibility of this process, too.

The period discussed in this book ends with the eruption of the Islamic Revolution. To what extent did the new education contribute to popular resentment against the shah? Most immediate was the frustration of the great number of high school graduates who had failed to gain admission to the universities. The 1974 law obliging graduates to take jobs specified by the government added another group of malcontents. Academic staff had their own grievances. To these must be added the thousands of graduates of vocational schools who found no interest in what they were doing; the lower-class students resented their richer fellows at the university and doubly so when, after graduation, they found certain prestige jobs virtually reserved for the sons of the wealthy.

Transcending personal frustration, many were disturbed by the cultural, social, economic, and political impact of the educational system as it emerged at the end of the monarchy. Thus, for example, the atmosphere of "servitude to the West" that the educational system was allegedly fostering was sharply criticized by many. Others were critical of the secular values imparted by the schooling system. Still others were disturbed by the political (i.e., nondemocratic) atmosphere at the schools (in particular at the universities). Some were disappointed by the failure of the educational system to generate more rapid economic development; others, by its failure to narrow social gaps. Supporters of the new education had expected education to be the cure-all for the country's ill—only to find that it wasn't. It is hard to imagine any group among the 1978–1979 revolutionaries whose list of grievances did not include education-related issues. For many, these had top priority.

The shah had been warned of the dangers ahead. Already in 1975, educationalists had warned of the political consequences of the rapid multiplication of dissatisfied high school graduates.[3] The following year they warned him about possible subversive tendencies among high school graduates not admitted to the university.[4] Others pointed to the dangers to the economy from the expansion of higher learning unrelated to economic needs.[5] In 1975, a report to the shah spoke of the anger of students at having to take government-designated jobs.[6] There is nothing to suggest that the shah took these warning seriously. In any case one must assume that by the mid-1970s it was too late to remedy the situation.

Although there may be different evaluations of the—direct and indirect—contribution of education to the outbreak of the Islamic Revolution, it is undeniable that the products of the shah's educational system failed to support his regime. At the moment of truth, with public grievances growing and resentment becoming open, it became evident that the schools had neither created substantial loyalty to the shah nor significantly diminished popular attachment to Islam and to

3. SSHBA, *Tarikh Amuzesh-e 'Ali*, 5–7, 107–26.
4. *Kayhan*, 4 and 7 September 1976. Similarly, Professor Safavyan, chancellor of the National University, as quoted in *Kayhan*, 7 September 1976.
5. SSHBA, *Tarikh Amuzesh-e 'Ali*, 10–14.
6. Baheri report, 1975, 8.

men of religion. On the contrary, alongside the clerics it was the educated class who was in the forefront of the opposition. The shah found that control of education by an autocratic regime did not necessarily guarantee genuine support. Will the Islamic regime have the same experience? Obviously, the clerics in power believe that they will not. In their first dozen years in power they spared no effort to use education to advance their goals. By doing so, Khomeyni and his men wished to turn the wheel back to where it had been at the outset of the period discussed here, when a distinction was made between (desirable) western technology and (undesirable) western culture. There is no reason to think that it is any more feasible to make that distinction now than it was then.

Epilogue

Having come to power in 1979, the Islamic regime concentrated in the first dozen years of its rule on two interrelated targets: First, the consolidation, institutionalization, and—insofar as possible—perpetuation of clerical rule. Second, the implementation of Khomeyni's ideology, which, in turn, would further promote legitimization and consolidation and would bring the country closer to its leaders' perception of a genuine Islamic society. Indeed, for the new rulers of Iran, "Islamic Revolution" was not just a title for their movement; it reflected their intent to concentrate all power and to bring all spheres of life in conformity with Islamic tenets and ideals. Making "new Iran" in the mold totally conforming to Khomeyni's perceptions of a genuinely Islamic society was a major objective of the Islamic Republic. To achieve this goal, the new rulers placed special emphasis on the overhauling of the code of laws and the judiciary, and the revision of the educational system. Under the Pahlavis, these had been the two areas whose reform was considered the primary prerequisite for the country's successful secularization and westernization. In revolutionary Iran, their reform was to be of a different kind, meant to accelerate Islamization in all spheres of life. Now, as then, education was both a subject of change itself and perceived as an instrument for change.[1]

In a message for the Iranian new year (21 March 1980) Khomeyni

1. Passages of the Epilogue are taken from my book *Iran: A Decade of War and Revolution* (Holmes and Meier, 1990). This book may also help the reader by supplying the general context of the educational policy in revolutionary Iran.

made it clear that in order to advance the country, a "fundamental revolution" in all the universities was essential. He emphasized that "all the miseries of society" and "all of our backwardness" were caused by the universities and their graduates.[2] On 26 April, the imam explained the scope and meanings of the Iranian Cultural Revolution. He said the Iranian universities lack independence; "they are imperialist universities; and those whom they educate and train are infatuated with the West." They "lack Islamic morality and fail to impart an Islamic education." These universities have become "propaganda arenas" and "served to impede the progress" of Iranians. Many of the teachers, at all levels of schooling, "are now effectively serving the West by brainwashing and miseducating our youth. . . . They want us to remain in a state of perpetual dependence on the West." The young generation may have had succeeded in "acquiring some knowledge, but they have not received an education, an Islamic education." Moreover, since the universities "do not impart an education that corresponds to the needs of the people and the country," their graduates turn into "a burden to the people."[3] Rather than helping to eliminate the problems facing the nation, they add to them. The Cultural Revolution was therefore planned to Islamicize and purify the educational system, with greater emphasis being laid on higher education. The scope of Iranian Cultural Revolution was as large as that of the Chinese Cultural Revolution; with "politics in command" being changed to "religion in command."[4]

Khomeyni was a great believer in education—in its power both to destroy (if controlled by the imperialist powers) and to advance the people and the country (if employed by an Islamic regime). He therefore viewed education as a major instrument to implement his ideology and perpetuate Islamic rule. According to his doctrine, a proper education can lead to the creation of a perfect human being (*ensan kamel*) or exemplar individuals (*ensanha-ye nemune*), who will serve to create an ideal Islamic society (*jame'e ideal Islami*).[5] "A good man can save a country whereas a bad man can destroy it. . . . Therefore it is very im-

2. Ruhollah Khomeini, *Islam and Revolution: Writings and Declarations of Imam Khomeini*, trans. and annotated by Hamid Algar (Berkeley: Mizan Press, 1981), 291–94.

3. Ibid., 295–99.

4. For a comparison of the Iranian Cultural Revolution and that of China, see Khosrow Sobhe, "Education in Revolution: Is Iran Duplicating the Chinese Cultural Revolution? *Comparative Education*, 18, no. 3 (1982), 271–80. Nader Entessar similarly suggests that it was a Cultural Revolution "à la China" in his "Educational Reforms in Iran: Cultural Revolution or Anti-Intellectualism?" *Journal of South Asian and Middle Eastern Studies*, 8 (Fall 1984), 47–64.

5. See, for example, the social science textbook for the fourth year of secondary education, 1986 edition, p. 9.

portant that our schools, from the first grade to the university, become training and educating (*tarbiyyati*) institutions. They should become schools that train good men."[6] Furthermore, without educational reform, there is "no hope that an Islamic Republic shall ever take shape in this country"; but reforming the schools and universities will not only "guard our country from the hands of the devils, it shall enable it to stand on its feet without dependence on foreigners."[7] In fact, the new slogan of the Ministry of Education reveals such an attitude, upholding knowledge as tantamount to worship (*'ebadat*). It states that "*ta'lim va ta'allom 'ebadat ast*" (learning and teaching is a worship).[8]

The term *'ilm* had a double meaning for Khomeyni and his disciples: it referred both to study and acquisition of knowledge, and to the cultivation of a value system and the molding of the students' personality. The aim was to "create a New Islamic Person," and in fact one of the most important slogans of the postrevolutionary period has been: "Our revolution is a revolution in values."[9] In a meeting with educators in September 1982, he asserted that these two aspects were inseparable. But if compelled to choose between the two, a Muslim educator must hold it "more important to acquire values than science." After all, the aim of education was not to provide the students with a livelihood, but rather to elevate their cultural level so that they would attain the goals of the revolution.[10] At the opening of the 1982/3 academic year he reemphasized the importance, at all levels of schooling, of instructing the young generation in accordance with the principles of the revolution. Education, he then reiterated, must be loyal to the republic, and the students must become familiar with the clerics and their views, and follow their path.[11] Education, as all other spheres of life, should be Islamic—in line with his own interpretation of Islam.

Thus, in Khomeyni's view, "knowledge, on its own, if not detrimental, is at least useless." He added: "All the calamities confronting mankind have their roots in universities" and the expertise created by them.[12] In the Islamic state, education should go through a process of

6. From a sermon delivered on 1 July 1979, cited in Farhang Rajaee, *Islamic Values and World View: Khomeini on Man, the State and International Politics*, (Lanham: University Press of America, 1983), 36.

7. Speech by Khomeyni cited in Entessar, 47.

8. This slogan has replaced the old one, *tavana bavad an ke dana bavad* (capable is the one who possesses knowledge) drawn from Ferdowsi.

9. Mehran Golnar, "Socialization of Schoolchildren in the Islamic Republic of Iran," *Iranian Studies*, 22, no. 1 (1989), 35.

10. *Ettela'at*, 7 September 1982.

11. *Kayhan*, 23 September 1982.

12. *Ettela'at*, 18 February 1981.

"spiritual purification" through which man "controls his inner forces and harmonizes them in the direction of Allah." Education must "reflect the independent nature of Islamic thought . . . and cleanse itself from all western values and influences." Schools must be made to produce people who "will not be prepared to hand over the country to others."[13] What made a nation prosperous, Khomeyni said in December 1982, is a "correct culture," and "what makes a university useful and productive . . . is the content . . . not merely the lessons." He added: "Industry minus faith will lead to corruption. Science minus faith, too, leads to corruption." In contrast to the shah's universities, which had made their students "backward and . . . dependent," a pure Islamic system would lead to "progress and independence."[14]

The educational system as it existed under the shah had been "contaminated" by foreign thinking, when it had come under the "control" of the superpowers who had made it serve their own interests.[15] In those days, Khomeyni said in December 1982, "our universities were in the hands of a group of Anglophiles and later mere admirers of the Americans."[16] Such statements reflect views expressed earlier by neo-revolutionary intellectuals like Jalal Al-e Ahmad and ʿAli Shariʿati. Thus, for example, the former charged that in the shah's schools there was "no trace of any reliance on tradition, no sign of the culture of the past, no philosophical or ethical principles and not a word about literature; no link between yesterday and tomorrow, between the home and the school, between East and West, and between society and the individual."[17] But now it was the policy of the regime itself to make the educational system conform with, and help shape, an ideal Islamic community.

Two essays in separate social science textbooks for the ninth and twelfth years, by Mohammad ʿAli Fayyaz-Bakhsh and Gholam ʿAli Hadad ʿAdel, respectively, discussed at greater length the flaws of the educational system and the need for—as well as the direction of—the desired change.[18] Fayyaz-Bakhsh claimed that revolutionary Iran has inherited a wrong educational system in which "dependence and blind

---

13. *Kayhan*, 18 December 1980.
14. Radio Tehran, 19 December—SWB, 22 December 1982.
15. *Kayhan*, 12 October 1980.
16. Radio Tehran, 19 December—SWB, 22 December 1982.
17. Al-e Ahmad, *Plagued by the West*, 88.
18. Mohammad ʿAli Fayyaz-Bakhsh, "Amuzesh va Parvaresh," in social science textbook, ninth grade (edition of 1985/6), 41–56; Gholam ʿAli Hadad ʿAdel, "Masaʾel-e ʿOmumi-ye Amuzesh va Parvaresh," in social science textbook, twelfth grade (edition of 1986/7), 145–203.

imitation of the Western educational system, has alienated us from our real needs." The best product of "our secondary school machinery" was a young man who spent the best years of his life in search of a profession and ended high school "not possessing any occupation." It would even be better, he claimed, "to break down these idols (i.e. schools)" which serve only as a "factory for production of paper certificates," rather than having them function as they are. Hadad 'Adel wrote that education, more than any other social institution, gained the attention of the imperialist powers because it is in fact the "major factory for the creation of human beings (*karkhane-ye adam-sazi*)" (for the use of such a terminology a century earlier, see Chapter 1). Imperialism used these factories to produce such products that would "think according to their wishes and act in their favor." "*Amuzesh* [acquisition of knowledge] gives people the expertise (*takhassos*) and awareness (*agahi*), and *parvaresh* [character formation] gives them the commitment (*ta'ahod*), faith (*iman*), and virtue (*taqava*). It is clear that *parvaresh* has a priority over *amuzesh*."[19] In fact, he concludes, the main deficiency of Iran's educational system has been the supremacy of western material values. The universities did not suck milk from the breast of their mother (the Muslim community of Iran), but rather from the breast of foreign nurses.

First to come under Khomeyni's direct fire were therefore the western-educated intellectuals. Yet, apparently, his opposition to them was not merely due to their educational policy but also to their political rivalry. He repeatedly blamed them for being "puppets" of imperialism, introducing into Iran western concepts alien to the spirit of Islam. He blamed them for striving to create a society "in which there is no God."[20] It became even clearer that the motivation was political no less than educational, since he repeatedly blamed the intellectuals for maintaining "links to the East or the West" and presently being engaged "in factionalism and dispute, in total isolation from the people."[21] He again made clear the political reasons behind his criticism, while blaming the intellectuals in 1980 for transforming the universities "into a battlefield for ideologies harmful to the nation. If Islamic morality existed in the universities, these shameful clashes would not occur."[22]

19. Regarding the question of which will have priority, *amuzesh* or *parvaresh*, an article in *Ettela'at* (26 November 1987) provided a more typical answer: "is it possible at all to separate these two terms?"

20. *Ettela'at*, 13 January 1979.

21. Khomeyni, *Islam and Revolution*, 291–94.

22. Ibid., 295–99. For the political background to such criticism, Menashri, *Iran: A Decade of War and Revolution*, 177–81; Sobhe, 275–79.

To reshape the educational system to conform to genuinely Islamic norms, Khomeyni announced a cultural revolution in 1980 and created revolutionary institutions to carry out the Islamization. Radical student intervention in the academic affairs of Tehran University resulted in the collective resignation of university's board of governors in February 1980. In March, students occupied the offices of the chancellor of Teachers' Training University and "elected" a new chancellor.[23] In mid-April, disturbances spread to all campuses. The starting point was the University of Tabriz, where students demanded that the Cultural Revolution be stepped up and more energetic measures taken to purge the faculty and the student body. They also demanded the removal from the campus of the office of all political movements (most of them leftist and hence objectionable to them). Violent clashes ensued between opposing student groups, and between students and the Revolutionary Guards. Many activists were arrested.[24] In May, the Revolutionary Council decreed that the universities would not open at the beginning of the new academic year (in September 1980) to give the government time "to prepare the foundation of an Islamic educational system," and to facilitate purges.[25] Some institutions (mostly in fields of science and technology) were opened within the next two years, but a full program was resumed only after the most essential steps were believed to have been carried out, in September 1983. The completion of the Islamization process, said ʿAbbas Sheybani (then chancellor of Tehran University), would take twenty years. The resumption of studies meant no more than that the minimum had been done to meet the demand for graduates and to allow students to continue with their education.[26]

Yet, by the very nature of things, revolutionary movements tend to deviate from their radical doctrine once they have made the transition from opposition to power. The Islamic Revolution was no exception. As long as he headed an opposition movement, Khomeyni had depicted a "new Iran" as being modeled on early Islam. Once in power, he knew he could not rule by means of revolutionary slogans—certainly not slogans drawn from seventh-century thought. He and his disciples were now called to manage, rather than discuss, affairs of state. Soon they had to compromise with reality, not from a newfound moderation, but from pragmatism responsive to the exigencies of their situation. The pragmatic interests of the *state* have clearly gained supremacy over

23. *Ettelaʿat*, 25 February; *Kayhan*, 29 February, 16 March 1980.
24. *Ettelaʿat*, 16, 19, 22, 23 April, 5 May; *Kayhan*, 18, 19, 22 April 1980.
25. *Daily Telegraph*, 27 May; *Ettelaʿat*, 17 June; *Kayhan*, 26 June 1980.
26. *Ettelaʿat*, 19 September 1983.

the radical philosophy of the *revolution*; and the effective running of the country turned out to be no less crucial than adherence to the dogma. We have already raised the question, to what extent were the roots of the revolution "Islamic"? (see the Introduction). Here one might ask, to what extent did the revolutionary movement remain loyal to its ideology after it assumed power?[27] Although the considerable deviations from the initial dogma may suggest a decline of Khomeyni's doctrine, one must guard against equating the fate of Khomeyni's ideology with that of the Islamic regime. In ideological as well as practical terms, there have already been considerable deviations from some of the most basic elements in Khomeyni's philosophy. Yet this does not signal, or portend, the end of clerical rule. Paradoxically, the greater the deviation from *revolutionary dogma* (and the concomitant adaptability to new realities), the greater is the likelihood for the *Islamic regime* to continue. This was probably the resonance beyond the (relatively) pragmatic policies adopted over time by the revolutionary administration—educational policies included.

Appeals for moderation related first to specific and narrow issues, such as the recruitment of professionals, and they came to involve more general issues and basic dogmatic questions as well. Khomeyni put his own weight behind the policy of moderating the Islamization process when he advised the clerics in September 1984 not to press "too hard" on the people and to "refrain from extremism." Instead, he advocated gradualism and explained that this reflected the teaching of the Qur'an: just as the early Muslims were tolerant toward those who joined Islam and did not expect them to display an ideal Islamic behavior right away, so revolutionary Iran should be more tolerant to people newly entering its ranks.[28] Encouraged by the imam's guidelines, ʿAli Akbar Hashemi Rafsanjani elaborated on these themes in two Friday sermons later in September. He advised against pushing the revolutionary process forward too fast and against going farther than "necessary." Wisdom, he said, "calls for moderation at this stage."[29]

Higher education was thus just one other sphere in which balance was being sought between the drive for Islamization and a sense of the prevailing realities. The change was prompted, according to the

27. I discuss this issue at somewhat great length in my book *Iran: A Decade of War and Revolution*, 386–93 and in my article "Khomeini's Vision: Nationalism or World Order?" in Menashri, *The Iranian Revolution and the Muslim World*, 40–57.

28. *JI*, 3 September 1984.

29. For Rafsanjani's elaboration on these guidelines in the following Friday sermon, see Menashri, *Iran: A Decade of War and Revolution*, 323.

testimony of those advocating it,[30] by the relative stability already achieved, by the quest for "normalization," and by the pragmatic approach acceptable to the majority of people. Having sensed that the most essential steps had now been successfully completed, that the faculty and student body had been weeded out, the curriculum revised, the campus atmosphere changed, and antirevolutionary groups at the university wiped out, the leadership was now ready for a slowdown. The resentment in certain quarters against extremist policies and the deteriorating educational services undoubtedly also contributed to this trend.

Ayatollah Hoseyn ʿAli Montazeri, who had long advocated greater tolerance toward professionals, again set the tone. He explained in 1984 that the radical steps taken in the past "were good for that time" but were unacceptable today. The present interests of the republic dictated bringing in anyone willing to teach or study. It was unreasonable to expect everyone to be "a perfect Hezbollahi" (member of the Party of God; i.e., truly revolutionary). At a meeting with people in charge of the educational policy, he asked them to "refrain from extremism" and to "practice moderation" as Islam obliged them to do. Opposition quarters, he said, must not be allowed to take advantage of the situation, but no one now supporting the revolution should feel threatened, even if he had in the past cooperated with the old regime.[31] In line with this new approach, on 11 December 1984 Khomeyni appointed eight figures as new members of the Council for Cultural Revolution; among them were heads of the three branches of government. A week later President ʿAli Khameneʾi was elected chairman of the council.[32] This demonstrated the importance attached to education but also changed the council's balance in favor of those who were more pragmatic. Upon his election, Khameneʾi announced: "I oppose any intervention by the Islamic councils in the universities' affairs." Consequently Jehad-e Daneshgahi (the Unit for University Crusade), the bastion of university radicalism, was incorporated into the council and was thus abolished as an independent organ.[33]

Speaking to the revolutionary committee members in January 1986, Montazeri voiced his annoyance that extremist officials were not prac-

---

30. For an account of how the leadership formulated its policy toward the universities, see the statements made by Prime Minister Musavi and Ayatollah ʿAbd al-Karim Ardebili, as quoted in *Kayhan*, 17 December 1983.

31. As in speeches and an interview with Montazeri, as quoted in *Kayhan*, 3 March, 5 May and *Jl*, 12 August, 26 September 1984.

32. *Jl*, 20 December 1984.

33. *Kayhan*, 19 December 1984.

ticing Islamic behavior.[34] Rafsanjani argued similarly that it was "natural" for the universities not to conform completely with Islamic standards yet. Such a process took time. Meanwhile, everyone "who has the knowledge but does not endanger the revolution" should be absorbed into the higher education system. To insist on "judging professors" by their views was meant "to shut down the universities."[35] Some leaders even appealed to the university organizations to allow the faculty to run the universities, just as the ulama were running the theological seminaries.[36] This did not mean that the regime had given up the ideal of a strict Islamization of education, but rather that a measure of pragmatism had gradually become discernible. Neither did the interference of revolutionary bodies altogether cease. But the top leadership was now more willing to accede to the exigencies of the realities and reconsider their policy.

Appeals for moderation became even more evident in the era following the cease-fire, when reconstruction became the order of the day. Again it was Rafsanjani who reminded his people that the ideal days of early Islam had long passed: "Today," he said in September 1988, "we live under new conditions."[37] Early in October (1988) he stated that Iran should "maintain ideals, but also meet "the needs of the people."[38] The country, he said, "may need experts from abroad."[39] Following his election to the presidency, he made clear his priorities: "For the reconstruction," he said, "one cannot work with slogans (*sho'ar*), commotion (*hayjan*), and sentiments (*ehsasat*)." Iran, he added, cannot live in today's world without the "material capabilities and the advancement of science and technology."[40] Khamene'i similarly stated that Iran needed "the assistance and cooperation of others. . . . Domestic resources (*manabe'*) and expertise (*takhassos*) are not enough," at least for a reasonable space of time.[41] In January 1989, Montazeri (still Khomeyni's heir-elect) called on his personal representatives in the universities to create an atmosphere favorable to the free expression

34. *KH*, 15 January 1986

35. *JI*, 8 August 1984.

36. See, for example, statements by Khamene'i, as quoted in *Kayhan*, 14 and 19 October 1984.

37. Radio Tehran, 25 September—SWB, 27 September 1988.

38. Ibid., 9 October—SWB, 11 October 1988.

39. Radio Tehran, 14 October—SWB, 17 October 1988.

40. *Ettela'at*, 21 October 1989. For the centrality of education in the reconstruction policy, see similarly Hasan Habibi (the vice president) and Mostafa Mo'in (the minister of education), *Ettela'at*, 22 October 1989.

41. Radio Tehran, 16 September—SWB, 19 September 1988; *Ettela'at*, 17 September 1988.

of political views. He said that his representatives, "except for preventing anti-Islamic deeds and inviting others to the truth, should not
obstruct free . . . thought, expression, and action, especially in political
and social affairs." [42]

The educational policy, just like virtually all the other policies of the
regime, had become an issue of conflicting attitudes between the different power groups: first, between Abu al-Hasan Bani Sadr (as president) and his opponents in the domestic struggle for power; later
between the Ministry of Culture and Higher Education and the universities (with all the differences between them) on the one hand, and
the more radical revolutionary organizations (mainly Jehad-e Daneshgahi)[43] and student organizations supported by radical clerics on the
other hand.

Frequent requests to reopen the universities were made by academics, backed by President Bani Sadr, a short while after the universities
closed. But these were mostly the voices of those against whom the
revolution had been directed in the first place. In February 1981, for
example, a petition signed by a thousand professors and secondary
school teachers was published in *Mizan*, demanding the immediate
reopening of the institutes of higher education. The petitioners stated
that the closings had "resulted in the loss of energy for the country." [44]
On 30 March 1981 Bani Sadr urged that universities should resume
their activities. Soon prominent leaders in the clergy joined in the
campaign. In February 1982, Montazeri argued that the universities
should be opened with measures that still needed to be bolstered while
the academic year was in progress.[45] This caused a dispute between
the Ministry of Culture and Higher Education and the Council for
Cultural Revolution. The latter wished to force more radical Islamization upon the universities, for example, by preferring applicants from
the lower social classes. It also demanded that future admission policies
should take into consideration the applicants' "geographical origin"
and not only their scholastic levels (with a view, presumably, to attracting more students from rural areas and small towns). However,
the heads of the universities and the Ministry of Culture and Higher
Education were not advocates of overly radical Islamization and attempted to obstruct these measures. The minister, Mohammad Najafi,

42. *Kayhan*, 19 January 1989.
43. The law for the formation of Jehad-e Daneshgahi was approved by the Majlis in
January 1984 and named the "spread of Islamic culture" as one of its main objectives.
For the full text of the law, see *Ettela'at*, 4 January 1984.
44. Radio Tehran, 25 February—DR, 26 February 1981.
45. *Kayhan*, 12 September 1982.

said in October 1982 that efforts were being made to work out a policy acceptable to both sides, and that the dispute had already been "partly resolved."[46] Disagreements continued, but the universities could not remain closed any longer.

The actual Islamization effort focused on four areas: the student population, the faculty, the general Islamic atmosphere to be created on the campuses, and the curriculum. The goal was to harness the universities—and schools in general—to the task of shaping a new generation with "Islamic personality" in keeping with the principles of the revolution. But no less important was the need to remove the political challenge presented by the intellectual-liberals.[47]

With regard to university admissions, the competitive entrance examination was now complemented by "ideological tests" that were to establish the applicant's moral competency.[48] A precondition for taking the examination was for the student to have "faith in the regime"; to support its institutions; to have no links with opposition movements, or with the West or the East; and of course to be "morally suitable" to gain a university seat. Moreover, the student had to be a Muslim or belong to one of the officially recognized religions.[49] (This meant the exclusion of Bahais.) This "discriminatory two-tier" admission system required the applicant first to pass written examinations; then a "background investigation" was made in order to determine the candidate's "moral suitability" and loyalty to the Islamic Republic. "Investigators were dispatched to inquire from the applicant's neighbors and other 'committed' individuals . . . about his Islamic commitment."[50] A negative report from the applicant's neighbors would be used against the candidate without even checking whether the informants themselves were trustworthy.[51] Another problem with this process was that such an investigation sometimes delayed the decision regarding admission, since the investigation sometimes took a year or even two.[52] This caused not only injustice to the applicants but also administrative problems for the universities. In addition, disciplinary committees were estab-

---

46. *Ettela'at*, 24 October 1982.

47. Thus Rafsanjani in *Kayhan*, 4 December 1982, and *Ettela'at*, 9 January 1983; Montazeri, in *Kayhan*, 22 May 1983.

48. Rafsanjani in *Kayhan*, 4 December 1982.

49. The conditions were disclosed by ʿAbbas Taʾeb, deputy minister of culture and higher education, in *Kayhan*, 13 April 1983.

50. Entessar, 60.

51. See, for example, an article complaining against such malpractices in *Ettela'at*, 14 February 1987.

52. For such criticism, see, for example, *Ettela'at*, 13 January 1987.

lished as another "safety net." These committees were established in each university to identify and punish deviators from Islamic behavioral (including political and moral) norms.

Yet, over time, the approach became somewhat more pragmatic. According to a decision of the Council for Cultural Revolution from 1986, information on the suitability of candidates should be obtained only from the Ministry of Intelligence and the judiciary (on applicants' political record) and from the Ministry of Education (on the moral record). Neighbors and other informants should no longer be used. Moreover, as far as the applicants' morality is concerned, only the present situation should be taken into account; while regarding their political suitability, their past records would be examined (however, if they were not engaged in terrorist activities after summer 1981, they should be approved).[53] Similarly, the long-standing demand of the radicals (in fact, of the Council for Cultural Revolution itself in its former composition) for an admission quota for the revolutionary organizations at universities was rejected by the council.[54] Hojjat al-Islam Rahimi (deputy minister of education) said in December 1988 that it would not be advisable to help candidates of different organizations (such as war veterans) to enter the universities by letting them bypass the general examination procedures. The goal should be to help them pass the examinations.[55] (In practice, however, some quotas were still preserved, for war veterans, martyrs' families, revolutionary organizations, etc., though not of the scope that the radicals may have wished.)

In purging the academic staff, the prime motive was clearly political, aiming to prevent them from posing an obstacle to the consolidation of clerical rule and to the Islamization of education. What was initially a step directed against the supporters of the *ancien regime*, soon extended to *all* those now termed as "West-stricken" and "counterrevolutionaries."[56] The Islamization of the universities' staff, however, presented a serious academic problem. Most of the faculty staff had studied in western countries; curricula were patterned on western models; and textbooks were mainly in English. (At the University of Shiraz, English was also the language of instruction.) Those in charge of the process wished to avoid employing professors "influenced" by the West but were unable to find competent substitutes among the

53. *Ettela'at*, 28 July 1987; 12 January 1988. According to the former source, some of the candidates initially rejected on moral grounds were approved after another investigation was concluded.

54. See interview with the minister of education in *JI*, 17 February 1985.

55. *Ettela'at*, 18 December 1988.

56. Entessar, 56–57.

revolutionaries. Montazeri, who supported an accommodating line toward the professionals, pointed to the dilemma when he said in 1983 that if only those who had fought against the shah, or who had been in his jails, were allowed to teach, there would be no university teaching at all. Yet he felt that extra care should be taken over appointments to key posts (e.g., chancellors, deans, and university administrators).[57]

In actual practice, however, present views and past connections continued to be taken into account in making university appointments. Early in January 1984, Hojjat al-Islam 'Abbas Mahfuzi (Montazeri's representative at Tehran University) disclosed that only 6,000 members of the 1978 academic staff were still teaching in 1983. (The rest had been dismissed, had resigned, or had fled abroad.) From among 4,000 candidates who had applied for teaching positions since then, the "moral credentials" of only 1,273 had been found satisfactory.[58] Those who were left were closely observed by the government apparatus. An attempt was also made to make them more familiar with the regime's ideology. But, all in all, the regime has to compromise on this, too, to enable the institutions of higher learning to function normally.

The close ties already established between university heads and the clerics and the appointment of supervisors on Montazeri's behalf for each university were believed to guarantee an "Islamic atmosphere" at the universities. This could be witnessed by the clothing worn by women, by the attendance at mosques, and so on. Symbolic of the Islamization process was the change in the names of some of the universities, especially those with national-monarchical names, to Islamic-revolutionary ones. Tehran's Melli (National) University, for instance, was now renamed the University of Shahid (Martyr) Beheshti; Gondi Shapur was called after Shahid Chamran; Aryamehr was renamed Sherif University, and Pahlavi was to be known simply as Shiraz.

The Islamization of the curriculum placed greater emphasis on "moral education" and on courses intended to raise the students' consciousness of history, Islamic culture, literature, and arts. Courses on the principles of religion were made part of the standard curriculum at universities.[59] These were regarded as even more important than cognitive skills. Yet, even at the end of the period discussed, there were not enough books compiled by local professors, not even in the

57. *Kayhan*, 22 May 1983 and *Ettela'at*, 19 September 1983.
58. *Ettela'at*, 8 January 1984.
59. These views were set forth in interviews and speeches by Mehdi Hojjat (head of the Department of Culture in the Committee for Cultural Revolution), *Ettela'at*, 16 December 1982; by Mohammad Reza Mahdavi-Kani, *Kayhan*, 18 December 1982; and by Montazeri, *Kayhan*, 4 January 1983.

field of humanities and social sciences.[60] At the university level, many foreign books were used; at the lower levels, many science high school textbooks of the old regime (mainly for the higher grades) remained in use—despite an ambitious program of rewriting the textbooks for elementary and secondary schools.[61]

The revision of these textbooks is perhaps the clearest example of the way the curriculum was harnessed to serve the aims of the revolution.[62] Indeed, no detail skipped the eyes of the censors.[63] The aim was stated as "purifying" textbooks by "clearing them of the misguidance and decadence of the despotic former regime."[64] This task was to be carried out by the Organization for Research and Educational Planning in the Ministry of Education through the Bureau for Education, Planning and Textbook Composition (Daftar-e Ta'limat va Barname-rizi va Ta'lif Kotob-e Darsi). The most fundamental changes were made in textbooks in social science and humanities, which now clearly reflected the ideology and politics of the Islamic Republic. The textbooks aimed at fostering loyalty to Islam and the revolution and advancing those ideals that they deemed important as well as revealing and stressing the flaws of the old regime and the superpowers. The symbols and messages were not much different from those presented to the people by the indoctrination machinery. Yet, while addressed to the young students, the textbooks used extra sophistication to bring home the desired results. Even simple stories reveal on close examination a deep meaning, which the teachers would elaborate on in class. Among other things, they stressed the oneness of religion and state (as well as religion and science), and the ideal of martyrdom, and the need for political participation. They also emphasized the need to actively support the (Islamic) government and obey its rules. On the other hand, they criticized the shah and his policies, the *gharbzade* (West-struck) intellectuals, and the superpowers. Not only was pre-Islamic culture downgraded, but even Ferdowsi was hardly mentioned.

60. An interview with the secretary of the Council for Cultural Revolution, Dr. Hashemi Golpaygani: *Ettela'at*, 27 January 1987.

61. Golnar, 35–50.

62. This fascinating issue has not been sufficiently studied yet. A comparison of the textbooks used under the shah and those revised under the Islamic rule may reveal many of the differences between the two regimes and the changes the Iranian people are experiencing. A substantial number of the school textbooks can be found in the library of the University of Chicago. So far, at least two articles already have been published on this issue: Golnar, 35–50; and another by J[alal] M[atini], "Ketabha-ye Darsi dar Jomhuri-ye Islami-ye Iran," *Iran-Nameh*, 3 (Fall 1984), 1–25.

63. Matini, 6.

64. Golnar, 36–37.

(Although, one textbook maintained, it was important to use the *Shahn-ame*, since it reveals the malpractices of the shahs.) In addition to changing the texts, the illustrations were carefully selected to fit the goals of the revolution. Women always appear with a veil or scarf, men never with tie; interior walls often display revolutionary and/or Islamic slogans, and on bookshelves the Qur'an has a place of prominence; the pictures of the Behesht Zahra cemetery appear in many books, and there are many pictures of Khomeyni and expressions of the popular support for him.[65]

In general, the books are designed to supply answers to any quandary that young students may have, and further strengthen their ties with Islam, the revolution and the government. Thus, for example, the English textbooks explain (sometimes even on the cover page) why students need to learn English at all in an Islamic republic: first, to be able to have a dialogue with the peoples of the world in order to bring them the truths of Islam and thus help export the revolution; second, to be able to absorb the science and technology needed for leading the country to full independence.[66]

While presenting the role models (the prophet, Imam ʿAli down to Ayatollahs Shirazi, Modarres, and Khomeyni), the textbooks contrast them with the "countermodels" (the *gharbzade*, not to speak of the Pahlavis).[67] All in all, these textbooks reveal that "education in the Islamic Republic is openly and avowedly political and every topic is used for consciously political ends," the ultimate aim being "the creation of a model citizen eligible to live in the ideal Islamic society."[68]

Deviation from the dogma was clearly evident when it came to the need to solve the most pressing needs of the country. One example was the relative tolerance toward the professionals. The massive flight

---

65. Comparing the differences in the third-grade textbook before and after the revolution may reveal some of these tendencies: the girl in the picture on p. 3 in the edition of 1980/81 (of the textbook for Persian for third grade) dresses according to Islamic custom, whereas the girl pictured in the edition of 1969/70 wears western clothes. And in the new edition of the same book published in 1986/7, the wall of the room of the Hashemi family is decorated with the slogan "There is no God except Allah" and a picture of Khomeyni (p. 4), and a volume of the Qur'an appears on the bookshelf (p. 1), but these items do not appear there in the same picture in the 1980/81 edition.

66. This answer appears, among other places, in the preface to *Right Path to English* (English textbook for first year of intermediary school), as well as in textbooks for the third and fourth year of high school (all of the 1986/7 edition). Above this explanation, the following revolutionary slogan is often added: "We will export our revolution to the entire world."

67. Golnar, 37–49.

68. Ibid., 49–50.

of professional manpower severely hampered government attempts to reinvigorate the economy and improve public services. No data on the brain drain are available, except with regard to physicians. In 1982 there were said to be 12,000–14,000 doctors in Iran, while some 10,000 Iranian doctors were practicing abroad. According to the minister of heavy industry, Behzad Nabavi, the brain drain was greatest among those with the highest levels of specialization.[69] In dealing with the problem, the Iranian leaders departed from customary practice and appealed to professionals abroad to return to Iran, assuring them that no harm would come to them.[70] In October 1982, Rafsanjani asked the government to allow even those who were not true "revolutionaries" (*enqelabi*) to return and to serve the homeland.[71] Khamene'i went to even greater lengths (at least in the case of physicians), saying early in 1982: "It is not our conception that a doctor should cease to work because he is not *maktabi* [i.e., faithful to the religion]; *today* in Iran this way of thinking is invalid. We expect doctors to be specialists and to be willing to work. If a doctor [does that] . . . we will accept him willingly."[72] Such downgrading of religious motivation was unprecedented since 1979. The prime minister explained that "tolerance is very important in this connection."[73] Montazeri said that there was no need to delve into the experts' past. Forgiveness was the order of the day.[74] A special center was set up to facilitate the return of professionals. The response, however, was minimal.

Another example of a change in attitude had to do with private schooling. Faced with the growing demand for education and the limited facilities, the revolutionary regime had to reconsider its initial rejection of private schooling. Against all declarations made at the inception of the Islamic regime (when private schools were nationalized), the Council for Cultural Revolution approved in Autumn 1985 the rules for the establishment of "private nonprofit" (*gheyr-e entefa'i*) institutions for higher education.[75] The minister of education, Kazem

69. *Kayhan*, 16 August, 13 September, 19 October 1982.

70. Such appeals were made, for example, by Montazeri (*Kayhan*, 25 and 29 September) and by the president of the Supreme Court, Ardebili (*Kayhan*, 2 October 1982).

71. *Kayhan*, 30 October 1982.

72. *Ettela'at*, 6 February 1982.

73. Radio Tehran, 27 January—SWB, 30 January 1982.

74. *Kayhan*, 15 January, 12 April, 11 June 1983. Similar views were expressed, for example, by Mir-Hoseyn Musavi (*Kayhan*, 15 December 1982) and Khamene'i (*Kayhan*, 18 April 1983).

75. *KH*, 30 October 1985. The main reason for this was the limited government facilities (see interview with the minister of culture and higher education, Iraj Fazel, in *JI*, 5 January 1985).

Akrami, said that private institutions should also be allowed at other levels of education.[76] And in fact, in March 1987, the government approved the establishment of private schools.[77] While forming his government in August 1989, Rafsanjani said that the initial idea of preventing the private sector from investing in private schools was unrealistic. He now encouraged investment in education "from the primary stages up to university."[78] Private schools did in fact come into existence, despite criticism that the end result would be a "complete two-tier" educational system (*do qotbi-ye kamel*), since such institutions attract upper-class students and better teachers.[79] In fact, in any case, some schools obtained financial support from the students.[80]

The government also took another look at programs of study abroad. The undersecretary in the Ministry of Culture and Higher Education, Jahanshahlou, explained in December 1980 that the number of Iranians studying abroad should be reduced. Students seeking qualifications that could be acquired in Iran need not travel abroad; for those seeking "an advance in knowledge in accordance with Islamic principles," study abroad was not useful. In Jahanshahlou's view, it was preferable to invite foreign professors to Iran rather than send students abroad.[81] Others used economic arguments to support this position.[82] However, students still left for western countries for studies, and even received allowances for foreign currency. Mostafa Mo'in, the minister of education, said in October 1989 that for rehabilitating the economy, Iran needs experts: preferably, they should be trained in Iran; but also (with careful planning) abroad.[83]

Yet, even given the (relative) pragmatism, some of the problems inherent in the educational system, at all levels, remained pressing. A study of the postrevolutionary educational system may in fact reveal

76. *JI*, 27 September 1985; *Ettela'at*, 3 January 1987. For the need for private sector's participation in schooling, see also a report of the Ministry of Education (*Ettela'at*, 24 October 1989).

77. *Ettela'at*, 21 March 1987. The 1979 constitution (article 30) made it the responsibility of the government to supply education facilities at the pre-university level.

78. See my article "Iran," in Ami Ayalon, ed., *Middle East Contemporary Survey, 1989* (Boulder: Westview, 1991), 358.

79. For such criticism see, for example, *Ettela'at*, 16 July 1987.

80. Answering such charges, the minister of education, Akrami, said that this was only "some kind of support" that the parents voluntarily granted (*Ettela'at*, 3 January 1987).

81. Radio Tehran, 1 December—SWB, 2 December 1980.

82. See, for example, such arguments as stated by the minister of heavy industry, Behzad Nabavi, in *Kayhan*, 7 September 1987.

83. *Ettela'at*, 22 October 1989.

that it had the same major problems as the educational system under the monarchy—and that sometimes these problems had even intensified.[84] The Ministry of Education itself was aware that if no immediate and substantial steps were taken, "before long" the educational problems could be "expected to form a national problem (*yek moshkel-e melli*)." Quoting from the ministry's 1989 report, *Ettela'at* said that the educational facilities not only have not improved but have even deteriorated.[85] It is important to note that some of these problems resulted not from the policies adopted by the Islamic regime, but rather from the social, economic, and other problems unique to Iran. Most detrimental was unquestionably the rapid growth of the population (from some 37 million on the eve of the revolution to some 55 million in 1989). The rate of growth was one of the highest in the world: 3.7 percent yearly. Moreover, about 50 percent of the population were under seventeen years of age. Consequently, the number of students attending schools grew rapidly. In 1988/9, according to official figures supplied by the Ministry of Education, there were 8,896,000 students in elementary schools (which is 78 percent of the elementary school-age children—83.8 percent of the boys and 74.2 percent of the girls). In intermediary schools the enrollment was 3,108,000 (which is 76.6 percent of the relevant age group—91.9 percent of the boys and 61.6 percent of the girls). In high schools the student population numbered 1,575,000 students (33.6 percent of the relevant age group—37.4 percent of the boys and 17.4 percent of the girls).[86] Below is a list of some of the major problems:

The acute shortage of teachers has now been exacerbated by the rapid growth of the population, as well as by the segregation of schools by sex, which created more classrooms and hence the need for more teachers to staff them. Vocational education remained one of the major problems.[87] In a seminar attended by leaders in the field of vocational education, it was pointed out that the main problem was the lack of clarity regarding the future path of the graduates of vocational schools:

84. This was clearly evident when new governments were introduced in the Majlis. The ministers of education and the ministers of culture and higher education were customarily confronted with harsh criticism and opposition, and several times incumbents failed to achieve the necessary votes. See Menashri, *Iran: A Decade of War and Revolution*, 317, 346–47

85. *Ettela'at*, 24 October 1989.

86. The Islamic Republic of Iran, *Education in the Islamic Republic of Iran: Now and in the Future* (Tehran: Ministry of Education, 1990), 14–17, 42. For the population growth, see *Kayhan*, 19 December 1988.

87. See reportage in *Ettela'at*, 17, 18, 19 July 1989. See also *Ettela'at*, 15, 31 January 1987.

should the schools be training their students to enter institutions of higher learning, or to enter the job market?[88]

In higher education, the rapid expansion of academic education led to a lowering of standards; nevertheless, a growing number of high school graduates failed to be admitted to a university. The disproportionate increase of those receiving a primary and secondary education had created a large population of aspirants for higher education with decreasing chances of being admitted to a university, let alone to a specific faculty. In the 1984/85 academic year, 581,000 candidates took entrance examinations, but only 44,000 were admitted to universities and other institutions of higher learning.[89] In 1987/8, some 540,000 youngsters took the examinations, and only 10 percent of them were admitted.[90] In the general entrance examinations for 1988/9, there were 660,000 candidates for some 70,000 seats.[91] Whereas in the final years of the shah's rule about 250,000 youngsters were left outside the universities' doors, now the number was more than double.

Several institutions for higher learning were established after the revolution (mainly in small towns). Of these, the most significant was the Free Islamic University (Daneshgah-e Azad Islami), which had many branches in the provinces. In its early years, however, owing to the closing of the universities the number of students actually declined: from 175,675 (54,248 women) in 1978/9; and 174,217 (53,571 women) in 1979/80; to 117,148 (36,356 women) in 1982/3; 121,048 (38,643 women) in 1983/4; and 145,809 (45,216 women) in 1984/5.[92]

The willingness to expand higher education, on the one hand, and the shortage of academic staff, on the other, led to problems in recruiting adequately qualified academic staff. In many cases teaching assistants taught classes, the number of students exceeded the capacity of classes, and so forth. This led to what the academic staff itself called a deterioration in quality.[93] In an interview with the secretary of the Council of the Cultural Revolution, Dr. Golpaygani, a reporter for *Ettela'at* made the assertion that in the Iranian universities "quality has been sacrificed for the sake of quantity." Not denying what was said, Golpaygani responded that this was exactly the reason that a private education was needed: otherwise, as long as there is a gap between

88. *Ettela'at*, 21 January 1988.
89. *Iran Almanac, 1987*, 135.
90. *Ettela'at*, 7 April 1987.
91. Ibid., 23 July 1988.
92. Ibid., 28 July 1987.
93. Professors still teaching in Iran during the revolution who later fled the country emphasized this point in their interviews with me. See also *Ettela'at*, 28 July 1987.

educational needs and capabilities, the level of schooling will continue to go down.[94] While there were 16,877 members on academic staffs in 1979/89, their number declined to 9,041 in 1982/3 and rose slightly to 11,494 in 1983/4 and 13,698 in 1984/5.[95] Research similarly continued to be limited and weak.[96]

Not only did the monarchy and the Islamic regime have the same major educational problems, but sometimes they came up with solutions that were basically similar: Thus, for example, the initiative for the Literacy Campaign (Nehzat-e Savad Amuzi), according to which soldier-teachers (sarbaz-mo'allem) would be used to eradicate illiteracy, was not much different in structure (but very different in content, of course) from the shah's Literacy Corps (Sepah-e Danesh).[97] So also the Jehad-e Madrese-sazi (the unit for school construction),[98] which may resemble the shah's initiative in 1971 to have people contribute to establish new schools. Similarly, the idea of the Open University had in fact originated much before the coming to power of the Islamic regime.

Ultimately, the most significant testimonial to the value of the new education and to the degree to which it had become rooted in Iranian society came from Khomeyni. His regime had set out to undo all that had been done in Iran under the impact of the West. Yet the elementary school system (despite significant changes in educational contents) remained much as it had been. Sciences and foreign languages continued to be taught. All the universities, though closed at first for Islamization, eventually reopened with their overall structure intact. It was generally conceded that science continued to be "needed as a tool." Khomeyni himself made clear that "we are not rejecting modern science, nor are we saying that each science exists in two varieties, one Islamic and the other non-Islamic."[99]

Neither did Khomeyni himself object to the use of academics for the service of his cause. On the contrary, people with a modern education, many of them educated in the West, gained prominent positions in his administration. The trend toward greater professionalism could also be seen in the educational background of the Majlis members. We have

94. *Ettela'at*, 27 January 1987.
95. Ibid., 28 July 1987.
96. See reportage on this problem in *Ettela'at*, 28 July 1987 and 15–17, 19–20 November 1988.
97. On this program see, for example, ibid., 17 March 1987.
98. Ibid., 28 July 1987.
99. Khomeini, *Islam and Revolution*, 296.

data on almost all Majlis members.[100] In the first Majlis, 122 members had a traditional religious education; in the second, 153; but in the third (and last, before this book went to press), only 68. Those with new-state education numbered 139 in the first Majlis, 122 in the second, and 204 in the third. Those with the highest level of religious education (at the level of *ejtehad*) numbered 30 in the first Majlis, 28 in the second, but only 11 in the third. As far as "modern" higher education is concerned, 128 members of the third Majlis were university graduates, as compared with 74 in the second and 115 in the first.[101]

Even more evident was the high level of (modern) education of the heads of the administration. The last government formed before this book was sent to press (that of Rafsanjani, formed in August 1989), had twenty-two ministers. Clearly, Rafsanjani selected a cabinet of technocrats, many of them western-educated, rather than revolutionary ideologues: a third had studied in the West, eight had Ph.D. or M.D. degrees, nine were engineers, and only four were of the religious rank of Hojjat al-Islam. Rafsanjani made it clear that he wished to have a government of experts, not of politicians. It was enough, he said, that he himself was political; the ministers should be "experts in their field and in their professional and administrative knowledge" as is needed "in the period of construction." Criticized for having a large number of western-educated ministers, he responded that he did not think it advisable to limit ministerial appointments to people who had studied in Iran. He said: "Studying in American universities was not and is not a negative point."[102]

If the previous chapters may have suggested that the roots of the revolution did not in fact spring from, in the western conception of the word, uniquely religious roots, the epilogue may show that the actual policy implemented by the Islamic Revolution has been far from strictly faithful to the professed Islamic ideology with which the regime had come to power. It may also suggest that, notwithstanding the vehement opposition of the clerics to the new education imported into Iran over a century ago, that education has now been deemed to be

100. The number may exceed the total number of Majlis members, because some members had partly traditional and partly new education and because some new members were elected in by-elections to fill vacant seats in the House.

101. *Kayhan*, 29 May 1988. Data were available for 216 members of the first Majlis, 260 of the second, and 266 of the third.

102. IRNA (in English), 27 August—SWB, 29 August; *Ettela'at*, 27, 28, 29, 30 August 1989. Some people, Rafsanjani said, suggested ministerial appointments should be offered only to those who had studied in Iran.

essential even by the leaders of the Islamic Republic, proving yet again that the new education has emerged triumphant.

Finally, there remains the question whether the Islamization of the educational system may in the future prove to be beneficial for the perpetuation of the Islamic Republic? The answer to this question is, of course, beyond the scope of this book. Unquestionably, control over the educational system and the contents of schooling helps in the indoctrination program of the Islamic regime. However, it is important to remember that under the shah, similar control over the contents of schooling did not result in widespread popular support for his regime. On the contrary, those who rose up against him were for the most part products of the royalist educational system. This is not to say that the same is expected under the Islamic government. Rather, the progress of Iran and the longevity of the Islamic state will ultimately depend not on sloganeering and indoctrination, but on the concrete policies undertaken by the regime to solve the basic and pressing problems facing Iranian society today—of which education is certainly one.

Sources

PRIVATE AND PUBLIC ARCHIVES

Daneshgah-e Tehran, Ketabkhane-ye Markazi (Tehran University's Central Library), manuscript section, Tehran.
Daneshgah-e Tehran, Mo'assese-ye Tahqiqat-e Ejtema'i (Tehran University's Institute for Social Research), Tehran.
Dowlat-e Shahanshahi-ye Iran, Darbar-e Shahanshahi, Markaz-e Asnad va Madarek (Court Ministry's Documentation Center), Tehran.
Dowlat-e Shahanshahi-ye Iran, Darbar-e Shahanshahi, Sazeman-e Shahanshahi Bazresi Amuzesh-e 'Ali va Pezhuhesh-e 'Ilmi (The Royal Institute for Research on Education), Tehran.
Dowlat-e Shahanshahi-ye Iran, Vezarat-e Ettela'at, Markaz-e Asnad (Ministry of Information's Documentation Center), Tehran.
Dowlat-e Shahanshahi-ye Iran, Vezarat-e 'Ulum va Amuzesh-e 'Ali, Mo'assese-ye Tahqiqat va Barname Rizi 'Ilmi va Amuzeshi (Ministry of Science's Institute for Research and Planning in Science and Education), Tehran.
'Isa Sadiq, private papers.
Ketabkhane-ye Majlis-e Shura-ye Melli (the Majlis Library), manuscript section, Tehran.
Public Record Office, London.

OFFICIAL REPORTS, SURVEYS, AND PUBLICATIONS

The Royal Institute for Research on Education (SSHBA)

Ahval-e Shakhsi-ye Davtalaban-e Tahsilat-e 'Ali: Barresi Moshakhkhasat-e Fardi va Khanevadegi, 1351. Tehran, 1352 [1973/4].
Ahval-e Shakhsi-ye Davtalaban-e Tahsilat-e 'Ali: Emtehanat-e Sarasari, Tir 1352. Tehran, 1352 [1973/4].

329

Ara'-ye A'za'-ye Hey'at-e 'Ilmi dar bare-ye Ejra'-ye Moqarrarat-e Khedmat-e Tamam-Vaqt dar Daneshgahha. Tehran, 1353 [1974/5].

Arzyabi-ye Gostaresh-e Amuzesh-e 'Ali-ye Iran. Ed. Mohammad Taqi Tayyeb. Tehran, 1353 [1974/5].

Atharat-e Moqarrarat-e Khedmat-e Tamam-Vaqt dar Daneshgahha va Mo'assesat-e Amuzesh-e 'Ali. Tehran, 1353 [1974/5].

Barresi Amuzesh-e Fanni va Herfe'i dar Sath-e Teknisyan. Ed. 'Ali Akbar Shirtavane'i. Tehran, 1352 [1973/4].

Barresi Raveshha-ye Emtehanat-e Entekhab-e Daneshju dar Mo'assesat-e Amuzesh-e 'Ali, Sal-e Tahsili 1351/2. Ed. Morteza Nasafat and Parviz Razedan. Tehran, 1352 [1973/4].

Ejra'-ye Firman-e Amuzesh-e Raygan dar Daneshgahha va Mo'assesat-e Amuzesh-e 'Ali, 1353/4. Ed. Hushang Ranku and Parviz Razedan. Tehran, 1353 [1974/5].

E'tebar-e Emtehan-e Entekhab-e Daneshju. Vol. 1: Tahlil Nomarat-e Tahsilat-e Dabirestani va Emtehanat-e Vorudi va Rabete-ye An. Ed. Morteza Nasafat. Tehran, 1351 [1972/3].

Gozaresh be Pishgah-e Mobarak-e A'lahazrat . . . Dar Hashtomin Konferans-e Enqelab-e Amuzeshi. Ramsar, 1975. (Report presented by Mohammad Baheri.)

Gozaresh Taqdimi be Pishgah-e Homayun Shahanshah Aryamehr. Tehran, 1974.

Hey'at-e 'Ilmi-ye Daneshgahha va Mo'assesat-e Amuzesh-e 'Ali-ye Iran. Ed. Mahmud Qanadan. Tehran, 1354 [1975/6].

Moshakhkhasat-e Amari Barnameha-ye Amuzeshi dar Daneshgahha va Mo'assesat-e Amuzesh-e 'Ali-ye Iran. Tehran, 1353 [1974/5].

Omur-e Daneshju'i, 1352/3. Ed. Mohammad Hasan Sarmadi. Tehran, 1353 [1974].

Omur-e Daneshju'i, 1353/4. Ed. 'Ali Asghar Shirtavane'i. Tehran, 1354 [1975].

Tahavvol-e Amuzesh-e 'Ali-ye Iran, 1353/4. Tehran, 1354 [1975/6].

Tashkil Jalasat-e Dars dar Daneshgahha va Mo'assesat-e Amuzesh-e 'Ali: Sal-e Tahsili 1353/4. Tehran, 1353 [1974/5].

Tasvir-e Amuzesh-e 'Ali-ye Iran, 1353/4. Tehran, 1353 [1974/5].

The Ministry of Science

Daftar-e Konferans-e Enqelab-e Amuzeshi. Chaharomin Konferans-e Arzyabi-ye Enqelab-e Amuzeshi, Ramsar 1350 [1971/2]. Tehran, 1971.

——. Dovvomin Konferans-e Arzyabi-ye Enqelab-e Amuzeshi, 1348 [1969/70]. Tehran, 1969.

——. Haftomin Konferans-e Arzyabi-ye Enqelab-e Amuzeshi, Ramsar 1353 [1974/5]. Tehran, 1974.

——. Hashtomin Konferans-e Arzyabi-ye Enqelab-e Amuzeshi, Ramsar 1354 [1975/6]. Tehran, 1975.

——. Konferans-e Enqelab-e Amuzeshi, Ramsar 1347 [1968/9]. Tehran, 1968.

——. Nohomin Konferans-e Arzyabi-ye Enqelab-e Amuzeshi, Ramsar 2535 [1976/7]. Tehran, 1976.

——. Panjomin Konferans-e Arzyabi-ye Enqelab-e Amuzeshi, Ramsar 1351 [1972/3]. Tehran, 1972.

——. Sevvomin Konferans-e Arzyabi-ye Enqelab-e Amuzeshi, Ramsar 1349 [1970/71]. Tehran, 1970.

——. Sheshomin Konferans-e Arzyabi-ye Enqelab-e Amuzeshi, Ramsar 1352 [1973/4]. Tehran, 1973.

Daftar-e Omur-e Daneshjuyan. *Amar-e Daneshjuyan-e Irani Moqim-e Keshvarha-ye Kharej.* Tehran, 1351 [1972/3].

Mo'assese-ye Tahqiqat va Barname Rizi 'Ilmi va Amuzeshi, (MTBRA). *Amar Amuzesh-e 'Ali-ye Iran.* 7 vols. Tehran, 1971–1977. (Published yearly between 1970 and 1977.)

——. *Amar-e Amuzesh-e 'Ali-ye Iran dar Panjah Sal-e Shahanshahi-ye Pahlavi.* Tehran, 1977.

——. *Barresi Amari dar Mowred-e A'za'-ye Hey'at-e Amuzeshi va Pezhuheshi-ye Danshgahha.* Ed. 'Ali Akbar Bayhaqi. Tehran, 1974.

——. *Gozaresh-e Moqaddamati Amuzesh-e 'Ali-ye Keshavarzi dar Iran.* Tehran, 1971.

——. *Rabete Sanaye' ba Mo'assesat-e Amuzesh-e 'Ali-ye Fanni.* Ed. Afshan Hassam-Vaziri. Tehran, 1972.

——. *Siyasat-e 'Ilmi va Nowsazi-ye Ejtema'i.* Ed. 'Ali Barzegar. Tehran, 1976.

——. *Tasviri az Tarkib-e Daneshjuyan . . . Sal-e Tahsili 1348/9 [1969/70].* Tehran, 1971.

The Plan and Budget Organization (SBB)

Barname-ye 'Omrani-ye Chaharom-e Keshvar—1347–1352 [1968–1973]. Tehran, 1968.

Barname-ye 'Omrani-ye Sevvom-e Keshvar—1342–1347 [1963–1968]. Tehran, 1963.

Bayan-e Amari-ye Tahavvolat-e Ejtema'i va Eqtesadi-ye Iran dar Dowran-e . . . Pahlavi. Tehran: Markaz-e Amar, 2535 [1976/7].

Degarguniha-ye Ejtema'i va Eqtesadi-ye Zanan dar Iran. Tehran, 1973.

The Fourth National Development Plan. Tehran, 1968.

Gozaresh-e Barresi-ye Khastha-ye Shoghli Honarjuyan va Daneshmandan-e Madares-e Fanni va Harfe'i-ye Keshvar. Tehran, 1976.

Gozaresh-e Ejra'i-ye Barname-ye Haft Sale-ye Dovvom. Tehran, 1964.

Iran's Fifth Development Plan: 1973–1978. Tehran, 1975.

Pish-Bini-ye Deraz Modat-e Eshteghal. Tehran, 1975.

Tarikhche-ye nim Qarn-e Akhir. Ed. Homayun Khaje-Nuri. Tehran, 1345 [1966/7].

Tehran University

Daftar-e Motale'at-e Amuzeshi. *Barresi Vaz'-e Daneshjuyan va Faregh al-Tahsilan.* Tehran, 1973.

Mo'assese-ye Motale'at va Tahqiqat-e Ejtema'i (MTE). *Barresi Mavad-e Darsi va Rabete-ye An ba Niyazha-ye Shoghli va 'Amali Nowamuzan Kelasha-ye Ta'lim Tavam ba Herfe.* Ed. Hoseyn Adibi. Tehran, 1973.

——. *Barresi Naqsh va Athar Tahsilkardegan-e Kharej az Keshvar dar Jame'e-ye Iran.* Ed. Hoseyn Moradi-Nezhad and Parviz Pazhum-Shari'ati. Tehran, 1974.

——. *Barresi Tahavvolat-e Amuzesh va Parvaresh-e Iran.* Ed. 'Abbas Khaqani. Tehran 1973.

——. *Masa'el Marbut be Amuzesh-e Motavasete dar Iran.* Ed. Morteza Kotubi. Tehran, 1969.

——. *Nemayandegan-e Majlis-e Shura-ye Melli dar 21 Dowre-ye Qanungodhari: Motale'e az Nazar-e Jame'e-Shenasi Siyasi.* Ed. Zahra Shaji'i. Tehran, 1965.

——. *Savad Amuzi va Atharat-e Eqtesadi va Ejtema'i An . . .* Ed. Kazem Izadi. Tehran, 1972.

——. *Vezarat va Vaziran dar Iran.* Ed. Zahra Shaji'i. Tehran, 1976.

Mo'assese Tahqiqat-e Ravanshenasi. *Sanjesh Afkar-e Daneshjuyan-e Keshvar.* Ed. Morteza Nasafat. Tehran, 1354 [1975/6].

Vahed-e Barname Rizi. *Barresi Nemune'i Moshakhkhasat-e Fardi va Khanevadegi-ye Da-neshjuyan*. Tehran, 1974.

——. *Gozaresh Marbut be Davtalaban va Padhirofte-shodegan Daneshgah-e Tehran 1351/2*. Tehran, 1973. (Similar studies were published in other years as well.)

——. *Shenakht Amari A'za'-ye Hey'at-e 'Ilmi*. Tehran, 1354 [1975/6].

——. *Shenakht Amari Daneshjuyan*. Tehran, 1353 [1974/5].

Other Iranian Institutions

Daneshgah-e Azad-e Iran. *Daneshgah-e Azad-e Iran: Rah-e Now dar Amuzesh-e 'Ali*. Tehran, 1974.

Daneshgah-e Gondi Shapur. *Amuzesh dar Iran az 'Ahd-e Bastan ta Emruz*. Ahvaz, 1350 [1971/2].

Daneshga-e Pahlavi. *Daneshgah-e Pahlavi dar Chahar Sal-e Godhashte: 1342–1346 [1963/4–1967/8]*. Shiraz, 1967.

——. *Daneshgah-e Pahlavi dar Nakhostin Dahe-ye Enqelab*. Shiraz. 1973.

——. *Gozaresh Bara-ye Chaharomin Konferans-e Enqelab-e Amuzeshi*. Shiraz, 1971.

——. *Majmu'e A'innameha, Asasnameha va Moqarrarat-e Daneshgah-e Pahlavi*. Shiraz, 1971.

Daneshgah-e Tarbiyyat-e Mo'allem. *Seyr-e Tarikhi va Tahavvolat-e Daneshgah-e Tar-biyyat-e Mo'allem az 1298 ta 1353*. Tehran, 1975.

Majlis-e Shura-ye Melli. *Majmu'e-ye Qavanin*. Tehran, 1907–1974.

——. *Modhakerat-e Majlis-e Shura-ye Melli*. Tehran, 1907–1975.

Mo'assese-ye Pezhuheshha-ye Siyasi va Eqtesadi Beynolmellali. *Tajziye va Tahlil az Ayande-ye Eqtesadi-ye Iran*. Tehran, 1974.

Sazeman-e Barname va Vezarat-e Kar. *Barresi Manabe' va Ehtiyajat-e Niru-ye Ensani dar Iran*. Tehran, 1975.

——. *Nata'ej Amargiri-ye Niru-ye Ensani—1351*. Tehran, 1972.

Sazeman-e Omur-e Edari va Estekhdami-ye Keshvar. *Nata'ej Ejra'-ye Tarh-e Shena-sa'i-ye Vizhegiha-ye Mostakhdemin-e Dowlat dar Koll-e Keshvar*. Tehran, 1354 [1975/6].

——. *Tarh-e Tabaqe-Bandi va Arzeshyabi-ye Mashaghel*. Tehran, 1352 [1973/4].

Vezarat-e Amuzesh va Parvaresh. *Amar Amuzesh va Parvaresh, 1352*. Tehran, 1974.

——. *Dowre-ye Rahnama'i-ye Tahsili: 'Ellal va Jehat-e Ejra'-ye An*. Tehran, 1970.

——. *Education in the Islamic Republic of Iran: Now and in the Future*. Tehran, 1990.

——. *Gozaresh Mostanad dar Bare-ye Amuzesh va Parvaresh*. Tehran, n.d.

Vezarat-e Darbar. *Reza Shah Pahlavi: Safarname-ye Mazanderan*. Tehran, 1976.

Vezarat-e Ma'aref va Awqaf. *Salname-ye Ehsa'i 1311/2*. Tehran, 1933(?).

——. *Salname-ye Ehsa'i 1314/5*. Tehran, 1936(?).

International Organizations

International Labor Organization (ILO). *Employment and Income Policies of Iran*. Lau-sanne, 1973.

Organization for Economic Co-operation and Development. *Policy Conference on Economic Co-operation and Development: Summary Report*. Washington, D.C., 1961.

Overseas Consultants, Inc. *Report on Seven-Year Development Plan for the Plan Or-ganization of the Imperial Government of Iran*. New York, 1949.

UNESCO. *Compulsory Education in the Arab World*. Paris, 1954.

——. *Economic and Social Aspects of Educational Planning.* Paris, 1969.
——. *Iran: Science Policy and Organization.* Ed. Harry Melville. Paris, 1969.
——. *Structures d'Organization du Ministere de la Science et de l'Ensignement Superieur.* Ed. J. Defay and J. Spacy. Paris, 1969.

MAJOR PERIODICALS AND NEWSPAPERS

Dailies and Weeklies (all published in Tehran)

Ayandegan	*Khandaniha*
Behnam	*Peygham-e Emruz*
Echo of Iran	*Seda-ye Mardom*
Ettehad-e Melli	*Rastakhiz* (a weekly published in the 1920s)
Ettela'at	*Rastakhiz* (a daily published in 1975–1979)
Jomhuriye Islami	*Shafaq-e Sorkh*
Kayhan	*Tehran Journal*
Kayhan International	

Periodicals (all published in Tehran)

Amuzesh va Parvaresh (a quarterly of the Ministry of Education; see also *Ta'lim va Tarbiyyat*)
Armaghan
Ayande
Donya
Majale Daneshkade-ye Adabiyyat va 'Ulum-e Ensani (a quarterly published by the Faculty of Humanities of Tehran University)
Majale 'Ulum Ejtema'i (a quarterly published by the Faculty of Social Science of Tehran University)
Mehr
Nashriye Daneshkade-ye 'Ulum Tarbiyyati (a quarterly published by the School of Education of Tehran University)
Sokhan
Ta'lim va Tarbiyyat (a quarterly published by the Ministry of Education; since 1937 it has been published under the title *Amuzesh va Parvaresh*)
Yaghma

BOOKS AND ARTICLES

In Persian

Abadi, 'Ali. "Ta'limat-e 'Aliye va Rah-e Eslah-e An." *AP*, 1328 [1949/50], 3:6–11.
Adamiyyat, Fereydun. *Amir Kabir va Iran.* 2nd ed., Tehran: Amir Kabir, 1334 [1955/6].
——. *Andishe-ye Taraqqi va Hokumat-e Qanun 'Asr-e Sepahsalar.* Tehran: Kharazmi, 1351 [1972/3].

———. *Fekr-e Azadi va Moqaddame-ye Nehzat-e Mashrutiyyat.* Tehran: Sokhan, 1340 [1961/2].

———. *Ideolozhi-ye Nehzat-e Mashrutiyyat-e Iran.* Tehran: Payam, 2535 [1976/7].

Adamiyyat, Fereydun, and Homa Nateq, eds. *Afkar-e Ejtema'i va Siyasi va Eqtesadi dar Athar-e Montasher-Nashode-ye Dowran-e Qajar.* Tehran: Agah, 1977.

Afshar, Iraj. "Talebov." *Yaghma,* 4:214–21.

Akbar-Niya, 'Ali. *Tarikh-e Siyasi va Diplomasi-ye Iran.* Tehran: Daneshgah-e Tehran, 1969/70.

'Alame, Ma'sume. "Lozum Taqviyyat-e Faza'el-e Akhlaqi dar Madares." *AP,* 1330 [1951/2], 4:30–32.

Alan, T. B. "Barresi dar Bare-ye Amuzesh va Parvaresh-e Rusta'i." *AP,* 1323 [1944/ 5], 205–11, 271–75, 319–24.

'Ameri, 'Ali Mohammad. "Shakhsiyyat-e Mo'allem." *AP,* 1319 [1940/1], 6–7:33–43.

Ardekani, Hoseyn Mahbubi. "Dovvomin Karavan-e Ma'arefat." *Yaghma,* 1344 [1965/ 6], 10:592–98.

Badi'i, Rabi'. "Tarbiyyat va Tahiyye Mo'allem." *AP,* 1323 [1944/5], 156–58.

Badr, Mirza Ahmad Khan Basir al-Dowla. "Ta'lim Gheyr az Tarbiyyat Ast." *TT,* 1304 [1925/6], 8–9:12–13; 10:8–10; 11–12:8–12.

Bahar, Mohammad Taqi. *Tarikh-e Mokhtasar-e Ahzab-e Siyasi-ye Iran: Enqeraz-e Qajariye.* Tehran, 1942.

Bamdad, Mehdi. *Sharh-e Hal-e Rejal-e Iran dar Qorun-e 12–14 Hejri.* Tehran: Navar, 1347 [1968/9].

Baradaran, 'Amele. "'Ilm va Ma'refat va Ahmiyyat-e an dar Zendegi." *AP,* 1323 [1944/5], 10:512–14.

Bayani, [Khanbaba]. "Daneshgah-e Tabriz." *AP,* 1327 [1948/9], 7:21–34.

Bizhan, A. *Cheshmandaz Tarbiyyat dar Iran qabl az Islam.* Tehran, 1963.

Dashti, 'A. "Andishe'i dar Atraf-e Ta'limat-e Ejbari." *Mehr,* 1312 [1933/4], 930– 36.

Derakhshesh, Mohammad. "Aya Tahsilat-e Dabirestani va Daneshgahi Bayad Hamegani Bashad?" *AP,* 1332 [1953/4], 9:10–13.

Donboli, 'Abd al-Razeq. *Ma'aser Soltaniye.* Tabriz, 1241q [1825/6].

Dowlatabadi, Hajj Mirza Yahya. *Tarikh-e Mo'aser ya Hayat-e Yahya.* Tehran: Ibn Sina, 1336 [1957/8].

Eqbal, 'Abbas. "E'zam Mohsel be Paris." *TT,* 1305 [1926/7], 5:229–38.

———. *Mirza Taqi Khan Amir Kabir.* Tehran, 1340 [1961/2].

Esfahani, Mirza Abu-Taleb Khan ibn Mohammad. *Masir Talebi ya Safarname-ye Mirza Abu-Taleb Khan.* [Better Known as *Masir Talebi fi Bilad al-Faranji*]. Tehran: Ketabhaye Jibi, 1352 [1973/4].

Estronach [Stronach] A. "Ta'limat-e Fanni." *TT,* 1304 [1925/6], 1:8–12.

E'temad al-Saltane. *Khalase.* Ed. Mahmud Katira'i. Tehran: Tahuri, 1969.

Farhudi, Hoseyn. "Amuzesh-e Salmandan: Mobareze ba bi-Savadi." *AP,* 1318 [1939/ 40], 9–10:17–28.

Fashahi, Mohammad Reza. *Gozaresh-e Kutah-e Tahavvolat-e Fekri va Ejtema'i dar Jame'e-ye Feodali-ye Iran.* Tehran, 1976.

Fayyaz-Bakhsh, Mohammad 'Ali. *Amuzesh va Parvaresh.* Social science textbook for ninth grade (edition of 1985/6), 41–56. Tehran, 1364 [1985/6].

Hadad 'Adel, Gholam 'Ali. "Masa'el-e 'Omumi-ye Amuzesh va Parvaresh." Social science textbook for twelfth grade (edition of 1986/7), 145–203. Tehran, 1365 [1986/7].

Hedayat, Mehdi Qoli. *Khaterat va Khatarat*. Tehran: Rangin, 1329 [1950/51].

Hedayat, Reza Qoli Khan. *Rowzat al-Safa'-ye Naseri*. Tehran, 1339 [1960/61].

Hekmat, 'Ali Asghar. "Farhang." In *Iranshahr*, 2:1165–1242. Tehran: Daneshgah-e Tehran, 1342 [1963/4].

——. *Si Khatere az 'Asr-e Farakhande-ye Pahlavi*. Tehran: Pars, 1976.

——. "Ta'limat-e 'Aliye." *TT*, 1315 [1936/7], 249–60.

Hekmat, 'Ali Reza. *Amuzesh va Parvaresh dar Iran Bastan*. Tehran: MTBRA, 1972.

Hess, André, "Raport-e Monsiur André Hess dar bab-e Tashkilat-e Ta'lim dar Iran." *TT*, 1304 [1925/6], 2:10–12.

Jaza'eri, 'Abd al-Latif [Musavi Shostari]. *Tufat al-'Alam*. Bombay, 1846.

Kasravi, Seyyed Ahmad. "Bayad az Gozashte Anche Nik ast Bardasht va Anche Bad ast Baz Godhasht." *AP*, 1313 [1934/5], 136–38.

Kermani, Nazem al-Islam. *Tarikh Bidari-ye Iraniyan*. Tehran: Bonyad-e Farhang, 1346 [1967/8].

Khanlari, Parviz. "Hal va Ayande-ye Farhanq-e ma." *AP*, 1341 [1962/3], 12:14–16.

Khomeyni, Ayatollah al-Musavi al-. *Al-Hukuma al-Islamiyya*. Beirut, 1970.

Makki, Hoseyn. *Zendegani-ye Mirza Taqi Khan, Amir Kabir*. Tehran: 'Ilmi, 1958.

Malekzade, Mehdi. *Tarikh-e Enqelab-e Mashrutiyyat-e Iran*. Tehran, 1327 [1948/9].

Malkom Khan, Nazem al-Dowla. *Kolliyyat-e Malkom*. Tehran, 1907.

Maraghe'i, Zayn al-'Abedin. *Siyahat Name-ye Ebrahim Beg*. Cairo: n.d.

Masha'ekhi, Mohammad. "Ba'zi az Masa'el va Moshkelat-e Javanan-e Iran dar Dowre-ye Motavasete." *AP*, 1348 [1969/70], 8:1–5.

——. "Hadaf-e Ta'limat-e Ejtema'i." *AP*, 1335 [1956/7], 792–94.

——. Hadaf-e Ta'limat-e Motavasete dar Iran." *AP*, 1343 [1964/5], 9:1–17.

——. "Mafhum-e Amuzesh-e Motavasete." *Nashriye Daneshkade-ye 'Ulum Tarbiyyati*, 3 (Winter 1973), 6–11.

——. "Manzur az Tajdid Nazar dar Barname-ye Dowre-ye Avval-e Dabirestanha Che Bude Ast?" *AP*, 1335 [1956/7], 771–75.

M[atini], J[alal]. "Ketabha-ye Darsi dar Jomhuri-ye Islami-ye Iran." *Iran-Nameh*, 3 (Fall 1984), 1–25.

Minovi, Mojtabi. "Avvalin Karavan-e Ma'refat." *Yaghma*, 1332 [1953/4], 4:181–85, 231–32, 274–78, 314–18.

Mostowfi, 'Abdollah. *Sharh-e Zendegani-ye man, ya Tarikh-e Ejtema'i va Edari Dowre-ye Qajariye*. Tehran: Tehran Mosavvar, n.d.

Na'ini, Hajj Pirzade. *Safarname*. Tehran, 1343 [1964/5].

Nateq, Homa. *Qanun*. Tehran: Amir Kabir, 2535 [1976/7].

Nura'i, Fereshte. *Tahqiq dar Bare-ye Afkar-e Mirza Malkom Khan, Nazem al-Dowla*. Tehran: Ketabha-ye Jibi, 1352 [1973/4].

Nuri, Yahya. *Hoquq-e Zan dar Islam va Jehan*. Tehran, 1353 [1974/5].

Pahlavi, Mohammad Reza [Shah]. *Majmu'e-ye Ta'lifat, Notqha, Payamha, Mosahebeha va Bayanat . . . Mohammad Reza Shah*. 10 vols. Tehran: Vezarat-e Darbar, 1975–1977.

——. *Tamaddon-e Bozorg*. Tehran: Ketabkhane-ye Pahlavi, 2536 [1977/8].

Qasemi, Ahmad. "Moshkel-e Ta'limat-e Motavasete-ra Chegune Bayad Hal Kard?" *AP*, 1344 [1965/6], 50–57.

Rahnama, Majid. *Amuzesh dar Khedmat-e Ensan*. Tehran: Amir Kabir, 1971(?).

Rasekh, Shapur. *Ta'lim va Tarbiyyat dar Jehan-e Emruz*. Tehran: Amir Kabir, 1970.

Sadiq, 'Isa. *Chehel Goftar*. Tehran: Dehkhoda, 1352 [1973/4].

——. "Sahltarin Rah-e Ejra'-ye Ta'limat-e Ebteda'i, 'Omumi va Ejbarti Chist?" *Mehr*, 1312 [1933/4], 561–67.

——. *Tarikh-e Farhang-e Iran*. 7th ed. Tehran: Daneshgah-e Tehran, 1976.

——. "Vaza'ef-e Jadid Nesbat be Ta'lim va Tarbiyyat-e Dokhtaran." *Mehr*, 1304 [1925/6], 973–76.

——. *Yadegar-e 'Omr*. Tehran: Maravi, 1974.

Safa, Dhabihollah. "'Ilm." In *Iranshahr*, 1:695–713. Tehran: Daneshgah-e Tehran, 1342 [1963/4].

——. "Madrese." In *Iranshahr*, 1:714–44. Tehran: Daneshgah-e Tehran, 1342 [1963/4].

Saltikov-Shchedrin, Aleksey. *Safar dar Iran*. Tehran, 1957.

Sasani, Malek Khan. *Siyasatgaran-e Dowre-ye Qajar*. Tehran, 1338 [1959/60].

Sayyah, [Mahalati]. *Khaterat-e Hajj Sayyah*. Tehran: Ibn Sina, 1346 [1967/8].

Shajare, M. "Ravesh Novin dar Tarbiyyat-e Emruz." *Mehr*, 1315 [1936/7], 5:38–40.

Sharifi, Hadi. "Hadaf va Falsafe-ye Amuzesh-e Motavasete." *Nashriye Daneshkade-ye 'Ulum-e Tarbiyyati*, 3 (Winter 1973), 13–24.

Shirazi, Abu al-Hasan [Ilchi]. *Safarname*. Ed. Mohammad Shahrestani. Tehran: Razun, 1347 [1968/9].

Shuqi, 'Abbas. "Chera be Madrese Miravim?" *AP*, 1323 [1944/5], 65–67.

Siyasi, 'Ali Akbar. *Do Mah dar Paris*. Tehran: Daneshgah-e Tehran, 1950.

Suratgar, Lotf'ali. "Ahmiyyat-e Amuzesh va Parvaresh-e 'Omumi va Ejbari." *AP*, 1322 [1943/4], 1–3:1–10.

Tabataba'i, Mohit. *Majmu'e Athar-e Mirza Malkom Khan*. Tehran: Danesh, 1327 [1948/9].

Talebov [Talebzade], Mirza 'Abd al-Rahim Tabrizi. *Azadi va Siyasat*. Tehran: Sahar, 1357 [1978/9].

——. *Ketab-e Ahmad*. Istanbul, 1311 [1895/6].

——. *Masa'el al-Hayat*. Tiflis, 1324 [1908/9].

——. *Masalek al-Mohsenin*. Cairo, 1323 [1907/8].

Taqizade, Hasan. *Maqalat*. Vol. 3: *Zaban va Farhang, Ta'lim va Tarbiyyat*. Tehran: Opset, 1351 [1972/3].

—— "Mavad Mofide dar Ta'lim va Tarbiyyat 'Omumi: Che Chizha be Vasile Madares-e Ebteda'i va Ta'limat-e Ejbari Bayad . . . Amukht?" *AP*, 1313 [1934/5], 585–89.

——. "Roshd-e Ejtema'i va Vasa'el-e Hosul-e an dar Mamlekat-e ma." *TT*, 1306 [1927/8], 372–88.

——. *Tarikh Ava'el-e Enqelab-e Mashrutiyyat*. Tehran, 1328 [1949/50].

Vadi'i, Kazem. "Enqelab-e Keyfi dar Amuzesh va Parvaresh-e Iran." *AP*, 1354 [1975/6], 1–6.

——. "Nezam-e Jadid-e Amuzesh-e Motavasete-ye Iran." *AP*, 1354 [1975/6], 7–33.

——. "'Obur az Bohran-e Matbu' Amuzesh va Parvaresh." *AP*, 1354 [1975/6], 34–40.

Vahid, A. "'Ulum va Awqaf." *Armaghan*, 1305 [1926/7], 273–82.

Yasemi, Rashid. "Daneshju'i." *TT*, 1315 [1936/7], 781–91.

——. "Talebov va Ketab-e Ahmad." In *Iranshahr*, 2:283–97.

Zel al-Soltan. *Tarikh-e Godhashte-ye Mas'udi*. Tehran, 1907.

In Other Languages

Abrahamian, Ervand. *Iran: Between Two Revolutions*. Princeton: Princeton University Press, 1982.

Adams, Don, ed. *Education and National Development*. London: Routledge and Kegan, 1971.

Adams, Don, and Robert M. Bjork. *Education in Developing Areas*. New York: McKay, 1969.

Akhavi, Shahrough. *Religion and Politics in Contemporary Iran: Clergy-State Relations in the Pahlavi Period*. New York: SUNY Press, 1980.

Alaghmand, Ali. "The Public School Teacher in Iran: Social Origin, Status and Orientation." Ph.d. diss., Southern Illinois University, 1973.

Al-e Ahmad, Jalal. *Plagued by the West [Gharbzadegi]*. Trans. Paul Sprachman. Delmar, N.Y.: Caravan Books, 1982.

Algar, Hamid. *Mirza Malkum Khan: A Study in the History of Iranian Modernism*. Berkeley: University of California Press, 1973.

———. *Religion and State in Iran: 1789–1906*. Berkeley: University of California Press, 1969.

Arasteh, Reza. *Education and Social Awakening in Iran, 1850–1968*. 2d ed. Leiden: Brill, 1968.

Arfa, Hasan. *Under Five Shahs*. London: John Murray, 1966.

Assad Bey, Mohammad. *Reza Shah*. London: Hutchinson, 1938.

Avery, Peter. "Iran: A Culture Challenged." *Contemporary Review*, 233 (November and December 1978), 243–49, 298–303.

Bakhash, Shaul. *Iran: Monarchy, Bureaucracy and Reform under the Qajars: 1858–1896*. London: Ithaca Press, 1978.

Baldwin, George B. *Planning and Development in Iran*. Baltimore: Johns Hopkins University Press, 1967.

Banani, Amin. *The Modernization of Iran: 1921–1941*. Stanford: Stanford University Press, 1961.

Bartsch, William H. "The Industrial Labour Force of Iran: Problems of Recruitment, Training and Productivity." *MEJ*, 25 (Winter 1971), 15–30.

Bayat-Philipp, Mangol. *Mysticism and Dissent: Socioreligious Thought in Qajar Iran*. Syracuse: Syracuse University Press, 1982.

Bayne, E. A. *Persian Kingship in Transition*. New York: American Universities Field Staff, 1968.

Beck, Lois, and Nikki Keddie, eds. *Women in the Muslim World*. Cambridge: Harvard University Press, 1979.

Ben-David, Joseph, and Abraham Zloczower. "Universities and Academic Systems in Modern Societies." *European Journal of Sociology*, 3 (1962), 45–84.

Berger, Morroe. "The Middle Class in the Arab World." In Walter Z. Laqueur, ed., *The Middle East in Transition: Studies in Contemporary History*. New York: Praeger, 1968.

Berkes, Niyazi. *The Development of Secularism in Turkey*. Montreal: McGill, 1964.

Bharier, Julian. *Economic Development in Iran, 1900–1970*. London: Oxford University Press, 1971.

Bill, James A. "Class Analysis and Dialectics of Modernization in the Middle East." *IJMES*, 3 (1972), 417–34.

———. *The Politics of Iran: Groups, Classes, and Modernization*. Columbus: Merrill, 1972.

Binder, Leonard. *Iran: Political Development in Changing Society*. Los Angeles: University of California Press, 1962.

———. "National Integration and Political Development." *American Political Science Review*, 38 (September 1964), 622–31.

Blau, Peter M. and Otis D. Duncan. *The American Occupational Structure*. New York: Wiley, 1967.

Bosworth, Edmond, and Carol Hilleband, eds. *Qajar Iran: Political, Social and Cultural Change: 1800–1925*. Edinburgh: Edinburgh University Press, 1983.

Boudon, Raymond. *Education, Opportunity and Social Inequality*. New York: Wiley, 1974.

Bowles, Samuel, and Herbert Gintis. *Schooling in Capitalist America*. New York: Basic Books, 1976.

Brembeck, S. Cole, and Marvin Grandstaff, eds. *Social Foundation of Education*. New York: Wiley, 1969.

Browne, Edward G. *A History of Persian Literature in Modern Times*. Cambridge: Cambridge University Press, 1924.

———. *The Persian Revolution of 1905–9*. London: Frank Cass, 1966.

———. *The Press and Poetry of Modern Persia*. Cambridge: Cambridge University Press, 1914.

———. *A Year amongst the Persians*. London: Adam and Black, 1893.

Byrne, David, Bill Williamson, and Barbara Fletcher. *The Poverty of Education: A Study in the Politics of Opportunity*. London: Robertson, 1975.

Carnoy, Martin. *Education as Cultural Imperialism*. New York: McKay, 1974.

Carnoy, Martin, and Henry M. Levin, eds. *The Limits of Educational Reforms*. New York: McKay, 1976.

Clark, Berton. *Educating the Expert Society*. San Francisco: Chandler, 1962.

Coleman, James S., ed. *Education and Political Development*. Princeton: Princeton University Press, 1965.

Coleman, James S., et al. *Equality of Educational Opportunity*. Washington D.C.: Government Printing Office, 1966.

Collins, Rendall. "Functional and Conflict Theories of Educational Stratification." *American Sociological Review*, 36 (December 1971), 1002–19.

———. "Where the Functional Requirement of Employment Highest?" *Sociology of Education*, 47 (Fall 1974), 419–42.

Conant, James B. *Education and Liberty: The Role of the Schools in a Modern Democracy*. Cambridge: Harvard University Press, 1953.

Cottam, Richard W. *Nationalism in Iran*. Pittsburgh: University of Pittsburgh Press, 1964.

Curzon, George N. *Persia and the Persian Question*. London: Longman, 1892.

Dahrendorf, Ralph. *Class and Class Conflict*. Stanford: Stanford University Press, 1959.

Dekmejian, Hrair. *Patterns of Political Leadership: Egypt, Israel, Lebanon*. Albany: SUNY Press, 1975.

Deutch, K. "Social Mobilization and Political development." *American Political Science Review*, 55 (September 1961), 463–515.

Easton, D. "Function of Formal Education in Political System." *School Review*, 65 (1957), 304–16.

Eisenstadt, S. N., ed. *Readings in Social Evolution and Development*. London: Pergamon, 1966.

Entessar, Nader. "Educational Reforms in Iran: Cultural Revolution or anti-Intellectualism?" *Journal of South Asian and Middle Eastern Studies*, 8 (Fall 1984), 47–64.

Etzioni, A., and E. Etzioni, eds. *Social Change: Sources, Patterns and Consequences*. New York: Basic Books, 1964.

Farman Farmayan, Hafez. "The Forces of Modernization in Nineteenth Century Iran: A Historical Survey." In William Polk and Richard Chambers, eds., *Beginning of Modernization in the Middle East: The Nineteenth Century*, 115–51. Chicago: University of Chicago Press, 1968.

Farrokh-Pars, M. H. "The Budgets of Iran, 1930–1959: An Analysis of Their Financial and Economic Impact." Ph.d. diss., New York University, 1960.

Fischer, Joseph, ed. *The Social Sciences and the Comparative Study of Educational Systems.* Scranton: International Textbooks, 1970.

Fischer, Michael M. J. *Iran: From Religious Dispute to Revolution.* Cambridge: Harvard University Press, 1980.

Fischer, Sydney N., ed. *Social Forces in the Middle East.* New York: Cornell University Press, 1955.

Flexner, A. *Universities: American, English, German.* New York: Cornell University Press, 1955.

Floud, Jean, A. H. Halsey, and F. M. Merton. *Social Class and Educational Opportunity.* London: Heinemann, 1956.

Frey, Frederick. *The Turkish Political Elite.* Cambridge: MIT Press, 1965.

Garoussian (Riazi-Dawoudi), Vida. "The Ulema and Secularization in Contemporary Iran." Ph.d. diss., Southern Illinois University, 1974.

Gehrke, Ulrich. "Univesitaten und Hohere Lehranstalten: Iran in de Amtlichen Statistic." *Orient*, 3 (June 1971), 83–89.

Gobineau, Joseph Arthur de. *Religion et philosophies dans l'Asie central.* Paris: Gallimard, 1933.

Golnar, Mehran. "Socialization of Schoolchildren in the Islamic Republic of Iran." *Iranian Studies*, 22, no. 1 (1989), 35–50.

Green, Jerrold D. "Pseudo Participation and Countermobilization: Roots of the Iranian Revolution." *Iranian Studies*, 13 (1980), 31–53.

Guthrie, James, et al. *Schools and Inequality.* Cambridge: MIT Press, 1971.

Hairi, Abdul-Hadi. *Shi'ism and Constitutionalism in Iran.* Leiden: Brill, 1977.

Halpern, Manfred. *The Politics of Social Change in the Middle East and North Africa.* Princeton: Princeton University Press, 1963.

Halsey, A. H. "Sociology and the Equality Debate." *Oxford Review of Education*, 1, no. 1 (1975), 9–23.

Hanf, Theodor, Karl A. Amman, et al. "Education—an Obstacle to Development? Reflections on the Political Function of Education in Asia and Africa." *Comparative Education Review*, 19 (February 1975), 68–87.

Hanson, John, and Cole Brembeck. *Education and Development of Nations.* New York, 1966.

Harbison, Frederick, and Charles S. Myeres. *Education, Manpower and Economic Growth.* New York: McGraw-Hill, 1964.

Hayden, Howard. *Higher Education and Development in South-East Asia.* Vol. 1: *Directors' Report.* Paris: UNESCO, 1967.

Heyd, Uriel. "The Ottoman 'Ulama' and Westernization in the Time of Selim III and Mahmud II." In Uriel Heyd, ed., *Studies in Islamic History and Civilization, Scripta Hierosolymitana*, 9:63–96. Jerusalem: Magnes, 1961.

Hourani, Albert. *Arabic Thought in the Liberal Age: 1798–1939.* London: Oxford University Press, 1962.

Hurn, J. Christopher. *The Limits and Possibilities of Schooling: An Introduction to the Sociology of Education.* Boston: Allyn and Bacon, 1978.

Husen, Torsten. *Talent, Equality and Meritocracy.* The Hague: Martinus Nijhoff, 1974.

Hyman, Herbert H. *Political Socialization*. Glencoe: Free Press, 1959.

Jacobs, Norman. *The Sociology of Development: Iran as an Asian Case Study*. New York: Praeger, 1966.

Jacqs, Jane W., ed. *Iran: Past Present and Future*. New York: Aspen Institute, 1976.

Jenckes, Christopher, et al. *Inequality: A Reassessment of the Effect of Family and Schooling in America*. New York: Basic Books, 1972.

Kamshad, H. *Modern Persian Prose Literature*. Cambridge: Cambridge University Press, 1966.

Karabel, Jerome, and A. H. Halsey, eds. *Power and Ideology in Education*. New York: Oxford University Press, 1977.

Karanjia, R. K. *The Mind of a Monarch*. London: Allen and Unwin, 1977.

Katz, Michael. *The Irony of Early School Reform*. Cambridge: Harvard University Press, 1968.

Kazamias, Andreas M. *Education and the Quest for Modernity in Turkey*. Chicago: University of Chicago Press, 1966.

Keddie, Nikki R. "The Iranian Power Structure and Social Change, 1800–1969: An Overview." *IJMES*, 2 (1971), 3–20.

——. "Religion and Irreligion in Early Iranian Nationalism." *Comparative Studies in Society and History*, 4(1962), 265–95.

Keddie, Nikki R., ed. *Scholars, Saints and Sufis: Muslim Religious Institutions in the Middle East since 1500*. Berkeley: University of California Press, 1972.

Kendall, W. L. *Statistics of Education in Developing Countries: An Introduction to Their Collection and Presentation*. Paris: UNESCO, 1968.

Khomeini, Ruhollah. *Islam and Revolution: Writings and Declarations of Imam Khomeini*. Trans. and annotated by Hamid Algar. Berkeley: Mizan, 1981.

Kinnane, Derk. "Iran: Bringing Literacy and Work Skills Together." *Panorama*, 49 (1971), 18–27.

Lambton, Ann K. "The Impact of the West on Persia." *International Affairs*, 33 (January 1957), 12–25.

——. *Qajar Persia*. Austin: University of Texas Press, 1987.

Lasswell, Harold. *Politics: Who Gets What, When, How*. Hightstown: McGraw-Hill, 1939.

Lenczowski, George, ed. *Iran Under the Pahlavis*. Stanford: Hoover Institution, 1978.

——. *Political Elites in the Middle East*. Washington D.C.: American Enterprise, 1975.

Lerner, Daniel. *The Passing of Traditional Society: Modernizing the Middle East*. Glencoe: Free Press, 1958.

Levitas, Murice. *Marxist Perspective in the Sociology of Education*. London: Routledge and Kegan, 1974.

Lipset, S. M. "University Students and Politics in Underdeveloped Countries." *Contemporary Education Review*, 10 (1966), 132–62.

Lorentz, H. John. "Modernization and Political Change in the Nineteenth Century Iran: The Role of Amir Kabir." Ph.d. diss., Princeton University, 1974.

Malcolm, John. *History of Persia*. London: Murray, 1815.

Manzoor, Cyrus, "University Reform in Iran: Problems and Prospects." Ph.d diss., Tufts University, 1971.

Mathehews, Roderic R. and Matta Akrawi. *Education in the Arab Countries of the Near East*. Washington D.C.: American Council of Education, 1949.

Mehran, Ahmad. *Iran und dem Weg zur Diktator-Militarisiezung und Widerstand: 1919–1925*. N.C.: SOAK, 1972.

Menashri, David. *Iran: A Decade of War and Revolution*. New York: Holmes and Meier, 1990.

Merton, Robert K. *Social Theory and Social Structure*. Glencoe: Free Press, 1968.

Meyer, John, and Francisco Ramirez. "The World's Educational Revolution: 1950–70." In J. Meyer and M. Hannan, eds. *National Development and the World System: Educational, Economic and Political Change: 1950–1979*, 37–55. Chicago: University of Chicago Press, 1979.

Michels, Robert. *Political Parties*. New York: Free Press, 1915.

Mills, Wright C. *The Power Elite*. New York: Oxford University Press, 1956.

Millspaugh, Arthur C. *Americans in Iran*. Washington D.C.: Brookings Institution, 1946.

——. *The Financial and Economic Situation of Persia: 1926*. New York, 1926.

Morier, James. *A Journey through Persia, Armenia and Asia Minor*. London, 1812.

——. *A Second Journey through Persia, Armenia and Asia Minor*. London: Longman, 1818.

Mosca, Gaetano. *The Ruling Class*. New York: McGraw-Hill, 1939.

Moser, C. A. *Inequality in Educational Opportunity*. London, 1956.

Myrdal, Gunner. *Asian Drama: A Study into the Poverty of Nations*. Clinton: Penguin, 1968.

Nashat, Guity. *The Origins of Modern Reform in Iran, 1870–1880*. Urbana: University of Illinois Press, 1982.

Pahlavi, Mohammad Reza [Shah]. *Mission for My Country*. London: Hutchinson, 1961.

——. *The White Revolution*. Tehran: Kayhan, 1967(?).

Pareto, Vilfredo. *The Mind and Society*. New York: Harcourt and Brace, 1935.

Parsons, Talcott. "The School Class as a Social System: Some of Its Functions in American Society." *Harvard Educational Review*, 29 (Fall 1959), 297–318.

Parsons, Talcott, and Edward A. Shils. *Toward a General Theory of Action*. Cambridge: Harvard University Press, 1951.

Piemontese, A. "The Status of the Qajar Orders of Knighthood." *East and West*, 19 (September–December 1968), 439–40.

Polak, Jacob E. *Persian: Das Land und seine Bewohner*. Leipzig, 1865.

Quandt, William. *Revolution and Political Leadership: Algeria, 1954–1958*. Cambridge: MIT Press, 1969.

Qubain, Fahim. *Education and Science in the Arab World*. Baltimore: Johns Hopkins University Press, 1966.

Rajaee, Farhang. *Islamic Values and World View: Khomeini on Man, the State and International Politics*. Lanham: University Press of America, 1983.

Ramazani, Ruhollah K. "Iran's 'White Revolution': A Study in Political Development." *IJMES*, 5 (1974), 124–39.

Ramirez, Francisco, and John Boli. "The Political Construction of Mass Schooling: European Origins and Worldwide Institutionalization." *Sociology of Education*, 60 (January 1987), 2–17.

Ronaghy, Hossain, et al. "Physician Migration to the United States: One Country's Transfusion Is Another Country's Hemorrhage." *Journal of the American Medical Association*, 227 (1974), 538–42.

Rosenthal, Franz. *Knowledge Triumphant: The Concept of Knowledge in Medieval Islam*. Leiden: Brill, 1970.

Rypka, Jan, et al. *History of Iranian Literature*. Dordrecht: Reidel, 1968.

Sadiq, Issa Khan. *Modern Persia and Her Educational System*. New York: Columbia University Press, 1931.

Sanghvi, Ramesh. *Aryamehr the Shah of Iran: A Political Biography*. London: Transorient, 1968.

Sanghvi, Ramesh, Clifford German, and David Missen. *The Revolution of the Shah and the People: The Literacy Corps*. London: Transorient, 1967.

Schultz, Theodore. "Investment in Human Capital." *American Economic Review*, 51 (March 1961), 1–16.

Sewell, William H., and Vimal P. Shah. "Socioeconomic Status, Inequality and the Attainment of Higher Education." *Sociology of Education*, 40 (Winter 1969), 1–23.

Shils, Edward. "Plentitude and Scarcity: The Anatomy of an International Culture Crisis." *Encounter*, 32 (May 1969), 37–57.

Shuster, W. Morgan. *The Strangling of Persia*. London, 1912.

Siassi, Ali Akbar. *La Perse au contact de l'Occident: Etude historique et sociale*. Paris: Ernest Leroux, 1931.

Smith, W. C. "The Intellectuals in the Modern Development of the Islamic World." In N. Sidney Fisher, ed., *Social Forces in the Middle East*. New York: Cornell University Press, 1955.

Sobhe, Khosrow. "Education in Revolution: Is Iran Duplicating the Chinese Cultural Revolution? *Comparative Education*, 18, no. 3 (1982), 271–80.

Sykes, Ella C. *Persia and Its People*. London: Methuen, 1910.

Szyliowicz, S. Joseph. *Education and Modernization in the Middle East*. Ithaca: Cornell University Press, 1973.

Tachau, Frank, ed. *Political Elites and Political Development in the Middle East*. Boston: Schenkman, 1975.

Trow, Martin. "Reflections on the Transition from Mass to Universal Higher Education." *Daedalus*, 99 (Winter 1970), 1–42.

Vaqefi, Reza. "A Micro-Analysis Approach to Modernization Process: A Case Study of Modernity and Traditional Conflict." *IJMES*, 12 (September 1980), 181–97.

Von Grunebaum, Gustav E. "Acculturation and Self-Realization." In B. Rivlin and J. S. Szyliowicz, eds., *The Contemporary Middle East*, 141–48. New York: Random House, 1965.

———. "Islam in Humanistic Education." *The Journal of General Education*, 4 (October 1949), 12–31.

Waadenburg, Jean-Jacques. *Les Universités dans le monde arabe actuel*. Paris: Mouton, 1966.

Watson, Robert G. *A History of Persia: From the Beginning of the Nineteenth Century to the Year 1858*. London: Smith, Elder, 1866.

Wilber, Donald N. *Riza Shah Pahlavi: The Resurrection and Reconstruction of Iran*. New York: Exposition, 1975.

Wills, C. J. *In the Land of the Lion and Sun, or Modern Persia*. London: Ward and Lock, 1891.

Yar-Shater, Ehsan, ed. *Iran Faces the Seventies*. New York: Praeger, 1971.

Zabih, Sepher. *The Communist Party in Iran*. Berkeley, 1966.

Zartman, William, ed. *Elites in the Middle East*. New York: Praeger, 1980.

Zonis, Marvin. *The Political Elite of Iran*. Princeton: Princeton University Press, 1971.

Index

'Abbas Mirza, 21, 25, 28, 46, 52, 71
'Abd al-Wahhab, Mirza, 50
'Abdollah Khan, Mirza, 52
'Abduh (member of Majlis), 187–88
'Abduh, Muhammad, 28, 29
'Abdul-Hamid (Sultan), 117
Abrahamian, Ervand, 140, 141, 154
academic freedom: in developing
  countries, 291; in the early
  constitutional era, 76; in the early years
  of Mohammad Reza Shah (1941–53),
  286–90; in the early years of Tehran
  University (1935–41), 149, 150–51, 153,
  283–86; lack of, in Dar al-Fonun, 58; in
  the Muslim Middle East, 282–83; in the
  West, 282, 284; during the White
  Revolution, 240, 290–99. See also
  universities
academic research: attempts to advance,
  233–35; weakness of, in Iran, 58, 66,
  137, 145, 150, 152–53, 225, 227, 230–33,
  283, 302, 326
Adamiyyat, Fereydun, 294
Adhham (Majlis member), 174
'Adl, Mostafa, 105, 285n
adult education, 96–97, 103; early ideas
  of, 96; law of 1936, 96; and promoting
  national consciousness, 97
Afshar (Majlis member), 174
Afshar, Hajji Baba, 40, 50, 52
Afshar, Mohammad Hoseyn Beg, 47
Afshar, Mostafa Khan, 28, 44, 53–54
Afshar, Reza, 122n

agricultural education, 52, 59, 79, 81, 138,
  182, 200, 225
Ahangar, Mohammad 'Ali, 47
Ahmad, Shah, 87, 88; on sending
  students abroad, 83
Akhundzade, Mirza Fath 'Ali, 28, 37
Akrami, Kazem, 322–23
A'lam, Amir, 287n
Alan, T. B., 182
'Alavi, Bozorg, 141
Al-e Ahmad, Jalal, 209, 214n, 304, 310
'Ali Khan (Majlis member), 78, 84
'Ameri, 'Ali Mohammad, 122n
Amin Khan (Majlis member), 84
Aminzade, Farrokh, 190, 201n, 202
Amin al-Dowla, Mirza 'Ali Khan, 60, 71n
Amini, 'Ali, 290
Amir Kabir, Mirza Taqi Khan:
  assasination of, 56; and Dar al-Fonun,
  53–55; as a modernizing leader, 25, 28,
  29n, 47
Amman, Karl, 12
Amuzegar, Jamshid, 224n
Anglo-Iranian Oil Company, 115
Anvar (Majlis member), 174
Arasteh, Reza, 5
Ardebili, Ayatollah 'Abd al-Karim, 314n,
  322n
Arfa', General Hasan, 116n, 126
Aryamehr University, 213, 214, 239, 258,
  319
Asadollah Khan, Mirza, 52
Ashraf (Princess), 179n, 183

343

Ashtiyani, Mirza Hasan, 61
'Assam, Mohammad Kazem, 287n
Ataturk, Kemal, 97, 99–100, 107, 124, 150
'Azimi, Reza, 276

Badr al-Din, 196n
Baha' al-Molk (Majlis member), 78
Bahar, Mohammad Taqi, 132
Baheri, Mohammad, 184n, 228n, 229,
    234, 238, 249n, 253
Bahrami, Mohammad, 141
Bakhash, [Alfred] Shaul, 227, 292n
Bakhtyar, Shapur, 157, 297
Baluchestan, 178, 193–94
Bamdad, Mirza Mohammad 'Ali Khan,
    128, 132
Banani, Amin, 5, 153
Bani Sadr, Abu al-Hasan, 316
Basir al-Dowla, Mirza Ahmad Khan
    Badr, 112n
Bayani, Khanbaba, 213
Bazargan, Mehdi, 157
Bazar merchants, 21, 54
Behbahani, Abu-Taleb, 32
Behjat (Majlis member), 78, 81
Behnam, Jamshid, 218, 223n, 231
Bowles, Samuel, 10
Britain: higher education in, 148–49;
    involvement in Iran during WW II, 88;
    and Iran, in the early nineteenth
    century, 23–24, 46–47; Iranian students
    in, 133; opposition to Dar al-Fonun, 54.
    See also superpowers
Browne, Edward G., 57, 66, 70–71, 72n,
    74, 75n
budgets, 121–22, 230, 233
Byrnes, David, 11

Carnoy, Martin, 10–11, 12
Central Council on Education, 222
Coleman, James, 9, 300
colleges, 239, 244–45, 258; expansion of,
    214–19, 223–24; private, 223–24. *See also*
    universities
communism in Iran, 140–41
compulsory education: in the early
    constitutional era, 76, 79, 113, 173;
    early support for, 31–32; the
    Fundamental Law of Education (1911)
    and, 77–78; implementation of, 176–78,
    183–84, 186; the law of 1943, 79, 167–
    68, 173–78; in the Middle East, 173;
    scope of, widened (1974), 183–85;
    under Reza Shah, 113, 115; in the
    West, 172–73

constitutionalism: education and, 38–39;
    intellectuals' contribution to, 70–75
Constitutional Revolution (1905–11), 2;
    role of the educated class in, 63–64,
    70–72, 298–99
Council for Cultural Revolution, 314, 316,
    318, 322
Curzon, Lord George, 22, 55

Daneshgah-e Azad (the Open University),
    215
Daneshkade 'Ilm va San'at, 216, 292–93
Daneshkade San'ati Politenknik, 216
Dar al-Fonun: 49, 148; contribution to
    modernization, 57–59, 61, 63–64, 70–71;
    deficiencies of, 58, 83, 231; dependence
    on the government, 58; foundation of,
    53; graduates' careers, 53, 56, 57;
    graduates' political activities, 56; lack
    of academic freedom in, 58; marking
    the beginning of the "new education,"
    5, 53, 57; opposition to, 56; printing
    house of, 57, 70, 71–72; under Reza
    Shah, 144; social origin of the students,
    53–54, 55–56
Dashti, 'Ali, 98, 105, 109, 112, 113, 116,
    118, 128, 131n, 132, 174
Davar, 'Ali Akbar, 96, 127, 128, 147
Department of Publication and
    Information, 97
Department of Public Enlightment, 97
Dewey, John, 111, 197
Dowlatabadi, Sadeqe, 109
Dowlatabadi, Yahya, 55, 85, 89; criticism
    of traditional schooling, 42; and
    foundation of new schools, 60, 62;
    opposition to Reza Shah, 89n, 91

Ebrahim, Seyyed, 78, 81
Economy, and education, 7–8, 36, 122,
    189–90, 221, 223–24, 234–35, 303, 305;
    in developing countries, 7–8; planning,
    156, 200, 204, 220, 224–25; in the West,
    12. *See also* oil
education: conflict theories of, 6–12, 208,
    241; functional theories of, 6–8, 11–12,
    241; as a tool to secure administrative
    job, 113–14, 128–29, 134–37, 171, 182,
    187–89, 201, 311; as a tool to secure
    university seat, 114, 187, 188, 190–95,
    198, 200–2, 205–9, 311
Education, in developing countries:
    appreciation for, 12–13, 163, 170, 300;
    as catalyst for development, 11–12,
    163; as an obstacle to development, 12;
    planning of, 219–20

"educational revolution" (*enqelab-e amuzeshi*), 163–64, 210–11, 225–40; and academic freedom, 290–99; philosophy of, 163–65, 166; and political recruitment, 163, 166; and students' welfare, 247–49. *See also* universities
Eftekhar al-Va'ezin (Majlis member), 82–83
Egypt: compulsory education law, 173; dispatch of students abroad, 46; early westernization of, 19, 23, 60, 99; elites' education in, 269; girls' education in, 107; influence on Iranian modernization, 53; statistics of education, 191–92, 210n; vocational schooling in, 199
Ehtesham al-Saltane, Mirza Mahmud Khan, 60
Ehteshamzade (Majlis member), 118, 119
elementary education: expansion under Mohammad Reza Shah, 185–86; and the Literacy Corps, 178–83; statistics of, 190–94. *See also* Literacy Corps; new education
elites: alienation from the masses, 174–75, 276, 280–81; educational background, 269–81; and Mohammad Reza Shah, 160; opposition to change in the nineteenth century, 21, 38. *See also* ulama
Emami Aheri (Majlis member), 174
Entesar, Nader, 308n
Entezam al-Hokama' (Majlis member), 84
Eqbal, Manuchehr, 157
Eqbali, 'Adl, 126, 128, 129, 131n, 133
Eqbal, Mirza 'Abbas, 128
Esfahani, Mirza Nasrollah. *See* Malek al-Motakallemin
Esfahani, Rahim, 47
Esfahani Abu-Taleb ibn Mohammad, Mirza, 68
Eskandari, Iraj, 141
E'temad al-Saltane, Mirza Mohammad Hasan Khan, 55, 72–73
E'temadzade, 113, 122n

Faramushkhane (Free Masons), 56–57
Farhad, Ahmad, 290
Farhangestan (Academy for the Persian Language), 97
Farhudi, Hoseyn, 93n, 96
Farhudi (Majlis member), 174
Farrokh, 119
Fayyaz-Bakhsh, Mohammad 'Ali, 310–11
Fazel, Iraj, 322n
Ferdowsi (poet), 17, 98, 308n, 320–21

Firuzabadi, Reza, 128, 129
Fischer, Michael, 294n
Forughi, 'Ali, 106, 148, 285, 286
Foruhar, Daryush, 157
France: Iranian students in, 133; and Iran in the early nineteenth century, 23–24, 69, 71; universities in, 144. *See also* superpowers
Free Islamic University, 325

Ganje'i (Majlis member), 174
Ganji, Manuchehr, 225
Germany: Iranian students in, 133; opposition activities of Iranian students from, 133, 140; universities in, 144. *See also* studies abroad; superpowers
Gharbzadegi (West-strickeness), 2, 209, 304, 309–11; accusation of, in the shah's regime, 309–11, 320, 321
Gintis, Herbert, 10
Girls' education: in the Islamic Republic, 324; in the reign of Mohammad Reza Shah, 179, 181–82, 191–93, 200, 201, 255–56, 264–65, 304; under the Qajars, 41n, 60, 63; under Reza Shah, 105, 106–10; and women's status, 106, 304. *See also* women
Gobineau, Arthur de, 69, 74
Golestan and Turkmanchay, treaties of, 23
Golpaygani, Hashemi, 320n, 325–26
Gondi Shapur University, 213, 214, 319
Green, Colin, 10
Green, Jerrold, 295
Grunebaum, Gustav von, 16
Guthrie, James, 11

Habibi, Hasan, 315
Habibi, Mostafa, 213
Habl ul-Matin (The Strong Cord), 70, 75n
Hadad 'Adel, Gholam 'Ali, 310–11
Hadheqi (Majlis member), 174
Hajji Aqa (Majlis member), 78
Hakim al-Mamalek, Mirza 'Ali Taqi, 50
Hanf, Theodor, 12
Hashemi (Majlis member), 174, 176
Hashemi Rafsanjani, 'Ali Akbar. *See* Rafsanjani, 'Ali Akbar Hashemi
Hashtrudi, 287
Hedayat, Mehdi Qoli, 22, 42, 48, 55, 56–57, 62, 73–75
Hedayat, Reza Qoli, 20
Hekmat, 'Ali Asghar, 56, 58, 96, 98, 101, 109, 116, 119–20, 122n, 141, 144, 146–48, 285
Hekmat, 'Ali Reza, 14–15

Hess, André, 94–95, 115
Hoseyn Khan, Mirza, 50, 52
Hoveyda, Amir ʿAbbas, 184, 220, 226, 233–34, 276
Hurn, Christopher, 7

Ibn Ishaq, Jaʿfar, 31, 44n
Illich, Ivan, 10, 205, 209
ʿIlm (knowledge), 13–16, 241–42
Institute for Research and Planning in Science and Education (MTBRA), 218–19, 221–22, 258–61, 265–66, 267n, 292
Institute for Social Studies (MTE), Tehran University, 52, 130–32, 134–35, 189n, 273
intellectuals: accommodating western ideas with Islam, 28, 37, 74; contribution to early journalism, 69–70; cooperation with the ulama, 75, 305–6; criticism of traditional schooling, 36, 39–43; definition of, 27; demand for overall reform, 27; and educational reforms in the nineteenth century, 25, 27, 28–39, 43, 44–45; and enlightenment in Iran, 63, 73–74; on freedom, 27, 36–37; limits of influence, 64, 74–75; support of the new education, 30–39, 60; western sources of thought, 28, 32, 73
intermediate schools: made free of charge, 183–85; and revision of the school structure (1971/2), 195–98
International Labor Organization (ILO), 191
Irano-German Industrial School, 115
Isfahan University, 213, 214, 258
Islamic Republic: admission regulations to higher education, 317–18; background of the political elite, 326–27; and brain drain, 322; criticism of the shah's educational policy by, 307–8, 310–11, 320; cultural revolution in, 308–12, 316–28; deficiencies of educational system in, 324–25; expansion of pre-university education in, 324; growing pragmatism of, 312–15, 318; and Islamization, 302–9, 312–23, 328; and private schooling, 322–23; the purge of faculty staff by, 312, 317–18; and purge of students by, 312, 317–18; quality of academic education in, 325–26; and rejection of the West, 6, 307–11, 320; and revision of textbooks, 320–21; role of intellectuals in, 298–99, 304–306; and the shah's educational legacy, 300–304; and shortage of

teachers, 324–25; and studies abroad, 323, 327; and tolerance toward the professional class, 313, 314, 321–22; uniqueness of, 1–2, 6, 307
Ismaʿil Pasha (ruler of Egypt), 99, 107

Jacobs, Norman, 187, 189
Jalali, Mehdi, 286
Japan, 12, 43–44
Javaher Kalam, ʿAli, 62, 92n, 98n, 147
Jazaʿeri, ʿAbd al-Latif [Musavi Shostari], 68
Jebhe-ye Melli (the National Front), 156, 290, 297, 304
Jehad-e Daneshgahi (the Unit for University Crusade), 314, 316
Jones, Harford, 46

Kamali, (Majlis member), 114n
Kamshad, H., 74
Kanun-e Banuvan (Women's Club), 108–10
Kanun-e Javanan (Youth Organization), 141
Karbalaʾi, ʿAbbas, 47
Karbalaʾi, Sadeq, 47
Kashani, ʿAli Akbar, 50
Kashef (Majlis member), 93n
Kasravi, Ahmad, 105
Kayhan (newspaper), 286
Kayhan, Masʿud, 173, 286
Kazemzade, Hoseyn, 105
Kazeruni, Mirza ʿAli, 119, 129
Keddie, Nikki, 1–2
Kermani, al-Riyasateyn, 39, 40n
Kermani, Mirza Aqa Khan, 28
Kermani, Nazem al-Islam, 35n
Khaje-Nuri, Ebrahim, 107
Khalase (Ecstasy), 73, 74
Khameneʿi, Ayatollah, ʿAli, 314, 322
Khanlari, Parviz, 171
Khomeyni, Ayatollah Ruhollah: appreciation for education, 3, 308–9; calls for Islamization, 308–9; criticism of the shah's educational system, 180n, 307–8; and the Islamic Revolution, 155, 304–6; and moderation, 313; and modern sciences, 326; opposition to the shah in the early 1960s, 157, 294; and the spread of education under the shah, 179n; and "West-stricken" intellectuals, 307–9, 311. *See also* Islamic Republic
Konferans-e Arzyabi-ye Enqelab-e Amuzeshi (KAEA), 164–65, 188n, 198, 208–9, 211–

12, 222, 228, 233n, 234, 238, 239, 247, 291
Kurdistan, 170, 178, 183

Lambton, Ann K. S., 21
Lesan al-Hokama' (Majlis member), 84
Levin, Herbert, 10–11
Lewis, Bernard, 25, 27
Literacy Corps (*Sepah-e Danesh*): academic shortcomings of, 180–82; activities in rural Iran, 178–83, 186; formation of, 159, 178–79; indoctrination activities by, 179–83
Lorestan, 181, 183, 193–94
Lower strata, and education, 118–20, 174, 176, 194–95; and higher education, 242–45, 247–51, 256–57, 304–5; and studies abroad, 128–29, 205; under the Islamic Republic, 316

Madrese-ye 'Ulum-e Siyasi (School of Political Science)), 59, 144
Mahdavi, Mahmud, 60, 126, 128, 129, 133, 135n, 138n, 152, 283
Mahdavi-Kani, Ayatollah Mohammad Reza, 319n
Mahfuzi, 'Abbas, 319
Mahmud II (Sultan), 117
Mahmud Khan, Mirza, 129
Malcolm, John, 20, 21, 41, 42
Malek, Sa'id, 173, 286
Malek al-Motakallemin, Mirza Nasrollah Esfahani, 30; criticism of the Qajars, 73; in praise of new education, 36–37; on role of education in Japan, 43–44
Malekzade (Majlis member), 109n, 117, 131n, 148
Malkom Khan, Nazem al-Dowla: biography of, 29n, 35n, 48; calls to accommodate Islam and the West, 37; criticism of government's disregard for education, 40; criticism of the new schools, 64; criticism of traditional schooling, 39–40; criticism of the ulama's opposition to new education, 41; and Dar al-Fonun, 58; on Islam, 21, 28–29; on role of education in Japan, 44n; on social prestige of studies abroad, 51, 82; in support of reforms, 28–30, 32–35
manpower, 251–53; planning of, 220. *See also* technical (vocational) schooling
manual work: attempts to encourage, 115–16; education as a rescue from, 113–14, 116, 171, 182, 225
Maraghe'i, Hajj Zayn al-'Abedin, 72;

criticism of traditional schools, 42; on the role of education in Japan, 44n
Mar'at, Esma'il, 82, 116, 285n
Mardom (People's) Party, 157, 240n
Marshal, Alfred, 7
Masha'ekhi, Mohammad, 169, 188, 190, 195–96
Matin Daftari (Senator), 190
medical law (1911), 83–85, 104
Mehr, Farhang, 215, 218, 231, 246
Mehr (periodical), 113
Mehran, Mahmud, 286
Meshhed University, 213, 214, 258
Miftah al-Molk, Mahmud Khan, 60
Millspaugh, Arthur C., 88n, 123
Ministry of Science and Higher Education, 218, 222, 223, 234, 247, 249–50; dissolution of, 211, 225; formation of, 211, 220; functions of, 220–21, 225
Minovi, Mojtabi, 65
Mir-Taheri, 104
Mirza'i, 'Ali Reza, 122n, 147, 148
Missionary schools, 40n, 41n, 53n, 107n
Mo'adel (Majlis member), 93, 109n, 117
Mo'ayyed Ahmadi (Majlis member), 114n, 174, 187, 188n
Mo'azzez al-Molk (Majlis member), 78, 81, 84
modernization: expansion of education and, 11, 193–94, 300–303; first phases of, 5; rural education and, 178–80, 182–83; studies abroad and, 66–75, 83, 134–38; the White Revolution and, 159–60. *See also* studies abroad
Moftakhar, 221, 231
Mohammad, Shah, 22, 40, 47
Mohammad 'Ali (Iranian student), 49
Mohammad 'Ali, Aqa, 47, 50
Mohammad 'Ali, Khan, 55
Mohammad 'Ali Shah, 21
Mohandes Bashi, Mirza Reza, 47, 50, 71
Mo'in, Mostafa, 315, 323
Mojahedin-e Khalq, 304
Mokhtari, Ahmad, 223n, 253
Montazem al-Dowla, Firuz Kuhi, 60
Montazeri, Ayatollah Hoseyn 'Ali: and extremism in Islamization, 314–16, 319; and tolerance toward professionals, 314, 319, 322
Morier, James, 22
Mosaddeq, Mohammad, 2, 156
Moshir al-Dowla, Mirza Ja'far Khan, 47, 50
Moshir al-Dowla, Mirza Nasrollah Khan, 59
Moshir al-Molk, Mirza Hasan Khan, 59

Mostashar al-Dowla, Mirza Yusef Khan, 31; biography and views, 31n; *Yek Kalame*, 31, 36, 72
Mostawfi, 'Abdollah, 52, 59
Mo'tamen al-Molk (Majlis member), 78
Mozaffar al-Din Shah, 22; in support of new education, 60; visit to Europe, 24, 36
Muhammad 'Ali (ruler of Egypt), 33, 46n, 53, 91, 117
Musavi, Aqa Seyyed Hoseyn, 62
Musavi, Mir-Hoseyn, 314n, 322

Nabavi, Behzad, 322, 323n
Nafisi, Sa'id, 113–15, 174, 286
Nahavandi, Hushang, 217, 218
Na'ini, Zel al-Soltan, 40n
Najafi, Mohammad, 316–17
Najafi, Shaykh Mohammad, 62
Naqqash Bashi, Abu al-Hasan, 47
Naraqi, Ehsan, 176n, 221, 246, 287
Nasafat, Morteza, 207n, 216n, 218n, 231, 247–48, 251, 259–63, 265–66
Naser al-Din Shah: and Dar al-Fonun, 56–57; on education, 40; visit to Europe, 24
Naser al-Molk, Abu al-Qasem Khan, 38, 42
Nasrollah, Hajj Aqa, 101
National Iranian Oil Company, 202
nationalism: adult education and, 97; beginnings of national education in Europe, 93–94; education's contribution to, 7, 36, 78, 92, 93–98, 164–66, 303–4; and education under Reza Shah, 90, 92–98, 112, 123, 124; as a goal of Mohammad Reza Shah, 160, 161, 164–66, 303; national education in the Middle East, 94; studies abroad and, 83, 106, 126, 128
National (*Melli*) University, 213, 214, 239, 258, 319
Nazem al-Dowla, Malkom Khan. *See* Malkom Khan, Nazem al-Dowla
Nehzat-e Azadi (Freedom Movement), 157, 304
Nehzat-e Moqavemat-e Melli (National Resistance Movement), 157
new education: appreciation for, 29–39, 43–45, 77, 163–64, 300, 328; criticism of, by Khomeyni, 308–11; deficiencies of, 114, 300–302; early praise for, 29–39, 43–45, 77
newspapers: first Iranian, 69–71; intellectuals' contribution to, 69–70;

significance to the Constitutional Revolution, 70–71, 74
Nikgouhar, 'Abd al-Hoseyn, 218, 219n, 231, 233, 234
Nir al-Molk, Ja'far Qoli Khan, 60
Nuri Niya'i, 130

OECD, 8, 11, 201n, 203, 232n
oil, education and, 162, 184, 211, 248, 249, 251
Ottoman Empire: dispatch of students abroad, 46; early westernization of, 19, 23, 60, 68, 98, 105; girls' education in, 107; impact of reforms on Iranian intellectuals, 32n, 35, 53, 68. *See also* Turkey

Pahlavi, Mohammad Reza Shah, 5; and academic freedom, 286–99; appreciation for education, 3, 163, 164, 172; attitude to Islam, 158–59, 161, 166, 296; and compulsory education, 174–77; criticism of higher education, 225, 226, 231, 236, 237; as crown prince, 92, 166; on deficiencies of secondary education, 188; and the "educational revolution," 210–12; and the elites, 280–82; encouraging vocational schooling, 203–4; and expansion of higher education, 212–19, 221, 222, 225; on his father's reforms, 123–24; and free higher education, 249, 250; and the Great Civilization, 164; and the Literacy Corps, 178–83; and the Majlis, 276; and the modernization of Iran, 17, 159; on the rights of all for higher education, 245–46, 298; vicissitudes of reign, 155–62; and widening the scope of compulsory education (1974), 183–85
Pahlavi University. *See* Shiraz University
Pahlbud, Mehrdad, 276
Parsay, Farah-rou, 180n, 195, 196, 197, 199
Parvaresh (Nurture), 71
Perkins, J., 40n, 41
Pishavari, 213
Plan and Budget Organization, 201n, 203, 204, 205, 220
political activities of students: dangers of high school graduates' unfulfilled expectations, 190–91, 208–9, 246, 304; demonstrations by high school students, 208; education and political discontent before the Islamic revolution, 2–3, 208–9, 293–94, 296–99, 304–5; under the Islamic Republic, 312;

the law of free education (1974) and
students' resentment, 250–54, 257, 304;
officials' warnings of students'
resentments, 209, 211, 224, 305;
oppositionary activities in the 1960s,
290; resentment of lower-strata
students, 267, 305; students'
opposition to Reza Shah's rule, 154;
and university growth, 212, 246
private education: in the Islamic
Republic, 322, 325–26; under
Mohammad Reza Shah, 194–95, 197,
267; under the Qajars, 60, 78; under
Reza Shah, 95, 119; at university level,
214, 223–24, 239. *See also* Aryamehr
University; National (*Melli*) University;
Shiraz University
Provinces, education in: in the Islamic
Republic, 325; under Mohammad Reza
Shah, 174n, 193–95, 213–15, 248, 258–
62, 303; under the Qajars, 77–79, 81,
84–85; under Reza Shah, 118–20, 126,
130–31, 152

Qa'em-maqam, Mirza Abu-Qasem, 25
Qajar, 'Ali Bakhsh, 32, 44n
Qajar period, education during:
backwardness of, 17; and
constitutionalism, 38; deficiencies of
new schooling, 62–65, 83, 302–3; in the
early constitutional era, 76–78, 85;
education and the lower strata, 77–79;
and the elites, 273–75; foundation of
new schools, 59–63; intellectuals on
new schooling, 39–40; opposition to
reforms of, 22; as a prerequisite for
progress, 28, 29–30; private schooling,
78; as privilege of the elites, 62; in the
provinces, 79; social prestige of, 63;
unification of, 78, 79
Qanun, 34, 40, 70, 71n
Qaragozlu, Yahya, 146
Qasemi, Ahmad, 188
Qasemzade, 287n
Qavam, Ahmad, 286
Qoli Khan, Hoseyn, 47, 50, 69
Qoli Khan, Mehdi, 148

Radmanesh, Reza, 141, 175
Rafi' (Majlis member), 128, 131n
Rafsanjani, 'Ali Akbar Hashemi, 313,
315, 323, 327
Rahimi, Hojjat al-Islam, 318
Rahnama, Gholam Hoseyn, 287n
Rahnama, Majid, 164, 169, 188, 211n,
220, 221, 226, 233n, 234, 237, 290

Ramirez, F., 13
Rasekh, Shapur, 169, 190, 232, 246
Rashid Pasha, 53
Rastakhiz (Resurrection) Party, 161, 166,
292
Razedan, Parviz, 219n, 232, 253
Razi, 'Abdollah, 101
Razun (village), 170, 181, 183n
research. *See* academic research
Reuter, Julios de, 24
revision of the school structure (1971/2),
195–98
Revolutionary Guards, 312
Reza, Fazlollah, 232
Reza'i, 'Ali, 203
Reza Shah: academic freedom under,
283–86; adult education and, 96–97;
appreciation for education, 91, 111,
126–27; and coup of 1921, 76;
education and nationalism under, 90,
92, 93–98; educational background of
elites under, 272–75; education of, 90n;
emergence to power, 76, 87–90; and
employment of foreign experts, 98;
expansion of education under, 118,
120–22; fall of, 155; interest in Tehran
University, 144–45, 146, 147–49; judicial
reforms under, 103–4; and ministry of
education, 95; nationalization of
foreign schools, 95; nature of rule, 87,
89, 91, 111, 124, 139; policy toward the
ulama, 90, 94, 98–104; preference of
elementary over higher education, 116;
preference of *parvaresh* over *amuzesh*,
111; and secularization, 90, 98–104; and
students abroad policy, 92, 105–6, 125–
42; Turkish influence on, 94; and
unification of school syllabus, 95;
vocational training, policy of, 115; and
westernization, 90, 104–10, 123
Rezvi, Ahmad, 176n, 182n
Riyazi, 'Ali, 82
Rosenthal, Franz, 15
Roshdiye, Mirza Hasan, 60, 61–62
Royal Institute for Research on Education
(SSHBA), 204, 216, 218, 223–25, 228–
29, 232, 235n, 239, 247, 252, 253, 254,
261, 262–63, 266–67, 292
Ro'ya-ye Sadege, 73–74
Ruhi, 'Ata'ollah, 93n, 128, 148, 174
Rural areas, education in: under Reza
Shah, 120; under Mohammad Reza
Shah, 174, 178–83, 193–95. *See also*
Literacy Corps
Rusk, Dean, 8
Russia: influence on Iranian intellectuals

from, 32n, 53; interests in Iran in the
early nineteenth century, 23;
involvement in Iran in Second World
War, 88; universities in, 144. *See also*
superpowers
Ruzname-ye Akhbar-e Vaqaye'-e Ettefaqiye
(Diary of Current Events), 70

Sa'di (poet), 16, 98
Sadiq, 'Isa, 5, 56, 61, 62, 80, 83, 85, 91n,
97, 104, 105, 107, 108, 112, 113, 115,
117, 128, 133n, 136, 138–39, 144–47,
149, 152, 153, 158, 167–68, 174, 188,
190, 196n, 246, 258, 283, 285, 297
Sadiqi, Gholam Hoseyn, 91n, 114, 126,
128, 129, 135n, 152, 246, 257–58, 283,
293, 296
Safa, Dhabihollah, 5, 58–59
Safavyan, 'Abbas, 198, 209, 305n
Sahabi, 287n
Sakenyan (Majlis member), 174n
Saltykov-Shchedrin, Aleksey, 69
Sangyan (Majlis member), 176n
Sanjabi, Karim, 157, 296
SAVAK, 157, 160, 217–18, 246, 257n, 293,
295–96
Sayyah, Fateme, 109
Sayyah Mahalati, Hajj Mohammad, 38
secondary education: cost of, for
government workers, 184; deficiencies
of, 187–91; demonstrations of students
of, 208; early schools, 187; as means
for securing desk job, 113–14, 128–29,
134–37, 171, 182, 187–89, 203n; as
means for university admission, 114,
187, 188, 190–95, 198, 200–2, 205–9,
311; political consequences of
inbalanced development of, 190–91,
208–9, 211, 224, 246, 304–5; rapid
expansion under Mohammad Reza
Shah, 191–94, 205–209, 217, 267; as
weakest part of modern education,
134, 186–87
secularization: education and advancing
of, 90, 98–104, 124; in Europe, 98; first
secularist ideas, 28, 69; higher
education and, 126, 137; in Islamic
society, 99; and Mohammad Reza
Shah's reforms, 157–61, 179, 281; and
restriction of the power of the ulama,
90, 98; studies abroad and the spread
of, 126, 137; under the Qajars, 28
Selim III (Sultan), 67–68
Sepah-e Danesh. See Literacy Corps
Sepahsalar, Mirza Hoseyn Khan:
biography of, 30n; and Dar al-Fonun,

57; and modernization, 25, 29n, 30, 37;
in praise of education, 30–31, 35, 44n;
and reformist intellectuals, 30; studies
abroad, 48
Shajare, M., 93
Shaji'i, Zahra, 273, 276
Shari'ati, 'Ali, 310
Shari'atmadari, Ayatollah Kazem, 107
Sharifi, Hushang, 185
Shaykh al-Ra'is, Hajj, 81, 82–83, 84
Sherekat-e Ma'aref (The Association for
Education), 59–60
Sheybani, 'Abbas, 312
Sheybani, Gholam 'Ali, 82
Shi'ism, strength in Iran, 19–20, 99, 104,
124; and support for '*ilm*, 15; and the
usuli doctrine, 20. *See also* ulama
Shirazi, Mirza Mohammad 'Ali, 49
Shirazi, Mirza Saleh: on achievements of
the West, 28, 66–69; career of, 50;
influence of his studies in the West,
66–69, 128; and the press in Iran, 70;
studies in Europe, 47, 48, 49n, 66; and
the ulama, 67–68
Shiraz University, 213, 214, 215, 230, 239,
248, 255, 258, 318, 319
Shirvani, Mirza Abu-Taleb, 128, 131n
Shuqi, 'Abbas, 174n, 188
Shuster, Morgan W., 76, 88n
Siyasi, 'Ali Akbar, 80, 83, 91n, 120, 136,
144, 152, 158, 167, 168–69, 173–80, 257–
58; and the compulsory education law,
173–76; and the independence of
Tehran University, 283–90, 293, 296–97
Smith, Adam, 7, 28, 36
Social mobility, education and, 10, 14,
130, 163, 170–71, 174–75, 241–45, 257–
67, 270–81; in developing countries,
170; in the early constitutional era, 76,
77–79; intellectuals on, 31, 32, 37–38;
lack of, under the Qajars, 22; in the
Muslim Middle East, 15–16, 241–42,
269–70; and revision of the school
structure (1971/2), 197–98; under Reza
Shah, 118, 120, 128–30, 148
Sohayli, 'Ali, 286
Soleyman, Mirza (Majlis member), 81
Stronach, A., 115
students: social background of, 254–67;
unions of, 295. *See also* political
activities of students; studies abroad
studies abroad: and constitutional
revolution, 79, 81; and contribution to
modernization, 52, 63–64, 66–75, 82,
83, 134–42, 152, 189–90; fields of study,
48, 81, 127, 131–32; first students sent

for, 24, 46–52, 66–68; as good "investment" by the elites, 129; and graduates' membership in the political elite, 271, 272, 276, 277–78, 327; under the Islamic Republic, 323; the law of 1911, 80–83; the law of 1928, 125, 127; lower strata and, 81, 126–31; under Mohammad Reza Shah, 218–19, 243; and nationalism, 105–6; negative influence of, 54, 64–65, 82–83, 126, 127–28; and opposition to the regime, 133, 139–41, 298; and political activities of students, 56, 66, 134, 136–37, 139–41; professional careers of graduates of, 49–52, 82, 133, 134–38, 152; under Reza Shah, 92, 125–42, 152; social background of students dispatched for, 48, 49, 51, 80–81, 126, 128–31, 132, 135; social prestige of, 51, 81–82, 134–36, 138, 243–44; and westernization, 6
superpowers: and advancement of imperialist goals, 64; as catalyst for educational reforms, 17, 29, 63; and change in the Muslim world, 19, 33; early Iranian contacts with, 5–6, 19, 23–25, 51; education as a tool against their aspirations, 98; involvement in Iran in First World War, 87–88; opposition to education in Iran, 40; science in, 5–6, 51. *See also* Westernization
Szyliowicz, Joseph, 153, 303n

Tabataba'i, Ayatollah Seyyed Mohammad, 38, 42
Tabataba'i, Mohit, 80, 114, 142
Tabataba'i, Seyyed Zia al-Din, 89, 94
Tabriz University, 213, 214, 312
Tadayyon, Mohammad, 96, 285n
Ta'eb, 'Abbas, 317n
Taheri, Shaykh Hadi, 119, 122n
Tahtawi, Rifa'a Rafi' al-, 28
Talbot, G. F., 24
Talebov (Talebzade), 'Abd al-Rahim: biography of, 32n; on education and economy, 36; and new education, 36, 43; and secularism, 28, 37; and superpowers' opposition to the spread of education, 40; and traditional schooling, 36, 43
Taleqani, Ayatollah Mahmud, 157
Talmaon, J., 100
Taqizade, Hasan, 78, 89n, 93, 105, 108, 116, 122n, 128, 129–31, 175n, 180
Taqizade, Jamshid, 230n, 233n, 235
Tarbiyyat, Hajar, 108, 109

Taymur, Amir, 176
Taymur-Tash, 'Abd al-Hoseyn, 101, 140, 145, 146, 147, 149
teachers: in developing countries, 121; prestige of, 121–22, 132, 151; recruitment of, from Literacy Corps, 180, 196; shortage of, 113, 121–22, 127, 131–32, 135, 180, 188, 196, 324–25; in traditional schools, 41, 42–43
technical (vocational) schooling: in the early constitutional era, 79; encouragement of, under Reza Shah, 106, 115–16; in Europe, 47–48; under the Islamic Republic, 324; low standard of, 116; made free (in 1975), 184–85; under Mohammad Reza Shah, 198–205, 249–50, 304; and the revision of school structure (1971/2), 196–98
Tehrani (Majlis member), 98, 109, 148
Tehran University: academic independence of, 139–40, 149, 153, 283–90, 292–94; academic staff of, 229; admission of girls to, 108; and antishah demonstrations in, 296–97; colleges of, 59; early expectations of, 143–44; early ideas of, 142, 144–45; the early years of, 136, 150–53; establishment of (1934), 146; evening classes at, 248; expansion under Mohammad Reza Shah, 213–15, 217, 218; foundation of, 143–50; purge of faculty, under the Islamic Republic, 312, 319; purge of students, under the Islamic Republic, 312, 317–18; social background of students, 151–52, 255, 264–65; tuition payment after 1974, 255
Tobacco Rebellion (1891–92), 2, 63–64
traditional education (*maktabs* and *madreses*, 16; closing down of, 61, 63, 101–3, 301; intellectuals' criticism of, 36, 39–43; under the Qajar rule, 60n; reemergence of the *madrese*, 102–3
tribes, education among, 170–71, 178
Tudeh (Masses) Party, 141, 156, 175
Turkey: adult education in, 96; compulsory education law, 173; education of the elites, 269, 272, 276n, 277n; girls' education in, 107; impact of reforms in, on Reza Shah, 94, 96, 97, 99, 108, 109; national educational policy, 94; secularization in, 99–100, 150; statistics of education, 191–92, 210n

ulama: and Dar al-Fonun, 56; as driving force behind the Islamic Revolution, 2;

educational policy, 307–28; and expansion of schooling under Mohammad Reza Shah, 179n; and girls' education, 108; intellectuals' accusations against, 31, 39, 40–41, 67–68, 73; and modern education, 16, 37, 38–39, 41, 45, 61–62, 64, 103, 105, 120, 122, 150, 179n, 282; roots of power in Shi'i Iran, 19–20, 99–100, 281; and Tehran University, 150; and westernization, 19, 21
UNESCO, 8, 11–12, 164, 170, 221, 222, 228, 232, 233, 291
United States: higher education in, 144; Iranian students in, 127, 133, 138–39
universities: academic autonomy of, 149, 150–51, 282–99, 302; academic staff and, 226–30, 235–37; deficiencies of, 153, 225–27, 235–36, 302–3; in developing countries, 143, 210; dissident movement in, 2–3, 250–54, 290, 292, 304–5, 325; and the "educational revolution," 210, 224; high expectations from, 143–44, 147–48, 300–301; Islamic atmosphere in, 319; Islamization of curriculum, 319–20; lowering of standards of, 325–26; made unconditionally free (1978), 254; planning of, 219–25; private schooling under the Islamic Republic, 322–23; quantitative expansion of, 211–19, 223–24, 325; revision of admission policy, 237–40; rising of social prestige of, 243–45; staff purges, 312, 318–19; student purges, 312, 317–18; students' social welfare programs at, 247–49; studies made free in 1974, 249–54, 304; in the West, 143–44, 210. *See also* academic research; students; Tehran University: academic staff

Vadi'i, Kazem, 167, 188, 190, 196n, 198, 218n, 246, 293

Vahid, A., 93, 115, 122n
Vakil al-Molk (Majlis member), 78
Vakil al-Tojjar (Majlis member), 81
Vaziri, Sa'id, 237
Vothqa al-Islami, 'Adl, 174

Watson, Robert, 51
Westernization: early steps toward, 23–25, 63–64; higher education and, 144; intellectuals in support of, 33, 34, 37, 60; studies abroad and, 64, 105–6, 126, 127; under Mohammad Reza Shah, 159, 303–4; under Reza Shah, 90, 104–10, 123, 124; ulama opposition to, 19
White Revolution (*Enqelab-e Sefid*), 155, 157; and the "educational revolution," 163, 184; philosophy of, 158–62; rapid implementation of, 161–62; and suppression of academic freedom, 290–99. *See also* universities
Wilber, Donald, 88
Women, 118, 122, 130, 179, 244, 304; Literacy Corps for, 178–79, 182–83; and membership in the elites, 270–71; and studies abroad, 130; unveiling of, 108. *See also* girls' education

Yahya Khan, 47, 50
Ya'qub, Aqa Seyyed, 119, 127, 128, 131n, 132
Yasani (Majlis member), 118
Yazdi, Morteza, 141

Zaka' al-Molk (Majlis member), 78, 84
Zaman, Behnam, 82
Zartman, William, 270
Ziya'i, Majd, 176n
Zonis, Marvin, 155, 228n, 242, 246, 269, 270, 272–73, 279–80, 294

Library of Congress Cataloging-in-Publication Data

Menashri, David.
  Education and the making of modern Iran / David Menashri.
  Published in cooperation with the Moshe Dayan Center for Middle
  Eastern and African Studies at Tel Aviv University.
    p. cm.
  Includes bibliographical references (p.) and index.
  ISBN 0-8014-2612-X (alk. paper)
    1. Education—Iran—History—20th century. 2. Education and
  state—Iran—History—20th century. 3. Education—Social aspects—
  Iran—History—20th century. I. Title.
  LA1351.M46   1992
  370'.955—dc20   91-55567